Pit Stop

by
Dave Organ

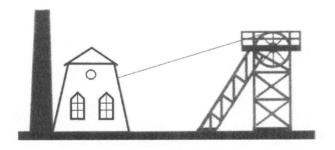

The Forest of Dean
Iron & Coal Mining Industries
The Birth of the Unions
The National Struggle

For
George

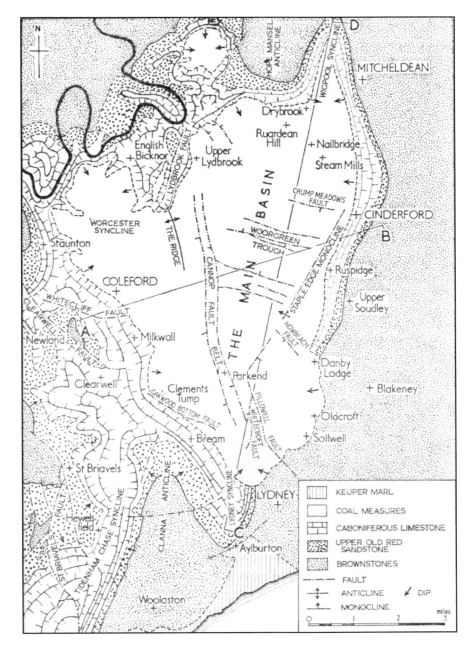

Fig. 1 Geology Plan of the Forest of Dean (after F.M. Trotter – Geology of the Forest of Dean Coal and Iron Ore Field - 1942)

Contents

List of Illustrations ix

Acknowledgements xiii

Author's Notes xiv

Prologue xvii

Chapter 1 The Ancient Forest of Dean 1

Chapter 2 The Iron Industry 10

Chapter 3 Tramways to Railways 19

Chapter 4 The Struggle for Unionism 27

Chapter 5 Forest of Dean Miners' Union 31

Chapter 6 Dean Forest Labour Association 42

Chapter 7 Accidents and Fatalities 47

Chapter 8 Pit Stop - National Miners Lockout of 1893 52

Chapter 9 Pit Stop - South Wales Miners' Strike of 1898 61

Chapter 10 Sir Charles Dilke M.P. 1843 – 1911 79

Chapter 11 New Beginnings 83

Chapter 12 The Union Colliery Disaster 96

Chapter 13 1903 – 1910 105

Chapter 14 Pit Stop - Cambrian Combine Strike
         The Tonypandy Riots 145

Chapter 15 1911 – Forest of Dean
         The Idea for a Dilke Memorial Hospital 164

Chapter 16 Pit Stop - The 1912 Strike
         The Minimum Wage Act 177

Chapter 17 East v West Dean 193

Chapter 18 1914 – 1918 - World War I 203

Chapter 19 1918 – The end of the Great War 242

Chapter 20 1919 – The Sankey Commission 254

Chapter 21 1920 - Pit Stop - The Datum Line Strike 272

Chapter 22 1921 – Pit Stop -The National Lockout – Black Friday 288

Chapter 23 The Aftermath - 1922, 1923, 1924
            Opening of the Dilke Memorial Hospital
            Opening of the Lydney Power Station.. 314

Chapter 24 1925 – The Subsidy 354

Chapter 25 1926 – Pit Stop – The General Strike 376

Chapter 26 The Lockout - The miners fight on alone 395

Chapter 27 The Aftermath 435

List of Illustrations

Fig. 1	Geology Plan of the Forest of Dean	v
Fig. 2	Effigy of Forest of Dean Freeminers Brass	xvi
Fig. 3	Geological Cross Section of the Forest of Dean	1
Fig. 4	Coal measures in the Forest of Dean	2
Fig. 5	Coal Seams and their depths in the F.O.D.	5
Fig. 6	Mural of Warren James	6
Fig. 7	Warren James calls for Freeminers Meeting	7
Fig. 8	Modern day copy of an original style Bloomery	10
Fig. 9	Cinderford Ironworks	14
Fig. 10	Lower Soudley Ironworks	15
Fig. 11	David Mushet c.1845	16
Fig. 12	Robert Forester Mushet	17
Fig. 13	Remains of the Darkhill Ironworks	18
Fig. 14	Sectional diagram showing the Plateway	19
Fig. 15	Map showing S & W Tramroads	21
Fig. 16	Remains of tramroad stone blocks in Bixlade valley	22
Fig. 17	Forest of Dean Railway system in 1880	24
Fig. 18	Severn Railway Bridge – Completed in 1879	25
Fig. 19	A Lasting reminder - the Dean Forest Steam Railway	26
Fig. 20	An early Davy Lamp	28
Fig. 21	Coal Hewing at Lightmoor Colliery	29
Fig. 22	Engraving depicting a boy pulling a hod of coal	29
Fig. 23	Types of Coal Mining Methods	30
Fig. 24	Trafalgar Colliery	34
Fig. 25	Tim Mountjoy	35
Fig. 26	Issue 2 of the F.O.D. Examiner – August 9th 1873	36
Fig. 27	Mr George Rowlinson	40
Fig. 28	Tons of coal raised	47
Fig. 29	Records of many fatalities spanning 85 years	48
Fig. 30	Accident record at the Parkend Deep Collieries, 1893	49
Fig. 31	Flour Mill Colliery	59
Fig. 32	Speech House Hill Colliery	60
Fig. 33	William Abraham (Mabon)	62
Fig. 34	Welsh Miners leaving their Colliery	65
Fig. 35	Cartoon depicting deadlock in negotiations	71
Fig. 36	Sir Charles Dilke 2nd Bt.	79
Fig. 37	Lady Amelia Dilke	81
Fig. 38	Mr Keir Hardie	85
Fig. 39	Norchard Colliery, Lydney	94

Fig. 40   Crump Meadow Colliery 95
Fig. 41   Union Pit Memorial on approximate site of pit shaft 97
Fig. 42   Union Pit Disaster Memorial Plaque 99
Fig. 43   Memorial Sculpture by Matt Baker................................... 102
Fig. 44   Miners at entrance to the Gold Mine 120
Fig. 45   Cannop Colliery – sunk in 1909 135
Fig. 46   King Edward VII 138
Fig. 47   Naval Colliery at Penygraig, Ely Pit 145
Fig. 48   Police guarding the Glamorgan Colliery Power House 148
Fig. 49   Glamorgan Colliery at Llwynypia 153
Fig. 50   Powell Duffryn Colliery at Aberamon 156
Fig. 51   January the 23rd 1911 Rail Disaster near Pontypridd 157
Fig. 52   Lieutenant Colonel Henry Webb...................................... 167
Fig. 53   New Fancy Colliery 181
Fig. 54   Mr Martin Perkins 188
Fig. 55   Lightmoor Colliery 195
Fig. 56   Universal Colliery, Senghenydd 201
Fig. 57   H.M.S. Dreadnought 203
Fig. 58   Government Recruitment Drive Poster 209
Fig. 59   The Legendary Speech House and adjoining field 218
Fig. 60   Mr David Lloyd George 229
Fig. 61   Foxes Bridge Colliery 232
Fig. 62   More Men and Still More 233
Fig. 63   Waterloo Colliery – Arthur and Edward 241
Fig. 64   Mr Herbert Booth 244
Fig. 65   Mr James Wignall 245
Fig. 66   Signing of the Armistice 248
Fig. 67   Mr David Richard Organ 256
Fig. 68   Mr Frank Hodges 258
Fig. 69   David Lloyd George signing the Treaty of Versailles 264
Fig. 70   Princess Royal Colliery (Park Gutter) 274
Fig. 71   Dean Forest Mercury Notice 280
Fig. 72   Lord Bledisloe feeding the boilers at Norchard 291
Fig. 73   Miners' Annual Demonstration Poster for July1921 303
Fig. 74   Group photo taken at that meeting 304
Fig. 75   Morris's Scheme in the National Press 311
Fig. 76   Pillowell Recreation Ground workforce 315
Fig. 77   Mr John/Jack Williams 316
Fig. 78   The Original Dilke Memorial Hospital 330
Fig. 79   Dignitaries and Staff at the Opening Ceremony 331
Fig. 80   Lydney or Norchard Power Station 334
Fig. 81   Power Station view showing two cooling towers 335
Fig. 82   Mr Arthur J. Cook 341
Fig. 83   FODMA Notice to discuss the Settlement 364
Fig. 84   Charles Bathurst – 1st Viscount Bledisloe 369

Fig. 85   Forest of Dean Miners Welfare Fund Foundation Stone...... 373
Fig. 86   Notice issued by the Home Secretary 380
Fig. 87   FODMA Poster Advertising the Speech House Meeting 381
Fig. 88   General Strike Bulletin issued on the 4th of May 1926 384
Fig. 89   Mounted Police in a baton charge 385
Fig. 90   Sir John Simon's Declaration 386
Fig. 91   Forest of Dean M.P. Mr Alf Purcell 387
Fig. 92   Armoured cars on the streets of London 388
Fig. 93   Prime Minister Baldwin's Declaration 389
Fig. 94   The T.U.C General Council's Response 390
Fig. 95   Volunteer Engine Drivers and Firemen 391
Fig. 96   Pugh, Citrine and Baldwin after calling off the strike 393
Fig. 97   Arthur Cook speaking in Sunderland   397
Fig. 98   Lydney Observer report of the Fryers Level incidents 403
Fig. 99   July 1926 Annual Demonstration Poster 406
Fig. 100   Notice of the 11th of July 1926 meeting 408
Fig. 101   Miniature Miners Lamps worn as a badge 409
Fig. 102   Eastern United Colliery 412
Fig. 103   Coal Owners' Propaganda Notice 415
Fig. 104   Delegates arriving at Moscow Railway Station 416
Fig. 105   Moscow – Meeting at the Miners Executive 417
Fig. 106   Vlassovka Anthracite Pit – Shakhta(Donbas) 418
Fig. 107   New Extension to the Dilke Memorial Hospital..................... 419
Fig. 108   View of 'The Dilke' today – c. 2023 421
Fig. 109   Mr Arthur Cook speaking at the Speech House 425
Fig. 110   Northern United Colliery 436
Fig. 111   The last Miners' Annual Demonstration, July 1939.............. 438
Fig. 112   Jack Williams on his retirement 439
Fig. 113   Banner of the Forest of Dean District of the
             National Union of Mineworkers 441

Acknowledgements

I would like to sincerely thank the following people without whose help and support in supplying me with much valued information, this publication could not have been produced: Mrs Vera Wildin, Mr George Organ, Mr Mark Organ, Mr Graham Morgan and Mr Ian Wright. I also wish to thank my long suffering wife Sue for putting up with my long absences while tucked away researching and writing this book.

I would also like to acknowledge and thank the following Organisations for the many photographs and images from their collections that are included in this publication.

Dean Heritage Centre, Camp Mill, Soudley, Cinderford, Miners Welfare Hall, Cinderford, Sun Green website www.sungreen.co.uk, South Wales Coalfield Collection, Swansea University – The Richard Burton Archives, National Museum of Wales, The People's Collection of Wales, University of Warwick Library, Durham Mining Museum, Wikipedia.

References;

Gloucestershire Live Online, Forest of Dean Local History Society, 'The Little Buttymen in the Forest' by Chris Fisher, 'Blood on Coal' by Ralph Anstis, 'Forest Voices' by Humphrey Phelps, Dave Tuffley's 'Roll of Honour', 'The Miners – years of struggle' by R. Page Arnot, 'Coal on one Hand, Men on the Other' by Ian Wright, 'Walter Virgo and the Blakeney Gang' by Ian Wright, 'God's Beutiful Sunshine' by Ian Wright, 'The Industrial History of Dean' by Cyril Hart, 'A look back at Norchard' by Dr Graham J. Field, The Gloucester Citizen, The Gloucester Journal, 'The Forest in Old Photographs' by Humphrey Phelps, 'The Dilke Memorial Hospital' by Nick Oldnall, The British Newspaper Archive, Forest of Dean Newspapers, Cinderford, Glos., General Register Office.

Author's Notes

There are many excellent publications relating to events concerning the mining industry in the Forest of Dean. Without a doubt they still stand as a lasting tribute to those who toiled beneath the earth to try and earn a decent standard of living and to provide food on the table for their families. My intention for writing this book was to try to encompass the accepted history of the Forest of Dean without trespassing on other writers' work. In the event this proved difficult to achieve. Obviously I could not have proceeded without the many references listed above but I have always tried to adopt my own way of expressing the facts enclosed.

It may be said that my inclusion of accidents and fatalities has cast a dark shadow over the book but in my view it illustrates the sacrifices that our men, women and children made in order to survive those hard times and should never be forgotten. These days it is so different and visitors to the beautiful Forest of Dean come to admire the beauty and tranquillity of the area without realising the reality of our industrial past.

In researching those accidents and fatalities there is good cause to believe that I may have omitted some events and people from the list. This is not intentional but due to the fact that details are sometimes difficult to find and often impossible. My apologies go to the relatives and friends of those that I have omitted.

In trying to convey to the reader the overall concept of the miners struggle nationally, I have sometimes strayed across our border to describe events that took place within our neighbouring coalfield, that in South Wales. This is important as there are so many myths and false reports of those events that I thought it right to record them as accurately as I could with reference to official documents. Also, the South Wales coalfield is geographically located and of a size as to create a lot of influence within the Forest of Dean. Obviously, many similar events were happening in all parts of the country in those difficult times but to try to record each and every event would take up several volumes.

I have also taken the liberty of straying beyond the miners' cause but still connected to it through the social system to record events within the Forest that would be of special interest to readers including WWI, the birth of the Dilke Memorial Hospital and the Lydney Power Station.

The character of the Forest of Dean has always been shaped by the people who live or have lived in it. Past events have shown the character and fighting spirit of those that have gone before. It is to them that we owe our good fortune to still be able to live within a community that looks after each other while at the same time strives to retain certain elements of our heritage for future generations to appreciate.

We all leave our mark in one way or another on this Earth but the Forest of Dean miners were a special breed who deserve our gratitude for persevering under extreme social conditions to try and achieve a better life for their children, grandchildren and successive generations and that is the reason why we are all still here today.

Dave Organ

Fig. 2   Effigy of Forest of Dean Free-miner's Brass of unknown origin depicted in Newland Parish Church of a 15th Century Miner with a hod strapped to his back, candle in his mouth and a pick in his hand.

Prologue

It was a Saturday morning in early September and the air was still. The only sound in this small mining village was the distant hum from the local pit which still worked the Saturday shift. It had a sound all of its own, generated by the steam powered machinery, intermingled with the regular echoed shouts from the surface workers going about their tasks. The air was smoky from a hundred or so cottage hearths burning the local house-coal and the unmistakable aroma of wood-smoke from garden couch-fires. A peaceful setting you would think. But, not far away, death was lurking underground.

The boy saw them coming up the rutted lane – an old nag plodding along and pulling a wooden cart with two men in pit clothes walking alongside, heads lowered. They passed him and pulled up at a cottage across the lane where his friend lived. He could see a form in the back of the cart but couldn't make out what it was until the two men carefully pulled it away on a makeshift board. It was a body covered in a large cloth bandage like an Egyptian mummy and they carried it in through an open gate to the cottage door. Within a few seconds, the back-kitchen door opened and there was a great wailing and cries of; **'no, no, no'**, and; **'Jack, Jack, Jack, what have they done.'**

As the wailing continued but more muffled as they all moved inside the cottage, the boy leaned on the garden fork he was using to lift some potatoes near the garden wall and waited. As he watched, the two men came away from the cottage with the empty board and slid it back onto the cart. One of the men took hold of the horse's bridle and turned the horse and cart round and returned the way they had come. As they went by, one of the men said; **'ow be Dave', sad day aint it?'** the boy said; **'whats 'appened then?'** The other man said; **'Accident up at the pit, rock fell on 'im an' crushed 'is bunes. Go and tell thee mam to go over and see what can be done var 'im'.** The boy let go of the garden fork and rushed into the house calling **'mam, mam, there's bin an accident up at the pit'.** Mam came rushing down from upstairs saying; **'who'** and he told her what he'd just seen and told by the two men. Mam was widely known for her medical knowledge and experience so she quickly grabbed her usual bag and ran up the lane to the cottage.

When she came back, the boy could see that she was upset and so he was a little reluctant to ask questions. Sat at the kitchen table with a freshly brewed pot of tea, she eventually said; **'Doctor's comin' soon so we'll know more then but there's not much 'ope I'm sad to say'**. He said no more and went back outside to his chore of digging potatoes. He soon heard the clatter of hooves and looked up to see the local Doctor coming down the lane in his customary pony and trap. He wowed the pony outside the injured man's cottage, dismounted from the trap, grabbed his medical bag and rushed inside. He came back out about 15 minutes later, climbed aboard the trap and with a click of his tongue, the pony trotted away. They drove past but there was no glance from the Doctor in his direction.

Later, when the family were sitting round the kitchen table having their tea, the boy was all ears as the news of a serious accident in the pit had swept through the village. He had heard of pit accidents before but had never seen the result of a man that had been injured in one. This brought home to him what working life in a pit would one day mean for him but it made little or no difference to the general way of life and he knew that one day, he would be working in the pit and facing those same risks.

Next day at school, Miss Phillips the head teacher called all the children into the main schoolroom and told them that young Arthur's dad had had a pit accident and had gone to Jesus during the night. She also said that young Arthur wouldn't be coming back to school again this week and that they should all pray for his father's soul and for the whole family.

Help for the tragic family was overwhelming from villagers and they would do what they could to provide food and clothes for them. There was little or no compensation from the pit owner and so the bereaved family had to rely on the good nature of neighbours until they could somehow support themselves again.

The funeral was set for the following Saturday and the boy's mam had gone over to the cottage to do the laying out of Arthur's dad (washed, cleaned, shaved and dressed) ready to be put into the coffin. It wasn't a pleasant task to have to do after the body had been subjected to broken flesh and bones but mam had been called to do it before in the village so she was accustomed to handling broken bodies. The coffin came on a cart the next day and mam and dad helped lay Arthur's dad in it. Another two neighbouring miner friends helped manoeuvre and carry the coffin downstairs and put it on two trestles in the front room. The lid was left off so that friends and neighbours could call in and pay their respects over the next couple of days. Some neighbours and friends had picked flowers from their own gardens and arranged them in pots around the room so as to give a more fragrant smell.

This could be the experience of any young lad growing up in the Forest of Dean during the 1800's. His life was no different from many other lads from any other of the tough families whose main source of income was from working in the pits or quarries. Mining had always been a dangerous occupation and the families of these miners lived at all times under the shadow of accidents but it was a way of life that they endured without giving it too much conscious thought.

D.M.O.

Chapter 1
The Ancient Forest of Dean

The Forest of Dean sits between the rivers Severn and Wye and a simplified geological cross section of it resembles a raised crater with steep sloping outer sides and a slightly depressed centre bowl – known as an Asymmetrical Syncline. Shaped like saucers stacked above one another, its underlying geology has undoubtedly influenced centuries of industrial activity especially around the rim where the sedimentary bands of crease limestone, old red sandstone and shale outcrops are easily accessible. Nearer the centre or core, are bands of carboniferous Westphalian coal measures. To complicate matters, the stratum contains many faults where the layers or bands have sheared and slipped, over time.

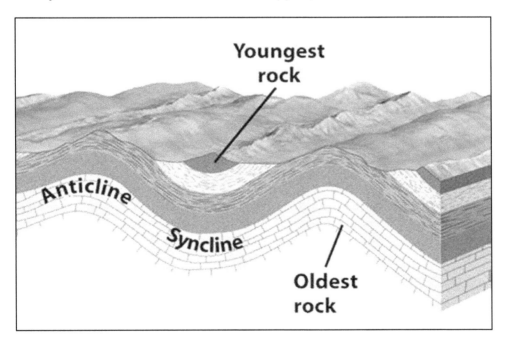

Fig. 3 Diagram showing how earth movements during the Hercynian period, formed the basic Geological shape of the Forest of Dean.

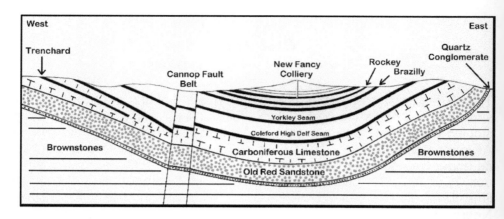

Fig. 4 Simplified east/west cross sectional diagram showing coal measures in the Forest of Dean

Dense woodlands once covered this area to the extent of over 100,000 acres and there is evidence of human habitation as far back as the middle Mesolithic period i.e. the Middle Stone Age dating from 9,000 BC to 4,300 BC. A recent survey has also uncovered a monument at Tidenham near Chepstow, constructed during the Bronze Age which has been roughly dated as between 2500 and 1500 BC. At the time of the Roman Conquest in 43AD, Britain was inhabited by tribal Celts, who had brought the working of Iron with them from mainland Europe. The Forest of Dean was part of an area occupied by the Dobunni tribe whose warlike neighbours to the west being the Silures. The latter were a short, swarthy warlike tribe who occupied a large part of present day South Wales and who may have migrated periodically to parts of the Forest of Dean. They put up fierce resistance to Roman occupation and their leader King Caractacus was eventually defeated in the Welsh Marches in 51AD and dispatched to Rome.

However, the Dobunnii, unlike their western neighbours were not warlike and were content as farmers, settling in small communities. One interesting implement they brought to Britain was the Iron plough. When the Romans came, the Dobunnii readily submitted to their rule and laws and adopted their way of life. Their territorial capital was at Cirencester which the Romans named Corinium.

The Romans of course left a great deal of evidence of their time in Britain and established local towns and cities such as Gloucester (Glevum),

Blestium (Monmouth), Aquae Sulis (Bath) and Londinium (London). Roadways such as Ermin Way, Fosse Way, Akeman Street and Watling Street are also reminders of their occupation that exist to this day. It has been suggested that their interest in the Forest of Dean was primarily due to its Iron reserves with apparent easy access to the outcrops on its western and northern rim. Evidence of their iron mining activities stretch across this area from Lydney in the southwest, the scowles at Bream and Coleford to Wigpool common in the northeast. A large settlement known as Ariconium existed near Weston under Penyard and Bromsash in the north which is known to have been a large industrial Iron working site with Bloomeries and Forges. It came under Roman control for 300 years but was abandoned when they returned to Rome.

The name 'Royal Forest' has existed since the time of the Saxon Kings. King Canute gave this Royal Forest its first Charter, written in Danish in 1016 and which was subsequently upheld by William the Conqueror but with severe tightening of their laws – poaching could then be punishable by a cruel death.

There are many references as to the origins of the Free-mining Rights and Privileges that were granted to the miners of the Forest of Dean – allegedly by either Edward I or Edward III for their contribution to the various sieges of Berwick upon Tweed during the Scottish Wars of Independence in the 13th and 14th Centuries. The date of 1244 keeps cropping up but the first capture of Berwick didn't take place until 1296 - however it is recorded that Free-mining Rights and Privileges already existed by 1244.

By the early 17th Century, the Free-miners rights and privileges were being challenged, not only by the Ironmasters who were allowed by the King to take whatever amount of ore they required but also by Local Landowners. They tried to persuade the King that mining within the Forest earned the King nothing while at the same time consuming the King's timber in the process. Leases to mine for ore and coal were granted to various Landowners but the Free-miners resisted this attempt on their Rights by causing some damage to their workings. Over time, the miners, being a tenacious lot, resisted many attempts to limit their rights and privileges and so they survived these onslaughts.

The earliest known document recording the Miners Laws and Privileges and dating from 1610 is set out in the **'Book of Denis'** which is effectively the Dean Miners Bill of Rights. This was succeeded in 1682 by the **Mine**

Law Court, established by the Free-miners for Free-miners and could be argued to be the earliest form of Unionism. Disputes could be settled by a court jury of 12 fellow miners that sat at the Speech House and was administered by the Constable of St Briavels.

As coal output rose, prices were set by the Mine Law Court and coal was sold by the Ton, Hundredweight (1/20th of a Ton), Barrels and Bushels (3 to a Barrel). By the end of the Seventeenth Century coal production in the Forest was around 25,000 tons per year and In addition to lime coal for domestic use, coal was shipped away from quays on the River Wye in small barges to Chepstow and Monmouth and beyond while on the river Severn from quays at Gatcombe, Purton and Lydney Pill.

By the middle of the 1700's, and spurred on by the Industrial Revolution, the Crown became determined to introduce a free market for minerals within the Forest and enabled outside Industrialists 'foreigners' to purchase land with mineral rights within the Dean. Violent arguments between Miners were frequent and when the miners' privileges were conferred onto these 'foreigners' by the Crown, the Mine Law Court became ineffective.

In 1775 the Court tried to prevent the 'foreigners' from owning mines and the Deputy Gaveller, who himself had an interest in several mines, raided the Speech House offices and confiscated their box of records. By 1777 the Court ceased to function but some of these records reappeared in the hands of the Crown some fifty years later. Regardless of this, the Free-miners continued to meet unofficially in order to resolve local matters but by 1820 this practice had largely died out. The granting of land (known as Gales) for mining became the responsibility of the Gaveller who also collected the fees and royalties due from each mine.

During the 1600's a population of around 6000 were scattered around the Forest rim and many small hamlets came into being during this period as squatter settlements of wooden cabins on Crown Land. These inhabitants worked in the Ironworks or collected cordwood for making charcoal - needed for feeding the furnaces for the smelting of iron. Crown Authority, usually in the form of the Deputy Surveyor, destroyed many of these cabins but he had to abandon the practice for fear of his life. Forester and Crown Authority were ever at odds over the erosion of Commoners rights which eventually led to the Foresters breaking down the fences and occupying the woods.

4

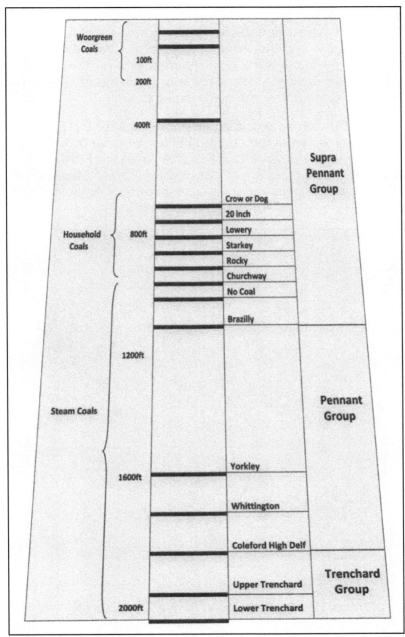

Fig. 5 Coal seams and their depths in the Forest of Dean

Warren James

Further evictions saw a general decline in Forest habitation but during the mid 1700's, miners and quarrymen returned and set up more permanent settlements using stone from local quarries to build their small primitive cottages – usually a single storey building with a hearth, one door with an earth floor and roof - and some adjoining land.

Many acres of Crown land was again enclosed after the **Enclosures Act 1808** in order to replenish the shortage of timber used by the Navy. Unrest within the Forest again came to a head between the Free-miners and the Crown due to the Act's effect of denying the Forest people their ancient mining and grazing rights and their access for hunting or removing timber for fuel.

Fig. 6 Mural of Warren James courtesy of the 'Fountain Inn' Parkend

Deputy Surveyor Edward Machin had by 1816 enclosed around 11,000 acres of woodland, with a promise of removing the fences after 20 years when the woodland had matured. This led to much unrest as many people now lived in extreme poverty and the Forest Riots of 1831 attracted much attention. Local hero Warren James was elected by the Free-miners to represent their cause and in June 1830, a petition from James opposing the Parliamentary Bill was heard in the House of Commons. This was rejected and so the Free-miners took the law into their own hands. In June 1831, James called a meeting of Free-miners with the intention of removing the fences illegally and they met at the Parkhill Enclosure and proceeded to demolish the fences. Machin arrived with other officials but they were outnumbered and withdrew. He then called in 50 troops from Monmouth to quell the riots. By the time they arrived the number of protesters had increased to over 2000 and so again they were greatly outnumbered and withdrew without firing a shot.

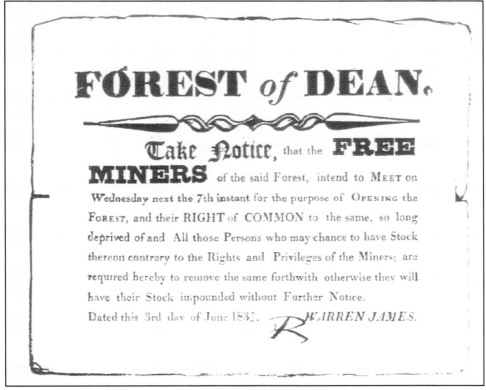

Fig. 7 Warren James calls for Free-miners meeting.

James was eventually captured, tried and sentenced to death for committing a Felony under the Riot Act. After a campaign for clemency, led by Edward Machin who captured him, within two weeks his sentence was commuted to transportation and he was transported to Van Diemen's Land (now Tasmania). Many others received prison sentences or fines and one other was also sentenced to transportation. Warren James was later pardoned for his 'crimes' but without the means to pay for his passage home. So, due to his lack of finances, he was never able to return home to the Forest of Dean and he died in a rented room in Hobart, Tasmania in October 1841. Ironically, within a decade most of the enclosures were released when the saplings had matured and mining and grazing rights were restored.

In 1831, a Royal Commission was appointed to enquire into the ongoing agitation between the 'foreigner' Industrialists and the Free-miners rights and customs in the Forest of Dean. As a result, the **Dean Forest Mines Act** was passed in 1838 and set out in clear detail the Free-miners rights to minerals and also to be able to sell their Gales to the larger Industrialists.

It states that *"All male persons born or hereafter to be born and abiding within the said Hundred of St Briavels, of the age of twenty one years and upwards, who shall have worked a year and a day in a coal or iron mine within the said Hundred of St Briavels, shall be deemed and taken to be Free Miners."*

This also included Quarrymen viz.

'All male persons born or hereafter to be born and abiding within the said Hundred, of the age of twenty-one years and upwards, who shall have worked a year and a day in a stone quarry within the said Forest, shall for the purposes of this Act, so far as relates to having gales or leases of stone quarries within the open lands of the said Forest, but not otherwise, be taken to be Free Miners.'

The middle and late 18th Century saw the first shoots of the Industrial Revolution starting to assert its influence. Inventions such as the Blast furnace, steam power and particularly in the Forest of Dean, advances in steel quality by Robert Forester Mushet all had a direct influence on the development of the mining industry and hence to the quality of the lives of the people of the Forest of Dean.

Chapter 2
The Iron Industry

The earliest form of iron smelters were known as Bloomeries – small furnaces heated with charcoal - where roasted ore was fed into the top and where the resultant iron and slag mass was referred to as a 'bloom'. A second heating process was needed to remove the slag (cinders) by hammering and forging to produce the resultant wrought iron.

Fig. 8 Modern day copy of an original style Bloomery

A Bloomery needed large quantities of charcoal, not only for heating the furnace but also to combine with the iron ore inside it in order to produce the correct grade of iron. Therefore the Forest of Dean not only had the iron reserves but also an abundant supply of wood where charcoal could be readily produced. The slag or cinders were discarded although they did contain a large degree of iron and their remains were left scattered throughout the Forest.

Before and during the Roman occupation of Britain, this was the accepted way of producing iron but it did have the effect of destroying those areas of the Forest where these activities were prominent. The Dark Ages and the Saxon period probably produced iron in much the same way and it wasn't until the Norman occupation in the 11th Century that iron manufacturing was considered more seriously. So it is little wonder then that the Royal Forest of Dean Iron reserves with their easy access near the surface eventually became of interest to the Crown. It was already a Royal Hunting Forest for Kings and by 1244 the mining of ore became regulated so that permission to do so had to be sought from the Crown.

During the middle of the 13th Century there was a boom in Iron production and by 1282 there were sixty two Bloomeries and Forges operating in the Dean. Feeding these with charcoal for smelting led to a great felling of timber and vast swathes of the Forest around its rim were reduced to open pastureland. Re-afforestation was never considered and maintaining what was left of the Royal Forest largely depended upon nature to reproduce itself with the Oak trees annually shedding their acorns. During Elizabethan times, the trees – especially the Oaks – were targeted again, but this time for the building of Queen Elizabeth I's Navy. Cut timber was easily slid down from Viney Hill to the ports of Purton and Gatcombe and then floated on the tide to the shiprights at Bristol.

The charcoal fired Blast Furnaces
The iron industry continued unabated in the late 1500's with the introduction from the Continent of the charcoal fired Blast Furnace. Originating from China in the 1st Century AD, Blast furnaces changed the way in which iron was extracted from ore by increasing the temperature inside the furnace with a blast of air provided by a pair of large bellows. Three of these furnaces were introduced to the Forest by the 1590's and by 1612 four Blast furnaces and three forges known as 'The Kings Ironworks' were in operation – each capable of producing around 700 tons of iron per year. Water with sufficient force to turn large waterwheels, needed to operate the forge bellows were the deciding factor for their location. They were located on the Cannop brook (one at Cannop and one at Parkend), the Lyd into Lydbrook (one at Upper Lydbrook) and the Soudley/Cinderford brook at Soudley (one). Other privately owned

furnaces and forges were built at Lydney, Flaxley, Gunns Mill, Brockweir, Bishopswood and Newland.

As mentioned earlier, the Forest of Dean had by now become littered with vast quantities of slag or cinders discarded from the Bloomery system of smelting and scattered at random. It was found that they contained a large percentage of un-smelted iron which the Bloomery process could not convert due to their low smelting temperatures. It was realised that this slag could now be used to supplement the raw iron ore and re-smelted within the new Blast Furnaces to produce the more refined type of pig iron.

Blast furnaces had a voracious appetite for charcoal and there were many disputes between owners and freeminers over the illegal felling of trees needed to feed them. The Crown interceded and temporarily suspended their working on two separate occasions but later in 1621 they were released.

Sir John Wintour (or Winter) of Lydney who owned vast swathes of forest was a well established Ironmaster by this time, inheriting Ironworks at Lydney from his father Sir Edward Wintour. Sir John was one of the chief offenders and local opposition to his enclosing of land and interfering with Commoners rights, provoked the riots of 1631. But he was also favoured by the King and had ambitions of acquiring many of the Forest's Ironworks and expanding the number of forges. By 1640 he had succeeded in acquiring *'All his Majesty's lands, waste, soil, minerals, trees and under-wood in Dean comprising nearly 18,000 acres'* to include the Kings Ironworks' for the sum of £106,000.

During the English Civil War (1642-1651), Royalist Sir John destroyed his own home 'The White House' at Lydney rather than it be acquired by Parliamentarian Forces. His chief adversary, Parliamentarian Sir Edward Massey acquired the leases for all Wintour's partly destroyed Ironworks and re-assigned them to favoured individuals. In 1646 however, he sold his interests for £2,000 but again the woods suffered large areas of de-afforestation and Ironmaking was suspended until 1653. Iron was still in demand especially for the military and Parliament ordered new furnaces to be built and others repaired and so the cycle continued.

Sir John Wintour survived the Civil War, recovered his Estates at the Restoration of King Charles II, with the exception of the Kings Ironworks. He petitioned the Crown for reimbursement of past losses and in 1662, was eventually granted a lease on the Parkend Ironworks. So he returned to attack the Forest but local opposition put a stop to his activities and a survey of 1667 showed that he had felled 30,000 trees and had left only 200 standing. In the same year the **Dean Forest Re-afforestation Act** became law and large areas were then enclosed, replanted and allowed to grow. All the Kings Ironworks were ordered to be destroyed in 1674 and Wintour lost his monopoly of the Forest.

Myths and legends surround the name of Sir John Wintour, chiefly the story where he was escaping on horseback from the Parliamentarian Forces. Desperate to get away, he leapt over the cliffs at Lancaut on the river Wye and landed safely on the other side. To this day that location is known as 'Wintour's Leap'. Had he in fact leapt over the cliffs, he would most certainly have perished in the fall to the river below.

However, the story was true, up to a point. He did in fact on two occasions escape across the river Wye from the Parliamentarian Forces but both were by boat – one in 1644 near the cliffs at Sedbury and the other was in fact at Lancaut in 1645.

Many of the other Forest Ironworks were owned by the Foley family who appeared to have a monopoly in the Forest but there were others who continued as privateers. Most were located around the fringes of the Forest and they continued production using the many old and decaying trees and coppice that still scattered the area for charcoal production. Charcoal remained the main source of fuel for Blast furnaces for the next 100 years and while some furnaces and forges disappeared, others were built to replace them.

The coke fired Blast Furnaces
Many experiments were being made during this period to try to successfully extract the sulphur and other impurities from coal so as to convert it to a more efficient fuel – Coke. Some experiments were undertaken by Sir John Wintour of Lydney by heating the coal without oxygen but none were successful, probably due to the low quality coal being mined at this time.

However, the beginning of the 19th Century marked a turning point for iron production when a more efficient method of producing coke by burning coal without air was found. The resultant Coke became the basis of the Coke fired Blast Furnace created by Abraham Darby and thence to the start of the Industrial Revolution.

Also helping this transfer was the invention of the Steam Engine which replaced the age-old waterwheel as a source of energy and so it was that coal began to outstrip Iron as a mineral resource in the Forest of Dean and so the move away from the destruction of the Forest woods began. Furnaces able to use coke for fuel began to appear at various sites within the Forest – those at Cinderford, Soudley, Parkend, Whitecliffe, Darkhill and Bromley being the largest and most productive.

These Industrial sized operations were financed and run by outside Industrialists, 'foreigners' as described in Chapter 1 who had the financial backing to purchase mineral rights and to set up these new furnaces. Prominent among them being William Crawshay, Edward Protheroe, Moses Teague, Charles Bathurst and David Mushet.

Fig. 9 Cinderford Ironworks – four coke-fired Blast Furnaces c.1875

14

Many advances were now being made to the quality of Iron produced and the old system of blast power from water wheels was being superseded by steam power so the need of a prominent watercourse was eliminated – water heads such as Cannop and Soudley ponds were constructed before steam power was introduced. With demand now increasing as the Industrial Revolution took hold, the number of furnaces at each of these sites either doubled or quadrupled. That of course, increased the need for more and more coke to fire these furnaces and so these prominent men also began investing in sinking the deep coal mines such as Crump Meadow, Lightmoor, Heywood and Parkend where the quality of Low Delf coal was found to be suitable for coking.

Fig. 10 Lower Soudley Ironworks – two coke fired blast furnaces

A little known bi-product from the blast furnace slag or cinders was a vitreous substance used as an ingredient for the manufacture of glass bottles. The slag needed to be crushed to a fine powder in a Stamping mill and after washing and grading, the resultant product was sent to Bristol for making green bottle glass. Any remaining amounts of iron were sent back to the furnaces for recycling. Stamping mills run by waterwheels appeared at both Redbrook and Parkend.

The name of David Mushet is of such importance within this industry that his name should not go unmentioned within these pages. He was a Scottish Metallurgist who was persuaded to invest in the new Whitecliffe Blast furnace and thus moved with his family to live in Coleford. His association with his business partner deteriorated so he started conducting experiments in a nearby barn.

The result was the discovery of a refined iron directly from the Blast furnace without the necessity of further refinement – as was needed with current output. He obtained land at Darkhill near Gorsty Knoll, Milkwall and built his small furnace and continued to produce his refined iron which he patented. He built a larger blast furnace using a steam powered blowing engine, a casting house and an office but used it mainly for experimentation purposes. He was also a shrewd investor in iron ore and coal mines and was one of the first to install tram-roads within the Forest.

Fig. 11 David Mushet. Courtesy of the DHC, Soudley, Cinderford.

His youngest son Robert Forester Mushet, encouraged by his father also took a great interest in metallurgy and in 1845, with his brother David, took over the running of his father's business at Darkhill. David senior died in 1847 and his mining interests were split between his three sons – the other being William but there were disagreements between them and in 1847 the partnership was dissolved. Robert started a new venture naming it Robert Mushet and Co., Forest Steel Works and in 1862 moved a short distance to what became known as the Titanic Steel Works. As a Metallurgist, Robert wrote many pamphlets and theses on the properties of steel alloys and how to improve their quality. When Henry Bessemer invented his method of producing steel using his special Converter in 1856, he ran into trouble with its quality and sought the advice of Robert Mushet. He had discovered a method which could guarantee good quality steel which he patented. When he couldn't afford to renew the patent, Bessemer acquired it and consequently made his fortune.

By 1868 Robert had discovered how to produce a self hardening high carbon steel that was named 'R. Mushet's Special Steel' - in today's terms means Tool Steel – a product that was hard enough to be used to cut other metals with machine tools and could be re-sharpened and re-shaped again and again. This Tool steel revolutionised industrial metalworking and was the forerunner of Tungsten high speed steel. Nevertheless, the Company ran into financial trouble and the works came to a standstill in 1871 and was wound up in 1874. Ironically, in 1876 Robert was awarded the Bessemer Gold Medal for outstanding services to the Steel Industry. He died in 1891 and is buried with his family in Cheltenham cemetery. Today, very little remains of the Titanic Steelworks.

Fig. 12 Robert Forester Mushet.
Courtesy of DHC,
Soudley, Cinderford.

Around this time – towards the end of the 19th Century – there was a general decline in the Forest of Dean Iron industry, caused mainly due to the lack of demand for its ore. Dean ore had a low concentration of phosphorous and became incompatible with the advances made in the Bessemer process of producing steel. It also had to compete with cheaper imported Spanish ore. In 1878 the only Forest of Dean Ironworks still in production was the Crawshay Cinderford plant and by 1890 only one of their furnaces was in use. The works closed for good in 1894 and literally saw the end of Iron production in Dean.

Fig. 13 Remains of the Darkhill Ironworks

Chapter 3
Tramways to Railways

As the newly legalised Free-mining Industrialists gained a foothold in the Forest they started investing large sums of money in sinking the deeper pits and coal was therefore being mined in ever increasing quantities. Towards the end of the 18th Century production was near 95,000 tons per year from around 90 active pits. Exported coal was being shipped through the river quays as described earlier but moving coal or iron ore within the Forest itself had always been carried out using packhorses through woods with unmade tracks. This inefficient and expensive means of transport meant that many export markets were being lost to other coalfields so an alternative had to be found.

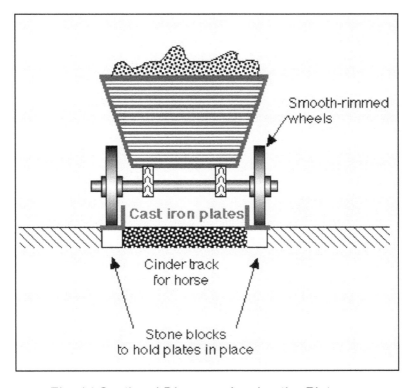

Fig. 14 Sectional Diagram showing the Plateway.

Industrialists such as the Protheroe family, David Mushet, Sam Hewlett, James Teague and others became established deep mine owners – Edward Protheroe owning at least 10 coal mines. They sought to create a network of tram-roads in the Forest for the efficient transportation of iron and coal for export and the first was built by James Teague in 1795. His tramroad ran from his pit at Edge End down to the wharf at Lower Lydbrook, a distance of three miles. It was a narrow gauge plateway tramroad with L shaped rails and using horse-drawn wagons equipped with flat iron wheels.

The Bullo Pill Railway Company constructed the Bullo Pill to Ruspidge tramway/plateway in 1807 that had a 4ft gauge and by 1809 had extended the line to Cinderford.

In 1809, the Protheroes, David Mushet and Sam Hewlett formed the Lydney and Lydbrook Railway Company and were authorised by Act of Parliament to construct a tram-road or plateway through the Cannop valley via Parkend and Myrestock to join the towns of Lydney with Lydbrook and consequently the two rivers. By the middle of 1810, the plateway track with a gauge of 3ft 6inches had been laid with other adjoining branches to the more remote coal, iron ore and ochre mines.

The Company changed its name to the Severn and Wye Railway and Canal Company and construction began on a canal and harbour to extend the line to the River Severn. By 1790, a canal known as Piddocks Canal had already been built to carry iron products from Upper and Lower Forges on the Cannop Brook (River Lyd) to the Severn at Lydney Pill. When this later canal was constructed, Piddocks was connected into it. By 1812 many of these tram-roads were in use and minerals were able to be more efficiently transported – especially from the more remote mines - using horse-drawn trams or drams.

The Coleford to Monmouth tramway/plateway was completed in 1817 and ran from the Howlers Hill quarries east of Coleford, through the centre of Coleford and via Redbrook on the river Wye to May Hill east of the Wye at Monmouth – again with extensions and an incline at Redbrook serving the smaller mines and quarries along the way. – all these tramways were originally built by separate Companies and were designed to serve the rivers of the Wye and Severn for both the coal and iron industries.

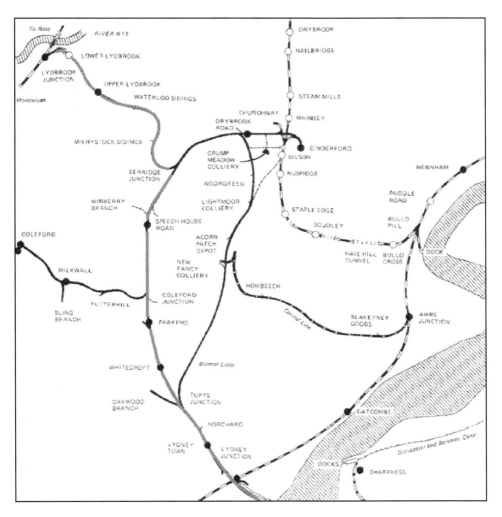

Fig. 15 Map showing S. & W. Tramroads

David Mushet was responsible for the construction in 1827 of the long Oakwood tramway/plateway linking his mines from Clements End and Noxon via Flour Mill to the Parkend Ironworks and the Severn and Wye railway. In 1891 the Oakwood branch line from Tufts Junction was extended from the Park Gutter to join the Oakwood tramway just south east of the Flour Mill.

The 'Severn and Wye Railway and Canal Co.' with their new canal and locks at Lydney operated their tramway/plateway narrow gauge system with tolls at intervals charging per wagon per mile but due to a lack of efficient weighing machines, early users of these tramroads went free. The Company were constantly short of investment money and so were slow to upgrade their system, so much so that in 1851 when the South Wales Railway built their locomotive run broad gauge line from Gloucester to Cardiff with an intersection at Lydney, the Severn and Wye Railway were unable or unwilling to modernise their tramway. Consequently, horse drawn wagons were manually unloaded and reloaded onto the main line for shipment – a state of affairs that couldn't go on.

Fig. 16 Remains of tramroad stone blocks in the Bixslade valley - Photo Author

From 1853 it was agreed to upgrade the line but to still retain the old plateway narrow gauge system. A locomotive engine was delivered in 1860 despite doubts about whether the line could sustain the weight of a locomotive engine. When it was proposed to construct a Mineral Loop line from the Tufts junction to Drybrook road in 1869, the Company had already converted to broad gauge from Lydney to Cannop. The South Wales Railway then became The Great Western Railway and in 1871 declared its intention to convert their line to standard gauge. By 1872, the new Mineral

Loop had been laid as standard gauge and the rest of the broad gauge line also converted to the new standard gauge system.

The Bullo Pill Railway had been taken over by the Forest of Dean Railway Co. in 1826 and in 1852 had been acquired by the South Wales Railway Co. They introduced a junction on the main line to connect with the Pill and also converted it to broad gauge. It was later converted to standard gauge by the Great Western Railway Company. Another railway was proposed – the Forest of Dean Central Railway – to run from a yet to be constructed port on the Severn, east of Blakeney to Foxes Bridge colliery west of Cinderford.

After many years of argument, legal actions and changes to the route, it eventually opened in 1868 from a junction with the Great Western Railway at Awre to Howbeach colliery with a further proposed extension to New Fancy. It was converted to standard gauge in 1872. In 1875 the steeply graded Parkend to Coleford extension was completed and served both the Milkwall iron mines and the Mushet Ironworks at Darkhill.

The last part of this vast jigsaw puzzle network of railways was the building of the Severn Railway Bridge which opened in 1879. It ran on a one track line from the Severn and Wye Railway and GWR Junction at Lydney to the docks at Sharpness where Forest of Dean coal was to be delivered and where it met a branch of the Midland Railway to Berkeley Road to accommodate passenger traffic for the Gloucester to Bristol route. Due to various financial difficulties and mergers during its five year construction, the Midland Railway was eventually granted the running powers.

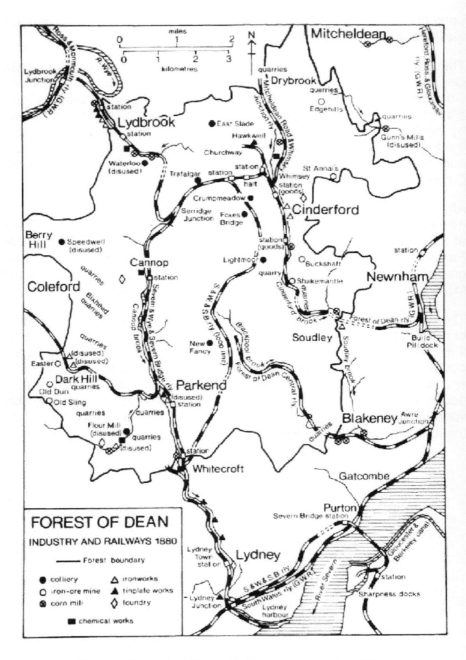

Fig. 17 Forest of Dean Railway system in 1880.

Unfortunately, and for a number of reasons, the coal trade suffered during this time and the volume of mineral traffic across the bridge didn't materialise. However, passenger trade was brisk and the Severn and Wye Railway ran seven passenger trains daily to Berkeley Road with reduced services from the furthest locations such as Lydbrook and Coleford – the main service being from their new station at Lydney Junction.

Fig. 18 Severn Railway Bridge – completed in 1879

In summary, the construction of the tramways was a great step forward to solving the problems of transportation and consequently the financial viability of the export trade of Forest of Dean minerals. Trade was boosted even further with the introduction in the mid 1800's of locomotive power on a more standardised rail system and the network was progressively added to during the latter half of the 19th Century.

Today, there are few reminders of those early tramway systems but a few stone blocks that supported the L plate rails can still be seen on some remote routes. The Author remembers a popular short-cut between Pillowell and Whitecroft called 'the dram' where an early tramway carried coal from Pillowell Level and Random Shot to the Whitecroft loading bay and where the rails were still visible during the 1940's and 1950's. Others may still survive but are probably buried deep in the woodlands.

Fig. 19 A lasting reminder - the Dean Forest Steam Railway.

Chapter 4
The Struggle for Unionism

As working conditions deteriorated and the number of fatal accidents in mines increased, there was an increasing determination for workers to create Miners Unions. Mine Owners were opposed to this, accusing the miners of following revolutionary doctrines so the miners were forced to hold meetings in secret and away from the workplace.

However, in 1800 Prime Minister William Pitt introduced the **'Combination Laws'** which made it illegal for workers to join together (to combine) and press their employers for shorter hours or more pay. This made these workers gatherings illegal and provoked an outcry that was supported by several Members of Parliament. In 1824 the Act was repealed and replaced with a **Combinations of Workmen Act 1825** which although recognising Trade Unions, restricted their activities and forbade the right of workers to Strike.

The Tolpuddle Martyrs

In 1834 six men were arrested and accused of being members of a Friendly Society and swearing secret oaths. They were tried and convicted and sentenced to Transportation of seven years penal servitude in New South Wales. These men were agricultural workers who protested against the lowering of their wages in the village of Tolpuddle in Dorset. After a popular appeal with over 800,000 signatures and a march, the workers were pardoned in 1836 and all returned home. This was just one example of how determined working men were to fight for better working conditions and a living wage.

Extremely poor working conditions continued unabated – children (boys and girls) as young as eight years of age were forced to work underground for up to fourteen hours a day, pulling sleds of coal along three feet high passages in the dust and damp - coal dust was in the air in high concentrations and black lung disease was the dominant health problem. This was later diagnosed as pneumoconiosis and was a major cause of death in men at the age of sixty five. Rock falls were numerous especially while a hewer was undercutting a seam of coal causing death or injury to many. Flooding could happen suddenly and again be the cause of many deaths. Explosions in the deep mines where firedamp and airborne coal dust were present caused countless deaths in the 19th Century eventually leading to the development of the miners'safety lamp.

The development of the safety lamp would in itself take up a whole Chapter but this foreshortened version should provide the the reader with general idea. The first miners' safety lamp was invented by Sir Humphrey Davy and first tested in 1816. Following several pit explosions caused by abuse of the Davy lamp, George Stephenson developed his own version which was well received within the mining community. Later, Dr William Clanny invented what is now known as the 'Clanny' or 'Geordie' lamp in 1839 and was the most favoured of safety lamps in Britain until the introduction of electric lamps from the 1890's.

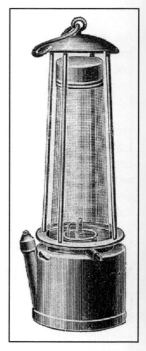

Many fatal accidents made national headlines including the Felling colliery disaster near Gateshead in 1812 when a large explosion caused the death of 92 miners. In 1838 at the Huskar colliery near Barnsley, a thunderstorm caused a stream to overflow into a ventilation shaft drowning 26 young boys and girls working underground. This reached the ears of Queen Victoria who ordered an enquiry into Britain's factories and mines. The investigation was chaired by Lord Ashley who met with opposition from Colliery Owners but eventually a Bill was passed.

Fig. 20 Early Davy Lamp

The **Mines and Collieries Act 1842** 'forbade the labour of women underground or of boys below ten years of age'. Colliery Owners in particular objected to this and other parts of the legislation but women could still be employed above ground and boys over the age of ten could still be employed underground. Enforcing these rules on Owners was near impossible due to the fact that there was only one mine Inspector for the whole country so women and children continued to work down the mines. In 1850 it was estimated that in the South Wales collieries, over 200 women and girls still worked underground so the number of Inspectors increased. In 1872, regulations raised the age of boys who could legally work in the mines to 12.

Fig. 21 Coal hewing at Lightmoor Colliery – courtesy of DHC, Soudley, Cinderford.

Fig. 22 Engraving depicting a boy pulling a hod of coal

Another disaster occurred in January 1862 at Hartley Colliery in Northumberland when the beam of the pumping engine broke and fell down the shaft trapping the men and children below and causing 204 deaths. This led to a change in the law which meant that mines had to have at least two shafts, one acting as a means of escape.

In December 1866, a series of underground explosions at the Oaks pit near Barnsley in Yorkshire caused the deaths of 361 miners which included 27 rescuers. This large Colliery had a history of explosions, deaths and strikes dating back to 1845 and in every case, firedamp and afterdamp being the cause. At the time it was the worst pit accident in England and left 167 widows and 366 fatherless children. The mine had to be sealed to extinguish the underground fires and was reopened in 1870 after all the remaining bodies had been recovered.

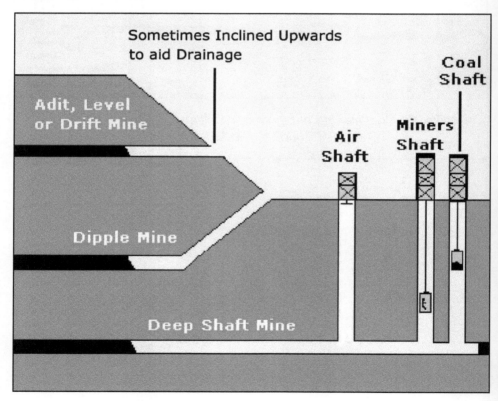

Fig. 23 Types of coal mining methods – image Author

Chapter 5
Forest of Dean Miners' Union

In 1869 two miners in Lancashire formed The **Amalgamated Association of Miners Union (AAM)** that held their first Conference in 1870 and which attracted delegates from the South Wales and Staffordshire coalfields. In 1871, the power of collective bargaining showed results when the Union was successful in their demands after a twelve week strike in South Wales and another in 1873 which saw another rise in wages. However the Coal Owners decided to form their own Associations to combat the workers Union and this, coupled with a downturn in demand for coal, led to the decline of the Union. Several disputes in the mid 1870's without strike pay saw disunity within its ranks and in 1875 the **AAM** became bankrupt and was dissolved in August of that year.

It is fair to say that prior to 1871 there was no Miners' Union in the Forest of Dean. Before then, Forest of Dean miners of minerals which includes Iron ore, coal, quarrying and ochre mining were loosely controlled by a peculiar custom known as 'Free-miners rights' as mentioned previously. This custom limited the rights to mine or quarry minerals to people born within the Forest and to exclude 'foreigners' from outside the area. This custom was further reinforced by the 'Book of Denis' in 1610 and later by the Mine Law Court in1682 and again more clearly defined with the **Dean Forest Mines Act** in 1838.

At that time of course, many Forest Free-miners, eager to exploit their hard won leases or gales and with the Crown's consent, formed partnerships with outside entrepreneurs and Industrialists who had the Capital to develop the deep mines. They had the means to purchase and install the necessary machinery for coal cutting, pumping out the water and also to install winding engines for raising and lowering men and coal in the shaft.

Up until the start of the 19th Century, the Free-miners markets were largely local, with iron ore going to the main Ironworks and coal sold locally for the burning of lime and household use. Transportation was via horse and wagons. The new Industrialists, given the local name of 'foreigners', could foresee the value of Forest minerals on markets beyond local use, and so began investing in better means of transportation in the form of tramroads (Chapter 3).

Water ingress and flooding that caused death by drowning had always been one of the greatest problems with Forest of Dean mines. The old Levels could more easily cope with this problem through natural drainage, but vertical shafts and dipples however, needed some form of pumping equipment to overcome it. By the late 1700's, technology of the day had introduced Newcomen's and Watt's steam powered beam engine pumps that were able to cope with the deeper mines.

The Buttymen

And so, by the early 1800's, the deeper mines began to appear and as the earlier partnerships dissolved, the ownership of the mines passed into the hands of several prominent capitalist 'foreigners'. They became employers of large numbers of men, women and boys but the skilled labour came in the form of a new system of contract miners called Buttymen.

Underground workers were paid by means of the 'Buttyman' system. A Buttyman was in effect a self employed contractor who negotiated a price with the Coal Owner for working a seam or seams. He had several men and boys working under him to help shift the coal from the stall/seam to the surface and prepare the new underground roadways. He was paid by the amount of coal his team could produce per day but paid his employees the negotiated day rate plus the standard sliding scale rate. In some collieries the fee was shared equally between the team but in others, the Buttyman took the largest share. Effectively known as 'piecework', this system became very unpopular and was the reason for many disputes and strikes within the industry.

The Sliding Scale

A sliding scale is an arrangement between employers and employees or their representatives (a Union) by which wages move up and down from a certain standard with the price of goods produced (in this case, coal). It was originally used in the iron trade and by the 1880's it became the accepted method of controlling wages, depending on the selling price of the goods produced. Coal Owners' Associations in the various Districts set the Standard rate and the percentage, plus or minus, that should be applied over a certain period of time. Rates differed from District to District depending on the quantity of coal produced and in this respect the Forest of Dean suffered more than most due to the underground difficulties in extraction. Therefore the Sliding Scale applied to Forest miners was generally of a lower percentage than many other Districts.

As an early example, a day rate for an unskilled dayman may be 1 shilling a shift and the sliding scale agreed at that time was plus 40%. The man would therefore receive 1s and 5p per shift. There were of course arguments over who was classed as skilled and who was unskilled and also who put in a 'fair day's work' and who didn't. Even Buttymen had their differences over their respective tenders for working a seam. Coal Owners and Buttymen set the rates in the early years but by the 1890's, they were reviewed regularly by a Joint Conciliation Board consisting of representatives of both the miners Unions and the Coal Owners Associations.

As can be seen, the Buttymen held sway over what rates of pay the men in their employ should be paid and this varied considerably from colliery to colliery and on the seasonal trade. For example, the steam coal pits to the south west of the Forest were largely unaffected as they supplied coal all year round to many industries for raising steam, while the house coal pits further north traded well in the winter months but suffered from the slackening of trade during the summer. These seasonal changes induced the Coal Owners to either reduce the working hours of the colliery or in some cases to close down temporarily while keeping a certain number of men employed to keep the water pumps going. So nothing was constant, with many unfortunate miners having to seek temporary employment elsewhere – probably on the land as farm labourers.

Rates of pay within the coal Industry nationally varied considerably from colliery to colliery and from region to region and nothing was standardised. Buttymen, hewers, daymen, pumpmen, enginemen, surface workers, women, boys and girls all worked on different rates and grades of pay depending on their skills and the output of coal each week. It was inevitable therefore that local disputes between grades of workers often arose.

So, it is understandable that the Forest miners were far from happy, not only with the seasonal fluctuations in wages that were reducing their standards of living to far below the accepted standard but also to the atrocious working conditions they had to endure. Minor strikes took place at various pits in the district but the Coal Owners were always holding all the cards and the miners were usually forced to accept their terms and return to work.

Pit Stop

The advent in 1869 of the **AAM** (as mentioned previously) with their regional Associations and a central strike fund saw the first stirrings of a move for the Forest miners to start their own Union. Buttymen led a strike in July 1871 at the Trafalgar Colliery over their contract rates of pay and their need for a checkweighman to fairly check the weight of coal they produced. The man they chose as checkweighman was John Williams. In September that same year, another strike, this time at the Parkend Colliery and again by Buttymen who were seeking the same demands. Both strikes ended in victory for the buttymen who were then allowed to employ their own checkweighmen and with the promise of weighing machines being installed at their collieries.

Fig. 24 Trafalgar Colliery – courtesy of DHC, Soudley, Cinderford.

This victory gave the miners the opportunity to consider forming their own Union. In July 1872 the miners at Trafalgar asked for a 20% rise in wages but were instead offered 10%. This was refused and the men were locked out for three weeks while negotiations took place. Tim Mountjoy headed the deputation that eventually agreed with the Coal Owners (the Brain brothers) that the men could return to work provided that both their weighmen be replaced.

34

To understand the Buttymen's point of view, coal hewed by the buttyman and his team was sent to the pit head in marked drams (or trams) and weighed by the employers' weighman and also by their own checkweighman. The checkweighman was elected by the Buttymen to verify the findings of the colliery owner's weighman. Therefore, a checkweighman had to be someone who the men trusted and he was therefore often called upon to resolve disputes over tonnage.

Abnormal Places

Men at the coal face were paid a rate of pay for every ton of coal produced at the surface and this rate varied in each and every District in Great Britain and within each colliery and every seam. So nationally, nothing was standardised as each colliery issued a signed price list and the price per ton was fixed by that. However, cutting of coal differs from any other class of work in that each and every seam of coal strata could be much disturbed and the miner was continually meeting with what was known as 'abnormal places'.

Abnormal places were parts of a seam of coal where a fault occurred and the seam was lost for a distance of maybe two or three yards, sometimes more. This had to be cut through without producing any coal in order to find the seam on the other side of the fault. So during that time of producing no coal, which could be up to several days, there were no wages to be earned and the miner was entitled to an allowance which was always at the discretion of the Coal Owner or colliery manager.

Tim Mountjoy – 1824 – 1896

A Miners' Committee had already been set up in 1870 at Cinderford by local public figure Tim Mountjoy in support of miners wishing to buy waste land locally. He had already established a number of Friendly Societies in the Cinderford area to help poor families and became a public figure when acting as Chairman of the Cinderford Ratepayers and Voters Committee.

Fig. 25 Tim Mountjoy

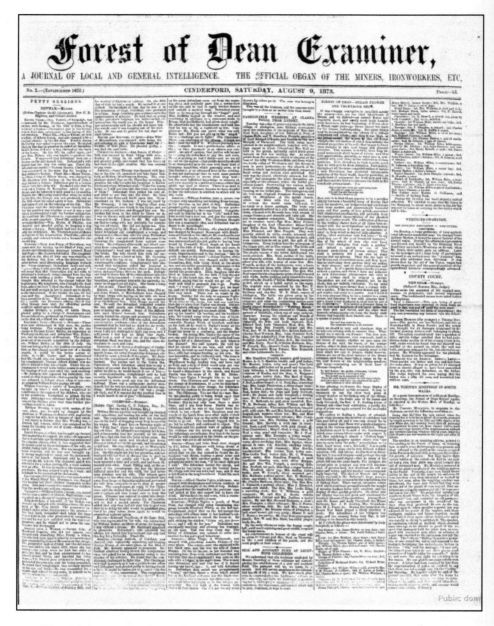

Fig. 26 Issue 2 of the Forest of Dean Examiner – August 9th 1873

Following the 1871 and 1872 strikes by the Buttymen, Mountjoy was responsible for forging the **'Association of Dean Miners'** and became their first General Secretary. In 1872 they joined the South Wales Miners by becoming affiliated to the Miners Union, **the Amalgamated Association of Miners (AAM).** In August 1873 Mountjoy created a weekly newspaper **'The Forest of Dean Examiner'** which formed the official mouthpiece of the new **Dean Miners Union.**

It is worth noting that 1872 was also the first year that the Forest of Dean Miners held their **Annual Demonstration** event on the Speech House field and which, in the subsequent years of the 19th and 20th Centuries became a great popular annual event held every first weekend in July with parades of local Bands, speeches by Union leaders and Politicians of the day, all supported by a popular regular fun-fare. This first event was reported in the local press thus;

'Saturday last will be a day held in long remembrance by the colliers and miners in Dean Forest. Never did such a muster of the Forest workers, with their wives and sweethearts, take place, and never did the favoured spot present such a spectacle as on Saturday. For several hours the Foresters reached the "Speech-house" by various pathways to the ancient structure. The various Lodges of the Forest, some ten or twelve in number, were headed by as many Bands and upwards of twenty banners, some 4,000 Union men joining in one general procession, midway between Speech-house and Cinderford. The Union men then returned to a large meadow, within the enclosure near the Speech-house. It was intended on this occasion to elect a Forest Union agent, the candidates being Messrs. Mountjoy and Morgan. It was found, however, impossible in the manner adopted to take the votes, and thus this matter was deferred. A platform had been raised from which addresses were delivered by Messrs. Mitchard (South Wales), W. Brown (Staffordshire). Pickard (Staffordshire), Keene (Darlington), and Mountjoy (Dean Forest). The Chairman (Mr. Mitchard) congratulated the Foresters on the extraordinary numbers which had that day assembled in honour of the first grand demonstration of miners in the district' Another report said; *'In spite of inclement weather, four or five thousand miners assembled at their head quarters, determined to assert their rights and denounce their wrongs with all the energy of which they and a quiver full of resolutions were capable. True, the ostensible object of the meeting was a day's enjoyment, fete and gala having been organised, but the opportunity was taken of discussing several subjects of interest to miners in particular and working men in*

general. The advantages of unionism securing miners the privileges and
rewards of their labours were dwelt upon several speakers, and a
resolution was passed unanimously pledging the men employed the
several mines in the district to be united in all matters of agreement
and controversy which may soon be expected to arise. The system of
paying wages fortnightly, which appears to widely prevail in the Forest, was
strongly objected to, it being stated that the result of ballot on the question
showed 3,720 out of 4,000 voters to be in favour of weekly payments. A
resolution stating that the fortnightly system grievance and injurious alike
to the social, moral, and economical condition of the miners was also
unanimously adopted. Mr. Keene addressed the meeting in support of
a resolution on the uniting of the Forest iron workers with the National
Association, and concluded by presenting to Mr. Timothy Mountjoy, on
behalf of Mr. Crawshay's workmen, a handsome silver watch and gold
chain with appendages, which was suitably acknowledged, and after the
resolutions had been passed the meeting was brought to a termination, and
some out-door games then became the order of the evening.'

Under this national Union umbrella, the Forest of Dean miners won several concessions from the Coal Owners including the installation of weighing machines for the newly appointed checkweighmen and improved contract rates of pay. As a consequence, the Union membership grew to 4,500 by 1874 but there were still differences to be settled between the Buttymen and their daymen. Daymen argued for a standard wage and this was resisted by both buttymen and the Union. There were also differences between the Buttymen themselves when it came to submitting their tenders to the mine owners – some accused others of deliberately undercutting the rates in order to gain a financial advantage. Disputes such as these were referred to the Union who decided that the Buttymen were all entrepreneurs and could submit whatever tender they wished and if their eventual contract turned out not to be rewarding to him and his men then that was his own responsibility.

Disputes also arose about rates of pay between workers classed as skilled or unskilled and Tim Mountjoy their Agent tried negotiating with the Coal Owners on a standardised system. They however, rejected his ideas and continued to set their own rates for the various skills each miner was capable of.

The situation came to a head in late 1874 when the market price of coal started to fall. Coal Owners insisted on a wage reduction which, in turn provoked a miners' strike in November 1874. This lasted till February 1875 when the miners were forced back to work with the Union beaten. Membership fell away during the next two years and as the Union was unable to prevent further wage cuts and the Coal Owners refused to talk to Mountjoy, in 1877 he was discharged from his position as Union Agent and the Union was disbanded.

The Buttymen were still the chief negotiators with the Coal Owners on wages and a new sliding scale of rates of pay had been negotiated. The daymen however still had to rely wholly on the Buttymen for their wages. Checkweighmen, who were elected by the Buttymen were now considered to be trusted negotiators with the mine owners and were also becoming responsible for holding meetings and keeping books.

In 1882 the Checkweighmen were responsible for bringing the District Lodges together in a new District Organisation and electing their own Checkweighman as President.

Edward (Neddy) Allen Rymer – 1835 – 1915
Edward (Neddy) Allen Rymer, a Union activist from County Durham was invited to Cinderford in 1882. He was instrumental in reconstituting the Union as the **Forest of Dean Miners' Association (FODMA)** and was appointed their new Agent and Secretary. His life was dedicated to fighting for the rights of the miners to better and safer working conditions and compensation for miners and miners families in the event of injury or death in the pits. He had toured the country carrying out recruitment drives for miners to form their own local Associations in every mining District of the country and although Rymer was militant from an early age, fuelled by his experiences within the northern mining community, he became a supporter of the Liberal Party. In 1884 he represented the Forest of Dean miners in a deputation to Prime Minister Gladstone over extending the Liberal Franchise in Dean. A year later he supported the successful re-election of Liberal candidate, Thomas Blake in the Forest of Dean Constituency.

Pit Stop
Unfortunately, Rymer was at once at odds with the Checkweighmen who disagreed with his style of leadership in favour of their allegiance to the Buttymen. He wanted them to accept his policies or face re-election by the workforce but was rejected. His somewhat aggressive policies towards the Coal Owners were certainly popular within the general workforce especially after he had won them a pay rise and by December of 1882 the Union

membership had reached 3,000. Once again the Coal Owners took action against the Agent as they did with Tim Mountjoy and in March 1883 took away the pay rise, refused to talk with Rymer and imposed a Lockout.

Rymer then led the men into a five week strike which was fuelled by much intimidation. Two men appeared at Littledean Court charged with attempting to destroy a collier's house at Ruardean Hill using explosives such as dynamite - the men were eventually bound over through lack of evidence. Rymer's militant influence caused much ill feeling among the miners that led to such incidents. Arbitration by Mr Colchester-Wemyss was ignored and the strike achieved nothing and the men had to return to work. The workforce then accepted an arbitration award without Rymer's interference, with further negotiations with arbitrators set for 1885 and 1886. These deals effectively made the Union redundant and while the Buttymen still had their own tendering system in place, the Union membership of the general workforce fell rapidly. Rymer was eventually sidelined when the checkweighmen saw their opportunity to reorganise the Union and when by mid 1886 there were insufficient funds left to pay him, he was forced to leave his position.

George Rowlinson – 1852 – 1937

George Henry Rowlinson was born in James Bridge, Darlaston, Staffordshire, an area surrounded by canals and working pit shafts and who began work in one of those pits at the age of seven. He was in his twenties before being able to read and write and then became a lay preacher with the Primitive Methodists. He became a member of the West Bromwich Miners Association and later became their President.

Fig. 27 Mr George Rowlinson

However in 1884 a strike by many West Midlands Unions including West Bromwich, brought their Union close to collapse, resulting in George Rowlinson being blacklisted and therefore unable to find work in that area. Later that year (1884), George Rowlinson arrived in the Forest of Dean and worked with Edward Rymer on the **Forest of Dean Miners' Association's** reconstitution. When Rymer left in 1886, George Rowlinson took on the role of Agent and Secretary and as a Methodist lay preacher with strong non-conformist views, it gave him a voice as a public speaker. He was also a member of the Liberal Party.

Under George Rowlinson's leadership, the **FODMA** kept a loose association with the Western Counties Miners' Federation that included both the Bristol Miners' Association and the Somerset Miners' Association. These were all represented at the Newport meeting in November 1889 when the **Miners' Federation of Great Britain (MFGB)** was formed and the **FODMA** were one of the first to join. Rowlinson stood for election as a Committee member of the **MFGB** on several occasions and eventually won a seat in 1891.

George Rowlinson worked closely with the Buttymen and Checkweighmen of the **Forest of Dean Miners' Association** but cosy as this arrangement was, differences between these and the rank and file members of the Association still surfaced due to the wide variations within the wages system. Whereas the Buttymen were paid by negotiation with the Coal Owners, the daymen were still being paid on the complicated 'Sliding Scale' system based on the 1888 pay level and the day rate was calculated as a percentage above that level and reviewed regularly by a joint conciliation board. However, this system was not standardised throughout the Industry and each coalfield had its own standard scale and rates of pay. This system of payment formed the basis of much discontent amongst miners throughout Great Britain and was the inevitable reason for many stoppages, strikes and lockouts for many years to come.

George Rowlinson's career led him, over the following years to become a prolific public servant and he served on the Board of many local organisations; United School Board, County Education Committee, East Dean Rural District Councillor, Forest of Dean Group of Council School Managers, Westbury Board of Guardians, 1907 Justice of the Peace, Gloucester Local Advisory Committee (Ministry of Labour), Chairman of the Forest of Dean Joint Hospital Board, Hon. Secretary Dilke Memorial Hospital Fund, Member of the Colliery Recruiting Court during WW1. In 1917 he was forced to resign his post as miners' Agent for the Forest of Dean due to his support for the unpopular 'comb out' of miners for the Army. In the 1918 New Year Honours List he was awarded an **MBE** in recognition of his work as Miners Agent and in the Forest of Dean Recruiting Court.

Chapter 6
Dean Forest Labour Association

The previous Chapter has extolled the virtues of forming a Miners' Union in the Forest of Dean and to briefly recap; In 1871 Tim Mountjoy forged the first Union of Forest Miners – the **Association of Dean Miners**. Unfortunately this Union was disbanded in 1877 but with the help of Edward (Neddy) Rymer, it was reconstituted in 1882 and became known as the **Forest of Dean Miners' Association (FODMA)**.

At the **Miners' Annual Demonstration** held at the Speech House field in July 1884, the chief speaker was Mr William Abrahams (Mabon) representing the Rhondda Valley in South Wales. He expounded the view that every man in every pit should be encouraged to join the Union and that advancement of wages could only be achieved through Union solidarity.

In 1885 the **Miners' Annual Demonstration** was held on the 13th of June at Latimer Lodge, Littledean Hill near Cinderford. Miners first gathered at Cinderford Town Hall and marched to Latimer Lodge preceeded by several Bands. The field was occupied by shooting galleries, coconut shies and skittle alleys representing a small fair. Over 2,000 miners with wives and girlfriends were gathered to hear the speakers at one o'clock and who were on a platform consisting of two wagons. Guests included Mr T. Blake the Liberal Candidate and his wife, the Revs C.J. Reskelly and W. Thomas and Messrs S. Brightly and Gould of London. Association members included Mr Edward Rymer, Agent, S.J. Elsom, F. Martin, E. Cockayne, J. Cooksey, R. Buffrey, H. Kear and W. Evans. The meeting was opened by Mr A.D. Williams and topics were mainly concerned with political arguments in favour of the Liberal Candidate for the District and much support for the outgoing Government of Mr Gladstone. Among the many resolutions; Mr W. Evans moved and Mr H. Kear seconded; *'That we, at this meeting of workmen and electors of the Dean Forest desire to express our willing and kindly confidence in Mr Thomas Blake, our chosen and accepted Liberal Candidate for this Division in the Reformed Parliament and that we here assembled agree to unite in voting for Mr Blake at the General Election and work faithfully and lawfully for his safe return.'*

Mr Edward Rymer moved and Mr J. Willmott seconded *'That we, the Forest miners desire to raise a Permanent Relief Fund to be self supporing for sickness, accidents, permanent injury, and for widows and orphans at every colliery to abolish the poverty and misery in our homes arising from mining calamities and contingencies, and that we form a strong, intelligent, representative committee of miners and local gentlemen to draw up rules and constitution and to apply money already banked for 21 years for raising this necessary fund'.*

As stated earlier, Edward Rymer eventually departed the Forest and in 1886, Mr George Rowlinson became the new Agent and Secretary.

By then however, many Forest miners had become disillusioned with the Union's continual confrontations with the Coal Owners and their failure to secure their demands for a decent living wage. Consequently, membership plummeted and Mr Rowlinson was faced with the task of rebuilding the Union. So he began a recruiting campaign.

At the **Miners' Annual Demonstration** held at the Speech House in July 1888, the **FODMA's** new President Mr John McAvoy was in the Chair and was supported by Mr G. Samuelson MP the newly elected Liberal MP for the Forest of Dean and other senior Association members. Mr J. Baldwin moved the first resolution *'that in the opinion of this meeting, the time has arrived and we are thoroughly convinced that nothing but unity will improve our position as workmen morally, socially and financially and that we pledge ourselves to do all in our power to make the* **Forest of Dean Miners' Association** *a strong one'.*

In the autumn of 1888, Mr Rowlinson announced his intention to run as a candidate for the Drybrook Division on the Gloucestershire County Council and in January 1889, he was successfully returned as Councillor George Rowlinson.

In June 1889 at a Speech House meeting of colliery representatives, the subject of the victimisation by Colliery Owners of miners joining the Union was discussed. It was acknowledged that relations between employers and employed had become strained and the Conference passed a resolution; *'that this Conference agrees to support all men who shall be victimised on the Parkend and New Fancy works for joining the* **Forest of Dean Miners' Association** *and we entreat them to join us so that all may be as one man to effectually prevent men being marked'.*

A month later, the July 1889 **Miners' Annual Demonstration** held at the Speech House was billed as the **Forest of Dean Miners' Association**

Annual Demonstration. Mr J. McAvoy was unable to attend and so Mr Rowlinson took the Chair. He said that he was pleased with the progress that the Union had made and over the past year it had made several contributions to members' causes. He again strongly reaffirmed his intention to rebuild the **FODMA** where out of a total workforce of 4,500 Forest miners, only 2,500 were at present paid up Union members.

However, Mr Rowlinson's efforts seemed to have had only a limited appeal to the Forest miners and while extolling the virtues of the **FODMA,** he also sought to appeal to a wider membership by introducing a subtle change in the Union name. At a packed meeting of miners, their wives and girlfriends at the British Schoolroom in Coleford on Saturday the 2nd of November 1889 he declared that; **'A National Federation of miners is an absolute necessity in order to secure an eight hour working day from bank to bank for all men, and to demand and maintain a price for labour that will give more comfort in our homes that will enable a rise to a higher social platform. This can be done by all men becoming members of the <u>Dean Forest Labour Association,</u> and by Federation with other counties'.**

He also remarked that **'the Association is now no longer solely interested in the coal workers' prospects. It is now agreed that the style should be the <u>Dean Forest Labour Association</u> and to that end, not only the miners but blast furnace men, stone workers, quarrymen and labourers of all sorts, even stone breakers if they choose so, are welcomed into the Association. The progress we are now making is most encouraging, but I want to see the whole of the 6,000 workers in this District converted to Trades Union principles. I see no reason why the different classes of labour should not be brought into one Federation'** The first President of the newly named Association was Mr John McAvoy.

Miners' Federation of Great Britain

After a series of unsuccessful strikes in other coalfields, the various District Federations organised a conference at Newport in South Wales on the 26th of November 1889 with a view to forming a National Union. The result was the formation of **The Miners' Federation of Great Britain (MFGB)** with Ben Pickard of the Yorkshire Miners Association as President, and Sam Woods of the Lancashire and Cheshire Miners' Federation as Vice President. Major aims of the Federation were to eliminate the 'Sliding Scale' system of payment to be replaced by a standard weekly wage, to fight for an eight hour day, better working conditions, a fairer compensation system for injured miners and bereaved families and to have representation in Parliament. They started initially representing 36,000 members and a year later, it had risen to 250,000. By 1893 the **MFGB** had a rising membership and had ambitions to have all Miners District Associations to become members in one single body.

Unfortunately this wasn't to be as some Districts decided not to sign up as they felt able to negotiate their own terms with the Coal Owners and were strong advocates of the 'Sliding Scale'. Among those were the Durham Miners Association, Northumberland Miners Association and the South Wales Unions. Eventually, after several local and National disputes, they all joined up and by 1898 the membership had risen to over 600,000 which gave them the influence they needed to negotiate with the Coal Owners on a National Level.

The Forest of Dean Union was one of the first of eleven member Associations to sign up on that historic day with Mr Rowlinson acting as Agent. It was noted however that he sought to use the title of **Forest of Dean Miners' Association (FODMA)** as representing the Forest of Dean District. It was also still sometimes useful to use the former guise as the **FODMA** on other occasions – as was noted during the two major strikes of 1893 and 1898 where their contributions collected for the Relief Funds were noted in the local press.

The **Miners' Annual Demonstrations** at the Speech House continued year on year where the Union was, from then on referred to as the **Dean Forest Labour Association** or just **'the Association'.** At the 1890 Demonstration, Mr Rowlinson was presented with a valuable gold watch and chain and a cheque (value unknown) from the Forest of Dean miners as a token of appreciation for services rendered as Agent.

At the July 1891 **Miners' Annual Demonstration**, the Liberal nominee for the next General Election Sir Charles Dilke and his son Mr Charles Wentworth Dilke were on the platform with Mr John MacAvoy, President of the Association in the Chair. Sir Charles was warmly welcomed to the Forest of Dean and Mr Rowlinson and other Association members were sincerely thanked for what they had done to secure his nomination.

At the July 1892 **Miners' Annual Demonstration**, attended by the new Parliamentary Liberal Candidate for the Forest of Dean Sir Charles Dilke and Lady Dilke, Mr Rowlinson who was now a Committee member on the **MFGB**, congratulated the Association for now including quarrymen, miners, pig-iron men, labourers and railwaymen – with each Lodge marching to the field with their own banner and some with their own brass band. Sir Charles Dilke was encouraged to say some words in favour of his candidature for the forthcoming General Election but said he couldn't electioneer at this meeting because of the Bands that were present. He said that the Law prohibited the presence of Bands at election meetings so he wasn't going to risk it. He did however speak on his support for the eight hour bill and supported other MP's who were elected by the working classes and fought for their rights in Parliament.

At the 1893 **Miners' Annual Demonstration**, Mr John McAvoy, President of the **Dean Forest Labour Association** took the Chair. Sir Charles Dilke MP, the newly elected Member of Parliament for the Forest of Dean was present as were several Committee members of the **MFGB** and **DFLA.** Mr Rowlinson spoke of his continiued disappointment at the lack of enthusiasm of the miners for joining the Union although their numbers had shown a slight increase. Sir Charles Dilke MP urged the miners' Associations to join the **MFGB** and supported those who intended representing the Miners in forthcoming elections.

At the same time, due to the fall in the coal trade, the Coal Owners were posting notices at the pitheads terminating the present working contracts and miners had been asked to accept a 25% cut in wages. 1,500 men were already idle and due to this action, another 3,000 would be out of work. This crisis had been repeated at most other Districts of the Country.

At the 1894 **Miners' Annual Demonstration**, Mr George Barnard was the new President of the Associatiion but Mr Rowlinson took the Chair. He said that he was still disappointed at the low numbers of men joining the Union and that they were now low in numbers and finances compared with the previous years but that he would not let the Association fall through.

As can be seen, Mr Rowlinson appears to have been fighting an uphill battle to strengthen the Union and his Liberal Party ideals did bring him into conflict with the miners who really wanted to affiliate with Keir Hardie's newly formed **Independent Labour Party (ILP)** and have their own representation in Parliament. His regular speeches at the pitheads struggled to convince the miners that he had their interests at heart and he failed to gain their serious support.

Chapter 7
Accidents and Fatalities

Coal was now becoming King in the Forest of Dean with half the population employed within the industry. Output in 1900 had topped one million tons per year while output of iron ore had dropped to less than one thousand tons. Collieries were now mainly privately owned although small numbers of Free-miners were still working Levels and Dipples. Wages were constantly under threat of being reduced with the Butty and 'sliding scale' systems still in operation. Working conditions were still not satisfactory and the safety of men and machinery still left a lot to be desired.

The Forest of Dean did not escape the tragedies caused by mining accidents and many miners' lives were lost in the pursuit of a living wage. Although there was no single mass loss of life, there were nevertheless cases where up to four men and boys were recorded as losing their lives in one single accident.

Even one death can be a tragedy to those that are left behind in a society where there was no state assistance or even medical help other than the local doctor who had to be paid to attend the sick and dying. A grieving family was largely left to cope with bringing up several children with only the help of generous neighbours and it was a state of affairs that all mining families had to

Year	Tons of coal raised
1841	145,136
1850	337,948
1860	590,470
1862	474,168
1871	837,893
1877	638,319
1885	826,167
1894	860,312
1900	1,050,000

Fig. 28 Tons of coal raised

get accustomed to living with. It would take up several volumes to list those deaths here and others have researched this and published their results elsewhere. However, as a small tribute to those lost, here are but a few examples of these records up to 1898, some of which can be a very harrowing read.

Date	Name	Age	Occupation	Pit	Cause
4/1805	J. Jenkins	17	Collier	Independent Pit	Fell from mouth of the pit 42 fathons to the bottom (250ft)
2/1813	W. Jenkins	11	Collier	Brockaditch	Fell between fly and cog wheels
4/1815	C. James	13	Collier	Moseley Green	Fell down pit
7/1838	W. Dean	11		Holt Pit	Struck by stick in revolving wheel and knocked 240ft down pit.
1/1858	G. Nelmes	10		Broominghall	Ran empty tub to mouth of shaft too fast and fell down dragging boy with it.
5/1862	J.Weaver	11	Collier	Strip and at it	Sudden fall of Bell mould
11/1863	E. Mallett	45	Banksman	Foxes Bridge	Fell 300yds down the pit and was dashed to pieces
12/1866	J. Price	13	Doorboy	New Engine	Walked into sump at pit bottom and was drowned
10/1875	T Meek	22	Collier	Foxes Bridge	Crushed by accidental fall of earth.
12/9/1890	S. Morse	53	Repairer	Pillowell Level	While riding on rubbish tubs was crushed against roof.

Fig. 29 Records of many fatalities spanning 85 years

The earliest recorded multiple death in a Forest of Dean pit happened on the 6th of April 1819 at Bilson colliery near Cinderford where four men were lost when a chain broke on a tub lowering the men down the shaft. They were James Meredith aged 11, Thomas Morgan aged 26, Robert Tingle aged 16 and his brother William Tingle aged 19.

Parkend Deep Navigation Collieries, Ld.,

ACCIDENT & DEATH SOCIETY

STATEMENT,

FOR THE YEAR ENDING DECEMBER 31st, 1893.

PAYMENT TO INJURED.

Name	£	s.	d.	Name	£	s.	d.	Name	£	s.	d.
Bath, A.	0	10	0	Joynes, R.	0	10	0	Preest, W.	0	9	0
Beach, J.	0	18	0	James, J.	0	10	0	Phipps, C.	1	5	6
Barnet, Joseph	0	16	6	James, T.	4	1	0	Preest, Hosea	1	8	6
Blanch, S.	1	10	0	James, H.	1	16	0	Prout, W.	1	1	6
Biddington R.	0	15	0	Jones, A.	0	12	0	Ruck, J.	0	13	6
Berry, W.	0	16	6	James, Jesse	0	9	0	Russell, J.	1	11	6
Blanch, James	0	10	6	Jefferies, T.	0	4	6	Richards, Alfred	0	18	0
Brown, E.	0	11	0	Jones, T	0	4	6	Russell, T.	1	13	0
Beddis, C.	1	18	0	James, C.	0	15	0	Russell, T.	0	4	6
Cole, F.	0	18	0	Jones, F	0	19	6	Smith, E.	2	2	0
Craddock, W	12	1	0	James, Amos.	0	15	0	Stephens, J.	0	18	0
Cooper, Henry	0	9	0	Jones, S	0	12	0	Smith, Levi.	0	18	0
Charles, F.	0	15	0	Kear, W	0	18	0	Screen, Robert	2	3	6
Charles, Alex.	1	7	0	Kear, A.	1	2	6	Thomas, J	0	13	0
Cox, Thomas.	0	12	0	Lee, Thomas.	0	7	6	Turner, W	0	12	0
Childs, G.	0	3	•	Lowe, J.	1	5	6	Turley, R.	0	15	0
Childs, James.	3	6	0	Lane, W	0	13	6	Thorn, G.	0	9	0
Duffy, Thomas.	0	9	0	Lewis, W.	0	9	0	Thomas, J	1	8	0
Dobbn, Rees	0	6	0	Morgan, W.	0	10	6	Turley, James	0	18	0
Ellway, W.	1	10	0	Morse, W	0	7	6	Turley, Joe	1	11	6
Edmonds, George.	0	8	0	Morgan, Richard.	3	13	6	Underwood, J.	1	2	6
Evans, J	0	13	0	Mansell, W.	0	7	6	Well, Thomas.	0	4	6
Embrey, Thomas	0	9	0	Mansell, C.	1	1	0	Watkins, W.	1	8	6
Genvel, Henry	0	16	6	Moulton, W	0	13	6	Willetts, T	0	9	0
Gandern, Henry.	1	2	6	Morgan, A.	0	10	6	Wintle, Mrs. (widow)	6	13	0
Griffiths, S.	0	6	0	Organ, D.	0	18	0	Wright, E.	4	17	6
Guest, L.	0	7	6	Pearce, Dan	0	9	0	Wilding, Richard	0	15	0
Hale, E.	0	18	0	Preest, C.	1	1	0	Wintle, Alfred.	0	9	0
Howell, Henry, sen.	2	14	0	Phillips, Richard	0	15	0	York, W.	0	12	0
Howell, Henry, jun.	0	16	0	Powell, C.	0	16	6				
Howell, S.	1	7	0	Phipps, Henry	2	2	0	£147	10	0	
Hewlett, T	0	15	0								

BALANCE SHEET.

	£	s.	d.		£	s.	d.
Jan. 1st.				By Cash paid to Injured	147	10	0
To Cash in Capital and Counties Bank, Lydney	592	2	8	" " Secretary's Salary	6	0	0
" " Treasurer's hands	5	16	11	" " Cooksey, Printing	1	6	6
" Subscriptions from Members	176	18	10	" " Gloucester Infirmary	10	10	0
" " Outside	3	11	3	" " Loan to Relief Fund	100	0	0
" Interest on Deposit	9	13	3	" " Deposit in Bank	301	15	11
" Part Repayment of Loan	17	4	8	" " In Treasurer's hands	66	6	2
	£603	8	7		£603	8	7

RELIEF FUND.	£	s.	d.	LOAN ACCOUNT.	£	s.	d.
Dec. 1891				Dec. 31st, 1893			
Loan to Fund per Mr Rowlinson.	100	0	0	By Repayment, to date	17	4	8
				" Amount due to Club	82	15	4
	£100	0	0		£100	0	0

We have examined the Accounts of the above Society, and found them correct as per Balance Sheet.

Signed, { THOMAS BLANCH, { JOHN HAMPTON.

Committee:

LEVI SMITH, GEORGE THORN, HARVEY SUMMERS, JONATHAN BIRT, ISAAC JONES, ELIJA SAYCE, THOMAS ROBBINS, ALFRED WINTLE, JAMES PAGE, WILLIAM FLETCHER, SAMUEL ELLWAY, T. H. DEAKIN, Treasurer. ALFRED MILES, Secretary.

Fig. 30 Accident record at the Parkend Deep Collieries, 1893

Further afield, mining accidents were commonplace in every coalfield in the Country, none more so than with our close neighbours, the South Wales Coalfields. Grades of coal produced in these areas varied from the bitumous coal produced in the east, close to the Forest of Dean, to the high grade anthracite found to the west. Bitumous coal seams were found at deeper depths than others and so the risk of encountering gas (firedamp) was higher.

As a consequence, the South Wales Coalfield suffered considerably from mining disasters, both in the 19th and 20th Centuries. One such was at the Albion mine in the village of Cilfynydd, just a mile north of Pontypridd where the two vertical shafts descended nearly 2000 ft. At 4pm on the 23rd of June 1894 a massive explosion rocked the pit causing the death of 290 men and boys and 123 horses. The cause was attributed to the shotfiring of unserviceable timbers which in turn led to the ignition of airborne coal dust and consequently to the explosion of gas. Many recovered bodies were unable to be identified and several were later delivered to their wrong homes. The colliery was reopened within two weeks.

Many of us have heard of Senghenydd, a mining village near Caerphilly where the Universal colliery employed over 1,000 men and boys. The colliery had a bad history of accidents, one of which happened at 5am on the 24th of May 1901 where three consecutive underground explosions of airborne coal dust, led to the deaths of 81 miners with just one survivor. The inquest found that safety precautions had not been followed and that if sufficient watering had been carried out, it would have reduced the amount of coal dust carried in the air. A far more serious accident happened at the same colliery in October 1913 when 440 men and boys were killed – described in later pages.

Yet another major disaster occurred at Whitwick Colliery near Coalville in Leicestershire on the 19th of April 1898 when 35 lives of men and boys were lost due to an underground roof fire causing suffocation by carbon monoxide poisoning. The pit shafts were 750 feet deep and the fire started in roof timbers and quickly gained ground due to the forced ventilation system operating at the pit. Valiant efforts by mine officials and miners to dam off the source of the fire saved the pit from further damage and to the recovery of the lost men. The inquest found that the spontaneous combustion of waste material in a worked out area called a 'gob' had, in consequence, ignited the roof timbers in the main road. It was recommended that steel girders be used instead of timber where practicable.

The above accounts represent a very small example of the many accidents, disasters, deaths and heartache suffered by coal miners and their families up and down the Country. In our present day it is hard to imagine what the loss of so many lives from those close communities would have had on individual families. Little regard was paid to the safety of miners with most of the profits going to the Coal Owners and shareholders. Lives were cheap and pit ponies and horses were far more valuable. Little wonder then that anger and discontent spread among mining communities.

Chapter 8
Pit Stop
National Miners Lockout of 1893

As the price of coal on the open market rose and fell it became the favourite ammunition for the Coal Owners to use against its workforce and the threat of reducing wages due to the 'Sliding Scale' system was a regular occurrence. Naturally, the miners only had one weapon in their arsenal and that was to withdraw their labour, so pit strikes became a way of life for many workers in coalfields up and down the Country. The advent of the **Miners' Federation of Great Britain (MFGB)** in 1889 made collective bargaining a serious threat to both Coal Owners and Government. To recount all of them within these pages would take up several volumes, so the mention of a few should suffice to understand the miners situation and how they were treated in relation to their terrible working conditions coupled with wages that were often less than subsistence level.

An undercurrent of unrest had been festering within the coal industry for some time as market prices fell and wages were constantly under threat. In early 1892 with mounting surplus coal stocks nationally, the **MFGB** instructed its members in the Federated Districts to take a week's holiday starting on 12th of March 1892. Naturally the Coal Owners objected to this but the holiday was observed. The Coal Owners in Co. Durham countered with a 10% cut in wages and the Durham Miners Federation went on strike after being locked out. After twelve weeks, the Union was broke and the miners returned to work on the Coal Owners' terms. This experience gave them the incentive to join the **MFGB.**

Nationally the situation continued to simmer until the 30th of June 1893 when the Coal Owners in the Federated Districts imposed a 25% wage reduction. This was vigorously opposed by the **MFGB** with the consequence that at the end of July 1893, miners in the Unions were locked out. The Districts that took part were Yorkshire, Lancashire and Cheshire, Staffordshire, Worcestershire, Cannock Chase and Shropshire, Nottinghamshire, South Derbyshire and Leicestershire, Forest of Dean, Radstock, Bristol, Warwickshire, North Wales, Stirlingshire and Monmouth.

Some Districts such as Durham, Northumberland and South Wales refused to support the ensuing strike as they sought to settle their differences with the Coal Owners independently. They were also largely in support of the 'Sliding Scale' system and had secured legally binding contracts with their employers. Even then, some Districts were divided in their loyalties – some supporting the strike while others refused and continued to work.

South Wales

This was the case in South Wales where out of 120,000 miners, only around 45,000 were affiliated to the **MFGB** (the majority supporting the 'Sliding Scale') and there were riots and violence between strikers and non-strikers at many of the collieries. Local Police forces were outnumbered and the Magistrates were forced to call in the Military to maintain order. Around 1,200 Cavalry and Infantrymen were stationed in several towns and villages where striking miners (mainly hauliers) had armed themselves and were assembling at pitheads preventing working miners from entering the colliery premises. Some of these disturbances turned ugly and there were frequent clashes between striking miners and iron and steel workers in the area who had been made idle due to lack of coal and who supported the working miners. Many had armed themselves with cudgels and some strikers were on the receiving end of persistent stoning. Striking miners' wives took up arms at Brynmawr early one Saturday morning with the intention of waylaying and stoning the wives of working miners but there was no opposition so the 200 women instead, attacked a travelling peddlar en route to Ebbw Vale, upsetting his cart and scattered his goods across the roadway.

As more Military personnel arrived at Cardiff and Newport, The Coal Owners' representatives on the 'Sliding Scale' Committee reiterated their intention to keep to their original contract on wages without any reduction and urged the Union representatives that included William Abraham (Mabon) and David Morgan the Agent, to communicate their intentions to the miners. There were however, signs that the strike was waning as Union funds were severely depleted and many strikers were now aware that they had broken legally binding contracts and many were dispirited by the presence of the Military who didn't hesitate to quell the least disruption with equal force. There was also a feeling of a lack of leadership and co-ordination between the various Unions.

In the last week of August 1893, a meeting organised by Union and 'sliding Scale' representatives on Merthyr Mountain in the pouring rain was attended by over 2,000 miners. They held a ballot which resulted in an overwhelming majority voting for a return to work. Some of the other areas were undecided and the Military were again in action firing on civilians to quell some of the rioters. Within a week however, men were returning to work in overwhelming numbers – the majority of which were supporters of the 'Sliding Scale'.

Yorkshire

Here, as in South Wales, there was violence between strikers and non strikers which continued throughout August 1893. In early September the Military were again called in to quell the disturbances but this only seemed to aggravate the situation. In the town of Featherstone where two collieries were at a standstill, rumour spread that stockpiled coal was being transported away from one of them, Ackton Hall. On the 7th of September 1893, an angry crowd gathered and confronted the men involved. Troops from the First Battalion of the South Staffordshire Regiment were called in and Bernard Hartley JP, a magistrate, read the Riot Act. There followed two volleys of shots where eight people were injured, two of them fatally - one of those killed wasn't even among the protesters. This event became nationally known as **'The Featherstone Massacre'.**

Forest of Dean

The price of Forest of Dean coal on the open market had been falling gradually over a period of years as a result of cheap competition from other coalfields. The Forest became a sandwich between the Midlands and the South Wales coalfields that were able, due to their geological conditions, produce more coal per man than could the Forest coalfield. Coal Owners were therefore under pressure to reduce wages and as early as March 1893, Forest miners were being locked out for refusing to accept the 25% cut in wages. Eventually, as staunch members of the Midland Counties Federation as affiliated to the **MFGB,** Forest miners joined the strike at the end of July but their strike pay provided by the Midland Federation only lasted for two weeks. A meeting of the Forest Miners' Union at Speech House on Saturday the 12th of August 1893, attended by over 2,000 miners, agreed that their Agent Mr Rowlinson, should seek a meeting with the Coal Owners to reopen the collieries. They in turn, met with the miners' representatives at Speech House on the following Wednesday and agreed to do so if the miners agreed to a 25% drop in wages. Over 3,000 miners met again at Speech House to discuss the deal and a great deal of pressure had been made upon Mr Rowlinson by many miners' wives and mothers to end their starvation. During the lively discussion, one miner Mr Peter Thomas remarked that **'he would eat his last 'tater' before he would give way'.**

The Coal Owners offer was unanimously rejected and it was agreed to continue the strike until the **MFGB** gave instructions otherwise. The following weekend the remaining Union funds were distributed at the rate of 5 shillings per adult and 1 shilling per child. In sympathy with the miners and as an example, Mr Rowlinson declared that during the strike he had not drawn his own salary and stated that he would continue that way until the strike ended – although a mystery persisted surrounding his being loaned £1,000 by two unknown persons.

By the fourth week of the strike, several Forest of Dean Coal Owners withdrew their lockout notices and some men returned to work at New Bowson, East Slade and Speech House Hill collieries. Up to 600 men were working three full shifts per day without resistance from the District Union. Messrs Crawshay however, gave notice to shut their three ironstone quarries and their foundry at Cinderford. Local coal stocks had now run dry and some men working the Severn and Wye and Bullo Great Western railways were laid off.

A meeting was held at the Travellers Rest in Blakeney on Monday morning the 28th of August 1893 to discuss why the working miners had stopped paying their 2 shillings Union Levy and many considered trying to persuade them to stop working. Mr Rowlinson said that it was a delicate situation and he didn't want to interfere unless it became necessary to draw the men out. Referring to his loan of £1,000, Mr Rowlinson said that it had now been distributed to the miners and he hoped that he didn't have to repay it. He said that another £100 could be taken from the funds of the clubs at each of the five large collieries in the District and a resolution to that effect was unanimously adopted. They were keeping a keen eye on what was happening in South Wales and had expressed the hope that the striking hauliers would succeed in their aims.

By mid September 1893 the distress of miners' families was becoming so apparent that the **Dean Forest Labour Association** received £100 from the London Vigilance Committee and 50 Guineas from the Northumberland miners. Local butchers gave away meat and Grocers gave goods from their stores. Coal Owner Mr William Crawshay, made a request that bread should be given away at Cinderford and Ruspidge and relief funds were set up at both Yorkley and Lydbrook.

On Thursday the 14th of September 1893, Coal Owners and representatives of the house coal pits and Union officials met at the Speech

House Hotel where terms for a return to work were agreed. On Saturday the 16th of September 1893, again at the Speech House, the Union with their new President Mr George Barnard in the chair, met with a large gathering of miners to inform the men of the settlement, which he said was **'an honourable settlement not to be ashamed of.'** Mr Rowlinson read out the terms which overall meant a return to work at a reduced wage of 20% for two weeks followed by an arrangement whereby wages were governed by the price of coal at the pithead at an agreed starting point of 9 shillings and sixpence a ton. A joint committee comprising a team of colliers appointed by the men and their Agent and representatives of the Coal Owners would then enter discussions to consider any rise and fall from that Standard at the rate of 5% per 1 shilling – in other words a form of 'Sliding Scale'. The argument was that this time, the miners had a say in the rate paid whereas before, power to decide the rate was solely in the hands of the Coal Owners. This arrangement was to be permanent and initially agreed to last until 1st of January 1894 and only to be terminated by notice on either side of six months from 1st of January in any year. After a ten week strike, a return to work was agreed for Monday the 18th of September 1893.

As a consequence, the **MFGB** frowned on the Forest of Dean agreement as submitting to the 'Sliding Scale'. At the **MFGB** conference in Chesterfield on the 29th of September 1893, a letter from Mr Rowlinson explaining the Forest of Dean decision was read out. This was followed by a resolution to refuse any further communication with the Forest of Dean and supported the Midland Federation's decision in condemning them for accepting a settlement based on the 'Sliding Scale' and a reduction in wages of 20%, which was against Federation principles. In consequence, the Midland Federation severed their links with the **Forest of Dean Miners' Association** who were now on their own.

However other Districts were undergoing similar discussions simultaneously and eventually the **MFGB** had to accept the gradual return to work for a large majority of miners. By the end of October 1893 around 87,000 miners were still locked out and the Coal Owners in those Districts made an offer of a reduction of 15%. A meeting of the **MFGB** at Derby on the 3rd and 4th of November 1893 rejected this offer but a later meeting at the Foreign Office in London on Friday the 17th of November 1893, agreed a settlement which involved no reduction in wages and a Joint Conciliation Board set up consisting of an equal number of representatives from the Coal Owners and miners Unions to last at least one year. It was recommended that the miners could return to work on Monday the 20th of November 1893 – so ending a four month long dispute.

The Aftermath
As can be seen from the above, the mining communities nationally were split over the question of the 'Sliding Scale'. The **MFGB** argued for its abolition while many District Unions including the South Wales and Forest of Dean Unions settled in its favour. These differences didn't go away and over the next few years the undercurrent of unrest continued. Mr Rowlinson was constantly pressurised into explaining the decision to call off the ten week strike even though the miners overwhelmingly voted to give him the power to settle the dispute and return to work. He also disclosed that the Union was in debt to the Bank for £1,100 with another £100 in credit tickets out at the shops.

Acting in good faith, the Forest of Dean Joint Committee met on the 6th of October 1893, and agreed to an advance of 15% in wages due to the increase in trade with coal price increasing by 3 shillings per ton since the end of their dispute. Non Union men however, still presented a problem and in the Forest there were approximately 450 non Union men out of a total workforce of 3,500. Try as he may, Mr Rowlinson was unable to persuade this minority to join the Union and pay their levy. He continually reiterated the fact that; **'those men have the advantage of the Society and they ought to help to pay for its working. I consider he is a mean fellow who takes the benefit of a Union without contributing. My conviction is that no District can live long unless they force their men into the Union and if you allow some to remain outside, you lose a lot of those that do contribute because they say 'why should we pay any more than these do?'**

In late November 1893, two important decisions had consequences for the Forest Miners. Firstly, the Joint Committee were forced, due to the fall in coal prices, to reverse their earlier decision to advance pay by 15%. And secondly, as a consequence, a meeting of miners at Cinderford voted four to one to give the Coal Owners six months notice to terminate the current 'Sliding Scale' arrangement. This would expire at the end of June 1894.

In the early months of 1894 the price of coal continued to fall due to increased competition from other, more productive coalfields and the Coal Owners sought to reduce miners' wages even further. Men at some collieries were only working two shifts per week while others were on three and so a joint agreement was reached by both sides to agree a 10% reduction, on the understanding that no further reductions would be made during the summer months. It was also agreed that if the coal trade revived, the 10% could be restored by September. At several meetings around the Forest, Mr Rowlinson reiterated that he was still on cordial terms with the Midland Federation despite their unfortunate severance and it was his desire that the Forest of Dean Union rejoin them when the 'sliding scale' contract ends in June 1894.

However, when this contract did end, the miners were reluctant to tow the line with a larger Union, pay their additional levies and come out on strike when called upon. And so the decision was deferred and the current system of wages continued. Mr Rowlinson's wish for the Forest of Dean miners to become affiliated had fallen on deaf ears and so in August 1894 he offered to resign. He said he would only carry on if he had the fullest backing of the Union Council. Delegates urged him not to resign and voted to give him all the help he needed in future.

There were also rumblings of discontent from the **MFGB** who issued a report to miners stating their reservations concerning the Conciliation Board's attitude to the Minimum wage. Chairman of the Conciliation Board Lord Shand had made remarks to the effect that he was not in favour of setting a minimum wage which the **MFGB** were lobbying for.

Pit Stop at Flour Mill and Bailey Hill Collieries
A dispute over wages occurred at these two collieries in February 1895 when the Joint Wages Board imposed a wage reduction of twelve and a half percent over the whole of the Forest of Dean workforce. When a 7% reduction was accepted by the vast majority of miners, the men at these two collieries refused to accept it. They made a counter offer which their management refused to accept and so around 300 men walked out on strike. The matter was taken up by Mr Rowlinson who met with the Directors and after discussions, terms acceptable to the men were agreed and the men went back to work. The strike lasted two weeks.

Speech House Hill Colliery
Another dispute occurred at the Speech House Hill Colliery that produced house coal from the upper levels of the Lowery, Starkey, Rockey, Churchway, No Coal and Brazilly seams. In December 1895, the Coal Owners indicated to the miners that they wished to reduce certain scales of pay for certain grades of work and asked the men to accept this

reduction. The miners said no and the Coal Owners fixed a notice to the pithead to terminate their contract. The 517 men and boys employed there decided to strike and Mr Rowlinson stepped in to negotiate. This became a long and drawn out bitter strike with some young Forest miners moving to South Wales seeking work while others were taken on at other local collieries. With Union and non Union men receiving the same strike pay, fellow miners in other local collieries were reluctant to support their cause. Mr Rowlinson took a dim view of this and at several local meetings castigated them for their poor support and neglect of the Union saying that existing contracts were due to run out in September 1896 and that they themselves could be in a similar position when the Coal Owners were intent on reducing wages. However, financial support did arrive from the South Western Federation which included Bristol and Somerset coalfields and also the Durham Miners Association.

Fig. 31 Flour Mill Colliery – courtesy of DHC, Soudley, Cinderford.

During March 1896 Mr Rowlinson organised a series of social meetings to raise funds and to create a bread fund for distressed families of the 300+ miners still affected by the strike. The strike lasted until August 1896 when the operating Company finally went into liquidation. The colliery then passed through a succession of owners and finally reopened in July 1898. In 1903, it was purchased by Henry Crawshay, owner of the adjacent Lightmoor colliery who opened up the barrier between them underground.

In the event, the colliery ceased to produce coal by 1906 when demolition started but the shaft was kept open as an emergency exit for Lightmoor until April 1937.

Fig. 32 Speech House Hill Colliery – courtesy of DHC, Soudley, Cinderford.

Chapter 9
Pit Stop
South Wales Miners' Strike of 1898

Ever since the settlement of the 1893 National Strike, the South Wales miners continued to have their differences with minor disputes surfacing throughout the coalfield. More and more miners were increasingly angered by what they referred to as the unfair 'Sliding Scale' wages system that was the result of the 1893 strike settlement. The aforementioned 'Butty' system of payment coupled with the falling open market price of coal saw their wages decrease in real terms compared to the cost of inflation. There was also disquiet over the recent Workmen's Compensation Act going before Parliament which, if passed with certain House of Lords amendments was likely to exclude many miners and miners widows and fatherless children still awaiting payment. William Abraham MP (Mabon) as leader of the largest District Union – the Cambrian Miners' Association, had been instrumental in encouraging miners to join the Union and he spoke on the miners' behalf at many meetings trying to resolve problems concerning the 'Sliding Scale' and controlling coal output. The Districts were still not united as one Union and that presented leadership problems as they all differed in their aims. (Mabon himself was a supporter of the 'Sliding Scale')

Pioneering Union leader William Abraham had a somewhat chequered start to working life. He was born in Cwmafan, Glamorgan and by the age of 10, he was working underground as a Trapper or 'air door boy' (he manned the door that let the coal trucks pass and let air into the working area of the mine). In 1864 Abraham sailed to Chile to work in a copper mine but after finding no work there, returned to South Wales and by 1869 was working as a tin-plater in Swansea. By 1871 Abraham was back working in the pits and was involved in fighting for the cause of fellow miners in disputes with the mine owners. He rose to become miners Agent for the Loughor District within the **Amalgamated Association of Miners (AAM).**

William Abraham (Mabon) – 1842 - 1922

Surprisingly, he had an interest in poetry and would sing at social events. This led to him taking on the Eisteddfod name of Gwilym Mabon and the name stuck. In the mid1870's he led a series of strikes that stretched the Union's funds to the extent that the **AAM** became bankrupt in August 1875.

Abraham was then forced to move Districts and he joined the Cambrian Miners Association in the Rhondda valley which, although surviving the collapse of the **AAM**, still existed as a local Union. He became their agent in 1877, campaigning vigorously to revive the spirit of the Rhondda miners to join the Union and by 1885 the membership had reached 14,000 – the largest of the seven Districts in the South Wales Coalfield. In that year (1885) Abraham

Fig. 33 William Abraham (Mabon)

(Mabon) stood as a candidate for the Rhondda constituency in the General Election and won the seat as a Lib-Lab MP, which he held until 1918.

In 1888 Abraham was credited with negotiating an agreement between the Unions and the Coal Owners that all South Wales mines be closed on the first Monday in every month so that the miners be given a holiday from their physical exhaustion. The intention was that miners could devote that day to more intellectual pursuits and it became universally known as **'Mabon's Day'**. However, in practice, the day didn't quite live up to Abraham's aspirations although Union meetings, fairs and other forms of entertainment did take place. But drunkenness and brawling was often the end result and this led to the Coal Owners complaining that the men's recovery time led to more coal production being lost.

The falling price of coal and reduced wages due to the 'sliding scale' system prompted more and more dissatisfaction amongst the miners. They argued their case with the Coal Owners in an attempt to control coal output at the pits to match actual demand. This was in the hope of stopping over production and the sale of cheap coal that reflected as a percentage drop in the 'sliding scale' figure, paid as wages.

In early September 1897, a ballot of the whole coalfield was held over the question of whether or not to hold a one week holiday (known as the Stop Week) in order to reduce coal stocks and to persuade the Coal Owners to accept their recommendation. This was overwhelmingly rejected by a majority of 9,514. The Coal Owners also decided not to adopt the principle of limiting output to demand which would have helped to abolish over production and cheap coal that had kept the miners wages down.

It was then decided to hold a ballot in the whole South Wales and Monmouthshire coalfield on a proposal to terminate the current 'Sliding Scale' contract within the requisite six months notice. The ballot was held on the 18th of September 1897 and over 53,000 miners voted and around 130 collieries participated. At the end of September the final figures were published which resulted in an overwhelming majority of 29,231 to terminate the Scale. The Coal Owners were then given the statutory six months notice that the miners would terminate the scale which would come into effect on the 31st of March 1898.

During this time several collieries in South Wales were in dispute with their Coal Owners which indicated what mood the miners were in over broken promises involving the 'Sliding Scale' and poor working conditions. One such was the lock out at the Six Bells pit at Abertillery involving 500 miners that lasted for twelve weeks. Another was at the Abernant No. 9 pit in Carmarthenshire that involved over 900 men and boys. Some men returned to work on the 31st of December but were approached by strikers and persuaded to come out again. Alderman David Morgan (Agent) was arrested and accused of intimidation. Funds to support the men were forthcoming from neighbouring collieries but the bitter dispute continued throughout 1898 and into 1899.

While strike action over wage differences and coal production was rife at many other South Wales collieries, Mabon held meetings urging miners to unite saying that even though he himself had not recommended the vote to terminate the Scale, he could understand those whose lives were made miserable by low wages. He also advised that when the end of the notice expired at the end of March 1898, miners' demands for unsustainable increases such as 20% or 30% as was being suggested by some, may involve a strike as Wales had never seen before.

A Conference of miners' representatives was held in Cardiff on the 10th of January 1898 to discuss among other matters, a proposal to unite as a single Union in view of a possible forthcoming confrontation with the Coal Owners. Two significant leaders were absent – Mabon had missed his train from Swansea and Alderman David Morgan had been arrested and imprisoned for alleged intimidation in connection with the ongoing Abernant dispute. However, Mabon arrived in the early afternoon and it became evident that differences among the miners still remained. A resolution was eventually passed that each District should organise themselves individually as best they could but also to consider joining forces as one Union in the future.

The Coal Owners had, over the winter months issued notices at many of the South Wales pits to terminate their contracts at the end of March 1898 to coincide with the miners terminating the 'Sliding Scale' agreement and rumours were spreading about the Coal Owners intentions after that date. It was suggested at another miners representatives meeting that they would be prepared to agree a deal if the Coal Owners Association accepted the control of output as previously desired by the miners. This was forwarded to the Coal Owners who rejected the deal.

As the March 31st deadline approached, ship owners at the South Wales ports were getting nervous about a potential shortage of steam coal in the event of a stoppage, especially for the Admiralty in view of the outbreak of war between Spain and America. Privateers were taking steps to seek contracts on the near Continent and to divert steam coal cargo ships to northern ports.

At the mid March 1898 meetings of miners' delegates on the 'Sliding Scale' Committee, 'Mabon' consistently portrayed a conciliatory attitude towards the Coal Owners and it was suggested that a member of the Board of Trade act as arbitrator between the parties to come to an amicable agreement that suited both sides.

A coalfield wide ballot on whether to grant plenary (negotiating) powers to the miners' representatives on the 'Sliding Scale' Committee to act as negotiators was defeated. A Provisional Committee Chaired by Mabon was then selected to negotiate with the Coal Owners for a settlement of the dispute. By the end of March however, both sides were still entrenched as in previous discussions with no movement on either side but both sides agreed to extend talks until the 9th of April and the Coal Owners Association agreed to keep their pits open until that time.

Discontent was widespread and although District meetings were held throughout the Coalfield, agreement amongst the rank and file could not be reached. However, the general feeling was that the 'Sliding Scale' had to go but every District's demands varied on what percentage rate of advance to accept. 'Mabon's' Provisional Committee agreed that they should demand an immediate 10% advance in wages, 10% above the present Standard of 12.5% provided that their scheme to control output should be incorporated and that coal should be sold at a minimum of 10 shillings per ton. This became known as 'the three tens'. The problem was that the Coal Owners Association under the Chairmanship of Sir W.T. Lewis refused to negotiate with the provisional Committee until they had the power to represent the whole of the South Wales coalfields and this seemed to be the main stumbling block.

Fig. 34 Welsh miners leaving their colliery

On Thursday the 7th of April 1898, 175 Delegates held a disorderly meeting and overthrew their long time loyal leader 'Mabon'. Thirty one resolutions were considered in both Welsh and English and they couldn't make up their minds whether or not to keep the 'Sliding Scale' or to join the **MFGB.** They appeared to be in revolt against their leaders but had no plenary powers to negotiate with the Coal Owners. As there was no chance of collective bargaining in sight, it was evident that a prolonged strike was in prospect. An article in the Yorkshire Post declared *'An industrial army insists on fighting and at the moment of going into battle deposes all its leaders without appointing new ones'*

Some non associated collieries in the Aberdare valley had agreed an advance of 10% and around 4,000 men had returned to work but over 100,000 men in the associated collieries still remained idle. Men were now allowed to descend their collieries to retrieve their working tools while horses and ponies were also being brought up. In addition, over 30,000 Ironworkers were unemployed as a result of the stoppage. On the 20th of April 1898, the Mayors of Cardiff, Newport and Swansea sent a joint letter to the President of the Board of Trade Mr C.T. Ritchie MP requesting his help to effect a settlement of the dispute. The reply they received merely acknowledged receipt of that letter but also said that they were fully aware of the situation and they would assist at and when it seemed to them that a settlement was in reach.

On Monday the 18th of April 1898, the Workmen's Provisional Committee Conference, meeting at Cardiff, decided to demand an immediate advance of 10% for three months after which discussions could take place regarding a wage regulator. These were conveyed by letter to the Secretary of the Coal Owners Association Mr Gascoyne Dalziel.

In reply on the 20th of April 1898 Mr Dalziel questioned their authority in demanding 10% but would put it to the Association for consideration at their next meeting. On Saturday the 23rd of April 1898, the Coal Owners Association made a counter offer of 2.5% as from the 1st of April to run for three months.

The **MFGB** held a meeting on Tuesday 26th of April 1898 at the Westminster Palace Hotel attended by 38 Delegates representing over 394,000 miners. Among matters discussed was a plea by Aberdare Agent Alderman David Morgan and William Abraham (Mabon), MP for Rhondda Valley, asking for financial support for the destitute families of South Wales.

They indicated that if help was forthcoming, it would bring the South Wales miners closer to joining the Federation. It was discussed the following day and a grant of £1,000 was made plus another £500 per week for 4 weeks.

On Friday the 29th of April 1898, the Cambrian Miners' Association voted £1,000 for distressed families of the South Wales miners and the East Lothian miners agreed to subscribe 1 shilling per man. Also, the North Wales miners agreed to contribute 6 pence per man. The stoppage caused great distress in the Valleys – in the Aberdare valley soup kitchens were reported to have fed over 6,000 and at Mountain Ash over 4,000 were fed.

A wind of change

A meeting of miners at Treharris near Merthyr on the 3rd of May 1898 decided to reverse their previous policy and to give plenary powers to the men's representatives to negotiate a settlement with their employers. This reversal was echoed in several Districts as miners families were on the brink of starvation and their men were eager to end the dispute. 'Mabon' was again called upon to lead the negotiating team but first insisted upon a favourable ballot of the entire South Wales and Monmouthshire Coalfield in granting plenary powers to the Workmen's Provisional Committee.

On Monday the 9th of May 1898, a deputation from Monmouthshire County Council and local Members of Parliament met Mr Ritchie MP, President of the Board of Trade in seeking his help to act as mediator in an attempt at settling the dispute. Mr Ritchie, although sympathetic to the situation declined to intervene until both sides of the dispute approached him directly. He did agree however that the Employers insistence on the workmen's representatives having plenary powers to negotiate was not unreasonable.

On Friday the 20th of May 1898, a meeting of miners Delegates from the whole of the South Wales and Monmouthshire coalfields met at Cardiff and voted to give the Workmen's Provisional Committee plenary powers to negotiate. Unfortunately, the vote included Delegates from non associated collieries and in a letter from Mr Dalziel of the Coal Owners Association, they refused to negotiate if they were included.

On Thursday the 26th of May 1898, another general workmen's conference in Cardiff voted in favour of a negotiating committee consisting of the Workmen's Provisional Committee plus one Delegate from each Associated pit. This was carried by a majority of 39,761 votes.

Contributions for starving families were arriving daily - on Saturday the 21st May 1898, the Durham Miners voted to donate £1,000 plus £100 per week and on Friday 27th May 1898, the **MFGB** Conference offered another £500.

Riots and the Military

On Sunday night the 29th of May 1898 there were riots in Dowlais when a pawnbroker ejected a striking miner from his home for not paying his rent. Police reinforcements were called in and the Magistrate requested help from the Military. A Detachment of 120 soldiers from the 24th Regiment South Wales Borderers was sent to help restore order. Both sides in the dispute met at Cardiff on Tuesday the 31st of May 1898 but the Coal Owners refused to agree to an advance of 10% or to abandon the 'Sliding Scale'. They also refused to agree to a joint Conciliation Board with an Arbitrator to oversee any disagreements. Inevitably, the meeting was adjourned, to be reconvened at a later date. News of this failure spread throughout the District and miners started organising marches, some ending in violent confrontations with the police.

In early June 1898 more soldiers from the Worcestershire Regiment were called in to the Rhondda valley and Aberdare making a total of 550 troops in the area. Similar numbers arrived at Aberamon and Mountain Ash, each soldier carrying 100 rounds of ball ammunition. From Plymouth another 400 soldiers of the Welsh Fusiliers were awaiting orders to move to the Valleys and 100 Carabineers from Aldershot were already on their way. From Cardiff, a squadron of the 6th Dragoon Guards had moved on to Pontypridd and were billeted in the Albwin colliery stables.

Mabon's Death Threat

On the 1st of June 1898, Mr William Abraham MP (Mabon) received an anonymous letter addressed from the Rhondda Valley;

June 1, 1898, Rhondda Valley. "Mr Mabon — It grieves me to write you these few lines, but we have made our minds up. We are 12 in the band and have signed before man and God that one of us is to do the deed and unless you do what is right to your fellow-workmen, this time your days are numbered. Don't forget it. It is no sham, for as true as this is written we shall stick to our word. We are just the men. There will be a Phoenix Park murder in Wales. You have lived long enough to keep you M.P. and starve poor workmen, with your loving dear brother, Sir W. T. Lewis. He is first on the list. By a vote of show of hands he only carried by one. I wonder how Lord keep men like you in the world—tyrants and vagabonds, swindlers, keeping your gold and starving families and their poor little children. This raises my temper, that I could go now straight and do it. 1 can do it. If it drops to my lot, I will do it and die like O'Connor in Liverpool. Mabon, our meeting is now. I have no more time but this will just warn you. Watch and pray. We will be close by you when you think we are far away. You eat a good breakfast with your loving brother in London, for if we can get you both together it will save some of us getting the rope. So no more. Do your duty, for we will surely watch you. Our funds are strong. Look out. This is hard lines, but it must be done."

The letter had a scrawled signature that was accompanied by two sketches – one depicting a coffin and the other a figure with a rope around his neck.

In his comments, Mabon said;

'this is the third letter of this kind that I have been honoured with during the present crisis. This one bears the Pentre postmark, the other two were from Porth. The handwriting, though disguised, shows that it is the production of no uneducated person. Though such threats will avail nothing with me or induce me to swerve one iota from my duty, they will serve to furnish the public and the miners with an idea of what a man has to put up with when he dares to follow the straight and conscientious path of duty. One day an attack comes from this quarter and the next day it emanates from another source.'

Throughout June 1898, the bargaining situation between the two sides remained unchanged although the Employers did agree an advance of 3.16% but no conciliation board and no arbitrator. Mabon and others deplored the presence of the military as the South Wales miners were, in the main a peaceable lot. Many of the younger out of work colliers had taken the Queen's shilling and joined the military while many others had left the pits to find work elsewhere. The Prince of Wales was called upon to intervene but although sympathetic to the miners' cause, declined the offer. Miners in other Districts of the Country joined the South Wales and Monmouthshire miners in demanding a 10% Advance. These included Lancashire, Yorkshire, Derbyshire, Warwickshire, Somerset, Nottinghamshire, Bristol and North Wales. What was not generally known was that during the month of June 1898, production of steam coal at the non associated collieries where the men were at work, averaged around 100,000 tons per week and sold at 20 shillings per ton (£1.00).

In early July 1898, the Workmen's Provisional Committee headed by Mabon succeeded in gaining an interview with Mr Ritchie MP in the House of Commons and presented him with a written request for an intervention in the dispute. This was later followed with the news that Sir Edward Fry, a previous High Court Judge, had been appointed by the Board of Trade as conciliator. He met with Mabon and the men's representatives in Cardiff but their communication with the Employers representatives resulted in a blunt refusal to abandon the 'Sliding Scale'. Sir W.T. Lewis, Chairman of the Coal Owners Association spoke with Sir Edward to confirm their refusal to accept his position as conciliator and that they would only be prepared to negotiate with the men's representatives directly and to retain the 'Sliding Scale'. Further joint meetings to discuss proposals made by Sir Edward ended in failure, with the Coal Owners declaring that the modified proposals would mean that their collieries would be under the perpetual control of an arbitrator and that was not acceptable.

On Monday the 18th of July 1898, the Coal Owners posted notices at their collieries offering fresh terms to include a 5% advance, the reintroduction of the 'Sliding Scale' that was terminated on the 31st of March 1898 for three years and the abolition of 'Mabon's Day'. A Conference of 146 Delegates representing 106,304 workmen met on the 25th of July 1898 in Cardiff. A difference of opinion meant that there had to be a contest to decide a Chairman and Vice Chairman with Mabon being re-elected Chairman and Alderman David Morgan as Vice Chairman. The meeting ended with resolutions restating their demands for no 'Sliding Scale', a conciliation board with an umpire and a minimum wage rate of 22.5% above the 1879 Standard. A deputation was sent to see Sir Edward Fry who had remained in Cardiff to thank him for his services but that under the circumstances he could be of no further assistance and so he agreed to withdraw from any further negotiations.

Later, in a Parliamentary Paper, Sir Edward would lay out the facts of his experiences as a conciliator which had been contained in letters he had sent to the Board of Trade during his time at Cardiff. He attributed his failure as conciliator to two sources. One was the failure of the Coal Owners Association through Sir William Lewis to hold any discussions and the second was that the Workmen's Provisional Committee didn't know their own minds and couldn't agree among themselves. He elaborated on this second point by saying that they had no figures to put to the employers, they had not arrived at a measure for the 'Sliding Scale' or at a definition of a minimum wage and they asked for an arbitrator which they knew the employers would not grant. Sir Edward came to the conclusion that the Provisional Committee were out of sympathy with the Delegates and did not represent the men.

Negotiations were therefore once again at a deadlock. The men were insistent on their latest demands while the Coal Owners said that they could not entertain any other terms than those posted at their pitheads. Miners' families were now at starvation level and soup kitchens around the Valleys and in the major cities where thousands of workers were idle, were kept going 24 hours a day. Cases of malnutrition were common - a poorly nourished woman was walking to the Merthyr Workhouse when her six week old child died in her arms, having been fed only on water.

Fig. 35 Cartoon depicting deadlock in negotiations

Meanwhile, Mabon was attending an International Congress in Vienna where the case for the Welsh Miners presented by him was favourably received. A promise of relief funds was made by the French and Belgian delegates and £500 was donated by the Austrians. Further contributions to the Central relief fund during the last week of July 1898 topped £7,000 with further contributions from miners now at work totalling over £40,000.

Reaction from the Forest of Dean

Being such a close neighbour, Forest of Dean miners had great sympathy for their South Wales colleagues and collections were being made at many rallies, carnivals and concerts held throughout the Forest. Substantial voluntary donations were also being made at schools, chapels and churches and forwarded to the Welsh miners' Central Fund.

The Forest of Dean Miners held meetings at various locations during this time, some of them being addressed by senior miners' representatives from the South Wales and Monmouthshire Coalfields. As a direct consequence of this dispute, the Forest of Dean house coal pits were reaping the benefit at a time when they would normally be suffering slackness in trade. Mr Rowlinson urged the men to contribute liberally to the suffering of the Welsh miner's families and collections were made at the pit gates.

At the **Miners' Annual Demonstration** held at the Speech House field on Saturday the 9th of July 1898, a fine day brought out huge crowds supported by Bands from Cinderford, Lydney, Pillowell and Bream. Officials and guests on the platform included Sir Charles Dilke MP, Mr Charles Fenwick MP, Mr George Rowlinson, Agent, Mr W. Brace, Monmouthshire Agent and Mr George Bernard, President of the **FODMA**, Mr Martin Perkins and Mr C. Fowler. Naturally the emphasis of the meeting was on the plight of their fellow colleagues in South Wales and speeches in their support were greeted with warm applause. Mr George Rowlinson moved a resolution *'That this meeting urges every collier and other workmen in the Forest of Dean and the general public to do their best to help feed the women and children who are wanting bread in South Wales'.* The resolution got overwhelming consent. He also remarked that if every Union man paid a 6d levy and boys paid a 3d levy, they would be able to send £100 each week to the South Wales Central Relief Fund but in the event, he said he was disappointed that the weekly total was usually less than £50.

Mr Brace said that he very much appreciated what the Forest miners had done in support of the distressed families in South Wales and commented that Wales produced the best steam coal but got the worst wages. Mr Martin Perkins argued that the Forest of Dean miners could learn from the South Wales situation and urged all working miners to join the Union in order to protect their own interests in the fight for better wages. Sir Charles Dilke MP remarked that he had never had a strong opinion on the 'Sliding Scale' but that if, as in the case of the South Wales miners who produced the best coal but hadn't received their sufficient share of the prices obtained, it was due to the imperfect nature of their Trade Unionism. And if, as many believed, the 'Sliding Scale' was the cause of this, then its existence would be a fatal drawback to Trade Unionism.

The speeches were followed by a Band Contest and the 1st prize of £10 went to Pillowell, 2nd of £6 to Lydney and 3rd of £4 to Bream. In the evening, protests were handed in against Pillowell and Bream so the Prizes were withheld. There were also two serious fairground accidents where one person fell out of a swing and another fell from the 'galloping horses'.

On Sunday evening the 6th of August 1898, a large meeting was held at the Yorkley Bailey addressed by Mr S.J. Elsom JP urging support for the Welsh miners' families. Afterwards, the Yorkley and Blakeney joint male voice choir gave a concert where a collection was taken for the Relief Fund.

At the old recreation ground in Cinderford on Sunday the 14th of August 1898, a large crowd gathered in support of the Welsh miners' strike. Mr George Rowlinson acted as Chairman and was supported by Mr W. Brace (Monmouthshire Agent), Mr Martin Perkins **(FODMA),** and other South Wales representatives. They all supported a resolution condemning the treatment of Alderman David Morgan and his colleagues and wished to be associated with the petition being made to the Home Secretary pleading for a reconsideration of the sentence. Bands from the Artillery and Rifle Volunteers supported the event by parading the streets and a collection amounting to £6-13shillings was sent to the Central Fund.

After 17 weeks of stoppage, there were signs that miners at some twenty collieries had agreed to reconsider the acceptance of the 'Sliding Scale' with a minimum wage. They put it to the Workmen's Provisional Committee that they would accept a ballot on the subject. Two to three hundred miners in the Merthyr District were also considering returning to work on the employers' terms but the Workmen's committee resolved that if they did, they would not work with them when the dispute was over. Mabon was still insistent that a conciliator was necessary for a settlement to be agreed and that 'Mabon's Day' should be preserved – and so the dispute continued.

Meanwhile, at the Glamorganshire Assizes at Swansea on Monday the 8th of August 1898 before Mr. Justice Wills, Alderman David Morgan and three other defendants, were charged with intimidation in connection with the dispute at the Abernant Collieries in December 1897. The accused were previously tried at the Cardiff Spring Assizes, when the jury disagreed. All were now found guilty, and David Morgan was sentenced to two months' hard labour, Jones to one month, and Joseph Price to two weeks. Thomas Price was bound over to come up for judgment when called upon. In Aberdare, the news brought thousands of people out at night to meet the last train from Swansea, by which it was expected that the parties in the case would return. One of the witnesses for the prosecution was loudly hooted as he stepped off the train but he was allowed to proceed to his home without any molestation.

On Wednesday the 10th of August 1898, the Workmen's Provisional Committee condemned the severity of the sentence and decided to petition the Home Secretary for a reduction. As a consequence, the medical officer at Cardiff Gaol excused Alderman David Morgan from hard labour on account of his age and health and Mr Joseph Price was discharged.

On Saturday the 27th of August 1898 a meeting of both parties in the dispute at Cardiff arrived at a tentative agreement on their main differences but which had to be agreed with the men. It allowed for an agreement whereby if wages fell below the minimum rate of 12.5% above the Standard set in 1879, the men could terminate the agreement by giving 6 months notice from January or July next or any following year and that this would be an arrangement for a period of 4 years from 1st January 1898. The workmen's Provisional Committee held a general conference at the Cory Hall, Cardiff the following Wednesday the 31st of August 1898 to consider the proposals agreed with the Coal Owners. A vote was taken and 61,912 voted in favour with 37,077 against, (8,800 being neutral) and so the proposals were agreed by a majority of 24,835. The final terms for settlement were;

1. The 'Sliding Scale' which terminated on 31st March 1898 to be re-embodied in an agreement to last until 1st January 1902 and to be determined by 6 months' notice either side of that date i.e. 1st July 1901 or 1st July 1902 or any other following 1st of July or 1st January.

2. 'Mabon's Day' to be abolished with no replacement.

3. An immediate advance of 5% above the wages in force on 31st March last.

4. That if the wages after September fell below the minimum rate of 12.5% above the Standard set in 1879, the men have the power to give 6 months notice on any 1st of January or 1st of July to terminate the agreement. But if not, the agreement would continue in force till 1904

The next day, Thursday the 1st of September 1898, the Coal Owners Emergency Committee and the Workmen's Provisional Committee met in Joint conference in Cardiff where the employers' proposals were accepted. Appeals by Mr Abraham for the retention of 'Mabon's Day' or alternatively for a once a year 'play-week' was rejected by the Coal Owners. The agreement was therefore signed but only by 11 of the 16 Delegates. So, after 22 weeks of bitter struggle, hardship, starvation and privation, the battle was over. Some pits were able to reopen immediately where upwards of 50,000 miners were employed while others would take between 2 to 3 weeks to get started.

Dramatic scenes followed the early release from Cardiff Gaol on the 9th of September 1898 of Alderman David Morgan. His surprising release which should have been on the 29th came as a welcome shock to many who were making arrangements for that date. However, news in the Valleys spread fast and large crowds gathered at each train station en-route from Cardiff to Aberdare to cheer him home. Alderman Morgan was a fervent opponent of the 'Sliding Scale' and many believed that had he been free to express his opinion, no such agreement would have been approved.

By the 13th of September 1898 the military presence in South Wales came to an end with the departure of the Infantry and Cavalry by train.

The Aftermath

It was estimated to have cost the District nearly £6,000,000. Taking into account the loss of coal production of approximately 7 million tons and also the miners' wages, the loss in production alone amounted to £3,830,000. Added to that, the loss of wages for the miners, loss of financial investment by individuals and Company shareholders, losses suffered by Ship-owners and Railway Companies, dockers, Iron and quarry workers wages, the cost of deploying the Military and extra Police plus a host of other ancillary workers wages, the figure ran near to £1.5 million.

The Strike was over but the recovery would take not weeks but months or even years and the suffering would continue. While miners' families throughout the District had suffered considerably, so had the people of Cardiff and Newport through no fault of their own. Port trade had been paralysed and the people were reduced to poverty and children were starving.

Contributions towards the relief of the miners' families totalled over £108,000 of which £12,000 was contributed by the **MFGB** while Districts such as Durham, Northumberland, Scottish, Staffordshire and many others such as the Forest of Dean had given generously. At a meeting of the Workmen's Provisional Delegates and other Delegates on Tuesday the 20th of September 1898 at the Park Hotel, Pontypridd under the Presidency of Mr W. Abraham MP (Mabon), moves were made in an effort to form one united Union for the whole of the South Wales and Monmouthshire coalfields under the banner **'South Wales Miners' Association'**. Also discussed, and an important consideration for all miners, were the pros and cons of joining or contracting out of the 1897 Workmen's Compensation Act. All collieries in the area were involved in conducting ballots as to whether they wished to contract out or not.

A General Conference was held in Cardiff on Tuesday 11th of October 1898 to appoint Officers pro tem and to agree draft rules of their newly formed **'South Wales Miners' Association'**. Notices were sent to all collieries requesting they appoint representatives to attend and 160 were present. W. Abraham MP (Mabon) was elected Chairman pro tem and Mr W. Brace Vice Chairman pro tem, with the proviso that permanent Officers would be elected at their first Annual Conference in Cardiff on the 7th January 1899. And so at last, but with some doubters, the miners of South Wales had begun to realise that in order to succeed with their demands, they had to be united within a strong organisation and with leaders they could trust to fight for their interests. There was still some dissent from those that opposed the September 1st agreement and the abolition of 'Mabon's Day' was still an issue at some collieries. An encouraging letter from the leader of the **MFGB** gave further hope that at some time in the near future, they could be part of the National Federation and fight for the abandonment of the 'Sliding Scale' in favour of a minimum wage. A meeting took place at the Westminster Palace Hotel in London on Friday the 18th of November 1898 between leaders of the **MFGB** and leaders of the **South Wales Miners' Association** which included Mabon, Alderman David Morgan and William Brace. The objective was to clear the way for South Wales to be affiliated to the **MFGB** at the January Conference and to form a basis on which both sides could agree, taking into account their September 1st settlement which would last for four years.

As the year drew to a close, almost 60,000 miners – men and boys - in the Districts had signed up as members of the new Association. On Tuesday the 29th of November 1898 the Sliding Scale Joint Committee held their regular audit and decided to raise the wages 2.5%, making the wages now 20% above the Standard set in 1879.

As new Lodges were rapidly being formed, each District held their own meetings to elect their own officials and the Delegates onto the new **SWMA** Committee prior to their first AGM on the 7th of January 1899. This took place at the Cory Hall, Cardiff with 182 Delegates in attendance representing 69,883 mineworkers and where it was overwhelmingly resolved to apply to join the **MFGB**. Election of officials of the new Union included Mr W. Abraham MP (Mabon), President; Mr W. Brace, Vice President; Mr A. Onions, Treasurer and Mr T. Richards, Secretary. The officials elected to attend the forthcoming **MFGB** Annual Conference were Mr W. Abraham MP, Mr W. Brace and Mr John Williams.

At the Annual Conference of the **MFGB** held at the Oddfellows Hall, Edinburgh on Tuesday the 10th of January 1899, presided over by Mr Ben Pickard MP, the South Wales Miners Association were officially admitted to the Federation with Mr W. Abraham elected to the Executive Committee. In his opening submission for membership, Mr Abraham said;

'We are three penitent Welshmen. (laughter). We are the children of the resurrection, having found conviction by fact and harsh treatment. We have been some days in the throes of resurrection and we hope now to sit in the palace of adoption. As yet, we only represent a portion of our men, the portion that we hope will be considered ample to allow of affiliation with the Federation. We have about 100,000 men working in and about the mines and of that number we have 60,000 men in Union and to prove that we are sincere, we have brought with us a cheque for £60'.(applause)

So, at long last, the South Wales miners had eventually come to terms with their fragmented attempts to beat their masters. They had now realised that as part of a much larger body of workers such as the **MFGB,** with a combined membership of 425,000, they were much more likely to succeed with any future dispute and that the 'Sliding Scale' system of payment was doomed to failure in the not too distant future. It wasn't long before the press began referring to their new Association as a Federation and so it was eventually to become known as the **'South Wales Miners' Federation'** or **'The Fed**.'

Chapter 10
Sir Charles Dilke M.P. 1843 – 1911

Many words have been written about Charles W. Dilke, both good and bad but on a local level he proved to be a very popular MP while representing the Forest of Dean in Parliament and gave the working classes, miners in particular, his undivided support. Charles Dilke was educated at Trinity Hall, Cambridge where he became President of the Cambridge Union Society. He became a Liberal Member of Parliament for Chelsea in 1868 and aspired to the Baronetsy when his father died in 1869 leaving him a fortune worth £7,000 (£8.8 million today). Dilke was known as a Radical who supported reform for the working classes both in

Fig. 36 Sir Charles Dilke 2nd BT.

Parliament and while touring the country. As an example, in 1870 he supported the East End of London matchmakers who were being imposed with a tax on matches that would affect their jobs and livelihood. With Dilke's support, the idea was dropped.

His controversial views about the Monarchy and Republicanism nearly finished his Parliamentary career. He complained in Parliament about the £1,000,000 tax free money given to the Queen and members of the Royal Family. Riots usually followed in his footsteps as he toured the country giving speeches on the subject and on at least one occasion he was threatened with death, as happened at a meeting in Bolton. His response was to walk out of the meeting hall, casually light his cigar on the steps and walk away through the crowd. Riots usually followed in his footsteps. He had sympathy for workers Unions, supported the **1871 Trades Union Act** and was influential in getting voting times at the polls extended so that workers could cast their votes. In January 1872 he married Katherine Sheil but she died in childbirth on the 20th of September 1874, two days after giving birth to a son. Her wish was to be cremated in the interest of science but the law forbade this in Britain. Her body was therefore embalmed and transported to Dresden in Germany where a new legal crematorium incorporating an observation window and invented by Friedrich Siemens was to be used. Sir Charles himself was so distraught with grief that he travelled to Paris and left the funeral arrangements to his younger brother Ashton. The actual cremation took place on the 9th of October 1874 and was witnessed by many scientific observers – the written account of this event is too graphic to include here and so is left to the readers' imagination.

Sir Charles served under William Gladstone's second Government as Under Secretary for Foreign Affairs from 1880 to 1882 and also became a Cabinet Member as President of the Local Government Board until 1885. He was instrumental in seeing through Parliament the **1884 Third Reform Act or Representation of the People Act** – which gave greater voting rights to men who owned land but not women. At that time no women had the vote and only 60% of men.

Unfortunately, his career came to an end in 1886 when he became embroiled in a notorious scandal and he lost his Chelsea seat at that years' General Election. Sir Charles was accused of having an affair with his brother's mother in law Mrs Ellen Smith, wife of Liberal MP and shipowner Thomas E. Smith before and after his own second marriage in 1885. This was compounded in 1885 by another accusation that in 1882 he seduced Mrs Smith's second daughter Mrs Virginia Crawford, wife of Mr Donald Crawford MP. This whole affair or affairs became the subject of a very messy court case in which a verbal confession of adultery was admitted by Mrs Crawford. However, in the event, there was no evidence against Sir Charles of that offence and so the Judge concluded **'I cannot see any case whatsoever against Sir Charles Dilke'.**

Sir Charles fought back to clear his name but the court case didn't go well for him, especially as it was found that he had cut pages out of his diary. The court found that Virginia Crawford's version of events were correct and granted her a 'decree absolute'. Queen Victoria was not amused and demanded he be stripped of his membership of the Privy Council. An enquiry in 1892 largely exonerated Sir Charles by casting doubt on Virginia Crawford's evidence.

In spite of this reputation damaging scandal, Sir Charles remarried in October 1885 to widow Mrs Francis Pattison nee Amelia Francis Strong and from then on known as Lady Emilia Dilke. She was a well known author, art critic, feminist and Trade Unionist who had already created a name for herself as a public speaker on social reform.

She established herself as an expert on French art and cultural history and was a prolific writer on the subject. She became President of the Women's Trade Union League and regularly spoke at the Annual Trades Union Congress. She also campaigned for votes for women and both she and Sir Charles were personal friends of

Fig. 37 Lady Amelia Dilke

Richard and Emmeline Pankhurst and who regularly donated money to the cause of Women's Suffrage. Due to her political views on universal suffrage, in 1903 she resigned from the Liberal Party and joined the Independent Labour Party. She died in October 1904.

Mr Godfrey Samuelson who was elected as MP for the Forest of Dean constituency in July 1888 didn't always share the miners demands for better working conditions and a reduction in working hours and other important causes and so, in 1889, as a stalwart in the Forest of Dean Liberal Association, Mr Rowlinson approached Sir Charles Dilke with a view to his standing for election for the Forest of Dean constituency at the next General Election. After consulting Liberal Leader Gladstone, he refused the offer but in 1891 he went against Gladstone's wishes and accepted the nomination. And so, in the July 1892 General Election, Sir Charles was duly elected MP for the Forest of Dean constituency.

As Forest of Dean MP, serving in Gladstone's minority Government, Sir Charles Dilke involved himself in supporting the miners' cause both with the local miners' Union and politically within Parliament but he never held a senior Government position again - some saying that was due to his chequered past. He attended nearly all the **Miners' Annual Demonstrations** at the Speech House and supported their cause in

Parliament whenever the opportunity presented itself. He died in January 1911. Such was the high esteem in which he was held within the Forest of Dean, that a fundraising campaign raised enough money to build a local community hospital to his memory (see later chapters). This was opened in 1923 as the **Dilke Memorial Hospital** at Yew Tree Brake and for over 100 years has operated as a functional Hospital serving the local community. At the time of writing however, it is due for closure – a new Hospital serving the needs of the whole Forest of Dean will open in Cinderford

Chapter 11
New Beginnings

As the clock ticked over into the year 1900, the coal industry nationally was buoyant with production at an all time high and wages correspondingly high. Over one million tons of coal was being extracted and fetching 30 shillings a ton at the pithead. The miners' wages for those Districts within the **MFGB** was 50% above the Standard of 1888 with a promise of an immediate rise of 5% with proportionate levels for those not yet affiliated. However, wages contracts for all Districts were due for renewal in January 1901 (except the South Wales Federation, which was due in January 1902) under the agreed system of Conciliation Boards or Joint Wages Boards. In January 1900 the Board had agreed that a maximum of 60% and minimum of 30% above the 1888 Standard would be applied as from January 1901 although seasonal fluctuations were still possible if coal prices either rose or fell. So although wages were still subject to the price of coal sold at the pithead, the old 'Sliding Scale' system which largely favoured the Coal Owners was slowly being replaced by Conciliation Boards consisting of an equal number of miners' representatives and Coal Owners representatives with an independent chairman. The Coal Owners Association were also pleased that peace had been established for another four years.

Unfortunately, fatal accidents and injuries continued to happen and the **MFGB** were continually pressing the Government for more Colliery Inspectors, but without success. The Workmen's Compensation Act of 1897 was still a bone of contention among the mining community with some Coal Owners delaying payouts to the families of those killed or injured and sometimes finding loopholes to avoid any payout. Deputations to the Home Secretary met with promises of consideration and so amendments to this Act were still in the pipeline. Other main aims were to secure an eight hour day for all mineworkers – 12 hour shifts were still being operated at some collieries - and a standard national wage.

An unfortunate side effect of the new wages system was that many miners were still reluctant to join their local Union, partly from the threat of being victimised by their employers and partly because they were already receiving the same privileges without necessarily being in the Union. The Unions countered this argument with the fact that had it not been for the Unions bargaining history in fighting for their rights, the current system of

Joint Wages Boards wouldn't exist and they would be back with the old system – and a lot worse off. Also, it was unfair to those who supported their Union and who had consistently paid their monthly levies. And, in the event of a local dispute at a colliery, the Union would usually be the negotiating power with the employers to secure a settlement. These arguments however didn't carry too much weight and so the battle of persuasion continued, both on a national level and locally with Mr Rowlinson having an uphill struggle still trying to encourage Forest of Dean miners to join the Union.

As far as the Iron Industry was concerned, Messrs Henry Crawshay and Co. had, in September 1899 shut down the Shakemantle, Perseverance and Buckshaft mines near Cinderford due to exhausted veins, putting 200 men out of work. They said that sinking shafts to the richer, deeper veins was uneconomical at the present time.

Looking at the overall picture of the past 100 years, there had been major advances in the mining industry. Safety in the mines and a fair working wage were the miners' two main grievances and the formation of Unions paved the way for improvements to both. Pit safety during the first half of the 19th Century had been non-existent with death and serious injury at horrendous levels and boys and girls as young as four being employed underground. A welcome piece of legislation in 1842 was the **Mines and Collieries Act** which forbade women and children under the age of 10 working underground and in 1860, the **Coal Mines Regulation Act** raised the limit for boys from 10 to 12 years. The advent of **Coal Mines Inspections Act of 1850** helped to some extent but only four Inspectors were appointed to cover the whole of Britain and Coal Owners were ordered to provide detailed underground maps for inspection. A further Act of 1855 broadened the sphere of influence to include ironstone mines and slate mines but with so few inspectors and some having cosy arrangements with the colliery owners to save money, a great many dangerous practices were still overlooked. With over 1,000 deaths each year by 1870, the **Coal Mines Regulation Act** of 1872 gave miners the right to choose pit Inspectors from among themselves and for the pit managers to have State certification of their training. Later, in 1881, the **Mines Regulation Act** gave the Home Secretary the power to hold enquiries into the causes of mine accidents and in 1883, the Home Office took over the responsibilities of the Mining Records Office.

Wage structures were the main causes of disputes, strikes and lockouts for a large section of the mining community but with the advent of strong Unions, initiated by the checkweighmen, collective bargaining became a force to be reckoned with. Coal Owners of course fought back with the formation of their own Coal Owners' Association and with considerable funds with which to withstand many long disputes. Innocent parties in these disputes suffered appallingly through no fault of their own with miners' families suffering the most with very high levels of privation and starvation. Other associated trades also suffered with the loss of jobs when coal became scarce and shopkeepers unable to extend loans had to close their premises. The advent of the **Miners' Federation of Great Britain (MFGB)** in 1889 was a great step forward which would eventually include all coalfield Districts in the Country. The Owners then began to listen and so the two warring parties could at last agree on a sensible compromise that involved decision making by a team drawn from both sides.

The **MFGB** held their Annual Conference in January 1900 at Cardiff, the Delegates representing 432,500 men. Conference again committed to persisting in their efforts to secure an eight hour day for miners but fought shy of fighting for boys under eighteen years from working over eight hours per day. Future conferences were to be held annually in October.

Keir Hardie – 1856 – 1915

Meanwhile, other powerful Union leaders were beginning to assert their influences in other Districts. In Scotland, Lanarkshire born Keir Hardie rose from extreme poverty through several menial jobs including hewing coal to become the leader of a miners Union in Hamilton and led unsuccessful strike action in 1880 and 1881 in both Lanarkshire and Ayrshire.

After winning the South West Ham seat at the 1892 General Election as an Independent candidate, Kier Hardie MP with the cooperation of the Trades Union Congress, formed the **Independent Labour Party (ILP)** in

Fig. 38 Mr Keir Hardie

January 1893. This event marked the beginning of a political movement that, with support from the Unions, represented the working man in Parliament. At the 1895 General Election, the **ILP** fielded 28 candidates but unfortunately they failed to gain a single seat. He campaigned on many controversial issues and was ridiculed in Parliament for wearing a tweed suit and deerstalker hat instead of the customary frock coat and top hat.

A special Conference was called by the Trades Union Congress in February 1900 to discuss the possibility of forming a political party that would sponsor candidates for election to Parliament who could justly represent the working class movement. This was attended by various socialist and left wing organisations including Keir Hardie's **Independent Labour Party.** Hardie's own motion; *'to establish a distinct Labour group in Parliament'* was overwhelmingly passed and resulted in the formation of the **Labour Representation Committee (LRC)** with Ramsay MacDonald as it's first Secretary. In the October 1900 General Election, the **LRC** fielded 15 candidates but won only two – Keir Hardie for Merthyr Tydfil and Richard Bell for Derby - but it marked the embryonic formation of the Labour Party six years later.

However, there was dissent regarding Hardie's views on women's suffrage and in 1908, he resigned his leadership although he continued to campaign for working people. He became prominent while working with Sylvia Pankhurst in the fight for Women's Suffrage and campaigned for self rule in India as well as to end segregation in South Africa. But his political views did alienate him from mainstream politics and his pacifist tendencies at the start of the First World War, won him no friends. He died of pneumonia in a Glasgow nursing home on the 26th of September 1915 after suffering ill health for some time. No politicians attended his funeral but his legacy still lives on in our political institutions today.

Alderman David Morgan

In July, a stalwart in the fight for justice within the South Wales coalfield and miners' Agent for Aberdare Alderman David Morgan was found dead in bed by his daughter. The previous night he had addressed a meeting and went to bed in the normal way at 10.30pm. At about 5am the next morning he woke with some discomfort and called his daughter. He eventually told her to leave but when she returned at 7am she found that he had passed away. It appeared that he had died aged 60 of a weak heart. Tributes echoed the fact that Alderman Morgan had served his community and fellow miners for nearly fifty years and that there never was a more sincere and conscientious person who had devoted his life to improving the lives and conditions of his fellow man. He left one son and five daughters and was interned at Mountain Ash cemetery.

Boer Wars
Meanwhile and somewhat forgotten was the existing war in South Africa between British Empire forces and that of the Africaaners/ Dutch settlers – known as the 2nd Boer War (1899-1902). It is important to remember that many young men who had become disillusioned with the recent strikes and disruptions, had opted to take the Queen's shilling and join our Forces, many of whom had then been shipped to South Africa to fight the cause. Casualties on both sides were heavy and in total, 45,000 British and Colonial men were either dead, injured or missing and over 6,000 Africaaners and foreign volunteers were dead.

Forest of Dean
Feelings were strong here in Britain in supporting our boys fighting abroad and all sections of the community were involved in fund raising for the War effort. None more so than in the Forest of Dean where Mr Rowlinson announced in a March 1900 meeting that the **Forest of Dean Miners' Association** had collected the handsome sum of £311.17s.8d, not only from colliers but also from Quarrymen and Iron and Colour workers.

In response to the healthy state of the Forest of Dean coal industry and the high prices being paid for Forest of Dean coal, the Joint Wages Board met in June 1900 to discuss the termination of the present wages contract between Miners and Coal Owners in September 1900. It was agreed to increase the miners' wages by 10%, the contract to run for four years and so therefore they would then be 40% above the 1888 Standard.

At the July 1900 **Miners' Annual Demonstration** hosted by the **Dean Forest Labour Association** with Mr George Barnard as Chairman, Mr Rowlinson said that he was pleased to announce the forthcoming wages increase but was again disappointed with the lack of enthusiasm for joining the Union. He pointed out that at one time 9 out of 10 miners belonged to the Union and urged the men not yet members to remember how their wage rises were negotiated. This was echoed by the other speakers including Sir Charles Dilke.

On the 30th of July 1900 with the help of Sir Charles Dilke, the Government passed the **Mines (prohibition of child labour underground) Act** which prevented anyone under the age of 13 from working in any underground mine.

In October 1900 a General Election (known as the khaki Election in the belief that the 2nd Boer war was at an end) returned Sir Charles Dilke as Liberal MP for the Forest of Dean District with an increased majority. During previous canvassing meetings, Mr Rowlinson announced that the Miners Association had arranged with the Colliery Owners for Polling Day to be a 'Play Day'. Sir Charles had apparently taken to electioneering in a carriage and pair accompanied by Lady Dilke while their Conservative opponent Mr Henry Terrell QC took to one of those new fangled motor cars (could possibly have been a Daimler) bedecked with his party colours - what a colourful sight they both must have been. Sir Charles was well known to be able to predict the amount of his own poll in advance and 4975 was his prediction. The results were announced at Newnham Town Hall and Sir Charles gained 4972 votes while Mr Henry Terrell QC gained 2520 votes, a Liberal majority of 2452. And his prediction was remarkably only 3 votes adrift.

Accidents/Fatalities

Life in the pits and quarries were seemingly as dangerous as ever and accidents, many of them fatal, were still an unfortunate regular occurrence. The following pages contain many examples of these for each year in the Forest of Dean but are by no means all inclusive - so apologies to the relatives of those that have unintentionally been missed.

One such occurred on Wednesday the 16th of May 1900 at a quarry at Fetter Hill where 53 year old Mr Oliver Hoare the quarry proprietor was attempting to erect a large crane at the top of the quarry with the help of carpenter Mr Henry Rudge. While putting in a post as a guide for the crane, he slipped and fell 30ft to his death – his body and head striking the stone projections during the fall. The inquest at the Bible Christian Chapel at Clements End recorded a verdict of accidental death.

And another on Saturday the 1st of December 1900 at the Foxes Bridge Colliery near Cinderford where 17 year old William George Tingle a horse driver was involved in a freak accident. While towing two empty drams underground in the main 'Lowery vein', his horse suddenly started off at a fast rate and both drams jumped the rails knocking down some stored timber. This in turn brought down half a ton of debris which buried Mr Tingle, crushing him to death. At the inquest at the Dog Inn, Cinderford, a verdict that death was caused by a fall of the roof, being instigated by the knocking out of timbering by a cart.

1901 - Into the 20th Century

As the clock ticked over into 1901 and Queen Victoria passed on, what was in store for the working classes in the 20th Century? The past 100 years had been horrendous as far as pit safety was concerned and boys as young as 8 were still being legally employed in the mines. Wage structures were the main causes of disputes, strikes, brutality and starvation for a large section of the mining community.

A persistent bone of contention for many years was the 'Sliding Scale' system of payment for the miners and after the South Wales Miners strike just a couple of years earlier, it seemed that when the current pay agreement terminated in 1902, they would negotiate another form of payment that would be more acceptable to the miners. That said, one of the main aims of the **MFGB** was getting rid of the 'Sliding Scale' for the whole of the Country's miners and so the battle went on.

Nationally, the Conciliation Board's agreement reached the previous year was activated and in January 1901 the miners received an immediate increase of 5% with another 5% in the first week of February 1901. This brought their wages up to 60% above the Standard of 1888. In South Wales where agreements with Coal Owners were different, the increases obtained would take their wages up to 74% above the 1879 Standard.

With collective bargaining now a reality, especially with the ever growing strength of the **MFGB**, the miners were confident that their demands would eventually be settled. There were however setbacks, one of which was in 1901 when the **Taff Vale Railway Company** raised a lawsuit against the Amalgamated Society of Railway Servants of South Wales who were involved in a strike of railway workers. The House of Lords judged in favour of the Company and the Union was fined £23,000 as compensation to their employers for losses during a strike. This proved to be a weakness in the collective actions of Unions and undermined their right to strike. Sir Charles Dilke spoke at length in the House of Commons and brought to the attention of Henry Campbell-Bannerman the hypocrisy of this decision by a Judge. He pointed out that although it was a legal right to strike, the judgement had made it impossible to take peaceful strike action without a Union becoming bankrupt. Later, when the Liberal party won a landslide victory at the 1906 General Election, Prime Minister Henry Campbell-

Bannerman backed a Bill that introduced the **1906 Trades Disputes Act** that removed Trade Union liability for damage by strike action.

Accidents/Fatalities

On Thursday evening the 17th of January 1901, Mr William James Lucas aged 32 and from Soudley, lost his life while working underground at the newly developed Crown Colliery at Moseley Green when about a ton of blue shale fell on him. At the Soudley Inquest Mr Thomas Johnson from Wigan who owned the colliery said that he had put a Mr Bedney who he relied upon in charge of the colliery and there was a lot of discussion about the setting of the timbers in the roadway. As the exact circumstances of the accident were unknown, the jury found that death was due to a fall of earth from the roof.

On Friday the 25th of January 1901, Mr William Jenkins, a trammer, working at the Darkhill Endeavour Colliery, died instantly when he was crushed by a runaway dram. The loaded dram was being sent down a 25 yard long incline and Mr Jenkins was at the bottom to receive it. His light went out and at the same time, one of the sprags in the dram wheels broke, letting it go rapidly and crushing Mr Jenkins between it and the side of the roadway.

On Saturday the 26th of January 1901, Mr James Williams aged 33, a foreman shunter, died instantly while shunting in a private siding at Lightmoor Colliery, Cinderford. At the Inquest it was revealed that Mr Williams had been using a plank between the trucks to save time. The plank had not been provided for that purpose and by using it, he had acted indiscreetly and he had lost his life due to the breaking of the plank.

On Wednesday the 3rd of July 1901, Mr John Kear aged 43, a collier from Edenwall, Coleford died as a result of an accident while working underground at the Speech House Main Colliery that same day. Mr Kear had been working with Mr Mark Eddy whose job it had been for several months to fill casks with water and transport them in two drams up a steep incline using an engine and then to return them empty. On the day of the accident, Mr Kear came to help and after several loads had been drawn up, Mr Kear wanted to ride alongside Mr Eddy up the incline. Mr Eddy said no, that it was a privilege for the man in charge only to ride up. As Mr Kear was an older man, Mr Eddy eventually allowed him to ride and the signal to start was given. After only 15 yards, Mr Kear's head came into contact with the roof and he was knocked off, the lights went out, the signal wire could not be found and they had to continue the journey to the top. Once there, Mr Eddy quickly raced back to help but found Mr Kear in a bad state. He was helped to the surface and taken home where he was attended by Dr Currie who found that his collar bone and ribs had been fractured and a lung had been injured. He died that night and the cause of death was heart failure following bronchitis, brought on by his injuries. At the Inquest, the Jury also added that the deceased had been riding improperly on the dram and that Mr Eddy was guilty of negligence in allowing the deceased to break the rules.

On Wednesday the 28th of August 1901, Mr George Phipps of Pillowell lost his life at the New Fancy Colliery by a fall of rock. Mr Phipps was a Buttyman with a stall at the Colliery and was working with his son Thomas and a Mr Henry Ruck. They started their shift at 7am after the stall had been examined and reported safe. At 12.45pm a cracking noise was heard in the roof and Mr Phipps called on his men to run. He himself also ran but unfortunately ran into the fall and was killed on the spot with a fractured skull. His son Thomas was also knocked down but was only badly bruised. The evidence showed that there was plenty of timber and the fall was attributed to a slip which could not have been seen until it had taken place. A verdict of accidental death was recorded.

On Tuesday the 17th of December 1901, Mr Joseph Willetts aged 18, a collier from Primrose Hill and living with his parents, was killed while working underground at the Norchard Colliery near Lydney. Mr Willetts and another collier Mr Albert Bath were both working together erecting timber supports on a roadway and had just placed two upright posts in position. They were about to place a piece of timber along the top when a large quantity of earth fell onto Mr Willetts. He was pulled out as soon as possible but was found to be dead. At the Inquest, the pit Inspector Arthur West of Whitecroft stated that about an hour before the accident, he had inspected the place where the men were working and considered it to be safe. A verdict of being crushed to death by a fall of earth was recorded.

1902

Peace was declared at 11.15pm local time in Pretoria, South Africa on the 31st of May 1902, between the British Empire Forces and the Africaan settlers, known as the Boers. This prolonged war, which started on the 11th of October 1899 was brought to an end when the Boers signed peace terms with Lord Kitchener and Lord Milner. However, news of this event didn't reach the Forest of Dean until a week later and although feelings were subdued, flags flew and children had a holiday from school,

The **Miners' Annual Demonstration** in July 1902, organised by the Labour Association and Chaired once more by President Mr George Barnard, attracted speakers such as Sir Charles Dilke MP, William Abraham MP(Mabon), Mr E. Fowler (Vice President), Mr G. Rowlinson Agent and other Committee members. Mention by the President was again made regarding the lack of loyalty to the Union and Cinderford, Drybrook and Lydbrook were named as the worst while West Dean had set them all such a good example. Mabon spoke of the ingratitude of those who enjoyed the benefits but paid nothing. Sir Charles Dilke spoke of the intricacies of the forthcoming **Education Bill** and what it meant for the Forest of Dean. He said that unless changes were made, the District could lose a great deal of money and lose control of its own Education policy. However, despite opposition from sections of Parliament, including David Lloyd George and many nonconformist religious organisations, the Act became law in December 1902 – as a result of which, 170 men went to prison for refusing to pay their school taxes. Sir Charles also referred to the previous year's Taff Vale Railway case in which he had been critical of the state of affairs regarding the Union's ability to take strike action without becoming bankrupt by judicial decisions.

Accidents/Fatalities

The year of 1902 will go down in history as one of the worst years for pit accidents and deaths in the Forest of Dean. Causes of these continuing accidents are many and varied and it would seem to be an impossible task to make the mines a safe place to work. Human error played a large part in these accidents and so did failings or weaknesses within the earth itself but sometimes accidents are just that – accidents, and they continued to happen as long as man needed to toil underground. It was a very dangerous occupation and any amount of precautions could not predict the unpredictable.

On Friday the 27th of June 1902 at the Lightmoor Colliery, a number of young men were bathing in the colliery pond when Daniel Smith aged 18, of Victoria Street, Cinderford got out of his depth and drowned. Others including Messrs Prosser and Jones had narrow escapes. While bathing in the pond, Smith got into difficulties and called out for help and one of his friends John Worgan, a collier, jumped in to help. Unfortunately they both went under and Worgan had to let Smith go to save himself as the water was 9 feet deep. At the Inquest, the Jury praised the courage of John Worgan for putting his own life in danger and that the death of Daniel Smith was due to drowning through being unable to swim.

On Wednesday morning the 8th of October 1902 at approximately 11.30am, two men working in the Trenchard seam at the Norchard Colliery near Lydney producing steam coal, were overcome by a fall of five tons of rock. The Colliery, known as a Level with several Dipples was owned by the Park Iron Ore and Coal Company. At 10.30am on the day of the accident, Mr Ben Bath an Examiner had inspected the roof and had pronounced it safe for the men to proceed to their workplace. They were Mr William Phipps and Mr Richard Shingles both living at Bream. At about 11am both men stopped work to have their 'bait' and at 11.40am when another collier Mr Allan Beverstock who was working nearby indicated to the men to bring out their coal, he received no reply. On going to investigate, he found that the roof had collapsed onto the men. He ran for help and with another collier managed to remove a large stone covering Mr Shingles' head and he was immediately released but seriously injured. The colliery manager was called and he and several other colliers managed to find and release Mr Phipps. He was found with serious head injuries and when Dr Thomas and P.C. Hazell arrived, he was pronounced dead at the scene with a fractured skull. Mr Phipps aged 30 was a married man with four children while Mr Shingles was single and 22 years of age.

Mr Shingles, who was conscious, was taken home that afternoon with bruises to his abdomen and legs and was unable to walk. On the Saturday, he became unconscious and was taken to Gloucester Infirmary on Tuesday the 14th of October 1902. He had become delirious and was suffering from multiple bruising to his head and legs, a large abscess on his chest, a cut on his back and partial paralysis of his legs. His condition deteriorated and he died two days later on Thursday the 16th of October 1902. At the Inquest, a post mortem found that Mr Shingles' death was attributed to inflammation of the lungs and haemorrhage, paralysis of the legs caused by shock and had died from blood poisoning caused by the abscess.

On Friday the 10th of October 1902, again at the Norchard Colliery, another collier, Mr George Hancock aged 20 also of Bream, suffered the same fate only a short distance away from the other two in the same vein of coal. He had been buried by a fall of coal and timbers and had also died of head injuries at the scene.

On Saturday the 18th of October 1902 at Bream, the Inquest into the death of Mr William Phipps was adjourned following the news that another death, that of Mr George Hancock had happened on the Friday. The Coroner, Mr M.F. Carter and the Jurymen visited the home of Mr Hancock to view his body before dismissing them for a month. Lady Dilke expressed her sympathy to the relatives of the men during her visit to their homes.

Fig. 39 Norchard Colliery, Lydney – courtesy of DHC, Soudley, Cinderford.

At the reconvened Inquest held on Thursday the 13th of November 1902 into the deaths of the three colliers, it was concluded that the mine was insufficiently timbered. Mr Martin H.M. Inspector of Mines remarked that the miners would do well to err on the side of being too liberal rather than too sparing with the use of timber and the Jury agreed that there had been insufficient timbering in the mine. A verdict of accidental deaths was recorded and that no one was to blame.

What could have been another serious disaster was averted on Friday the 24th of October 1902 at the Crump Meadow Colliery near Cinderford. Work to rectify a problem with the cage rope had been carried out overnight and at 7am on Friday morning, over 100 men were ready to descend the pit. However, it had been decided to do a trial run and as the engine was started, the cable jumped the winding wheel flange and wrapped itself around the axle, causing it to break. The cage then fell to the bottom of the shaft smashing to pieces and causing a lot of damage. In the stampede to clear the pithead, one boy was injured but had it not been for the trial run, many more Forest men could have lost their lives.

On Friday the 4th of December 1902, Mr George Edward Morris of Newtown, Cinderford, a single man was seriously injured by the fall of a large lump of coal onto his leg while working underground at the Crump Meadow Colliery. The injury broke his leg between the knee and ankle and he was attended at the scene by Dr McCartney and later at home by Dr MacMullen. He appeared to be getting on well but on the 17th of December, friends thought he had deteriorated and Dr MacMullen diagnosed peritonitis. Four days later on the 21st of December, Mr Morris died. At the Inquest it was stated that a Dr Scott had carried out a post mortem and concluded that the primary cause of death was a compound fracture of the leg, secondary peritonitis and finally heart failure. Death was recorded according to the medical testimony.

Fig. 40 Crump Meadow Colliery, courtesy of DHC, Soudley, Cinderford.

Chapter 12
The Union Colliery Disaster

On the afternoon of Thursday the 4th of September 1902 at the Union Colliery in the Bixslade valley near Parkend, a serious flood cost the lives of four men. The colliery, owned by the Parkend Deep Navigation Colliery Co. had been producing 100 tons of coal per day and employed around 100 men.

The dayshift started at 6.30am and 69 men and boys descended the 252 foot deep shaft. It had been noticed during that shift that water running alongside the roadways was greater than usual and near the end of the shift where nine men were working their stall, water broke in from old abandoned workings. Two men managed to run and escape to safety and were hauled up the shaft but seven were cut off by the flood and it was hoped that they had reached higher ground. The rest of the workforce managed to escape to the surface and as the alarm was raised, water had risen 35 feet up the shaft trapping the remaining men and flooding the pumps. Surface pumps were set in motion but they were hampered by the dirty water and continually getting clogged. After ten hours of continual pumping out 300,000 gallons, the water had only receded 3 feet.

On Saturday the 6th of September 1902, the Inspector of Mines and two colleagues descended the Hopewell Engine Shaft about two miles away in the hope of reaching the trapped men, but without success. It was realised that pumping out the water was the only solution but after 24 hours, the level had only receded by 7 feet. Pumps stopped working at midnight on Saturday for 4 hours in order to extend the plant and by Sunday morning the missing men had been 72 hours underground without food. However the pumps continued to lower the level and by early Tuesday morning the 9th of September, the bad air in the shaft had greatly reduced. At 5am, a party of men including Mr Walker (assistant Inspector), Mr E.A. Worthy (manager), Mr G. Rowlinson (Agent) and Mr Carl Deakin (son of the Managing Director) were able to descend the shaft. The roadway was in good condition and after progressing about three quarters of a mile, came across the body of Mr William Martin of Berry Hill. They carried on for another quarter of a mile and heard voices which they hurried to locate. Three men were found alive after being entombed for 120 hours, huddled into a small space. They were Mr James Gwilliam, Mr James Hawkins and Mr Thomas Cooper and although they were found in a crouched position, they were in better condition than expected but were unable to walk. They were all given medical aid and a dram was prepared to convey the men to the shaft where they were brought to the surface later on that Tuesday. They were taken to the Engine house where they were wrapped in warm blankets and given refreshments. News of this rescue travelled fast within the Forest mining community and crowds gathered at the pithead where the Doxology in praise of God was sung. Proprietor Mr Deakin praised the rescuers and pump-men for their skills, especially to their engineer Mr Burrows.

Fig. 41 Union Pit Memorial on approximate site of pit shaft, photo Author

The bodies of brothers Amos and Thomas James were found holding each others' hand near to where the body of Mr Martin was found – all had drowned. One man Mr Hubert Gwatkin aged 26 remained missing presumed dead after so much time underground but the rescue party continued their search. It wasn't until Monday the 15th of September, eleven days after the flood that Mr Gwatkin's body was eventually found at the bottom of an incline which had filled with water and where he had drowned.

While the rescued men were being nursed back to health at home, their wives had strict orders from their Doctor not to be interviewed unless they were by relatives. However, interviews were gained and as a tribute to those men who survived and to those who perished, this publication would not be doing its duty to the Forest of Dean miners if those harrowing accounts were not preserved and recorded.

The first is by survivor **Mr James Hawkins;**

'We heard a noise like a large pond being let out. I went out into the roadway and met Cooper. The water was pouring down the steep incline and before we could decide what to do, it threatened to carry us off our legs. We agreed to cross over the road to a sideway which led to much higher ground and by this time the water was shoulder high. Cooper stumbled but turned round and I caught hold of him and held him up until we could pull him out. He was half drowned but no one was shouting and we saw nobody where we were. We got as high as we could and believed that we were safe there. Our lights went out from the start but being in the wind road, we got a little air (from ventilation). I knew there was a small rill of water a yard or two away and one of us had an empty can and either me or Gwilliam fetched some water in it. But at length we became so weak and stiff with cramp that we couldn't walk so we rolled and crawled to and fro. Cooper was too bad to do anything and we were afraid he would go. I don't think we slept much and we had no idea of time and thought it was Sunday when we saw the light of the rescuing party appear. Then we said 'Thank God we are saved' and all three of us felt quite sure that we would live long enough to be got out alive. We had a terrible time and we got very hungry. We do not want to talk a lot about it'

Fig. 42 Union Pit Disaster Memorial Plaque
photo Author.

The second is by survivor **Mr James Gwilliam;**

'I've worked in the Union pit for seven months and have always followed pit work and am Forester born. That day there were no incidents that suggested evil and I had just eaten all my bait and started working again when the accident happened. James Hawkins was my mate and my brother William was our trimmer and we were 'holing' and lying full length on our sides. Some call it 'drowling' but whatever it was, we were making an airway into a cross heading. Hawkins heard the noise of the water and said 'I think the water's broke out' and then 'yes it's broke in'. The place where we were was 30 yards from the old workings and getting on for a mile from the bottom of the shaft. I dropped my tools, sprang to my feet, threw my jacket over my arm, grabbed my water bottle and bolted. I

remember that my mate Hawkins put his jacket on and when we got out into the road we saw Hubert Gwatkin who had been working close to us. Gwatkin lit his lamp from his candle and we ran as well as we could towards the shaft with water being around us all the time. We were rushing along behind Gwatkin and for some reason or other, our candles went out. We tried one road and then another but there was water everywhere and Gwatkin was carried off his legs by the water when jumping across the road. His light went out and we heard nothing of him after that. Hawkins also parted company with me at that time and I was then on my own.

I saw nobody for a long time after that and it was impossible to hear and as I couldn't see, there was no way of knowing if anybody was near or far from me. My worst plight was being carried along by the flood and knocking against the roadside timbers but managing to keep my head above the water. I caught hold of anything I could and when I was swilled against a large post, I clung on, although the current was so strong, I thought I might have to let go. I held on for a long time, I don't know how long but I knew that if I let go, I would be drowned. When the water slackened I tried to feel where I was and when I got to a cross heading, I came across Cooper and was very glad. Not long after, Hawkins came groping along and we decided that come what may, we would stick together. Cooper was high and dry and we wanted to get together but he was scarcely strong enough to help himself and was almost perished with cold and his clothes all soaking wet. Cooper had his jacket on and I was only wearing my trousers and a guernsey, having thrown my jacket and bottle away.

As the hours passed, I got bolder and poking about the roadway, I got into a stall and scrambling over carts, timber and coal and searching with my hands, found a water bottle and a bread bag. I've since found out that these belonged to Ted Baldwin. There was a drop of tea in the can and a bit of bread in the bag and I was so excited about this find that I made my way back to my comrades as fast as I could to let them know. I gave it to Jim Hawkins to hold and went back for a further search but found nothing more. We didn't part the bread until we couldn't keep it any longer and although it was only a tiny bit, we made the most of it. We all had a sup of tea and then it was all gone. When we began to feel thirsty, I took the bottle out into the roadway where the dank and stale water was running, filled the can and went back with it. Whatever it was like, it served a purpose and in the long hours that passed I made several journeys, although towards the end, my legs became cramped and I was none too smart.

We were never short of water but I was hungry mind. We had a nice bit of sleep at times. I was confused with whose face I saw first but I do well remember Mr Rowlinson and we were glad to see anybody. We all rejoiced together when we met'.

The third survivor **Mr Thomas Cooper** didn't survive so well as the other two but was still able to say a few words;

'I'm not quite so well and have had a bad night. So many people have called in to see me that had made me upset. I've worked at the Union pit for 12 months and my mate was Bill Martin and I worked with Shadrach Hathaway. When we heard the rush of water, I rushed off but lost my jacket and bottle. I shall be glad not to say any more as my poor head is all about just now'

When Mr Rowlinson was on his way through the woods to the scene of the disaster, he tripped and fell about six feet over a boulder at the Spion Kop quarry. It shook him up somewhat and caused pain in his chest but he continued on and descended the pit with some of the rescuers. Later, on being examined by Dr McCartney, he was found to have broken a rib on his right hand side. The Court of Enquiry was delayed due to the Coroner Mr M.F. Carter being ill with a severe cold but it was reconvened at the Coleford Police Court on Wednesday the 15th of October 1902. The Enquiry heard that it was discovered that a meridian line drawn on a Crown Office survey map obtained by the colliery in 1896 had been positioned incorrectly and also that a boundary stone had been incorrectly placed. The Hopewell colliery, about two miles away had not been included on the map and another pit, Miles Level was only 180 yards from it.

Fig. 43 Memorial Sculpture by Matt Baker of two miners embracing - photo Author

These errors were acknowledged by the Enquiry and Mr Llewellyn, the Crown Office Surveyor admitted that he had drawn the Meridian incorrectly.

Unfortunately, the colliery manager Mr E.A. Worthy was unaware of these errors and omissions and planned the Union Colliery's underground workings accordingly.

Separation between individual mine workings had always been accepted as a minimum of 80 yards but in this case, the two mine workings had, without the Manager's knowledge, come to within 8 yards of each other, causing the flood to break through. Mr Llewellyn said that they were under no obligation to provide plans for the opening up of a colliery but they had done so out of friendship. He admitted he had made a mistake but said that it was also the responsibility of the colliery officials to verify those plans before use. The Jury returned their verdict; *'that the cause of death was drowning the result of the inundation of the colliery in which the men were engaged at work. The owners of the colliery were guilty of neglect in not taking the necessary precautions to ascertain the proximity of the old workings of Miles Level from whence the water came'.* The Jury gave their fees of two guineas to the families Relief Fund.

Nearly 1,000 rank and file employees of the Parkend Deep Navigation Colliery Company were unimpressed with the verdict and a special meeting in support of the management was called at the Board Schools of Parkend on the 29th of November 1902. A resolution carried with applause stated; *'That we, the workmen employed by the Parkend Deep Navigation Colliery Limited hereby place on record an expression of our grateful recognition of the thoughtful consideration and practical sympathy which our Employers have, at all times and in various ways extended to us and of the readiness with which they have adopted any new methods that were likely to secure our safety. We desire at the same time to express our full and unwavering confidence in the certificated Manager and in his assistants who have always exercised the greatest care and watchfulness in supervision and carried out the duties of their offices in a highly efficient manner'.*

A presentation of a marble clock and two bronzes was made to Mr E.A.Worthy who thanked the men for their confidence in him which, he said, after recent events, was most reassuring. Mr T. Deakin, Managing Director was presented with an illuminated address which expressed the men's admiration of his personal qualities and of his sympathetic and practical interest in his employees. Mrs Deakin also received a combination fruit and flower stand.

On Tuesday the 23rd of December 1902 at Coleford Police Court, Mr E.A. Worthy, the Union Colliery manager was summoned by the Mines Inspector; *'for offending against the Mines Act at the colliery named for failing to keep in the office the plans needed for the carrying on of the Colliery'.* A nominal fine of one shilling without costs was imposed.

In a now somewhat secluded Bixslade valley, a commemorative statue of two trapped embracing miners and a plaque now marks the colliery site where otherwise no one could ever imagine the scene that unfolded from that fateful Thursday in September 1902. Word had spread fast in the communities around Coleford, Berry Hill and Broadwell that men were trapped underground and wives, girlfriends, daughters, family members and large numbers of the mining population all descended on this spot in the hope that their loved ones or friends would be rescued, many keeping overnight vigils. Sadly, four of those families lost their loved ones.

Chapter 13
1903 – 1910

During the year 1903, there were two main topics that concerned the Forest of Dean miners and both were fully aired at the **Miners' Annual Demonstration** in July. As most miners were aware, Mr Rowlinson had always been an advocate of affiliation with the larger Associations and since the unfortunate separation from the Midland Federation in 1893, the miners had consistently opposed the move, thinking they would be better off staying as an independent Union.

At the July **Miners' Annual Demonstration**, chaired by Mr George Barnard, a resolution proposed by Mr Martin Perkins and seconded by Mr Riley Brown was carried unanimously; *'that this meeting of miners of the Forest of Dean District think the time has come when we should consider our position regards affiliation with other Districts, because in 12 months hence the present wage agreement with our employers will end. Also, the ballot just taken shows that a large section of the men desire to go under the Compensation Act at the end of the year, and if we are to maintain our position as a District and to have our fair share of the prosperity of the country, we need a strong organisation and that can only be built up by all men becoming members.'*

As for the Compensation Act, the miners had conducted ballots at all the Lodges, the result of which was that they had voted to abandon the current Mutual scheme of Contracting out which had been operating for the past 10 years and to avail themselves under the provisions of the 1897 Compensation Act from the end of the year. Mr Rowlinson proposed that every Union man pay 6 pence per month to the Labour Association and that fund would pay 10 shillings per week for any injured employee for the first two weeks with the employers paying 11 shillings and 6pence per week thereafter, a week being calculated as four and a half days. Non Union men would not get the first two weeks benefit paid by the Labour Association. Mr Rowlinson also predicted that if all Forest miners joined the Union and paid their 6 pence per month, then in three years time they would have enough funds to guarantee an old age pension at 60 years of age.

Accidents/Fatalities

On Thursday the 5th of February 1903, a collision occurred on the 'loop line' near Cinderford between two locomotives. One was carrying Mr J.W.Keeling JP of 10 Lansdown Terrace, Cheltenham, who was in the process of carrying out his Official Inspection of the railway as Engineer of the Forest of Dean portion of his District. The other locomotive was a goods train carrying a number of loaded coal wagons. Mr Keeling's train had already climbed the incline from Speech House Road towards Drybrook Road and was on the 'Loop line' that connected to Lightmoor and other nearby collieries when they were met head on with a goods train coming round a sharp bend in the line. Both engine drivers Thomas Norkett and Henry Octree acted promptly and brakes were applied and steam was shut off before they jumped clear of the inevitable collision. However, there were injuries – Mr Keeling happened to be standing at the rear of the open ended rear coach facing along the already travelled line and was thrown backwards into the coach, suffering severe head injuries. The fireman on his train Frederick Templeton didn't manage to jump clear and suffered bruising to his back. Mr Keeling's assistants Messrs W.J. Jakeman and T. Scholes were also thrown down but suffered little or no injuries.

Messages were sent to Lydney where an engine and coach was dispatched up the line while doctors Thomas and Brownlie waited for their arrival back at Lydney Town Station. Mr Scholes and Mr Templeton then needed some attention to head wounds but Mr Keeling was still unconscious when back at Lydney. A coach with a bed was quickly arranged and Mr Keeling was transported up the GWR line to Gloucester where he was eventually taken to his home in Cheltenham. The other casualty, Mr Templeton was taken to Gloucester Royal Hospital where it was found that he was suffering from a cut head and an injured shoulder but he was later released.

Mr Keeling however, remained unconscious and in a bad way and it was found that he was suffering from a fracture of the base of the skull. Over the following days, his condition continued to improve and when he had regained consciousness, he was able to recognise those around him. Bulletins issued from his residence indicated continued improvement and that he was recovering from the shock of the accident.

The result of the Inquiry into the cause of the collision which was carried out by Lieutenant-Colonel H.A. Yorke R.E. on behalf of the Board of Trade criticised as highly unsatisfactory the negligent manner in which the 'loop line' operated and centred the blame for the accident on the two operating staff at Drybrook Road Station. No blame whatsoever was attributed to the drivers or guards of either train. It was hoped that the two operating Companies who owned and ran the railway would take early steps to put an end to the existing dangerous arrangements. Also to introduce a keener sense of their responsibilities and duties than currently exists for the men in charge of traffic at Drybrook Road.

A Collier's self sacrifice

On Thursday the 12th of February 1903, Mr Stephen Adams, a middle aged collier from Ellwood near Coleford, died as a result of heart exhaustion brought on by his exertions in rescuing a fellow miner. Mr Adams was working underground in a local pit when he heard a fall of earth and rushed to the scene where he found that around seven hundredweight of earth had fallen on fellow miner Mr Thomas Morgan. Mr Adams struggled bravely and successfully managed to release Mr Morgan from the fall and saved his life. Mr Adams gave no immediate cause for any concern for his own health but the next day he started getting chest pains but continued going to work for some days before consulting his doctor. He then grew rapidly worse and seven days later he died. Dr Currie performed a post mortem which revealed that Mr Adams had died from heart exhaustion which was set up by the great pain he had suffered due to strained muscles. It was considered that if Mr Adams had received medical attention at the time of the rescue, he may have had some relief of the pains.

On Tuesday the 17th of March 1903, Frank Hale aged 16 and from Highbeech near Lydbrook, died while working underground as a hod boy at the Trafalgar Colliery. At around 7.30am in the deep head road which contained a 17 inch vein, Mr Hale hadn't at that time started his job as a hod boy on account of some dirt having to be removed from the road. He had already stacked some coal to the side of the road and then he went about four feet under the coalface to remove more dirt that lay on top of the coal. A fall of the roof then occurred trapping Mr Hale's head but he was got out straight away but died almost immediately. The Inquest stated that the deceased was crushed by a fall and that no one was to blame for the accident. It was also mentioned that over 700 men worked at the colliery and that until now, no one had died as a result of an accident there for nearly seven years.

On Thursday the 14th of May 1903, Mr William Hall aged 21 and living at the Feathers Inn, Ruspidge, died as a result of a fall of coal and earth while working underground at the Lightmoor Colliery. He was working with 'buttyman' Mr Hubert Harris and several other colliers driving a deep heading when there was a fall of earth. Mr Harris and the others managed to escape but Mr Hall was covered by the fall and died at the scene. The Inquest verdict recorded an accidental death.

On Tuesday the 28th of July 1903, Mr Amos Baynham aged 47, a collier from Broadwell near Coleford, died as a result of injuries he received while working underground at the Wimberry Colliery on the 3rd of July 1903. The Inquest, held at the Britannia Inn, Coalway Lane End, heard that on the 3rd of July Mr Baynham had been working underground on the Coleford High Delf seam with fellow colliers Messrs Henry Brown and Benjamin White. Mr Baynham had been in a stooping position wedging some coal when about two hundredweight of top coal fell on him. He was immediately released but it was seen that he was seriously hurt, so he was taken to the surface and then to his home where he was attended by Dr Currie. Since then he was attended each day by both Dr Currie and Dr Trotter but had died on the 28th. The Inquiry verdict was that Mr Baynham had died from a fracture of the spine resulting in paralysis as a result of the fall of coal.

On Thursday the 12th of November 1903, Mr Richard Elvey aged 60 and from Berry Hill, died as a result of a fall of earth while working underground at the Primrose Iron mine at Oakwood near Bream. The mine was owned by Mr R.J. Shingles and was a small affair with only two men and two boys working it. A shot had been fired the previous evening and Mr Elvey was the first to enter the mine on the Thursday morning. He had apparently shouted to the other men that the mine was safe but while trying to break down some ore, a quantity of earth fell on him. He was freed from the fall and said **'thank God no bones are broken'** but was then taken home and attended by Dr Buchanan. He died shortly afterwards. At the Inquest, held at the Cross Ways Inn, Coleford, Mr Thomas Baker the 'buttyman' stated that Mr Elvey had shouted up that the mine was safe but both boys, Mr George Rosser aged 16 and Mr Bertram Driver aged 14 said that they did not hear the shout but they knew that he had made an examination. It was judged that the mine had been operating in a loose and unsatisfactory manner and that the accident may not have happened if more care had been taken. A verdict of accidental death as a result of a fall was recorded and that no blame was to be attached to Mr Baker.

In an extraordinary coincidence to this accident, it was revealed that Mrs Elvey had been married twice and that her first husband had been killed in a mine on the last day of his work there as they were about to move to South Wales. In this most recent case, this was the last working day of Mr Shingles' mine as it was closing down and Mrs Elvey had reminded her husband of her first husband's death. He had chosen to ignore his wife's reminder with the result that he unfortunately also met his own fate.

On Tuesday the 22nd of December 1903, Mr Thomas John Trafford aged 65, a Fetler from St John's, Cinderford, died as a result of an accident underground at the Lightmoor Colliery. Mr Trafford had worked at the colliery for over 20 years and on Monday the 21st of December 1903, the day of the accident, he had been let down the shaft in the cage in the usual manner. He then gave the signal for the empty cage to return but when the cage had risen a few yards, Mr Trafford walked underneath it to attend to some water pipes. The engine that worked the cage was a single piston engine that, at that point had to be lowered in order to continue to ascend. Mr Trafford was unaware of this and consequently received a severe blow to the head from the cage that weighed around sixteen hundredweight. He was subsequently brought to the surface and taken home where he was attended by a doctor but he died the next day. The Inquest recorded a verdict of accidental death caused by asphyxia, the result of his bronchial tubes being blocked by blood as a result of the accident.

Quarry Fatalities

On Wednesday the 23rd of December 1903, at the Wilderness Stone Quarry belonging to the Forest of Dean Stone Firms, a fall of rock killed Mr John Smith aged 70 of Plump Hill instantly while another man Mr John Morgan aged 47 of Hazell Hill, Plump was seriously injured and died a few hours later in Gloucester Royal Infirmary. The Inquest at Gloucester heard Mr Thomas Williams, a labourer at the quarry describe how he had been working with the two men for about three hours when a huge stone estimated at over 150 tons and some smaller debris slipped out of the face of the quarry and fell onto the two men, killing Mr Smith outright and crushing Mr Morgan's leg below the knee. Mr Morgan was attended at the scene by a local doctor and then rushed into Gloucester Royal Hospital where Dr Bower had to amputate the leg. Mr Morgan's condition however deteriorated and he died later that evening. The inquest heard that quarry foreman Mr Richard Webster state that it was his duty to examine the quarry, which he did the night before the accident and found that it was quite safe. It was considered that the fall of the rock was due to the wet weather. Mr Douglas E. Finlay, house surgeon at the Infirmary attributed

Mr Morgan's death to heart failure and shock caused by his injuries. The Jury returned a verdict of accidental death on both men.

1904

And so the miners came under the provisions of the **1897 Compensation Act** as described previously. Many had admitted there were shortcomings such as excluding certain members of a workforce and misinterpretation of the rules by the Judiciary. Sir Charles Dilke in his speech to the assembled miners at Whitecroft in September, alluded to these shortcomings and would be urging the Government to introduce some amendments to the Act. He also went on to suggest that the Act would be much improved by the introduction of a State Insurance or National Insurance scheme recognised by the State.

Mr Rowlinson mentioned the number of injury cases had dropped considerably with 177 so far as compared with 540 the previous year. He supposed this may have been due to the Labour Association's refusal to take on non Union men who he still considered to have no backbone or moral courage to join them. If they did, he said that their interests would then be looked after.

The Joint Wages Board or Conciliation Board agreed a new system for calculating wages and would be based, not on the price of coal as a whole, but as separated into five classes of coal. This system would be used at specific collieries such as Trafalgar, Lightmoor, Foxes Bridge, Crump Meadow and Fancy and Mr Rowlinson admitted that this agreement was one of the most favourable to the men that he had seen during his 18 years as their Agent. The new agreement would start on the 1st of October 1903 and operate for a period of three years.

Free-miners and the Dean Forest Mines Act 1904

August saw the introduction of the above Act which was intended to facilitate the opening up of the lower coal seams by amending the current law for the granting of gales. The Deputy Gaveller was given the power to subdivide, amalgamate or re-arrange gales but only with the consent of the current galees. The subdivided gales would be renamed and the Free-miners would be able to sell their portion to the new galee at a sum to be agreed by the Deputy Gaveller. Forty one gales were affected by this legislation and the intention was to access the Coleford High Delf seam with deeper shafts that could only be constructed by the Capitalists who could provide the greater financial investment in plant and machinery i.e. the 'Foreigners' as described earlier.

The Free-miners Association held a meeting to discuss these issues at the Speech House in September 1903 where there was a great deal of hostility, bad temper and ill behaviour which ended in uproar. The Chairman Mr S.J. Elsom JP resigned over differences of opinion on certain provisions of the Act but was later re-elected as President and Mr Martin Perkins was elected as Vice President. Above the din, Mr Elsom said he believed the Act was a blessing to the Forest of Dean and that he was already in correspondence with certain Capitalists for the development of the deep seams of coal. At a more convivial meeting held on Boxing Day, the Free-miners agreed amendments to the Act in accordance with Clause 7 and Mr Martin Perkins remarked that if the Free-miners had drafted the rules themselves, they could not have done so in a more broad minded spirit. In accordance with the Act, all the deep seams of valuable steam coal were amalgamated into seven areas each of which would be negotiated separately between the Deputy Gaveller, the Free-miners and the Capitalist Investors.

Mr Rowlinson's position for the Newnham Division on the County Council was coming up for re-election this year. At one of his many campaign meetings held in Blakeney, he was very critical of the present Council, particularly for their reckless overspend on the Thames and Severn Canal and their hurried acceptance of the Education Act. He said that he was a great advocate of building a bridge across the Severn at Newnham. In August, Mr Rowlinson had an unfortunate accident while out walking. He tripped and fell over a stile breaking a bone in his right forearm and injuring his spine.

Road making
In May the Crown reported progress on their portion of the New Road being constructed from Lydney to Lydbrook. The West Dean portion from Lydney to Parkend was already constructed and in use but the Crown portion of over half the total length had been delayed by bad weather. The portion to Cannop Ponds was completed but the remainder was still in a poor condition. The contractors had laid a railway track the entire length and were using a locomotive as a power source. It was hoped to complete the roadway before the end of the summer and the Crown were making plans to complete roads at Pope's Hill and Joys Green.

Lady Dilke

The sad news of the death of Lady Dilke, wife of Sir Charles Dilke MP on Monday the 24th of October 1904, reached the Forest of Dean the next day. She had been suffering from a nervous inflammation but was reported to have died from heart failure at their home at Rough near Woking. Well known for her work as a Trade Unionist, women's suffrage, an author and art critic, Lady Amelia was respected and well liked in the Forest of Dean where she was an avid supporter of Sir Charles' causes, often at his side at the **Miners' Annual Demonstrations**. Many tributes were made from the various Liberal Associations and individuals from the Forest of Dean and representatives from many of those attended the funeral including Mr and Mrs George Rowlinson, representing the Miners and Quarrymen and Dr McCartney from Cinderford . Lady Dilke's coffin was taken from Woking to Waterloo on the Saturday morning and from there to Holy Trinity Church in Sloane Street for the funeral service. Afterwards, the cremation took place at Golders Green Crematorium. Sir Charles Dilke then left for Italy where he later met up with friends.

Accidents/Fatalities

On Friday the 8th of January 1904, a lad named Taylor had an extraordinary lucky escape while working on the surface of the New Mount Pleasant Colliery near Cinderford. Taylor was assisting at 'landing' and was returning an empty dram to the pit mouth when he misjudged the distance and the dram rolled over the edge. Taylor was unable to release his hold in time and went over the edge with it. The shaft was 40 yards deep and while the dram got stuck with the cage in the shaft, Taylor ended up in the water reservoir at the bottom. Fortunately there were two colliers at the bottom who rescued him from an otherwise watery grave. He was brought to the surface and examined by Dr Scott who found that the lad was only suffering from shock and no bones were broken. However, the cage and guides were severely damaged.

Another lucky escape on the same day

On Friday the 8th of January 1904, Robert Morgan aged 14 and from Pillowell was working on the screens at the Crown Colliery, Moseley Green near Parkend. He had wandered away from his workplace and was casually looking down the pit shaft when the cage, descending from above, struck him on the back of the neck. The cage continued with its descent to the bottom of the shaft which was over 90 yards deep. The incident was witnessed by other workmen and the pit manager Mr T.J. Wykes called to be taken to the bottom, expecting to find the boy in pieces. When he arrived at the bottom he was more than astonished when the boy came up to him and said; **'I'm alright gov'ner, I'm not hurt'.** The explanation was that when the boy was struck, he was turned over and landed on the roof of the cage. He had the presence of mind to grab the chains and hold on till the cage reached the bottom – where he jumped down onto the landing stage and awaited events. He had escaped without a scratch and his only concern was that someone might tell his mother what had happened.

On Monday the 21st of November 1904, Mr William Sims aged 70 of Tufthorn Terrace, Milkwall, a checkweighman working at the Dark Hill Colliery, suddenly collapsed at his workplace and died a few minutes later. Mr Sims had been known to be in poor health but on this day he started from his home at 6.30am in his usual health and had some breakfast at the pit before starting his shift. He was seen by another collier Mr Edward Riley at 8.30am weighing coal but shortly afterwards he heard a noise and saw Mr Sims staggering. Mr Riley ran towards him and managed to save him from falling. With other assistance, Mr Sims was taken to the machine house where he took a few more deep breaths and died. Dr McQuaide of Coleford was sent for and on arrival he determined that life was extinct and later confirmed that it was caused by heart failure. No Inquest was necessary.

1905

January saw the re-election of officers of the **Forest of Dean Miners' Association.** Mr George Barnard was re-elected President, Mr Riley Brown as Vice President, Mr R. Buffrey as Secretary, Mr J. Baldwin as Treasurer and Mr George Rowlinson as Agent.

At meetings held at various venues, Mr Rowlinson highlighted the fact that during 1904 it was a matter of satisfaction that there had been no fatal accidents in the Forest of Dean coalfield where 5,000 men were employed and that was something that hadn't happened for the past 25 years. The Workmens Compensation Act had run for its first year and figures showed that under the previous scheme the accident rate over a five year period averaged out at 700 per year but the 1904 figure was 400.

The question of Union membership was once again a constant subject for discussion and Mr Rowlinson said that their membership now stood at 3,000 and that they would only discuss the question of re-joining the **MFGB** when every miner became a Union member. He said that if men did not join, then the old age pension scheme would have to be revised.

Strike or no Strike

It was generally accepted by the miners that over the past two years the coal trade had suffered through lack of orders and the Coal Owners had been seeking ways to attract orders through reducing the price per ton. At one of his regular meetings In April, Mr Rowlinson commented on the fact that there had been some friction in certain Districts over the recent cut of 5% in wages which had been negotiated with the Wages Committee. He explained the reasons for it and said it had been generally agreed that if coal was reduced by one shilling per ton and wages by 5%, it would mean that the men would probably get another days' work per week. He had agreed that this was the proper course to take and it was generally accepted by the men. However, some colliery managers had taken advantage of non Union men who had been induced to work for lower tonnage rates against the advice of the Union and the Wages Committee/Conciliation Board who had just negotiated an agreement on the same matter.

It was widely reported that 500 men at the New Colliery in Lydbrook owned by the adjoining Tinplate works of Messrs Richard Thomas and Co. had come out on strike and that the manager had cancelled their contracts. Strike action was later denied and Mr Rowlinson was not amused and took exception to the actions of certain colliery managers that the Wages Committee/Conciliation Board had been sidelined in order to get a quick and inferior deal. He was insistent that wages problems should have been left to the Wages Committee/Conciliation Board which had the machinery to deal with these situations and had been established and run successfully for many years past. Order was eventually restored and the men and manager came to a mutually agreed arrangement in line with the Union settlement.

At the **Miners' Annual Demonstration** in July, the hosts were now being referred to as the **Forest of Dean Miners' Association** with the Chairman being referred to as Mr George Barnard President of the **Labour Association.**

The topic of non Unionism was once again on the Agenda and the first resolution submitted was that; *'This annual meeting of the Forest of Dean Miners' Association condemns the action of the workmen who keep outside the pale of the Union but still receive the advantages obtained for them by the men who have stood firm by the Union. We are convinced that they are a danger to all agreements made by our leaders with the employers by their offering to work for lower tonnage rates and allowing their yardage prices to be interfered with, and we strongly recommend all men outside the Union, for their own sakes and for the welfare of their fellow working men to become members of the Association.'* This was carried unanimously.

Sir Charles Dilke was in attendance once again and another resolution expressed sympathy for the irreparable loss he had sustained by the death of his dear wife Lady Dilke and sincerely trusted that his life may be spared to help that great cause of labour for which he has done so much. Sir Charles was deeply moved and responded by thanking them for their kind references which had been made to Lady Dilke. He said he hoped that he could continue his connection with the Constituency while life lasted and trusted that any independent action he might take in the future would have their approval.

Accidents/Fatalities
On Thursday the 2nd of February 1905, Mr Frederick Morgan aged 24, a married man living at Sling was killed while manoeuvring a three ton piece of stone at a quarry near Coleford. He and another labourer Mr William Howell were trying to get the stone from the quarry onto a trolley and were obliged to use a crane and a pair of 'nips' for that purpose. The stone was successfully landed onto the trolley but was not quite level. Mr Howell called to the crane driver to raise the load so as to reposition the trolley, which he did and the trolley was put in the right position. Mr Howell then moved around to the other side at the same time as the nip slipped out and struck Mr Morgan a fatal blow to the forehead. At the Inquest held at the Orepool Inn near Coleford, it was confirmed from Dr Buchanan's evidence that death was due to a fractured skull. Both Mr Howell and the deceased were noted as negligent in their duties and that there should be more supervision at the quarry than at present existed.

On Friday the 10th of February 1905, Mr John Crump Watkins aged 59 and a collier, died as a result of a fall of earth while working underground at the Howbeach Level. He was ripping down the roof of an old roadway when there was a fall from the roof which trapped his legs. He called out; **'come and lift the stuff off my legs'** and several fellow colliers ran to his aid. When they saw the state of the roof, they just managed to jump clear to save themselves due to a further fall of the roof. At the Inquest, held at

Moseley Green, it was stated that Mr Watkins had gone four yards further down the road than his own timbering which, according to the mine owner Mr Wykes, was where he shouldn't have been. He said it was one of an experienced man's weaknesses to be curious as to what lies ahead and that's what led to his demise. The jury was told by Dr Lunn that Mr Watkins died of shock as a result of his hip being smashed to pieces and the verdict was to this effect.

On Monday the 30th of October 1905, Mr Milson Aston aged 54, a collier from the Pludds near Lydbrook, was killed while working underground at the New Pit at Lydbrook. Mr Aston started working the night shift on the evening of the 29th of October 1905 and early the next morning was working with a fellow collier Mr Samuel Lloyd in bareing down some loose rock. Without warning, a large piece of rock fell down and struck Mr Aston who fell, severely injured. Mr Lloyd called for help and Mr Aston was helped to the surface and then taken home. He was then seen by Dr Lacey of Ruardeen but his injuries were such that Mr Aston died later that afternoon.

1906

The year started off with a bang – that of the results of the January General Election in which the Liberal Party won a 'Landslide victory' over the Conservative Party with an overall majority of 125 votes. Sir Charles Dilke was returned unopposed for the Forest of Dean Division and was therefore back with the ruling Party headed by Prime Minister Henry Campbell-Bannerman.

The other important result was that of the **Labour Representation Committee (LRC)** which fielded 50 candidates and won 29 seats, mainly in the north of England and London's East End but also including that of Keir Hardy at Merthyr Tydfil. He immediately changed the Party name to that of the **Labour Party** and became its first Leader.

One of the most important pieces of Legislation that the new Liberal Government introduced was the **Trade Disputes Act** which effectively gave Unions immunity from being sued for financial loss during a strike. This was originally prompted by three House of Lords decisions of imposing damages on Unions for going on strike, most notably the Taff Vale Railway Company strike in 1901, when they were fined £23,000, as mentioned earlier.

A Bill was introduced to Parliament on the 28th of March 1906 but several factions within the Government opposed its wording which, they said gave the Unions too much power. A private members Bill led by Trade Union MP's was then introduced which was eventually supported by the Prime Minister and the **1906 Trade Disputes Act** was given the Royal Assent on the 21st of December 1906.

Legislation also saw the introduction of the Workmen's Compensation Act which expanded the scheme operated since 1897 and which was in dire need of amending. Many more classes of employees were now included and the limits of compensation were increased. Compensation would also apply to an employee howsoever an accident was caused except in cases of wilful misconduct. Originally Forest of Dean miners voted to opt out of the Government scheme in favour of a Mutual Scheme but decided to abandon that and revert to the Government Scheme at the beginning of 1904. This new Act took the best part of 1906 to become law but even so, it did not come into force until the 1st of July 1907 although it was still referred to as the **1906 Workmen's Compensation Act.**

In the Forest of Dean, the coal trade continued to be slack, especially at the house coal collieries and Mr Rowlinson was in despondent mood when he said that there was more destitution and want in the Forest than he had seen for the past twenty years. There were men with no work who wanted work and their women who showed more heroism and backbone than on the battlefield. He said that he was also doubtful as to the men's chances of an old age pension when they were only being paid 4 pence per hour. However, towards the end of the year, an increase in trade prompted the Wages Board to advance miners wages by 5%, bringing them up to 30% above the 1888 Standard.

At the **Miners' Annual Demonstration**, there was another call for the men to unite under the umbrella of the Union and a reduction in the entrance fee hoped to induce more recruits. Sir Charles Dilke once again supported that idea and went on to describe the intricacies and his involvement with the **Trade Disputes Act.** In his final remarks he said that someone had suggested that he become a Lord of Dean Forest but he responded by saying that the King was Lord of the Forest of Dean and that he wished to stay as their MP in the Commons until his death.

Accidents/Fatalities

On Monday the 13th of August 1906, Mr George Powell aged 64, proprietor of the Well Level Colliery near Berry Hill, died as a result of a fall of earth while working underground at the above colliery. He was working with his son and another collier when about two hundredweight of earth fell on him. At the Berry Hill Inquest, Dr Buchanan confirmed that death was due to suffocation caused by his right side ribs being crushed in. The verdict was in accordance with that evidence.

1907

The overall picture revealed many good and some bad events. The welcome increase in the coal trade prompted three increases in miners' wages totalling 15% but was linked to corresponding rises of three shillings per ton for house coal and half that for steam coal for the year. So although wages were higher, the cost of providing coal to the household was also higher, so cancelling out a portion of the wage increase.

The campaign for an **eight hour day** for miners took a step forward in January 1907 when the Board of Trade appointed a Departmental Committee to look into its possibility. It was argued by several Forest of Dean 'witnesses' or Coal Owners that an eight hour day from bank to bank would be detrimental to the coal industry and would raise the price of coal by 3 shillings a ton. It was calculated that the current daily hours worked was 9 hours and 20 minutes and by reducing it to eight would cost the Midlands coal industry four million tons of output per year. The Coal Owners expressed their disapproval of the scheme and said that they believed that the miners were opposed to the reduction in hours and would only lead to the closing of some of the older collieries. Its complicated conclusions which trended against the eight hour day was published on the 22nd of May 1907 in what was known as the **'Blue Book'**

In February 1907 Mr Rowlinson received a boost to his career by being appointed a Magistrate by the Lord Chancellor and at an Association meeting at the Nags Head, Yorkley, Vice President Mr Riley Brown congratulated Mr Rowlinson on his appointment and said that he felt sure that the whole Forest felt proud of the honour paid to their Trade Union representative who enjoyed a singular degree of confidence from both masters and men alike. In reply Mr Rowlinson said that he was much obliged for the congratulations and that he thought that he was the first labour representative in Gloucestershire to be made a County JP. He said that he acknowledged that he had sometimes heard complaints about his holding certain offices but he believed that by that means he could help them. If it were not so, he would withdraw from them at once.

Another breakthrough, this time for the **Miners' Federation of Great Britain** where the Northumberland Miners' Association who, for many years had fought to be an independent organisation able to negotiate their own wages agreements finally became an affiliated member.

Forest Gold
During March there was quite a lot of excitement about a secretive London Syndicate interested in buying up several of the Free-miners gales for an attractive sum of money under the guise of iron ore exploration. Trafalgar owner Mr T.B. Brain sold his mansion at Euroclydon together with a farm and underlying minerals for £15,000 (just under two million today) and moved to Cheltenham. Other nearby pits at Wigpool, Fairplay and others were also sold as were the gales of Injunction belt, Wigpool belt, Meend and Westbury Brook belts. A short while later, the gales of Shakemantle, Buckshaft, Perseverance and Cinderford were also included in the sale. The whole area covered 102 acres of freehold and 1,814 acres of leasehold from Euroclydon to Wigpool Common to Upper Soudley. There were 493 Free-miners sharing a payout of £1,518, which was handed over to them at a special meeting at Coleford on Monday the 25th of March1907. It was thought that this transaction was the largest and most important that the Forest of Dean Free-miners had ever undertaken.

Sir Charles Nicholson, Chairman of the Syndicate known as the **'Chastain Syndicate'**, held a meeting in April 1907, setting out the Syndicate's aims and progress so far. He said that the gold bearing reef was twelve miles long and resembled that of the Witwatersrand at Johannesburg in South Africa. He said that Gold was now thought to exist in the auriferous conglomerates in this area at a rate of six grains per ton and that after a long delay due to the complicated land tenure, work had now started.

An adit had been driven from Bailey Hill Wood, close to the Whimsey rallway line into the hillside and was intended to intersect the Wigpool Iron Mine Shaft which was sunk from several hundred feet above. The operation was carried out by blasting and the Syndicate said that they had every confidence in it as a paying proposition and that there was an almost inexhaustible supply of the ore. Samples already tested showed an average yield of 3 dwt. per ton (where 1dwt = 1.555 grams) and from those figures it was estimated that a profit of £145,000 per annum could be made from a turnover of £435,000 per annum.

Fig. 44 Miners at entrance to the Gold mine

It was hoped to reach the gold bearing conglomerate by the middle of May 1907 and Drybrook was amazed at being the closest village to this veritable gold rush and to have first claim to being recognised as the **'Rand of the Forest'**. Optimism was still high in August 1907 when expert opinion on the gold reef compared samples removed as likened to that of the South African Transvaal. The quartz conglomerate beds are sedimentary deposits made up from older rocks that sit atop of the old red sandstone layer that form a basin beneath the Forest of Dean well below the coal measures and completely encircles it.

They do get exposed at many places around the edge of the basin and Buckstone overlooking Monmouth is one such place and another is at the site of the present excavation where the old red sandstone can be seen exposed along the west and north facing hillside of Wigpool Common. In September, Sir Charles Dilke was shown around the site and agreed that with improved processes, the low grade ore could be made to pay but by

December 1907 doubts began to be expressed as to whether the minimal amounts of gold and silver found in the strata could become a financial proposition.

Deep Seam Coal – sale of gale leases by Freeminers

In May 1907 a meeting of nearly 1,800 Free-miners at the Speech House discussed the matter of the seven amalgamated gales created for the development of the deep coal seams. The options for discussion centred on whether or not the gales should be sold outright or to sell their rights and receive a royalty from the Capitalist buyers on the coal won. Eventually there was a split decision but the larger group who were in favour of the royalty option won the day.

So, in accordance with the **1904 Dean Forest Mines Act,** in June 1907 a group of Free-miners sold their rights of the South Eastern gale to the Princess Royal Colliery Co. for an undisclosed sum with a view to developing the deep coal seams. The sale comprised 533 acres containing 6 seams of coal and was estimated to produce over twelve million tons of steam coal. A royalty of one half penny per ton would be paid to the Free-miners on the coals extracted. The transfer was overseen by representatives of the Free-miners, the Deputy Gaveller and the Princess Royal Colliery Co. at a meeting convened at Gavellers office in Coleford.

Later the same month other sales were agreed. The Pillowell United Deep Colliery gale comprising 800 acres of coal containing 5 seams was sold by 756 Free-miners to the Wallsend Colliery Co. for £1,749. A royalty of half a penny per ton to be paid to the Free-miners on coals extracted and the handover of the cheque took place at the Speech House.

The Western United gale of 860 acres with an estimated yield of twenty million tons was sold to the Cannop Coal Company with a royalty of half a penny per ton.

The Eastern United gale of 2,000 acres with an estimated yield of forty four million tons was sold to Messrs Crawshay and Co.

The Holly Hill United gale of 900 acres with an estimated yield of twenty million tons was sold to the Lydney and Crump Meadow Collieries.

Under this new system, four new collieries were started – Cannop Colliery and Eastern United both in 1909, Waterloo Colliery (formerly Arthur and

Edward) in 1908 and the Princess Royal Colliery Co. deepened their shaft at Park Gutter in 1914 to access the lower seams.

The three year wages agreement would come to an end in September 1907 and at a meeting between the Coal Owners and the miners, it was agreed that the present system of a Conciliation Board which had been in operation for 14 years was considered to have done good service and that it should continue.

At the **Miners' Annual Demonstration** at Speech House, a resolution was passed confirming that their membership and funds were on the increase and to thank the Joint Wages Board for securing a wage agreement for another three years from the end of September 1907. It also urged more men to become members so that all miners could benefit equally from the Compensation Act. Sir Charles Dilke was once again in attendance and gave a speech based on the current political situation and apologised for some promised legislation that had not yet been carried out. Also in July, the Mines Inspector's report was published but as all the quoted figures related to the combined coalfields of the Forest and Bristol, any form of conclusion to its usefulness for the Forest of Dean seems impossible. However, he did comment on the slackness of trade in the house coal pits during the summer months and said he didn't know how the men and their families could manage to eke out an existence on working only three days a week and that it could possibly only be achieved by saving some of their winter earnings.

Referring to the future development of the deep seam pits and in particular the new Cannop Colliery, he indicated that if successful, Cannop would be the forerunner of others for the working of the lower seams. It would extend the life of the local coal trade now that the upper coal measures are rapidly becoming exhausted. The seams are for steam coal and not house coal and it may have the effect of providing more regular work throughout the year than has been the case in the house coal trade.

At a miners meeting at Two Bridges In September 1907, Mr Rowlinson acknowledged the good state of the coal trade and said that there was nothing that he could grumble about. He was however very concerned at the alarming rate of accidents and that the last three weeks had been most painful. He couldn't see any one particular factor that contributed to these accidents or that could be accounted for any lack of care by either Master or men.

On Thursday the 12th of December 1907, the Flour Mill colliery at Bream became flooded by an abnormal amount of water and around 700 men were sent home. Thirty seven horses had to be taken to the surface and it was as much as the steam pumps could do to contain the flood.

Accidents/Fatalities

The first of these occurred on Friday the 8th of February 1907 at the Crump Meadow Colliery near Cinderford where 18 year old Arthur Vernon met with a freak accident underground. Arthur, who lived at Heywood Lane, Cinderford, worked as a hodder under his father and at the time of the accident was standing in front of three empty drams in an underground siding. Miner Frank Adams was approaching the siding with two drams full of coal pulled by a horse and Mr Vernon called and said it was clear for him to pass. As he did so, one of the full drams clipped the front empty dram in the siding and overturned it. Vernon was caught between the empty dram and the roadway wall and was severely crushed. He was immediately taken to the surface and transported home where he died the next day from severe internal injuries.

On Tuesday the 25th of June 1907 at the Norchard Colliery near Lydney, 19 year old Frank Aston from Blakeney was seriously injured while working at the coal face. He was crushed when a large fall of coal fell on him. His back had taken the brunt of the fall and he was transported home in a serious condition. He had only been working at Norchard for 8 days and previous to that at Lightmoor, working with his father James Aston.

On Wednesday the 26th of June 1907 at Messrs Richard Thomas's New Pit in Lydbrook, Mr William Ward was driving a new underground heading with other colliers. They were careful with the timbering supports due to the nature of the ground and were in the process of installing big heavy posts when the roof gave way. The men rushed clear but Mr Ward was caught in the fall. It took two hours to release him but he was found to have died due to suffocation. He had left a widow and nine children.

On Thursday the 5th of September 1907 at the Lightmoor Colliery near Cinderford, Sidney Beddis aged 39, a married man with three children who was a Fireman at the colliery was working on the winding engine. His job was to oil the engine when it was motionless and he was in position at 11.15am waiting for it to stop when another workman noticed that he had disappeared. He looked around and noticed a foot and instantly stopped the engine. Sidney was found outside the engine cage with terrible injuries to the back of his head and a broken leg. He had done the oiling many times before and it was a mystery why he would do it when the engine was running. It appeared that he could have been struck by the engine crank and death was instantaneous. The Inquest Jury recorded a verdict of accidental death.

On Monday the 9th of September 1907 at the Foxes Bridge Colliery, two brothers Charles and Frederick Wilce from Ruspidge were seriously injured while working at the coal face. Both were laying charges of gunpowder in three holes bored in the rock when one of them exploded prematurely throwing both of them violently backwards. Both were carried out of the pit and taken to Gloucester Royal Infirmary where Frederick (Alfred) recovered. His brother Charles aged 24 had serious injuries to his spine causing paralysis. His condition deteriorated and he died on Sunday the 20th of October 1907 leaving a young widow. No cause was ever found for the pre-detonation and the Inquest Jury found that Charles Wilce died as a result of injuries caused by the explosion.

On Wednesday the 18th of September 1907 at the Lightmoor Colliery, 20 year old Harry Barton from The Meend, Cinderford was crushed by a fall of rock while working underground. He started work at 7.30 am and was working with William Hewlett and William Smith a buttyman. Harry was working clearing up some coal which had fallen down when a large piece of coal fell from between two sprags above, hitting him on the head. His workmates called out his name and struggled to release him from one and a half hundredweight of coal but when they did, he was found to be dead from a severe head injury. The place of work was considered a safe place and Inspector William Morgan from Moseley Green said that he had made his inspection at 9.30am and that it was safe. The law said that the supports should be no more than six feet apart and those at the place of the fall were five feet apart and the roof was seven feet in height. The verdict of the inquest was that of Accidental death with no blame to be attached to anyone.

Mr Rowlinson made a point of paying his respects by visiting Harry's parents at their home at The Meend, Cinderford. After his visit, he was visibly upset and collapsed in the street and taken into a nearby home. Mrs Rowlinson was alerted and Dr McCartney was called and assured her that it was nothing serious and later that day he was able to get home to recover.

On Monday the 23rd of December 1907 at the Foxes Bridge Colliery, 49 year old Henry Morgan from Ruardean Hill was working with another collier Sidney Merrell shot firing the coal face. They had drilled two holes and had charged them with powder. A squib was put in the lower of the two holes and lit and the two men hid in their place of safety while the charges went off. When Henry returned to examine the result of the explosion, the charge in the upper hole went off and he was thrown violently backwards. Sidney went to his aid and Henry said; **'Sid, I don't know how I got this. Has the bottom shot knocked anything down?'** Sidney went for help and Henry was taken to the surface where Dr Ibbotson came and dressed his wounds as best he could. He was then taken to Gloucester Royal Infirmary suffering from head injuries and a badly mutilated face. He died at 9.45 am the next morning. The Inquest concluded that Henry had put the squibs into both holes instead of just the one and that a spark from the first squib had fired the second. The Jury returned a verdict of Accidental Death.

1908

In January 1908, the **Dean Forest Labour Association** held their Annual meeting and reported a favourable increase in the membership over the past year and Mr Rowlinson remarked that he had noticed greater attendances at all 28 Lodge meetings and was pleased that the colliers were expressing more interest in Trade Union activity. The re-election of Officers were recorded as; Mr George Barnard, President, Mr W. Smith, Vice President, Mr George Rowlinson, Agent for the 22nd time, Mr J. Baldwin, Treasurer, Mr R. Buffry, Secretary. Auditors, Messrs A. Adams and A. Cooper. Finance Committee, Messrs W. Taylor, E. Taylor and T. Wright. Executive Committee, Messrs M. Perkins, G. Barnard, C. Lees, T. Preest, E. Williams, R. Powell, J. Roberts, D. Organ and B. White.

As the New Year began it became clear that the miners agent Mr Rowlinson was not in the best of health and was compelled to give up his work for a short period. The Executive of the Miners Association decided to offer him three months leave which he graciously accepted. By the end of March he was already sailing westward for a well earned holiday visiting the United States and Canada in the hope that when he returned, his health would be re-established.

There was further Parliamentary activity regards the Eight Hour Day legislation with arguments for and against being lobbied to the Committee. The Bill before Parliament would get a second reading before Easter and there were strong influencers who were prepared to speak out in its favour including Mr Gladstone and Sir Charles Dilke. Mr Gladstone, in reply to Mr Hicks Beech's amendment purporting that the Act should not apply to Forest of Dean mines said that he thought the miners themselves were in favour of the Bill and that he had received no representations from the mine owners to the contrary. The amendment was dropped. Another Liberal M.P. Mr J. E. Sears, speaking at Symonds Yat said there was a lot of bunkum talked about the Eight Hour Bill and about the prospect of dearer coal. But first of all they had to be humane and let the opponents ask themselves how they would like to be working more than eight hours a day under such conditions as coal mining involved. He also remarked that in the long run, the Bill was not going to make any difference to the price of coal or if it did, only by a few pence per ton while it would result in many more miners getting work.

The newly elected Liberal Party were keen to continue with their legislation to help the working classes and as far back as 1891 Joseph Chamberlain tried to introduce a contributory Old Age Pension scheme but was faced with serious opposition from the Friendly Societies. In 1899 a non contributory scheme was introduced in New Zealand and a Government Select Committee was established to explore its possibility here and concluded that it was.

Successive Governments had therefore just paid lip service to the idea of old age pensions until the Liberal Government under Henry Asquith, intent on social reform introduced the **Old Age Pension Act** to Parliament at the end of May 1908. Chancellor of the Exchequer David Lloyd George had the unenviable task of seeing this non contributory scheme through Parliament and the **Old Age Pension Act 1908** finally received its Royal Assent on the 1st of August 1908.

This Act ran far, far short of the pensions we have today but it was a start. For example, a recipient had to be 70 years of age or over to receive 5 shillings per week and 7shillings and 6 pence for a married couple. There were many qualifications for this including a 20 year residency in Great Britain and their yearly means should not be more than £31 and 10 shillings. Disqualifications included a history of avoiding work when able, making themselves poor in order to qualify, being imprisoned or convicted under the Inebriates Act or in receipt of any Poor Law relief or under medical assistance.

The Durham Miners' Association who expressed some opposition to the Eight Hour Bill finally decided to re-affiliate with the **Miners' Federation of Great Britain.** They were expelled in 1893 after refusing to join the National strike and tried to re-join in 1897 demanding certain concessions that were not acceptable to the **MFGB.**

The question of whether the **Miners Federation** was now ready to become affiliated to the **Labour Party** became increasingly discussed and a ballot of the whole Country's membership took place in May 1908. The result was generally a foregone conclusion judging by the early results but the official results were published on the 12th of June 1908.

They were;

        For affiliation 213,137,
        Against affiliation 168,294,
        Majority in favour of affiliation .... 44,843.

Notable Districts who voted against were the Midland, Derby, Nottinghamshire, Leicestershire and North Wales. There were 13 sitting Liberal MP's who were affected by this decision and their positions would be considered when the official affiliation took place.

During May 1908, Free-miners who sold their rights to their gales in 1907, received their share of the first year royalties already earned amounting to £180. This was distributed to just over 1000 miners. Some had rights to all four of the gales, others three, others two and others one so that their shares were split accordingly. Two more large gales were due for sale later in the year, the South Eastern United of 460 acres yielding 11 million tons and the Alexandra No 3 of 205 acres yielding 5 million tons.

At the **Miners' Annual Demonstration** at the Speech House in July, a resolution was passed expressing the miners delight in securing another three year wages agreement last September including the raising of the standard rate by two and a half percent. Sir Charles again spent some time talking politics especially on the new Old Age Pension Bill going before Parliament. The question of providing state pensions had been discussed in Parliament for many years past and Sir Charles alluded to the fact that in general, he had supported the poor of the country whenever possible. Unfortunately, certain aspects of the current Bill before Parliament contained elements that disqualified those who were in receipt of Poor Law Relief and that unless that was amended, he was unable to back the Bill.

He said he was also not in favour of the starting age of 70 years which would exclude workers of many trades.

Gold Mining

Enthusiasm for this venture during 1907 lost a lot of its momentum in January 1908 when further exploration could only be carried out with an injection of cash. This became clear when the Syndicate made an appeal against a rating assessment due to there being as yet, no return on their investment. They succeeded in getting the value reduced by half. However, by June 1908 the matter of funding became the subject of a legal debacle at the Kings Bench in front of Mr Justice Bigham and a special Jury. The Chastain Syndicate Limited tried to sue a Colonel Trower, an investor for not paying for 7,743 shares at 5 shillings each. Syndicate members were cross examined and it became obvious that a shambles had been made of setting up this Company. Company Secretary Mr Herbert Thompson was asked by the Judge if the Company was in Liquidation. The answer he got was **'no'**. The defence lawyer asked **'what is it doing?'** answer – **'not anything at present, the auditors are at work and the balance sheet is being prepared'**. The witness was asked about the gold producing quality of the property and said that samples had produced some pennyweights per ton. The Judge asked what that would be worth and was answered 3 shillings but on further cross examining said that experts had put the yield at two pence per ton. Asked further if any independent experts had had a look at the property – answer **'yes'**. And have they pronounced it worthless? – answer **'they don't say definitely that it is worthless'**. Do they say it is worth anything? - answer **'they say gold might be found there'**.

The Judge interrupted and remarked that that would be true about the foundations of his house in London – to great laughter. This was the path the rest of the case took with a final admittance by Mr C.F.Kennedy the Managing Director of the Syndicate that he wished to pursue other interests and that as there was no money to fund further excavations, the exploration had ceased its operations. Eventually judgement in the case went in favour of Colonel Trower with costs.

On Saturday the 26th of July 1908 the Chastain Syndicate held their Annual General Meeting at the Cannon Street Hotel in London to consider the way forward. There were disagreements among the few attendees as to how the Company could operate without funds and one suggestion was to apply to the Court for a voluntary winding-up - another was to adjourn the meeting till the following Thursday. The latter was eventually agreed upon and at that meeting it was eventually agreed to set up a committee of shareholders to investigate their current state of affairs with a view to considering a scheme for reconstruction.

On the 30th of September 1908, the shareholders met again to hear the committee's report. Mr Vogel re-called events that led the Company into a one sided agreement with the discoverer without getting the gold bearing seams properly tested. The Company was without funds although the work done had been to drive two shafts, one of 96ft and the other of 141ft and an open cut of around 1,000ft at an expenditure of £3,273. A resolution was eventually passed to place the Company in voluntary Liquidation and to appoint a Liquidator.

In Parliament, the controversial **'Coal Mines Regulations Act 1908'** became law on the 21st of December 1908 for the purposes of limiting the hours of work underground to eight hours. The first clause of this Act read; *'Subject to the provisions of this Act, a worker shall not be below ground in a mine for the purpose of his work and of going to and from his work, for more than eight hours during any consecutive twenty-four hours'.* Naturally, there were many other clauses and sub clauses to this Act - too many to list here and it would remain to be seen whether the opponents arguments regarding loss of production would be justified.

Accidents/ Fatalities

On Thursday the 9th of April 1908 at the Crump Meadow Colliery near Cinderford, 39 year old Joseph Alfred Parsons, a married man, was killed while operating a coal cutting machine underground. He and fellow miner Henry Rogers were both working at the coal face and were in the process of starting up the coal cutting machine. Rogers was eleven feet away and had called to Parsons twice if it was clear to start and received two 'yeses'. He then turned on the electric power and instantly Parsons became entangled in the machinery which stopped immediately as the fuse had blown. Parsons was killed instantly with multiple injuries and it was supposed that part of his clothing may have got entangled and drawn him in. Both men had been using the machine for two months without problems, both knew the routine to follow and the workplace was well lit. Ironically Parsons' widow later recalled how her husband had recently woken up in the night after a bad dream of being dragged into the machine. Accidental death was recorded with no blame being attached to anyone.

On Monday the 31st of August 1908 at the Flour Mill Colliery, Bream, 16 year old Richard Howard from Sling was killed by a fall of rock while working underground. Richard was with his older brother Alfred and Henry James working a stall and had just cut some coal and were clearing up the roadway. They had cleared away a few drams when Alfred left to fetch a candle and heard a crash and his brother Richard calling his name **'Alf oh Alf'**. He ran back and found a large stone on top of the two men. With the help of other miners, they managed to release the trapped men and found Henry James not badly hurt but Richard Howard had suffered a broken neck, thigh and leg and was dead. The roof had been sounded frequently and there was nothing to indicate a slip and there was a plentiful supply of timber available. It was recorded that this was the first fatal accident occurring in that pit for nearly nine years. Accidental death was recorded with no blame being attached to anyone.

On Friday the 11th of December 1908 at the new Cannop Colliery, Thomas Williams aged 20 of upper Lydbrook was seriously injured while working on an incline taking refuse by dram and tipping it onto a waste heap. The dram was pulled up the incline by a rope attached to an engine. Thomas and another worker named Smith were in the process of tipping the dram when a sprag in a wheel sprang up and caught Thomas between his legs, lifting him up and entangling his legs in the wheels. He was taken to the Gloucester Royal Infirmary where he later died from haemorrhaging of the wound. Mr H. Williams on behalf of the colliery expressed his sympathy with the relatives and said that 160 men worked at the colliery and this was the first serious accident that had occurred there. Accidental death was recorded.

1909

Following the ballot in May 1908, the **Miners' Federation of Great Britain** whose membership topped 600,000, applied to affiliate itself with the newly formed **Labour Party** and at the Party's Annual Conference in January 1909 a set of proposals including the fees payable annually was accepted by the **MFGB**. However, several **MFGB** MP's were elected as Liberal or Lib/Lab MP's at the previous Election and it was decided to continue until the next General Election where those MP's could, if their consciences allowed, then sign the constitution and join the **Labour Party.** From then on all Union and Independent Labour Party candidates were to run on the **Labour Party** ticket.

However, discontent over signing a 'pledge' harked back to the days of the **Labour Representation Committee (LRC)** when, in 1903, the then Union funded MP, Richard Bell who had been courted by Liberal MP's, refused to sign the 'pledge' introduced through the **LRC's** new Constitution. His stand ultimately saw his fall from the Union Executive but he remained an MP.

Bringing matters up to date, another Union man in the form of Mr Walter Osborne, a branch secretary of the Amalgamated Society of Railway Servants and a Liberal supporter, decided to take legal action against his Union over the matter of signing the 'pledge' to contribute a subscription to support the Labour Party. This ultimately led to the Law Lords Ruling of 21st of December 1909 that held that Trade Unions were not allowed to collect a levy for political purposes. It became known as the **Osborne Judgement** and was largely condemned by both Unions and Politicians as another blow against the working classes.

As the **Coal Mines Regulations Act 1908** or more commonly known as the **Eight Hour Day Act** was due to partly come into force on the 1st of July 1909, it gave the Industry time enough to sift through the small print and raise any points that needed further clarification or amendment. The Scottish and Welsh Miners' Associations were expressing their disappointment to certain aspects of the Bill and the Coal Owners were also threatening to terminate contracts and introduce a wage decrease of 12.5%, having foreseen a drop in coal production. Strike action from both areas was threatened. The **MFGB** conducted a ballot of its 603,000 members in June 1909 as to whether or not to take strike action nationally in support of their colleagues and the result was a 90% vote in favour of a national stoppage.

Meanwhile the **MFGB** were acting as mediators with the Government in a bid to avoid a strike in South Wales and a national stoppage was averted in early July 1909 when both sides came to an amicable agreement. The situation in Scotland however had not been settled and a national strike was still a possibility with a promise of 10 shillings per week strike pay being offered to each striking miner by the **MFGB**. Mr Churchill representing the Board of Trade agreed to see both sides in the dispute and with the threat of over 80,000 Scottish miners coming out on strike, talks had reached a crucial stage. The Coal Owners and Workmens' representatives met with the Board of Trade on the afternoon of Friday the 30th of July 1909 and by 9.30 in the evening, an agreement had been reached. And so a National Strike had been averted at the eleventh hour.

The **Eight Hour Day Act** threw up another anomaly concerning the hours of working on a Saturday. As the legislation stood, miners would finish their shift at 3pm in the afternoon which left little time for attending or taking part in their national sports such as soccer and, in the summer, cricket. This and other matters in dispute were the subject of a short Bill introduced by Mr Gladstone in early July 1909 that would allow miners to start work an hour earlier on Saturdays than the Act allowed. Also of concern was the 60 hours per year clause which enabled Coal Owners the option to add an extra hour to a miner's working week. The **Miners' Federation** made a strong objection to this but Mr Gladstone insisted that it was introduced for the specific purpose of *'helping old collieries in Districts like the Forest of Dean'.*

With Coal Owners wishing to put their own interpretation on the **Eight Hour Act,** instead of benefiting the miners, the Act had the effect of throwing up more problems than it solved causing unrest at many collieries throughout the country. At some collieries in South Wales, there was an undercurrent of unrest over the introduction of an afternoon shift with the Coal Owners terminating contracts from the 1st of October 1909 if the men did not comply. At other pits, miners had terminated their own contracts from the 1st of October 1909 due to the presence of non union men. In order to support their continued opposition to the **Eight Hour Act**, Coal Owners nationwide were now producing figures showing an 8%-10% reduction of coal output over the first three months of the Act being in force, compared to the same period in 1908, with a corresponding price increase of 6 pence per ton.

On the 29th of April 1909, David Lloyd George the Chancellor of the Exchequer for the Liberal Government introduced to Parliament what became known as the 'People's Budget'. This Budget incorporated a system of heavy taxation on the rich and wealthy, intended to fund a radical social reform programme which was seen as an intent to distribute the country's wealth equally among the population. Lloyd George called it a war Budget – a war against poverty which was voted for by Parliament the same day but came up against stiff opposition when submitted to the House of Lords. As many of those Lords were Conservative landowners who would be seriously financially affected by the legislation, they vetoed the Budget on the 30th of November 1909 despite urgings from the King. As the Liberal Government relied on other minor Parties for support in achieving a majority, the result was a 'hung Parliament' and the constitutional crisis could only be overcome by calling for another General Election.

Forest of Dean

In April 1909, the **Forest of Dean Miners' Association** held a Demonstration meeting at Yorkley where a large crowd of miners were in agreement to re-affiliate the **FODMA** with the **MFGB**. Later in the year a ballot of members was held and a 93% majority were in favour of re-affiliating but Mr Rowlinson did insist on the proviso that the area was to be allowed to negotiate its own wage agreements and he could see no reason why the Federation should deny them that. He would make the application to be re-admitted to the fold to a position they had occupied before the strike of 1893 and it would remain to be seen whether those miners who had consistently refused to join the Union because they were not affiliated, would now be compelled to join up because their argument was no longer valid.

In a speech at Soudley in September 1909, Mr Rowlinson referred to the **Eight Hour Act** and its implications within the Forest of Dean. Regarding the 60 hour per year clause he advised the men to refuse to work the extra time unless compelled to do so by litigation and there was every reason to believe that they would take his advice. The other bone of contention was the Saturday hours of work and the amendment being considered in Parliament may resolve the issue and allow the men to start work on Saturdays an hour earlier. One local casualty of the legislation was the Drybrook Rugby Football Club, who in 1908 had had a successful season but with the lack of Saturday afternoon spectators they were having trouble paying their way. They had paid their seasonal rents in advance but with the lack of gate money from the mining community, it had been decided to disband the Club.

Pit Stop

A court case brought against The Flour Mill Colliery that was owned by the Princess Royal Colliery Company by five colliers was held at Coleford Magistrates Court in August 1909. The five men claimed payment for work done in driving and timbering an underground roadway in 1907. The original agreement between management and men was for payment of 1 shilling and 6 pence per pair of timbers erected. The colliers claimed that they had erected 25 pairs of timbers but had only been paid for 3 of them. The majority of the Bench found that the men's claim had not been made out but one of the magistrates was Mr S.J. Elsom, President of the Free-miners Association. He voiced his strong objection to the decision of the Bench and thought that the men had indeed made out their case. The colliers were John Prince, Edward Ward, Henry Hart, Fred Hewlett and Henry Rogers all from Bream.

As a consequence of the Court's decision, the Colliery Company sacked the men involved. This action provoked bad feeling among the workforce at the colliery and Mr Rowlinson was called in to try and negotiate an amicable settlement. As the Court action was taken at a time when the Colliery manager was away on holiday Mr Rowlinson suggested that an apology would secure their reinstatement. This, the men refused to do and the management also refused to abandon their position and so the 400 men gave notice to terminate their contracts as from the 25th of September 1909 – in effect, taking strike action.

At a meeting at Cinderford, miners were unanimous in setting up collections at the pit banks to support the striking miners and it was thought that the dispute could easily spread to other collieries. However after further negotiations which related to the manager's absence during the Court case, it was agreed that a misunderstanding had taken place and after concessions were made on both sides, the men returned to work on Monday the 18th of October. The dispute had lasted just over three weeks.

During the month of December 1909 and despite problems with the influx of water and two fatal accidents, the Cannop Colliery Co. Ltd. reported that they had struck the Coleford High Delf seam in one of their shafts at a depth of just over 200 yards. The seam was expected to be around 5 feet thick which would lend encouragement to the other Companies engaged in the same exploration of the deep seams.

Fig. 45 Cannop Colliery, sunk in 1909.
Courtesy of the DHC, Soudley, Cinderford.

Accidents/Fatalities

On the evening of February 3rd 1909 at Cannop Colliery, 22 year old Charles Henry Mumford was killed when he fell out of a skip while ascending the vertical shaft. The shaft was being sunk to reach the Coleford High Delf coal seam and was about 100 yards deep when Charles was ascending in the skip to collect a bucket of clay. When the skip reached the top of the shaft, the engine operator noticed that the skip was upside down and realised that the occupant must have fallen out. At the bottom of the shaft no one was injured by Henry's fall but the sinkers who were very shocked, stopped work for the day. Unfortunately Charles' father was a surface worker and witnessed the swaying of the rope and knew that his son was ascending the shaft. Accidental death was recorded.

At 6.30am on the morning of Tuesday the 17th of August 1909, 22 year old Joseph Pullen, a trammer from Edge End, formally from Gloucester was killed while working underground at Cannop Colliery. He was working on a slope or incline and was operating from the bottom. The incline had two sets of rails, one for a full dram descending which drew an empty one up the other rail. Mr Pullen was in the act of uncoupling the last dram of the shift, when the empty one somehow got unhitched and ran back down the line at speed. Several colliers called out **'stand clear, an empty dram is coming'** but for some unknown reason he didn't hear the call and walked into its path and was instantly crushed to death.

On the morning of Thursday the 2nd of September 1909 at the Flour Mill Colliery near Bream, 60 year old James Edwards from Mill Hill, Bream was killed by a fall of rock. He had just started work that morning when a 'bell' of rock weighing about two tons fell directly onto him killing him instantly. He was described as a loyal and reliable worker and the coroner's verdict was accidental death.

1910

The year of two General Elections.

The first of these took place on Monday the 17th of January 1910 and in the Forest of Dean, Sir Charles Dilke was again standing as the Liberal candidate. He did have opposition this time in the form of Conservative and Unionist candidate Mr J.R. Renton and it turned out to be a very acrimonious campaign. Part way through his campaign Mr Renton fell ill with a very bad cold but insisted on carrying on. On a visit to Cinderford his condition worsened, causing him to faint. He was taken to the Lion Hotel where he eventually recovered and was transported back to his home in Newnham.

The results were;
Sir Charles Dilke – Liberal... 6,141,
Mr J.R. Renton – Conservative and Unionis............... 3,279,
Liberal majority.. 2,862.

The results were made public at Newnham Town Hall and afterwards Sir Charles made his way to his base at the Victoria Hotel where he made a speech from a window on the first floor.

Nationally, the result was another 'hung Parliament' with no Party gaining a majority but Mr Asquith was able to form a Government with the help of the Labour Party who had 40 seats, a gain of 17 and the Irish Parliamentary Party with 71 seats. The People's Budget of 1909 was eventually accepted by the House of Lords exactly one year to the day that it was originally introduced – 29th of April.

Forest of Dean

A sad loss to the **Forest and to the Miners' Association** was the death on Friday the 8th of April 1910 of Mr George Barnard, President of the **Forest of Dean Miners' Association**. During his time working in the local pits George was unfortunate to have lost an eye and an arm but had continued working at the Foxes Bridge Colliery as a checkweighman for a number of years. He served as President of the Association for seventeen years and was so respected by fellow miners that they carried his coffin four miles in the pouring rain from his cottage to a service at the Congregational Chapel in Drybrook and then on to the internment at Holy Trinity Churchyard, Drybrook. The occasion was packed with representatives from all mining sections in the Forest, including the **FODMA** and the Coal Owners' Association. Many tributes also came from the various mining communities in the Forest and also from Sir Charles Dilke who sent a wreath of yellow blooms.

At the end of April, a ballot of members of the **FODMA** was taken to elect the next President and although there were several candidates who were suitably qualified, the Executive Committee had to make the final choice. It therefore came as no surprise that the current Vice President Mr William Smith from Broadwell Lane End was duly confirmed to be the next President.

Death of the King

On the 6th of May 1910, it was announced from Buckingham Palace that **King Edward VII** had passed away. On the morning of that day he had suffered more than one heart attack but refused to rest. When he heard that his horse had won at Kempton Park he said **'Yes, I have heard of it. I am very glad'.** They were reportedly his last words as he then became unconscious and was put to bed where he died at 11.45pm.

Edward VII was a popular King who, although suffering the venom of his mother's tongue for several cases of impropriety while he was Prince of Wales, he did later exonerate himself

Fig. 46 King Edward VII

by conducting a successful tour of India in 1875 resulting in Queen Victoria being given the title **'Empress of India'**. When he became King in 1901, he became more interested in Politics and reform of the Army and Navy which some prominent members of Parliament and the Lords were opposed to. Nevertheless he was successful in creating Anglo-French unity at a time when the continued dominance of the German Empire, fuelled by his nephew Emperor Wilhelm II was of great concern. He was related to most European Royalty and was friendly with all of them, with the exception of one and he became known as the 'Uncle of Europe'. He also played an important role in modernising the Royal Navy that introduced the building of 'Dreadnought' battleships and also of reform of the Army after the failings during the Boer Wars.

In the Forest of Dean, the news was received with great sadness for the popular Monarch and flags flew at half mast at Municipal and other buildings throughout the Forest. Speeches expressing sadness were also made and in Cinderford, a Labour meeting chaired by Mr Martin Perkins passed a resolution; *'that this meeting of miners at Cinderford and district desires to place on record its feeling of deepest sympathy with all the members of the Royal Family in their hour of sorrow and bereavement and also sincerely deplores the great loss which the Empire and the world at large has sustained by the death of the King'*. Mr Rowlinson seconded the resolution saying; **'I do so with feelings of deep sorrow. No man had endeared himself more in the hearts of the people than the late King. This nation has lost a good and capable ruler and the World a kind friend'**. Similar meetings at Coleford, Whitecroft, Yorkley and Speech House also expressed the same condolences and sympathies.

At the **Miners' Annual Demonstration** held at the Speech House on Saturday the 9th of July 1910 where, once again fine weather encouraged the attendance with the Drybrook Brass Band heading the procession into the field at 1pm. Chaired by the new President Mr William Smith and supported on the platform by Sir Charles Dilke, Mr Robert Smillie Vice President of the **MFGB,** Mr G. Rowlinson, Agent and other members of the **FODMA** Council. A resolution put forward by Mr Thomas Wright, Vice President that in order for Forest miners to see any improvement in their new wages agreement and also to benefit from the working of the lower seams, the membership needed to be increased in order to strengthen the hands of the leaders of our Union, was seconded by Mr David Organ and supported by Mr Robert Smillie. Sir Charles Dilke gave a talk referring to the recent Lords approval of the Budget and some of the failures of the opposition Parties in supporting it. In view of the forthcoming **Coal Mines Regulations Bill,** he also touched on the subject of safety in the mines, especially now in the development of the deeper seams in the Forest of Dean and made comparisons to the dangers such as in South Wales and the recent disaster at Whitehaven where 147 miners lost their lives in an underground explosion four miles out to sea. He said that there should be more Inspectors and the laws should be more strictly enforced.

Many mourned the death of Mr William Crawshay who passed away on Monday the 11th of July aged 70 years. He had suffered with a serious internal complaint for nearly four years. Mr Crawshay was the son of Mr Henry Crawshay the well known iron and coal Master in the Forest of Dean and the grandson of Mr William Crawshay of Cyfartha. When Henry died in 1879, his son took on both Lightmoor and Foxes Bridge collieries as Managing Director. Mr Crawshay who lived at The Hyde, Newnham was a local magistrate and outside his business interests, was well known in the hunting and racing world. He suffered tragedy during his life when his wife was killed during a hunting event at Tewkesbury Park on the 5th of March 1878 and his son Henry died of a fever in 1901 while serving with the Scots Guards during the Boer War.

Mr Crawshay's funeral took place on the 14th of July at Awre Parish Church with the procession from The Hyde being joined at Bullo Cross by miners and miners' representatives from both Lightmoor and Foxes Bridge collieries. The large attendance at the funeral showed the high esteem in which he was held by both his workmen and business associates. His oak coffin was interred in the family vault.

A reflection of how the slackness of the coal trade was affected during the summer months was illustrated by the action of the Directors of the Norchard Colliery at the end of July 1910. Around 100 men and boys who had been working no more than two shifts a week on the Trenchard seam, were dismissed on Saturday the 23rd of July 1910 and part of the Colliery was closed. Mr Phipps the Managing Director wrote a letter to the dismissed men expressing his regret at having to take such measures but said that due to the bad ground which added to the cost of getting coal, it had become too expensive to continue at that time.

Meanwhile, miners' agent Mr Rowlinson was doing the rounds, holding meetings with various Lodges in the District under the auspices of the **FODMA**. The main theme of which concentrated on the pros and cons of the **Eight Hour Day Act** and how conditions would be different had it not been introduced. He said that at this time when trade was slow and there was plenty of coal on the market, the men would have had to work fewer days a week but each day would have been longer. He also remarked on the rise of the Trusts and Combines with their intentions of keeping prices and wages low and of trying to quash Unionism. He said that the Masters now had great power in their hands and if things carried on that way, he could foresee a great conflict ahead. Referring in particular to the trouble in South Wales, he said that he wouldn't be drawn into expressing his opinion other than to say that the fire had been smouldering for some time before it has now burst forth. At one meeting Mr Rowlinson was questioned as to whether he owned any shares in a Forest of Dean colliery, to which he quickly denied, saying that he would never be a shareholder while acting as miners' Agent.

Due to the national Political stalemate, a second General Election was held in December 1910 with the Forest of Dean Constituency being held on Tuesday the 13th of December 1910. As usual, Sir Charles Dilke represented the Liberal Party and he was opposed this time by Mr D.H. Kyd representing the Conservative and Unionist Party. Due to the particularly bad weather and the fact that the collieries were working, it was anticipated there would be a low turnout. As usual, the nerve centre of operations was at the Newnham Town Hall where counting the votes started at 9.45am on the Wednesday morning with the results being declared some three hours later.

The result was;
Sir Charles Dilke – Liberal 5,544,
Mr D.H. Kyd – Conservative and Unionist 2,820,
Liberal Majority .... **2,724.**

After the customary vote of thanks and hand shaking from both candidates, Sir Charles then boarded his motor car and proceeded to his headquarters at the Victoria Hotel. He then addressed the crowd from an upstairs balcony where he praised them for their fortitude in actually being there in the pouring rain and that he wouldn't detain them any longer than was necessary. He continued to say how pleased he was with the election result in spite of the miners not having their usual 'play day' this time and that those elderly voters weren't able to get to the polling stations due to the lack of conveyances. He said he would be pleased to continue to represent the Forest of Dean in his usual manner for as long as it took. Sir Charles left the district during the afternoon for a short holiday before returning to the new Parliament.

Looking at it nationally however, the overall Election results showed little in the way of a working majority for either Party again. Mr Asquith was just about able to form a Government with the help of the Irish Parliamentary Party and the Labour Party. The Liberals 272 seats, Conservatives 271 seats, Irish P.P. 74 seats and the Labour Party 42 seats, a net gain of 2 from the last Election.

At the end of December 1910, the Council of the **FODMA** held their Annual Meeting with the election of officers for the forthcoming year. President Mr William Smith, Vice President Mr Thomas Wright, Secretary Mr R. Buffry, Treasurer Mr J. Baldwin, Auditors Messrs A. Adams and J. Harper, Finance Committee Messrs R. Jones, E. Taylor and H. Beddington. It was acknowledged by congratulations that by August of 1911, Mr Rowlinson would have served the Association as its agent for 25 years. The Council resolved to make payments of £100 to the families of miners who were out of work as a result of flooded pits and an unnamed amount was granted to the striking miners families in the Aberdare district of South Wales. Mr Rowlinson disclosed that further amounts had been raised in support of local hospitals – Lydney Cottage Hospital £8-6s-6d, Gloucester Royal Infirmary £26-2s-3d and Monmouth Hospital £19-6s-8d.

Accidents/Fatalities

On Tuesday the 18th of January 1910 at the Trafalgar Colliery, Mr Hubert Powell, a Butty collier from Ruardean Woodside was killed by a large fall of rock while working in the Lowery coal seam. He left a widow and family. Although over 800 men and boys worked at the colliery, it was seven years since a life had been lost there.

Not strictly a mining accident but as quarrymen were part of the Labour Association, it should have a mention.

On Monday afternoon the 21st of March 1910, two men were instantly killed by a fall of rock at the Mople Hill or Maypole Hill quarry in the Kidnalls woods just north of Lydney and adjacent to the Norchard Colliery. One of the victims was the proprietor Mr Charles Thorne aged 63, married with no children of Viney Hill, Blakeney and Mr Matthew Johnson aged 44, married with four children of Primrose Hill near Lydney. From witnesses it was established that the two men were working half way up the quarry face undercutting a mass of stone when suddenly the rock gave way bringing down the two men and crushing them on impact with the quarry floor. Miners from the nearby Norchard Colliery were just leaving their shift and ran to help and it was some minutes before they were able to remove the bodies from beneath the stone which was estimated to weigh around four tons. A doctor attended the scene and pronounced both men dead and that their death had been instantaneous. The bodies were later taken to their homes.

On Monday the 4th of April 1910, Mr Frank Phelps aged 21, of Hawkwell road, Cinderford died as the result of a catastrophic explosion while working in the fuse factory at the Trafalgar Colliery. The inquest established that Mr Phelps had been employed in preparing and mixing ingredients for fuse composition and had been in charge of the department for over a year. The explosion took place at 3pm at his workbench where he was in the process of mixing ingredients that were lying in a paper tray near to a weighing scales. He had a scoop in his left hand partly full of the ingredients and was about to pour it into a sieve when the explosion occurred. The building was completely destroyed in the blast and the severely mutilated body of Mr Phelps was found nearby. The manager said that Mr Phelps was a steady and reliable worker who was a teetotaller and a non smoker.

Inquest returned a verdict of accidental death as a result of the blast and no blame should be attached to anyone.

On Monday the 13th of June 1910 during the day shift at the Duck Pit Colliery near Cinderford, Mr Frederick Chamberlain aged 60 of Upper Bilson, Cinderford was killed while working as a shot firer at the coal face. Fellow workers Andrew and William Yemm had prepared the firing charge and the usual warning shout was given by Mr Chamberlain who was in charge of the battery. The battery was started and the shot was fired. When the air cleared William Yemm found the dead body of Mr Chamberlain lying over the battery. Searching for an explanation, the brothers found that he had received a severe blow to the side of his head from a stone weighing 10 lbs which had broken from the rock by the force of the explosion. Mr Chamberlain was described as careful and reliable employee with long experience in his job. No blame was attached to the accident and that death was due to a fractured skull the result of which was caused by the firing of the shot.

On Wednesday the 8th of June 1910 at the Flour Mill Colliery near Bream, Mr William Rhodes aged 20, a single man of the Scowles near Coleford was injured while walking down the incline in front of a dram. He was employed as a trammer and was working with another trammer Mr Montague Jones letting a dram of 25cwt of coal down an incline. Mr Rhodes was walking in front of the dram instead of behind or alongside when it ran away. He tried to jump out of its way but got caught and was crushed. He was then brought to the surface and rushed to Lydney Cottage Hospital where he was operated on. He appeared to be improving but had a relapse and died a week later.

Mr Jones said that for safety reasons, they should have been behind the drams and they only had one 'scotch' (a triangular sectioned piece of wood about 24 inches long that was placed in front of the dram wheels acting as a brake) in front of the wheels instead of two. He also admitted this was normal practice to save time but was not necessarily the safest. The Coroner stated that this accident was as a result of carelessness, a case of 'familiarity breeds contempt' and if proper care had been exercised, the accident would not have happened. He urged the Company to enforce a rule that no workmen should go down such places in front of the dram. Company Secretary Mr J.H.Fewings said that the practice had been contrary to orders and that there was little that could be done other than following the workmen around to see that regulations were being followed.

Sympathy was expressed for the family of Mr Rhodes and the verdict of accidental death being recorded.

On Wednesday the 17th of August 1910, Mr Henry Holder aged 43, a sinker from Coleford was killed while working with others at the bottom of a 205 yard deep shaft at the Cannop Colliery. They were in the process of excavating for a new pump room when at around 3.30am, a rock weighing one and a half hundredweight fell from above onto Mr Holder's head, inflicting severe injuries. His workmates transported him to the surface where he died. It was thought that a shot firing may have dislodged the rock but it could not be proved. He leaves a widow and a young family. No blame was attached to anyone but it was pointed out that this was the fourth fatal accident at Cannop during the sinking of the new shafts.

On Thursday the 8th of September 1910, Mr Edward Kear aged 36, a pumpman from Albert Street, Lydney was killed while walking down the Dipple at the Norchard Colliery near Lydney. He said to a boy Henry Robbins that he was going to have his bread (lunch), which meant that he had to walk down the Dipple to a lower pump house. This happened while the cables were operating and were pulling drams up and letting drams down. Mr Kear started walking down behind a descending dram and after he had gone about fifty yards, the boy Robbins and a hooker-on Albert Fisher noticed several jerks on the cable. A signal was given to stop the engine and on walking down, they found the body of Mr Kear slumped in the upcoming dram road. They called to Mr Ernest Hancock for help but on examining the body, they found that he was already dead. At the Inquest it was thought that Mr Kear had crossed over the dram roads with the intention of going into a manhole on the opposite side but had been caught between a full upcoming dram and a prop, crushing him. It was pointed out that Mr Kear was one of few men whose duties allowed him to walk down the Dipple when the drams were running. Death was recorded as a result of crushing of the abdomen and shock. He left a widow and four children.

Chapter 14
Pit Stop - Cambrian Combine Strike
The Tonypandy Riots

In 1905 a move was made by a number of privately run collieries in South Wales to amalgamate into a business network known as the Cambrian Combine. The move was made in order to regulate the price of coal and miners wages on a large scale while still allowing individual collieries to operate independently. It was the brainchild of Mr D.A. Thomas, Liberal MP for Cardiff and owner of the original Cambrian Colliery in the Rhondda Valley whose ambition was to affect more control over the steam coal trade in South Wales.

Fig. 47 Naval colliery at Penygraig, Ely pit – courtesy of Richard Burton Archives, Swansea University.

By 1910 the Combine consisted of three groups of collieries – the Cambrian, the Glamorgan and the Naval Collieries (11 pits in total) employing around 12,000 men and were producing just under 3,000,000 tons of coal a year – it also controlled the Britannic Merthyr colliery at Gilfach Goch.

This dispute, like most others in South Wales was over the wages paid to miners for producing a set amount of coal. Managers would fix prices for getting coal at so low a figure that made it impossible for the miners to make a living wage. This was the case at the Naval Colliery, Ely pit in Penygraig earlier in 1909 where an experiment was carried out for a trial period to determine the exact amount of coal produced by 70 miners on a new five foot seam of coal, known as the Bute seam. The miners asked for 2s. 6d. per ton raised but the management offered only 1s. 9d., on the understanding that if they could not make a living wage, the management would make it up to the District rate. After a while the management accused the miners of deliberately working slowly which they denied saying the seam was difficult to work (abnormal places).

After 18 months, the management were still paying the men 1s. 9d. per ton per day when it was commonly known that the output per man was about two tons per day and that would work out at 3s. 6d. per day. The District rate was 4s. 6d. per day plus the usual 50% above the 1879 Standard. When the experiment ended, the management still refused to increase the rate after efforts were made through the proper channels. The management responded by giving notice on the 1st of August 1910 to terminate the contracts of the 70 men involved and also to all 800 miners in the colliery. On the 31st of August 1910 the miners were locked out with the result that on the 4th of September 1910, the men at the Nant Gwyn and Pandy pits threw down their tools and walked out in support of the Ely men. On the 1st of October 1910, the remaining pits in the Cambrian Combine also walked out and in all 12,000 men became idle. The situation was this; *'you must work this seam of coal at our price, or starve'.*

In the Aberdare valley at the Powell-Duffryn Collieries, a different dispute was in progress. It had been a tradition or privilege for miners to take home the cut-off ends of pit props for firewood – wood that would otherwise have been buried in the general waste of the pit. A management decision had been made to charge the men 6 pence per hundredweight for the wood and this, coupled with many other recent restrictions was the spark that lit the fire. The men, led by their fiery Agent Charlie Stanton, walked out without notice in an unofficial strike that was eventually joined by miners in other collieries in the valley, numbering around 9,000. Attempts to reach an amicable agreement with the Powell-Duffryn manager Mr F.M. Hann had so far come to nothing and so in total there were over 20,000 miners either locked out or on strike in the two valleys alone. Strikes and stoppages elsewhere brought the total up to 26,000. Prior to this dispute, the **South Wales Miners' Federation** (the Fed) were in funds of £120,000, of which £9,000 was allocated to the Aberdare miners with the balance being shared between the Cambrian Combine men, the Gelli men and the Powell-Duffryn men.

The **SWMF** held a conference to discuss the matter and decided to ballot the whole of the South Wales coalfield on whether to call a general strike. It was agreed to support the Cambrian miners financially with strike pay but not the rest of the coalfield and so on the 1st of November 1910, 30,000 miners of the Cambrian Combine were out on strike with all the pits concerned being picketed within a week. On the 2nd of November 1910, a pay deal negotiated by Mr William Abraham MP (Mabon) of 2s. 3d per ton was rejected by the **SWMF**. Unfortunately, there were three other Unions active in the collieries representing the Winding Enginemen's Union, the Enginemen's and Stokers and Craftsmen's Union and the Firemen's Union, all of which needed to be in solidarity with each other in order to effect an efficient strike. This was not the case as around 300 Enginemen, Ostlers, Stokers and white collar staff at each of the three groups of collieries – around 1,000 men in total – were still working in order to keep the mines from deteriorating.

As a result, picketing of each pit started at 5.00am which included many women and children out on marches in the streets leading to pits and on mountainsides to intercept those breaking the strike, often in the pouring rain. Local Authorities became nervous that the situation could get out of control and sent for reinforcements to support the local constabulary. Mr William Abraham MP (Mabon) and others on the **SWMF** Executive appealed to strikers not to provoke a national stoppage by encouraging unofficial strikes elsewhere but matters eventually got out of hand.

One Death

By the 6th of November 1910, all pits except one had been shut down and strikers descended on the Glamorgan colliery at Llwynypia with the intention of completing the job by shutting down the electric power house. This supplied power for ventilation and pumping to five collieries and until Sunday the 6th had been manned by under managers and other officials led by the general manager Mr Leonard Llewellyn. Police were stationed inside the colliery fence and a large crowd of strikers picketed the entrance to prevent strike-breakers entering the site.

Fig. 48 Policemen guarding the Glamorgan Colliery Powerhouse – Credit, 'The Miners' by R. Page Arnot.

Scuffles took place and stones were thrown breaking all windows facing the roadway. The engine men phoned for more police and a patrol of mounted police galloped into the affray wielding their batons. Some horsemen were injured by clinker stones and the Chief Constable of Glamorgan Captain Lionel Lindsay appealed to the strikers to disperse, but without effect. Colliery fencing was then destroyed and debris littered the streets but eventually the police managed to force the strikers back into the Rhondda Valley town of Tonypandy. Around 100 casualties of strikers, policemen and the local press were left lying and bleeding by the roadside. Through it all, the colliery officials kept the machinery working. One striker Samuel Rhys a single man and a haulier working at No. 2 pit was seriously injured and taken back to his lodgings on a stretcher in the early hours of Wednesday morning. He reported that he had been knocked down by a club and was seen at 10.30am by two doctors. He was taken to the Porth Cottage hospital on the Thursday but died of his injuries the next day. At the inquest, the Coroner concluded that it could not be proved that a policeman's truncheon had caused the injury because strikers were also carrying weapons. He advised that in order to prevent further trouble, the inquest should be adjourned until the 15th of December.

Winston Churchill's involvement

On Friday the 4th of November 1910, the South Wales and Monmouthshire Coal Owners Association communicated with the Chief Constable of Glamorgan Captain Lionel Lindsay requesting adequate protection for those men willing to work and who were being intimidated by strikers. The Chief Constable then sent a request to the local military authorities for assistance and on hearing this, Mr Churchill sent the following telegram in reply to the Chief Constable during the morning of Tuesday the 8th of November 1910; *'you may give the miners the following message from me. Their best friends here are greatly distressed at the trouble which has broken out and will do their best to help them to get fair treatment. Asquith, Board of Trade wishes to see Watts Morgan with six or eight local representatives at the Board of Trade two o'clock tomorrow. But rioting must cease at once so that the inquiry shall not be prejudiced and to prevent the credit of the Rhondda Valley being injured. Confiding in the good sense of the Cambrian Combine workmen, we are holding back the soldiers for the present and sending police instead.'*

However, in the early hours of Tuesday the 8th of November 1910, a gathering in Tonypandy town square was broken up by truncheon wielding policemen and injuries were sustained on both sides. On the Tuesday evening, youths returning from a miners meeting at the Mid Rhondda Athletic ground ran riot through the streets smashing windows, wrecking and looting shops indiscriminately, anything that couldn't be carried away was strewn in the street. Rioters entered the outfitters shop of Mr Phillips throwing stock into the street and throwing lighted matches around the floor. One of the strike committee Mr W. Johns appealed three times for order in the town square but was not listened to. Police were not on the scene until 10.30pm when violence erupted as they tried to disperse the crowd with blows being struck on both sides. Eventually the mob melted away through the many side streets. One report suggested that the rioters, about a hundred in all, were strangers, mainly from Cardiff who had been drinking most of the day in the local pubs and were in no way connected with the strikers. The vast majority of striking miners were aghast at the havoc that had been wrought and as one old collier said **'Tonypandy has disgraced itself'**.

It was later acknowledged that the special train carrying the Metropolitan policemen was held up at Swindon due to a small accident. Consequently it was late in arriving in Pontypridd and the police were unable to get to Tonypandy in time to quell the rioters.

A later statement from the Home Office; *'A request was addressed by the Chief Constable of Glamorganshire to the local military authorities for the assistance of 200 cavalry and two companies of infantry in keeping order in the Cambrian Collieries. The Home Secretary in consultation with Mr Haldane decided to send instead a contingent of the Metropolitan police consisting of 70 mounted and 200 foot constables to the district to carry out the instructions of the Chief Constable under their own officers. But in consequence of later information received at the Home Office reporting continuance of the rioting, the pacific action of the Home Secretary was rendered useless and the troops were sent to the following area, as indicated in the following official message – 'Information was received at the Home Office early in the evening that though the Home Secretary's telegram was well received and the leaders of the men promised there would be no rioting, disturbances began as soon as it was dark. In these circumstances, authority was at once taken to General Macready, the officer who has been specially placed in charge of the troops at Cardiff to move the Cavalry into the disturbed districts.'*

The telegraph to General Macready on the evening of the 9th of November 1910 conveyed the message that it was desirable for him to proceed to Tonypandy that night if the emergency came to the point where the police and civil authorities should apply for the direct use of the military. *'you should then assume general control and act as you think best for the preservation of order and the prevention of bloodshed. You will at the last moment consider whether the police forces can be used any further to quell riot without actually involving the military'.*

On Wednesday morning the 9th of November 1910 the scene in Tonypandy was of utter devastation with window glass, bottle glass, tailors dummies and discarded clothing littering the street. The Council workmen were out trying to clean up the mess while shopkeepers on both sides of the street barricaded up their shopfronts with corrugated iron sheets in anticipation of further violence. Some of those wrecked shops were of Mr D.P. Jenkins, Haydn Jones general clothier, the Public Benefit Boot Co., Bristol Furnishing Co., Jones and Evans Jewellers, Prothero pork butcher,

Michnadoi Ice Cream vendor, the Home and Colonial Stores, Oliver's Boot stores and J. Phillips clothier. Damage was estimated to cost several thousands of pounds. A detachment of 200 men of the 18th Hussars rode into Tonypandy two abreast followed by an ambulance but were met with no resistance and proceeded to Llwynypia swimming baths which was converted into their barracks. The Rhondda Valley was then being patrolled by over 400 police, a detachment of Cavalry and a Company of Lancashire Fusiliers. Several patrols were sent to various villages during the day but apart from one minor disturbance, they met no further trouble.

At the Powel-Duffryn Colliery at Cwmbach in the Cynon Valley, about fifty boys and youths walked to the colliery to picket officials working there. Police had already lined the roadside and a new fence had been erected around the pit. The youths asked to speak to the officials at work but the policemen's answer was to turn a fire hose on them. The youths ran away but ran into the electrified fence connected to the dynamo at the pit power house. They then resorted to destroying the fence and throwing stones at the police who reacted by baton charging, forcing the youths along a disused canal towpath. A bridge crossed the canal at the Whitehorse Inn and at this time was crowded with villagers, including women with children watching the happenings at the colliery. As the scuffle approached the bridge, another group of police made their way to the Whitehorse Inn, entrapping those on the bridge. They were beaten back, some even falling into the canal. Most made their way to the far side of the canal which was only waist deep, suffering from bleeding skulls and the uninjured climbed the bank and threw volleys of stones at the police. Women and old men didn't escape the bludgeoning, some being chased to the doors of their homes. One sixteen year old boy had come from playing football to see what was going on and was set upon and bludgeoned about his body and was thrown into the canal. He managed to climb out but was set upon again, pleading for his life before his hand was smashed to pieces protecting his head from a blow. Other children were treated in a similar manner being thrown into the canal – it was a miracle no one lost their life. Eventually the police retreated leaving many bleeding heads lying beside the canal. Some later reports suggested that the police were 'stinking with drink' but no action was taken against this form of butchery.

On Wednesday morning the town streets of the valleys were full of subdued and sullen strikers but there were no reports of rioting. There was the isolated scuffle with police and some nasty reports of strikers attacking strike-breakers homes. During the day police were stationed at strategic points at colliery entrances and also patrolled the streets in pairs where troublemakers were moved on. At the instigation of the local magistrates, public houses were closed all day while all the military were kept in barracks. In Tonypandy after 7pm a troop of Hussars rode four abreast through the main street, sabres and rifles on display followed ominously by an ambulance.

Of serious concern was the state of some 900 horses that had been kept underground at the affected collieries and not fed for several days, caused by the pickets of strikers preventing men from descending the pits for this purpose. However some agreement between management and strikers finally allowed men to descend the pits to feed them. Assistant Manager Mr Leonard Llewellyn descended one mine and found it half flooded and had to wade waist deep to find and feed the horses. One ostler said; **'have you ever heard a horse crying? If you have, you will never forget it. It is pitiful. It was breaking my heart when they were not fed. They are very knowing, these pit ponies'.**

Friday the 11th of November saw the first issue of strike pay for the Combine employees at various stations in the valleys at the rate of 10 shillings per man which was conducted in an orderly manner and guarded by a company of Lancashire Fusiliers with fixed bayonets. Public houses closed from noon onwards.

There were several reports of sabotage of pit property in attempts to close the pits down completely. One such incident was at Llwynypia Colliery where strikers stopped the supply of water to the boilers by damming a stream on the mountainside. It was discovered in time however and the boilers were able to keep going. As a further precaution, further police and troops were drafted in and there were now 400 Cavalry, 600 Infantry, 120 mounted police and 1,800 foot police stationed at various points in the valley.

Fig. 49 Glamorgan colliery at Llwynypia – courtesy of the Peoples Collection of Wales.

Attempts were made by the Board of Trade and Coal Owners representatives in a bid to end the dispute and to secure some form of settlement with the Union representatives. But because the workmen didn't trust their representatives to make decisions on their behalf and give them plenary powers of negotiation, the meetings ended in failure.

On the night of the 21st of November 1910, serious rioting was revived when a crowd of around 1,000 strikers descended on Tonypandy railway station waiting for the train from Cardiff, supposedly bringing in blacklegs to work the Combine pits. Extra police were called in and a pitched battle took place with serious injuries received on both sides. Fearing a repeat of the night of the 8th of November 1910, town traders rushed to barricade their newly repaired shopfronts as police tried to hold the crowd from entering the streets. Eventually the Chief Constable had to call on the military at Pontypridd and around midnight the town was occupied again by Lancashire fusiliers, a West Riding Regiment and a force of Hussars. The very presence of this strong force stemmed the violence and without firing a shot, the strikers dispersed.

In the remote Little Ogmore valley was the village of Gilfach Goch where the Britannic Colliery, part of the Cambrian Combine, was the sole support for the village. When the 900 men came out on strike they left the pit to flood – the engine men who were lifting 500 gallons of water a day were compelled to leave their jobs. After a week, the pit manager, concerned that the water would threaten the workings and deprive the community of their very livelihood, attempted to fire up the boilers with the aid of several under managers under the protection of fourteen policemen. Within an hour, the power house was surrounded by hundreds of angry strikers wielding their mandrels and threatening to roll boulders down the hillside unless the manager stopped work and surrendered himself to them – which he did.

On Friday morning the 2nd of December 1910, the same community and colliery were protected by the military. In the hills were the Munster Fusiliers with fixed bayonets ready to stop any strikers approaching from Tonypandy and in the village were eighty Hussars with swords and rifles and fifty Metropolitan police with heavy truncheons. The boilers were once again fired up under the supervision of Mr Leonard Llewellyn the General Manager of the Combine and the lifting of water was again in progress. Over 500 tons of water a day had accumulated during the last month and they were lifting three tons on each hoist. Mr Llewellyn said that he hoped to save the pit and when the dispute was over, the men would thank him.

On Wednesday the 14th of December 1910, 13 miners were summoned to Pontypridd Police Court on charges of violence and intimidation towards Mr William Gould, assistant manager at the Britannic Colliery. Large crowds and demonstrators from the whole of the Combine workforce assembled at 5am at various points along the valley and at a bugle call, marched to the town preceded by bands. They carried placards resembling horses with the words *'what about the horses?'* and chanting **'are we downhearted'**, with the inevitable reply **'No'**. A crowd of around 2,000 started loud singing outside the Court and proceedings had to be halted for some time while police dealt with them. Some of the accused openly admitted they were intent on killing Mr Gould and were sent to prison for up to 14 days. Others were either fined or discharged and were carried home on the shoulders of the crowd.

Acts of indiscriminate violence against workers families caused much disapproval among the majority of the mining communities who were just decent folk struggling to keep from starvation. It seemed inconceivable that by their actions, the strikers were literally attempting to cut off their own livelihoods by wrecking the collieries, sabotaging pumping operations and preventing the feeding of the underground horses.

Violence of a personal nature was another element in this dispute and tended to happen when no help was at hand for the victims. For instance, the house of the manager of the Ely pit was attacked by pickets when only his wife and children were at home. Windows were smashed and furniture and paintings were damaged by stones. At Clydach Vale the houses of persons known to be working at the pits were tarred and painted and several men were attacked and thrown into the nearby river. In mid Rhondda a mine official's house was broken into while he was away but his wife and children were in bed. The bedclothes were stripped from them and thrown into the street where they were burnt on a bonfire made from some of their furniture. The house of Mr Fred Allen who was an official at the Llywnypia pit was broken into while he was at the power station. The strikers ransacked the house before lighting a fire, cooking some ham and left after a good meal carrying with them the fender, kitchen clock and other articles. They then marched to Pandy square where they hung the clock on the fountain as a memento. An official's wife going away by train was set upon at the station, her case broken open, contents strewn about and she was doused in flour. These indiscriminate acts continued throughout the Christmas period and into the New Year.

The advent of the new year showed promise when a Delegate meeting of the workmen of the Cambrian Combine decided to give plenary powers of negotiation to their elected representatives of the **South Wales Miners' Federation** in their talks with the Coal Owners. Their one condition was that they should be paid a minimum of 8 shillings per day.

Fig. 50 Powell Duffryn Colliery, Aberamon

At the Powell-Duffryn Collieries in the Aberdare valley, the 6,000 men who had been on strike without pay for eleven weeks, turned up for work on Monday the 2nd of January 1911. They had originally agreed to start work the previous Thursday but due to the condition of the collieries they were turned away. The management stated that the condition of the pits were the men's own fault for not allowing the men and officials to get to work to pump out of water which had made the workings dangerous and unworkable.

The annual conference of the **Miners' Federation of Great Britain** was held in London during January 1911 and they agreed to advance the **South Wales Miners' Federation** £3,000 per week to help supplement their expenses with strike pay. They also stipulated that working miners in South Wales should up their weekly levy from 3 pence to 6 pence.

Another disaster struck the Rhondda Valley on Monday morning the 23rd of January 1911 on the Taff Vale Railway at the Hopkinstown junction just outside Pontypridd when a passenger train from Treherbert ran into a stationery goods train from the Lewis-Merthyr collieries.

Fig. 51   Rail Disaster at Hopkinstown near Pontypridd, January the 23rd 1911

It happened on a bend where there were six sets of rails and the passenger train driver couldn't see the goods train because of a high bank, until it was too late. Some of the coaches were telescoped and eleven passengers were killed – three of them representatives of the striking miners who were on their way to a miners conference in Cardiff. Many were injured with some helping to rescue others trapped in the wreckage including Mr W. Brace MP, Mr Mark Harcombe, secretary of the Tonypandy strike committee and Mr Will John, Chairman of the Cambrian Combine committee. Train drivers and firemen all miraculously escaped injury but at the Inquest it appeared there had been confusion over signals between the goods driver and the signalbox and the driver took a portion of the blame for the accident.

In early February 1911 in the House of Commons, the Home Secretary Winston Churchill stated that 854 metropolitan police had been sent to the disturbed district on the 8th, 9th and 12th of November 1910 and all except 143 had now been withdrawn. Those remaining would be withdrawn by the end of the second week of February 1911 and many that had suffered injury would now go onto the sick list. They would also receive extra wages for their 'outside services' according to rank, to be paid by the Exchequer. It was later disclosed that £15,000 had been granted to them as special allowances.

On the 11th of February 1911, a Conference consisting of the two sides in the dispute and the Board of Trade representatives took place at the Engineers Institute in Cardiff and a settlement seemed likely. Assurances were given by the Employers of the Cambrian Combine that they would pay a 'fair day's pay for a fair days work' whether in normal or 'abnormal places' and if a man is not satisfied with his pay or allowances, then the area Agent would be called in to settle the matter. As to the question of a guaranteed wage, the Employers said that that issue was for the coalfield as a whole to decide and not this particular dispute. The men's representatives would have to ballot their members before any confirmation could be given.

On Thursday evening the 23rd of March 1911, rioting took place at Blaenclydach where seventeen policemen were seriously injured. Rioting broke out as it was realised that some members of the **'Fed'** had gone back to work at the Cambrian Colliery and the crowd reached the pit before the police could stop them. Some charged up the hillside and started to roll large boulders down into the colliery buildings doing a large amount of damage. When the police eventually arrived from Tonypandy, they were met with a barriage of stone throwing men and women. When they failed to break up the rioters, the police divided their forces and with a flanking move up the hillside, managed to break up the strikers into a hasty retreat into Tonypandy.

Overnight 200 extra police were drafted in from other counties to guard the colliery and the next day at a mass open air meeting at the mid Rhondda football field, the miners protested at their Executive's decision to call for a ballot which had been arranged for the Saturday morning and passed a resolution condemning their action. They then all marched to Clydach Vale where, in the afternoon a gang of men invaded the butcher's shop of Mr Jones in the Clydach road, throwing all the meat into the road and setting fire to paperwork. The stables and slaughterhouse was burnt to the ground after releasing the animals and when the police arrived, they were unable to douse the flames but were able to stop them spreading to other premises. Not satisfied with their work, the crowd then seized the butcher's two carts, dragged them up the mountainside and let them roll down into the already blazing buildings. The attack was provoked by the rumour that the butcher's brother had helped the police the night before by leading them up a path on the mountainside that wasn't picketed by the strikers which helped the police in quelling the nights' riots. As it turned out, the rumour was unfounded but the value of the destruction was estimated to be over £800.

From there, the rioters made their way on up Clydach Vale where they attacked another shop belonging to Messrs Shears and Co. confectioners where they broke windows and again threw the shop contents into the street, some carrying away some of the stock. Later a detachment of Munster Fusiliers arrived and the crowds dispersed. In the midst of this rioting, Mr W.K. Harvey MP and Mr T. Ashton, two members of the Miners Federation were in Tonypandy making arrangements for the Saturday ballot and inevitably were caught up the demonstrations. Mr Harvey declared that he had not been treated that badly in his whole life while the local traders expressed their regret and blamed the riots on an insignificant section of strikers.

However, as 250 more police were drafted in from neighbouring counties to quell any further disturbances, the ballot did take place on Saturday the 25th of March 1911. The result was an overwhelming majority vote against accepting the proposed deal.

Voting result was;

For the settlement 309,
Against 7,091,
Majority against .... 6,782.

More rioting followed with suspected blacklegs being the targets and again in Clydach Vale, a man with a revolver and truncheon was attacked and badly beaten before escaping.

The press were now reporting the need for an arbitrator to settle the wages dispute at the Cambrian pits otherwise there was a great risk of a national stoppage. The miners themselves had pledged to return to work on the Bute seam for a trial period of twelve months at a daily rate of not less than 6s. 9d. But of course, the Employers openly rejected this as a blatant condition which prevented a just settlement between the two sides. A special conference of the **MFGB** was held in London on the 25th of April 1911 to discuss both the South Wales situation and Mr Churchill's **Mines Regulation Bill.** The two delegates who visited Tonypandy to set up the ballot gave their report and it was agreed the following day that the question of arbitration should be considered and put to the Employers as a means of settling the dispute. Inevitably, the Employers openly rejected this suggestion but were willing to discuss the dispute with representative of the **MFGB.**

Further rioting took place on the 4th of May 1911 at Blaenclydach where hostility towards the strike-breakers appeared to take on a more sinister approach. Strikers waylaid a strike-breaker on his way home from the pit, covered him in a white shirt and marched him at the head of the crowd towards Tonypandy. They were confronted by a detachment of police who managed to rescue the man but bloody scuffles took place before the rioters dispersed through the side streets where they pelted the police with stones. Both sides received injuries – a rioter was hit on the head by a stone thrown by a comrade and six policemen were injured including a Superintendant and two Inspectors.

A new initiative in the dispute took place on Monday the 15th of May 1911 when representatives of both Employers and men met in London. This was the third time they had met and after a three hour session, terms for a provisional settlement were agreed. It had to be put to the Executive committee of the **MFGB**, the Executive committee of the **SWMF** and to the Monmouthshire and South Wales Coal Owners and then finally to the men for approval. It was further understood that should the agreement be refused by the men, the **MFGB** would withdraw the £3,000 weekly support and also the levy from the men still at work. The proposed deal included a one year trial period working the Bute seam and paying the men just over two shillings per ton and taking into account working in 'abnormal places' where coal cannot be cut. It also allowed for the promise to raise any shortfall in wages up to the minimum already agreed within the coalfield.

The terms were unanimously agreed at a meeting of the **MFGB** but there were violent scenes at the Cardiff meeting of the **SWMF** where William Abraham (Mabon) their President, urged the Conference to support their leaders who had secured the best possible terms. Even so, the 288 delegates who represented 138,171 miners unanimously rejected the proposals and those delegates from the Rhondda District walked out in disgust at the proposed terms and vowed to fight to the bitter end. A resolution was eventually passed urging the **MFGB** at their general conference in June 1911 to consider the question of a minimum wage of 8 shillings a day for every collier and 5 shillings for every unskilled worker and to bear in mind the miners resolve to call for a national strike should their demands not be met.

The dispute had gone on for nine months with no signs of a settlement. Thousands of families were reduced to starvation levels, shopkeepers had either been reduced to ruin or had their properties destroyed by rioters, landlords were getting no rent and the loss to the coal trade was estimated to have been in the region of £2,000,000.

On Saturday the 3rd of June 1911, the General Secretary of the **MFGB** Mr Thomas Ashton issued a private open circular accusing some of the South Wales miners' leaders of being anarchists who did not want a settlement of the dispute but instead insisted on calling for the enactment of Rule 20 which called for a general strike. He said that the latest settlement terms were exactly what the men had originally asked for and now they were afraid to accept it. They were now asking for something completely different by way of a minimum wage with the threat of a general strike if they didn't get their way. In another open letter to Mr T. Richards MP Secretary of the **SWMF**, Mr Ashton indicated that if attempts were made to pay the miners less than 6s 9d per day, the miners would be justified in appealing to the **MFGB**. By way of a contradiction, Mr D.A. Thomas MP Director of the Cambrian Combine made it clear that the Company would not only attempt to pay less than 6s. 9d. per day but that they were not intending to guarantee to pay the men a minimum wage other than through the existing price list. President of the **SWMF** William Abraham (Mabon) stated that the demand for a national strike in order to get a guaranteed minimum wage was; '*a policy of despair and starvation which cannot but fail.*'

On Tuesday the 13th of June 1911, the **MFGB** held a special conference in London to specifically discuss the situation in the South Wales dispute. 170 Delegates representing 602,000 miners attended and after a free discussion, a resolution was passed stating that in regard to the settlement terms agreed between parties but rejected by the miners, the conference would no longer accept responsibility in reference to the dispute.

The voting result was;

In favour	465,000 men,
Against	137,000 men,
Majority in favour	**328,000 men.**

In accordance with a previous statement the £3,000 per week support for the South Wales dispute would be withdrawn at the end of the month.

On the 26th of June, the **SWMF** held a meeting in Cardiff to discuss the decision of the **MFGB**, William Abraham MP presiding. After lengthy discussions a resolution was passed stating that the assurances given previously by Mr D.A. Thomas MP gave no monetary promises and Mr Ashton's letter gave only an assumption that a minimum of 6s. 9d. per day could be earned should they accept the deal. Also, to make representations to the **MFGB** to continue their support of £3,000 per week at their next Annual Conference in London on the 28th of July 1911. And so the dispute continued.

On Monday the 10th of July 1911, the **SWMF** issued their Manifesto which tended to suggest that the National Federation did not fully understand the situation in South Wales and would now campaign for a National minimum wage of 8 shillings a day instead of their original claim for payment in 'abnormal places'. This detailed document was circulated to all the coalfields in England and Scotland in the hope of securing a favourable vote at the next Annual General meeting of the **MFGB** in July. The **SWMF** also wrote to the secretary of the **MFGB** urging that the question of the Cambrian strike and the National action concerning the minimum wage should be added to the agenda for the meeting on the 28th of July 1911. Unfortunately however, the Executive of the **MFGB** issued a statement refusing to allow the Cambrian dispute to be discussed.

The Cambrian men were determined in their resolve to secure a minimum wage although they and their families were on the fringes of starvation. The Union funds were exhausted and to continue the fight, the levy of 4 shillings a month for every working miner would have to be increased. The Scottish miners refused to strike in support of their South Wales colleagues and the **MFGB** had abandoned their financial support. The only way they thought they could achieve their aim was by way of a National Strike or at least a South Wales Strike in favour of a minimum weekly wage. The so-called 'anarchists' still insisted that either the **MFGB** or the **SWMF** enact rule 20 and call a National strike for a minimum wage.

However, in early August 1911, Mr D.A. Thomas MP hinted in an interview that he would be prepared to hold meetings with the workmen's representatives with a view of ending the dispute. The Conciliation Board consisting of men and Coal Owners representatives then held a meeting where the Owners informed the men's representatives that they would accept a return to work on the terms agreed to in October 1910 or in May 1911, whichever the men decided upon.

The Executive Council of the **SWMF** met in Cardiff on the 14th of August 1911 to consider the proposals which met with hostility from some members of the Council who still insisted that the only way forward was through a National Strike. This was eventually put to the vote and unanimously rejected. It was then agreed that to continue the Cambrian dispute would be futile and recommended that the men return to work as soon as the pits were back in working order.

And so, at a mass meeting of around 7,000 Cambrian men, held in Tonypandy on the morning of the 17th of August 1911, it was decided by a show of hands to return to work on the terms of the May 1911 agreement.

The struggle for a minimum wage for miners continued from a section of the South Wales miners who organised a Strike Committee and issued a Manifesto demanding strike action. This was also being echoed by other coalfields such as the Lancashire and Cheshire Federation who stated that they would be supported by other Federations when the time came to take action.

According to local folklore, Winston Churchill was labelled a *'villain'* and *'an enemy of the miners'* and was accused of sending in the military to quell the rioting. The military were also said to have fired on the strikers and been responsible for several miners' deaths.

All is untrue.

What is true is that the military were called in by the Chief Constable of Glamorgan Captain Lionel Lindsay and on hearing this, Winston Churchill took advice from the War Office before sending in any reinforcements to the area. He did however send 270 Metropolitan Policemen but held back the military that had already been requested by Lindsay.

All injuries during the dispute were either inflicted by the baton wielding Police or by stones and other missiles thrown by the strikers. No shots were fired and no bayonet charges took place. One miner died of head injuries during the riots, possibly caused by a truncheon blow. Property damage was the result of rioting by strikers which also included colliery damage that prolonged the eventual return to work.

Chapter 15
1911 – Forest of Dean
The Idea for a Dilke Memorial Hospital

Firstly, while the Cambrian dispute had still not been resolved and at a time when the coal trade was just picking up after a long spell of short work, six weeks of heavy rainfall caused severe flooding to several Forest collieries, some of which had to close temporarily. The Norchard and Wallsend Collieries were at a standstill and Cannop and Foxes Bridge were severely hampered when existing pumps could not cope with the deluge. 200 men at Norchard and 100 at Wallsend were out of work for two weeks and it took several more weeks before more powerful pumps could deal with the situation.

During his round of speeches to the Lodges, Mr Rowlinson remarked on the difficulties that water presented in the Forest pits and the risk it presented to the lives of the miners and also the wages lost as in the present situation. He suggested that the Crown, who was in effect the landlord of the Forest of Dean, should take on the responsibility of controlling water levels. Whether it was a *'tongue in cheek'* remark or not, he continued to suggest that they should follow the example set by South Staffordshire and have a drainage scheme. Water could then be ejected into the Wye in the west and into the Severn in the east. If the Crown could not finance the project then let Sir Charles Dilke go to the Treasury where they usually found cash for all manner of projects.

At the Coal Owners and Crown Office meeting at the Speech House, the question of water difficulties was raised by Mr F. Brain and it was also suggested that Mr Rowlinson's remarks on the subject, should be seriously considered.

Death of Sir Charles Dilke

However and very sadly, shortly after successfully defending his seat as Liberal M.P. for the Forest of Dean in December last, Sir Charles Dilke sadly passed away in the early hours of Thursday morning the 26th of January1911 aged 67. He had apparently showed some signs of illness during his election campaign and had decided to have a short holiday in Paris after winning his seat. He returned to his home at 76 Sloane Street, London on Friday the 20th of January 1911 and took to his bed straight away. He was constantly attended by two nurses and a Doctor but passed away at 4.45am on the Thursday morning. News travelled fast to the Forest of Dean via the early morning mail train and the calamitous news could scarcely be believed by his political supporters. The official news came during the morning with a wire from Mr H.K.Hudson, Sir Charles' private secretary to Mr John Cooksey of Cinderford, the Honourable Secretary of the Forest of Dean Liberal Council. He in turn passed the sad news on to the 20 polling Districts that made up the Constituency and the news appeared to paralyse everything. Work came to a standstill and blinds were drawn in private homes and businesses throughout the Forest. His affection for the people of the Forest of Dean went without saying as both he and his wife were regular visitors to events including the **Miners' Annual Demonstrations** which he always made a special effort to attend each July.

At Election time, Sir Charles made his base at the Victoria Hotel in Newnham and always covered as much of the Forest as was possible to meet as many people as he could, either by carriage and pair or latterly by motor conveyance. He had a special interest in the Forest of Dean miners and their struggle for better wages and conditions and this was reflected in his actions within Parliament on social reform. He was instrumental in legalising the Unions, the introduction of the eight hour day for miners and improving working conditions. He strongly supported the redistribution of votes as seen in the Third Reform Act of 1884 which gave the vote to a much larger section of the population as did his work on women's suffrage.

Chapter 10 of this publication describes a large part of Sir Charles' life but a lot still remains untold. For instance he was a prolific writer and an expert on military matters and foreign affairs as well as presiding over several Royal Commissions. After getting his Degrees at Trinity Hall, Cambridge, he travelled around the World and on his return stood as Liberal candidate for the Borough of Chelsea and won the seat. During the years 1869, 1870 and 1871 he travelled throughout the Russian Empire, gaining his knowledge on foreign affairs. His writings included 'The Present Position of European Politics' 1887, 'The British Army' 1888, 'Problem of Greater Britain' 1890, Imperial Defence and British Empire' 1898 and 'Memoir of Lady Dilke' 1905. He was an accomplished rower and was often seen on the river Thames in a paired boat.

His body was taken to Holy Trinity Church in Sloane Street on Monday the 30th of January 1911 where a memorial service took place at midday. The coffin, covered in a purple and gold cloth was laid before the alter and the service was conducted by the Rev. H.R. Gamble, Archdeacon Escreet, Archdeacon Bevan and the Rev. Percy Dearmer. Chief mourner was Sir Charles' niece Miss Gertrude Tuckwell as Sir Charles' son, Sir Wentworth Dilke was unable to attend due to being in foreign parts. As can be imagined, the service was attended by the great and the good from all walks of life and from all corners of the Globe. The Liberal Party and the Prime Minister sent their representatives and the Forest of Dean was represented by Messrs S.J.Elsom – Yorkley, J.Cooksey – Cinderford, C.Staley – Micheldean, G.H.Rowlinson – Miners Agent, B.H.Taylor – Coleford, C. Hirst – Pillowell, J.L.Stelfox and H.Davis – Newent, S.Jordan – Election Agent and J.Smith Charley – Blakeney.

Wreaths were received from many Political and Public Associations including many from Trade Unions and ordinary working class manufacturing Companies. Afterwards the cortege conveyed his remains to the Golders Green Crematorium for a private cremation as per his wishes and his ashes contained in a bronze urn were interred in the family vault at Kelsall Green Cemetary.

The question then arose as to who was to succeed Sir Charles as the next Member of Parliament for the Forest of Dean Constituency. The **MFGB** suggested that a Labour Candidate should be selected and at a special conference of the Labour Party, they were of the same opinion.

After a tetchy meeting in Parkend of the various local Trade Union branches, the name of the proposed Labour candidate Mr Robert Smillie, Vice President of the **MFGB** was eventually withdrawn. This was after representations from Mr Rowlinson and Mr Martin Perkins – both strong Liberal supporters who argued that a third candidate would weaken the Liberal vote and strengthen the Conservative and Unionist vote. And so the Bye Election was fought as a straight fight between Liberal and Conservative Unionists. The Conservatives adopted Mr D.H.Kidd who fought Sir Charles at the December 1910 Election and the Liberals eventually adopted Mr Harry Webb after the withdrawal of several local candidates.

The Bye Election took place on Friday the 24th of February 1911, the results being declared as usual on the steps of the Newnham Town Hall at 12.50pm.

The results were;

Mr Harry Webb – Liberal 6,174,
Mr David Kyd – Conservative and Unionist 3,106,
Liberal majority of .... 3,068.

After the usual civilities from both candidates, Mr Webb made his way to the Victoria Hotel where he made a speech from an upper window – as was the custom of Sir Charles Dilke. He thanked his staff and all who had faith and voted for him and made some fun of his opponent who, he said had been beaten twice and probably wouldn't come back for a third beating. Mrs Webb was also encouraged to speak and thanked all who had supported her husband in the fight. She said she had seen her husband lose the seat in South Herefordshire twice before and knows how it feels like to lose an election.

Mr Henry (Harry) Webb (1866 – 1940)

Henry Webb was born in Hereford and educated in Cardiff and Paris. He joined consulting Engineers Forster, Brown and Rees and received a sound training in colliery affairs before joining the Deep Navigation Colliery at Treharris. In 1896 that colliery came under the auspicies of the Ocean Coal Company. He eventually rose to become their colliery manager under his Uncle who was a Director of Ocean and later moved to another of Ocean's collieries in the Rhonda Valley. In 1898 he was appointed Company Secretary and on the death of his Uncle, he took a seat on the Board.

Fig. 52 Harry Webb – as Lieutenant-Colonel Henry Webb, later Sir Henry Webb 1st Bt.

Being a wealthy man, Webb had many outside activities including a keen interest in agriculture that led him to becoming a life member of the Royal

Agricultural Society and the 'Shorthorn Society'. He was also a member of the Glamorgan Chamber of Agriculture, Vice President of both the Dog Fanciers Association and the Glamorgan Beekeepers Association. He was also a generous donor to the Cardiff Infirmary and served as a member of the Council of the University College of South Wales. He was seen as very knowledgeable on colliery matters, having trained as a mining engineer and especially with regard to the deep seams. He expressed his agreement with Mr Rowlinson that something had to be done to alleviate the water problems in the Forest of Dean collieries which the Crown Authorities should address.

At this time, it was reported in one of the local newspapers that trouble was brewing at the Flour Mill Colliery over the employment of non-union men. Mr Rowlinson took exception to this report stating that the correspondent was incorrect and that the 'so called' dispute had been settled amicably and that there had been no strike action taken. In a number of local meetings, Mr Rowlinson said he was pleased with the reaction by the Deputy Gaveller Mr Westgarth Forster-Brown to his concerns over the flooding issue and it was agreed that much of the flooding was caused by 'land water'. It was suggested that if, during the summer months, the house coal colliers could be put to work clearing out the drainage ditches, it would prevent flooding at a time when coal was needed.

Mr Churchill's **Mines Regulations Bill** was progressing through Parliament but feelings within the Forest of Dean were mixed. The whole idea of this Bill was to amend and strengthen previous legislation relating to mine safety and for the ordinary miner it was welcome news. Although not strictly related to the Forest pits, the ever present dangers of fire damp in many of Britain's collieries was considered and the need to set up rescue stations at each and every colliery was given priority. That meant that Colliery Owners were responsible for establishing rescue stations with trained staff and regularly maintained rescue equipment such as breathing apparatus. Other measures under consideration were that colliery managers, deputies, firemen and shot-firers were to be suitably qualified with certificates of competence, boys under the age of 14 not to be employed underground and the welfare of pit ponies. Naturally, the Coal Owners were largely against such regulations arguing it would increase the cost of coal by 3 pence a ton. Forest of Dean Coal Owners canvassed for an exemption due to the fact that no gas was present in the Forest pits and some of the provisions of the Bill were unnecessary. This was supported by the new MP Mr Harry Webb but in December, the exemption was excluded from the Bill on the grounds that coal dust could cause pit explosions as well as gas and that the Bill would stand. Subsequently, the **Coal Mines Act 1911** received its Royal Assent on the 16th of December 1911.

The coal trade in the Forest of Dean was going through another slack summer period with miners on half time. On the 1st of June 1911 the Joint Wages Board decided to reduce the miners' wages by 5% and also the price of house coal by 1 shilling per ton. This was on the understanding that it applied until the 1st of September 1911 and if trade increased at that time, the wages would be restored.

Once again the miners held their **Annual Demonstration** at the Speech House field on Saturday the 8th of July 1911. Chaired by Mr W. Smith, President of the **FODMA**, the guests included Mr Harry Webb MP, Mr Charlie Stanton, Aberdare Agent, Mr Fred Maddison, ex Labour MP for Burnley and Mr G. Rowlinson, miners' Agent. Unlike any previous Demonstrations, this one turned out to be a very acrimonious one. Fiery Charlie Stanton in his speech criticised the old leadership of the miners and clashed with the views of Fred Maddison who deplored Stanton's critical remarks that were egged on by a small section of the crowd. Stanton's cause had always been for a national minimum wage which he believed could only be achieved by a nationwide strike. Words such as *'traitors'* were used and Mr Maddison called Stanton's speech disloyal to the members of the Federation who were probably older and wiser than he was. This ding dong battle went on for some time and amid cheers and jeers and calls for order from the Chair, a resolution was proposed by Mr F Iles from Bream and seconded by Mr E. Williams from Lydbrook offering Mr Webb a hearty welcome to his first Demonstration and hoped that his work and influence in Parliament would be for the good of the Forest of Dean miners and workers. Embarrassingly for many of those present, the resolution was rejected and Mr Webb was asked to respond. Mr Webb spoke eloquently and said that it was unusual to reply to a resolution that didn't have the good fortune to pass but nevertheless he acknowledged that there was an element that was unfriendly to him but that he was not unfriendly to them. He was asked by Mr Stanton about his connection with a certain colliery Company in South Wales and his membership of the Coal Owners Association. He said that was true and that he had done a great deal to bring industrial peace to the South Wales coalfield and that anyone who said that he was connected with causing unemployment was telling an untruth. Mr Rowlinson then moved a vote of thanks to the speakers but remarked that the conduct of certain elements had been disgraceful but the meeting concluded to loud cheers for Mr Stanton.

It was now acknowledged that since the recent Election there was a strong section of opinion that favoured a Labour candidate to represent the Forest of Dean at a future General Election. At a meeting held in Coleford in July 1911 it was agreed to the formation of a Forest of Dean Labour Party and the National Executive had convened a conference of Trade Union representatives and other Labour organisations to take place at Parkend with a view to that aim.

Miners meetings were also called around the District to assess the case for Labour representation, each being chaired by Mr Rowlinson. He acknowledged that there were sufficient grounds to put the matter before the men and he would report his findings back to the Executive Committee at the end of the year. However he was at pains to point out what it meant financially to support their own candidate which they would have to pay for themselves as Union funds could not be used for electioneering purposes

The Idea for a Dilke Memorial Hospital
Since the death of Sir Charles Dilke, suggestions had been made as to the erection of a Hospital to his memory and a Provisional Committee met in Gloucester on the 28th of September 1911 Presided over by Sir William Wedderburn to consider the matter. The Lord Lieutenant of Gloucestershire Earl Beauchamp K.C.M.G. consented to act as Chairman of a General Committee and Sir William Wedderburn agreed to act as his Deputy. Mr Harry Webb MP volunteered to act as Treasurer of the Fund which he said had already attracted several substantial donations.

A further meeting at the Cinderford Town Hall in December 1911 which included three local Doctors and other representatives of the District considered how to make Sir Charles Dilke's memorial most beneficial to the community. It was pointed out that the suggestion for a local Hospital had already received wide approval and seeing that the nearest General Hospital was twenty miles away at Gloucester, it would be fitting for the working population of the Forest of Dean to have a new facility on their doorstep. Speech House had been suggested as a suitable location but it was argued that either Coleford or Cinderford should be preferable as Lydney Cottage Hospital was already serving the western side of the Forest. Only the local Doctors made objections to the Hospital idea, stating that the purchase of one or more motor ambulances would serve the community better.

However, the overwhelming majority of those present, preferred the establishment of a Hospital. A figure of £3,000 was suggested as a possible amount needed for work to begin and Mr Webb the Treasurer stated that £900 already stood in the fund and further amounts were promised to bring the total up to £1,050. At the end, a sub committee was formed of local dignitaries including Mr Martin Perkins, Mr S.J. Elsom, Mr T.H. Deakin, Mr G. Rowlinson, Mr F. Brain, Mr G. Ayland, Mr J. Cooksey and the three Forest Doctors with a view to making a decision as to the best scheme to adopt and to report in the New Year to the Executive Committee.

Fight for a minimum wage

Nationally, pressure for a minimum wage for miners was being applied to the **MFGB** from many mining Districts including the Lancashire and Cheshire and particularly the **South Wales Federation** who had just been involved in a long and acrimonious strike over the matter. At their Annual Conference at Southport on the 1st of October 1911, the **MFGB** were asked to consider a resolution invoking rule 20 (a National stoppage) if all other avenues of negotiation had failed in the fight for a minimum wage for miners. They believed they had sufficient support from Durham and Northumberland and Scottish Federations to pass the resolution.

So, the Annual Conference was under great pressure to resolve this issue and in his Presidential address, Mr Enoch Edwards M.P. had considerable sympathy for the call for a minimum weekly wage and agreed that it should happen sooner rather than later. However, he said that at that time there was no need to plunge the nation into a strike when there were intelligent men on both sides of the argument who should be able to settle the matter. There were four resolutions on the agenda calling for a minimum wage and a national stoppage to secure it. The question was, how much was considered to be the **'minimum wage'** with the various Federations at odds with each other over what the figure might be. Suggestions varied from 6 shillings per day to 8 shillings per day with other concessions thrown in. In the end, the Conference passed a resolution requiring that each Federated District negotiate with their employers to secure a District minimum wage for every man and boy employed in their pits. If those negotiations failed, then another meeting of the **MFGB** would be held on the 14th of November 1911 to decide on whether to take national action. This led each District free to negotiate its own demands for a minimum wage for each class of workman.

Some Districts were already in negotiation with their employers or Conciliation Boards to the same effect and were close to settlements but the danger came from South Wales. There, the Coal-Owners had consistently refused to negotiate a minimum wage and Conference agreed that if any large District failed to effect an agreement by the 14th of November, they would be likely to support a call for a national stoppage. This would be put to the ballot and if the result was in favour of a strike, then one month notices to terminate contracts would start from the 1st of December 1911.

In view of that situation, a subtle change to the wording of the 20th rule making it into the 21st rule was also agreed, providing for aggressive as well as defensive action when a District is attacked on wages or conditions of labour.

In the Forest of Dean
As good as their word, the Joint Wages Board met on Friday the 1st of September 1911 and due to the increase in trade, wages were restored to the pre June 1911 level.

Pit Stop
There were disputes in mid September 1911 at two Forest Collieries. At the Flour Mill Colliery near Bream, around 700 men and boys walked out in a dispute over prices being paid for the splitting of pillars of coal.

Unable to resolve the dispute within the local Union, at the Southport conference of the **MFGB**, two of their prominent leaders agreed to come to the Forest of Dean to assist Mr Rowlinson and the Executive committee of the **FODMA** in a bid to settle the differences between management and men which had been going on for three weeks. Mr William Abraham (Mabon) and Mr Herbert Smith arrived at the Speech House on Saturday the 7th of October 1911 and met with the **FODMA** Executive that evening.

They eventually formulated an agreement which they thought would be acceptable to both sides and it was agreed to call a meeting of strikers on the Monday morning to put to them their new proposals. On that Monday morning a large crowd of strikers gathered to welcome Messrs Abraham and Smith to the Forest and after they addressed the meeting, their proposals were unanimously accepted. It was also agreed that Mr

Rowlinson should open negotiations immediately with the management and to let them know the terms on which the men would return to work. This was eventually arranged with the employers who accepted the terms proposed and 700 men and boys returned to work.

At the Cannop Colliery Mr James Sayes, a checkweighman was dismissed from his job for encouraging 300 men to 'down tools' and walk out in relation to the continued employment of 17 non Union men, contrary to their contract of employment. The employers brought a Court Action against Mr Sayes for impeding and interrupting the working of the mine by inciting the men to 'down tools' and break their terms of employment. The Court sat on the 10th of October 1911 at Coleford Police Court where Mr John Joynes the Colliery manager also applied for the removal of Mr Sayes from employment at the pit.

It was claimed that the pit employed virtually all Union men but some had got behind with their fees and that Mr Sayes had approached the management asking that those men be removed from employment. It was also claimed that Mr Sayes had put a notice on the pit-head calling a meeting to decide what to do if the management didn't remove the men. The result of this meeting eventually led to the men agreeing to 'down tools' and walk out.

Mr Sayes denied some of these accusations but nevertheless the Court found the case proved and Sayes was ordered to be removed from the office of checkweighman at the colliery. The **FODMA** offered the management guarantees that the men would return to work on the same terms as were originally agreed subject to certain points of dispute being sent to arbitration. And so, after three weeks, the strike was at an end and the men returned to work on Monday the 16th of October 1911.

Industrial unrest was rife at this time, with the Cambrian Combine strike in South Wales just settled but with other colliery strikes happening up and down the country. There was a threatened engine keepers strike in Scotland, men were on strike at Lofthouse Colliery in West Yorkshire over wages and also at Viewpark Colliery, Uddingston, near Glasgow. 800 men were out at the Waterloo Main Colliery near Leeds and 2,000 men were idle at the Mansfield Colliery part of the Bolsover Company. Men were on strike at the Cakemore Colliery near Blackheath over wages not paid for work done. In Lanarkshire 5,000 miners voted to strike in support of a nearby dispute.

There was a General Transport strike centred on Liverpool that involved the four rail Unions and by August over 70,000 workers were on strike including the Dockers and sailors. Troops in the form of the 18th Hussars were called out as rioting took place and two rioters were shot dead.

In Bermondsey, over 15,000 women in confectionery and jam factories went on strike in August 1911 over wages and working conditions aided by the National Federation of Women Workers (**NFWW**). Even schoolchildren went on strike in September against corporal punishment and poor conditions.

The **MFGB** Conference meeting on the 14th and 15th of November 1911 held at the Westminster Palace Hotel was attended by 159 Delegates representing up to 700,000 men. This meeting was arranged to consider invoking Rule 21 – a nationwide strike – but after many hours of deliberation an amendment to a motion calling for an immediate ballot was put to the vote.

The result was;
For a ballot 238,000,
Against a ballot .... 366,000.

So the ballot call was defeated. Instead it was finally agreed to postpone the immediate possibility of a strike and to re-open negotiations with Coal Owners in each District. Each District was to formulate its own wage structure for a minimum wage based on the conditions prevalent to that District and to negotiate on that basis.

Conference then agreed to meet to consider the results on the 20th of December 1911 in the hope that success could be achieved without resorting to drastic action. At that meeting on the 20th of December 1911, it was decided to call a ballot on the minimum wage issue which would take place over the three days of January 10th, 11th and 12th 1912. If the ballot results were in a two thirds majority, then notices would be given in every District to terminate contracts as from the end of February 1912.

The **Forest of Dean Miners' Association** decided to issue a statement as to how matters stood in the Forest of Dean. They stated that there had been meetings between the Employers and men's representatives following the **MFGB** meeting at Southport that dealt with the minimum wage question and that some reports had been misunderstood in the Forest of Dean. The correct situation was that the minimum wage must be the present recognised Standard of each District. The Employers in their response have said that they were not prepared to grant a minimum wage for all workmen but were prepared to consider the question of 'abnormal places' and as far as they could, would make up the wages of those men who, through no fault of their own, could not make their wage. They expressed the opinion that if they had to grant all that had been asked, it would mean closing every colliery in the District.

Accidents/Fatalities

On Thursday the 13th of July 1911 at the Princess Royal Park Gutter Colliery near Whitecroft, Mr Richard Roberts aged 30 a single man from Bream was killed by a fall of earth from the roof while walking his horse and water cart down a Dipple. No explanation could be given for the fall which completely buried Mr Roberts and a verdict of suffocation was given as the cause of death. He was one of a family of fourteen.

On Thursday the 27th of July 1911 at the Trafalgar Colliery near Brierley, Mr Moses Walkley aged 49 a married man from Ruspidge was seriously injured while employed as foreman pit Carpenter. He was working with his son Mr Herbert Samuel Walkley, also a carpenter who said that his father was in good health. At around 11 o'clock they were in the process of moving a 'principal' – a wooden frame weighing between 16 and 18 cwt used for carrying weights - which was standing upright on two flatbed trolleys. The trolleys were on a tramway and drawn by a horse. Mr Walkley senior and another man were on one side of the trolleys holding the 'principal' steady while Mr Walkley junior and another man were on the other side. They had moved the load about 150 yards when the 'principal' fell over towards Mr Walkley senior. The frame had an internal space which fell over Mr Walkley senior and he was not hurt but the horse carried on, dragging the frame over his left foot. He was freed and the foot was badly crushed and bleeding. Nearby ambulancemen were called and managed to stop the bleeding and two Doctors were called and dressed the wound, one of them taking him to Gloucester Royal Infirmary. Dr W. Taylor, House Surgeon at the hospital said that on admission, Mr Walkley had lost a lot of blood and was in a weak state. There were several wounds to the left foot but they were dressed and the bleeding stopped. Unfortunately, it did not progress well and there were signs of blood poisoning. He gradually sank and despite all efforts, Mr Walkley died on the 1st of August 1911. The House Surgeon commented that if the deceased had been treated locally, his life may have been saved and the Coroner emphasised the need for a small hospital in the Forest. A verdict of blood poisoning resulting from a wound to the foot caused by the 'principal' falling on it was recorded.

On Friday the 25th of August 1911 at the Eastern United Colliery near Ruspidge, Mr James Barker aged 28 a single man from Blakeney Hill was killed by a fall of earth from the roof. He had been working with buttyman Mr James Virgo and Mr Walter Collis and when they started work they said everything was fine and timbered correctly. Just before 1 o'clock, Mr Virgo, who had gone to fetch a stick heard someone shout **'run, I believe Barker's killed'**. He ran back and found between two and three tons of earth from the roof had fallen on him. With assistance they managed to remove the earth and found Mr Barker's body but he was already dead. Ten minutes earlier, a shot had been fired and Mr Virgo thought that it could have caused an unseen slip which later collapsed. A verdict was recorded of death by fracture of the spinal column near the neck and to suffocation caused by the fall of earth.

On Thursday the 31st of October 1911 at the Crump Meadow Colliery, 39 year old John Waite from Horsepool Bottom near Micheldean was seriously injured by a fall of rock while working as a fettler in the south Starkey road. At the time of the accident, the roadway was being widened and a corner was being straightened. Waite had holed 18 inches under a rock when an unseen rock broke away from behind and fell on him. Fellow workmen released him in 20 minutes but he had suffered severe back injuries and when brought to the surface, Dr Mitchell sent him to Gloucester Royal Infirmary where he remained for the rest of the year – see 1912 Accidents/Fatalities.

On Thursday the 21st of December 1911 at the Trafalgar Colliery near Brierley, Mr Thomas Gunter aged 27, a married man with two children was killed when a cart of timber broke away on an incline knocked him over causing severe head injuries. It was recorded that everything was in order and no blame should be attached to anyone. A verdict of accidental death was recorded.

Chapter 16
Pit Stop - The 1912 Strike
The Minimum Wage Act

In the run-up to the National vote in January 1912, Miners' Association meetings were held throughout the Forest of Dean with Mr Rowlinson laying out the current situation in their own District. At a meeting in Cinderford Town Hall on Monday evening the 8th of January 1912 he emphasised the position of the Employers in not being able to concede what had been asked of them but were prepared to consider alternatives on 'abnormal places'. Other matters discussed were the Compensation agreement, the Insurance Act and the possibility of a new Hospital. Regards the latter he said that a secret benefactor had offered £1,000 to the fund if the public could find another £1,000 and he hoped that could be done. A resolution in favour of a Dilke Memorial Hospital was unanimously adopted.

At another meeting at Two Bridges on Saturday evening the 13th of January 1912, Mr Rowlinson expressed his disappointment that a certain newspaper had seen fit to leak the results of the Forest of Dean vote before the official declaration and that regardless of the local figures, they would eventually all be pooled to come to a final decision. He said that he was not in favour of a national strike and hoped that an understanding could be achieved before too long as the day men were already on a minimum wage and it wasn't too much to ask for the Employers to safeguard the wages of the underground workers.

Meanwhile the Forest of Dean Colliery Owners held a meeting at the Lydney Dock offices of the Parkend and New Fancy Colliery Co. on Monday evening the 15th of January 1912. They decided that in view of the way the balloting for the minimum wage was being reported and the fact that the South Wales Owners had already decided to substantially increase their coal prices, they in turn had decided to increase their house coal prices by 2 shillings per ton and other grades accordingly. It was also agreed that in accordance with the current 'sliding scale' agreement, they would increase the miners' wages by 5% per 1 shilling increase, meaning an increase of 10% - all as from Tuesday the 16th of January 1912.

Very inclement weather in January may have contributed to the poor turnout of miners in the Forest of Dean on the ballot to decide whether or not to have a National strike for a minimum wage for underground workers. Voting days of the 10th, 11th and 12th of January 1912 were preceded by very cold temperatures and heavy rain and by the 18th of January 1912, heavy snow covered most of Scotland, England and Wales. The result of the National vote was declared on Thursday the 18th of January 1912 at the **MFGB** Conference in Birmingham.

The results by District were;

District	For	Against
Yorkshire	63,736	10,477
Lancashire and Cheshire	50,517	11,193
Midland Federation	26,019	5,275
Derbyshire	17,999	6,816
Nottinghamshire	17,086	5,386
Leicestershire	3,681	907
South Derbyshire	2,178	593
North Wales	7,327	1,566
Cumberland	4,918	813
Bristol	1,084	342
Somersetshire	3,378	370
Scotland	60,611	12,035
South Wales	103,526	18,419
Northumberland	22,595	7,557
Durham	57,490	28,504
Cleveland	2,021	5,225
Forest of Dean	1,585	245
Total	**445,801**	**115,921**

Although the **MFGB** expected a two thirds majority, many were surprised that the vote was nearly four to one in favour of a strike with unexpected variations in Districts where feelings were strongest one way or another. Only one District voted against, Cleveland, where it was reported that most members there were connected to the iron ore trade.

In the Forest of Dean there appeared to be a low turnout but at the **FODMA** meeting at Viney Hill on Monday the 22nd of January 1912, Mr David Organ presiding, Mr Rowlinson said that a third of the Association's members' ballot papers had not been returned – around 900 in total. If you added that number to the non Union men who were unable to vote, then there didn't appear to be the strong views for a strike as it was thought.

However, in view of the results, the **MFGB** adopted a unanimous resolution in favour of tendering notices in accordance with resolutions passed at their previous Conference. Notices were to be served in every District to terminate contracts at the end of February 1912 but that they were still ready to negotiate a settlement if the Employers agreed to talks. In the Forest of Dean only one weeks' notice to terminate contracts was required so these were delayed to correspond with the expiry of the rest of the country.

The month of February 1912 was taken up with three way negotiations between the **MFGB**, the Coal Owners Association and the Government. Early in February 1912, the **MFGB** had worked out a system of payment for the minimum wage for each District but the Forest of Dean, Bristol and Somerset were exempt. This was because the arrangement of a minimum of 5 shillings per shift per man and 2 shillings per boy would, in those Districts lead to some unemployment.

Negotiations with the Coal Owners began at the Westminster Palace Hotel on Wednesday the 7th of February 1912 with the South Wales Coal Owners walking out and the remaining representatives being unable to reconcile their views on what would constitute a 'fair days' wage for a fair days' work'. But they were all in agreement that they couldn't agree to a minimum wage until the principal of payment in proportion to the amount of work performed had been settled. The miners however did agree on a resolution to the effect that there could be no settlement of the dispute unless the principle of an individual minimum wage was accepted by the Employers. Convinced that there could be no settlement, the miners' leaders called on the Miners International Committee which included France, Germany, Austria and Belgium to promise to prevent any shipment of coal coming into the country from the Continent, to which they all agreed. They did however stipulate that Great Britain should reciprocate the favour should a similar dispute happen to them.

The **MFGB** appeared to be in permanent Conference during February 1912 with Delegates to-ing and fro-ing between their Districts conveying news or miners attitudes back to the Executive. A change of direction came when General Secretary of the **MFGB** Thomas Ashton received an invitation from Prime Minister Asquith to mediate in the dispute. The meeting between the

MFGB and the Prime Minister, Chancellor of the Exchequer, Foreign Secretary and the President of the Board of Trade took place at the Foreign Office on Tuesday the 27th of February 1912. Amid members of his own Party sitting opposite, Asquith agreed that the miners were right in their demand for a minimum wage but stressed that they should abandon their demands concerning specific day rates that had been published earlier that month. This, the miners refused to do stating that the figures had already been cut to the bone and any further reduction would mean a reduction in earnings. Following this, the Government drew up four proposals for both sides in the dispute to consider. The Coal Owners were divided on the issue but the majority of Federated Districts accepted the proposals but not surprisingly, the Scottish and Welsh Coal Owners flatly rejected them. The miners leaders on the other hand, accepted only two, stating that rates of pay already established should remain and that they were against compulsory arbitration. Talks continued on the 1st of March 1912 but by then, miners in many Districts were already out on strike and the Government had to concede their failure to bring both sides to an agreement.

In the Forest of Dean, the working week ended at the end of the Saturday shift so as far as the strike was concerned, the men ceased work and withdrew their tools on Saturday afternoon the 2nd of March 1912.

Nearly 5,000 men and boys were affected and It had been thought that judging by the small number of ballot papers received, there would be some hesitation in handing in notices to terminate their contracts and that there was division among the miners. Generally, Forest miners had no grievance with their Employers but the strong influence of the Union had persuaded all but a few to follow the National decision. As it turned out, all collieries except one in the Forest were idle and at a mass meeting of the **FODMA** at Speech House on Monday the 4th of March 1912, it was confirmed that the non Union men would stand by the National decision to support their fellow miners. Where work continued at the Lydbrook colliery of Messrs Richard Thomas, it was agreed to appeal to the colliery manager and men on a peaceful basis with no picketing, to join the strike.

On the 11th of March 1912, the **FODMA** held another meeting at the Speech House field where around 2,000 miners were gathered to hear the President Mr William Smith and agent Mr Rowlinson give their views on the latest situation. Mr Smith, referring to rumours coming out of recent Downing Street meetings said they didn't want a Parliamentary Bill or compulsory arbitration by people who knew nothing about coal mining. He complimented the miners for their exemplary behaviour during the strike but said that with more time on their hands, he had noticed that the public houses appeared fuller than was usual. He said that he had been approached by the Employers of some of the larger collieries with a request for roadmen to be allowed into the collieries to keep the roadways open and for pumping water to stop them getting into a bad state of repair. Mr Rowlinson said that he favoured that idea and the request was granted. Mr Rowlinson said that strike pay would be paid at the end of each week and also confirmed that the men at the Lydbrook colliery had agreed to come out and join their fellow miners as from Tuesday the 5th of March 1912.

So the Forest miners were as determined as ever to stick by the National Federation's decisions and because no coal was being produced, other industries were being affected and workers made idle. Train services of the Great Western and the Severn and Wye were reduced to the point that the Forest of Dean was virtually cut off. The Midland Railway Co. withdrew their services to Gloucester Docks but later allowed the transportation of food only and the timber yards were also idle. The Parkend Deep Navigation Co. and the New Fancy Collieries asked to be able to cut coal to feed the boilers to cope with the excessive influx of water due to heavy rainfall but at a meeting at Speech House, the **FODMA** voted unanimously to refuse the request. They did however vote a £500 donation from the local General Accident Fund to be distributed among the non Union miners in appreciation of their loyalty.

Fig. 53 New Fancy Colliery,
courtesy of the DHC, Soudley, Cinderford.

Nationally, nearly 100,000 miners were on strike and almost as many workers in other industries were also made idle. There was however one District that sought to break with the National Federation and return to work. In North Wales where many quarries, iron and brickworks had closed down, nearly 40,000 men were unemployed and as the Coal Owners had agreed to pay the minimum wage according to the scheduled list, the miners had indicated their willingness to return to work.

Meanwhile, negotiations between the Parties at Westminster had achieved nothing and Prime Minister Asquith announced on Friday the 15th of March 1912 that the only way the miners could get their minimum wage was for Government to introduce a Bill compelling the Coal Owners to pay. So the **Minimum Wage Bill,** without including any details concerning the wages figures was introduced for its first reading in the House of Commons on Tuesday the 19th of March 1912. In response, the Executive of the **MFGB** voted an amendment stating that all wages schedules for each District that had already been published must be included in the Bill. Unfortunately, that amendment and others were defeated at a later stage, even with the support of the Labour Party. After passing through the House of Lords, the Bill was given the Royal Assent on Friday the 29th of March 1912 and so the **Mines Minimum Wage Act 1912** became law.

In the Forest of Dean, the **FODMA** advised that the 5 shillings weekly payment would exhaust their funds by the end of the month and on Saturday the 30th of March1912, a mass meeting of miners at the Speech House decided to return to work on Monday the 1st of April although they did not participate in the national vote. Other Districts such as the Midland Federation, the North Wales Federation, the Bristol and Somerset District, the South Derby District and most surprisingly the South Wales Federation all voted for a return to work.

The Coal Owners accepted the new **Act** but the **MFGB** rejected it. They decided to call a quick ballot of miners as to whether to accept or reject the terms of the new **Act**. The results were in by Wednesday the 3rd of April 1912 with a majority voting to continue the strike.

The figures overall were;
Against resumption of work 244,011,
For resumption of work 201,013,
Majority against resuming work .... 42,998.

After much consultation, the **MFGB** eventually decided that because they asked for a two thirds majority in December 1911 in order to declare a National Strike, they would adopt the same two thirds majority to continue the strike. This they did not have in the overall result so it was decided to recommend an immediate resumption of work as from the 4th of April 1912.

Forest of Dean colliers met on Friday the 5th of April at the Cinderford Town Hall with Mr Rowlinson and Mr Martin Perkins as speakers. It was stated that the 5,000 striking miners had now returned to work except for around 200 from the Park Gutter Colliery that would not be reopened for some time. Resolutions were passed enabling the rebuilding of Union funds by granting free admission and reduced contributions. A request from the Coal Owners representatives that the collieries should work on Easter Monday was soundly rejected among a chorus of hoots of disapproval.

Forest Postscript

Undoubtedly, the decision to return to work was mainly driven by the lack of basic food, bare cupboards, near starvation levels plus the threat of no more strike pay from the exhausted funds of the Union. East Dean miners appeared to be most affected by the strike and were the keenest of all Forest miners to return to work. The generosity of local traders would not be forgotten for their gifts of meat, fish and poultry plus ready meals for children. They also contributed to the Relief Funds of the various areas while at the same time suffering themselves from income they would normally receive in good times. While the County Education Committee refused to support free meals for children of striking miners through the Meals Act, Mr Harry Webb the local MP was generous in donating another £100 to be distributed to the needy miners.

Coal Owners were also pleased with the return to work and the sounds of men going about their normal work, boilers and engines working, pithead gear running and the clatter of the screens must have been music to their ears especially when their bank accounts were getting low. However, coal production remained low while many collieries were in the process of repairing roads and removing debris before full production could begin. The question of the minimum wage still had to be agreed between the parties and a District Board had to be set up to consider what was to be determined as the 'minimum wage'. In order to fight future disputes, the **FODMA** also had to consider how to attract more members from the non Unionists and the decision to reduce contributions with free admission would certainly be tempting to many.

On a political note, a Bye-Election was called in the Forest of Dean due to Mr Harry Webb MP being appointed as Lord of the Treasury.

Pressure for Labour representation in the Forest of Dean was on the rise and a meeting of several hundred miners at the Speech House on Sunday morning the 21st of April 1912 supported that call. Acting under the guise of the **Dean Forest Labour Association**, Mr William Smith, President of the **FODMA** gave a rousing speech in which he denounced the present Liberal MP as not truly representing the miners as he was a mining magnate who could not be expected to vote for better working conditions for them. He went on to describe himself as a militant who was not satisfied with their present position and that the system was rotten. He said that the hierarchy of his own Union the **FODMA** was not of his own opinion (a slight at Mr Rowlinson) but the rank and file were, and that the time had come to have a Labour candidate who would fight for the rights of the miners. Mr James Sayes who was dismissed from his job as checkweighman at the Cannop colliery six months earlier was invited to move a resolution *'That in the opinion of this meeting, the Forest of Dean should be represented in the House of Commons by a member who should be entirely independent of both Liberal and Tory parties, and this meeting calls upon the Executive of the Forest of Dean Miners' Association to take immediate steps to open up negotiations with the Miners' Federation to recommend a Labour candidate and contest the pending bye-election'* The resolution was passed with a unanimous show of hands.

Mr Arthur Peters, the organising secretary of the Independent Labour Party admitted that he was no Forester but had done the next best thing and married one. He went on to list the failures of the incumbent MP and urged those present that if this resolution failed to meet with a favourable response, then they should let their officials know in no uncertain terms what their intentions were. He referred to a letter in a local newspaper and signed by Mr Rowlinson who said that *'the meeting to be held on Sunday morning at the Speech House has no connection with the Forest of Dean Miners' Association. The officials were entirely unaware of it until advertised'*. Mr Peters asked; **'well who in the world said it had any connection with that Association?'** He said that every person there represented themselves and no one else and therefore they were entitled to express their views independently. Mr Smith closed the meeting by saying that even if the local Miners' Association and the Miners' Federation threw cold water on their movement, they were not going to stop fighting.

A statement later the following week from the **FODMA** read:

'*The* **Forest of Dean Miners' Association** *was approached by the* **Independent Labour Party** *to provide a Labour candidate for the bye election. This was duly considered but as the Association Rules precluded any political action, the request had to be turned down*'.

On Saturday the 20th of April 1912, the Liberal Council met at Cinderford to decide their candidate and Mr Harry Webb was again invited to stand, which he accepted.

For the Liberal cause, at an open air meeting at Whitecroft on Saturday the 27th of April 1912, presided over by Mr S.J. Elsom, Mr Harry Webb MP defended his position as referred to at the recent gathering at the Speech House that described him as a capitalist who didn't vote in favour of the minimum wage payment system in the House of Commons. He said that his own background and parliamentary record so far had demonstrated that he had acted in the best interests of the miners of the Forest of Dean. He said that if he had voted for the minimum wage as suggested for the District of 5 shillings per shift per man and 2 shillings for boys, then that would be less than the 6 shillings that they were already getting and that would mean a probable decrease in their wages.

In the event, and as there was no opposition candidate, at Newnham on Tuesday the 30th of April 1912, Mr Harry Webb, as the only person nominated for the vacancy was returned unopposed to represent the Forest of Dean Constituency in Parliament. It was then revealed that Mr Webb had purchased a small estate on the Littledean road which he intended to build a new residence that would command extensive views. It also came to light that a ploy by the Conservative and Unionist Party to split the Liberal vote by putting forward a late candidate if a Labour Candidate had also been nominated, came to nothing.

A District Board was set up to determine miners' wages in accordance with the **Mines Minimum Wages Act 1912** and which had to consist of an equal number of miners and Coal Owners representatives (10 from each group). The first of these took place on Wednesday the 17th of April 1912 at the Speech House and those present representing the Owners were; Messrs. T.H.Deakin, L.Winterbotham, J.Hale, E.Morgan, W.R.Champness, A.Brown, J.J.Joynes and F.Brain (two others were unable to attend). For the workmen, Messrs. Martin Perkins (Lightmoor), E.Taylor (Foxes Bridge),

C.Lees (Crumpmeadow), W.Bradley (Trafalgar), Oliver Walford (Cannop), Samuel Rickards (Flour Mill), David Organ (Norchard), Horace Jones (Parkend and New Fancy), E. Williams (Arthur and Edward), G. Rowlinson (small collieries). An independent Chairman Mr Russell J. Kerr was accepted by both sides and the rules agreed upon.

The Board met again at the Speech House on the 13th and 14th of May 1912 and the rules and rates of pay relating to the various collieries in accordance with the **Mines Minimum Wages Act 1912**, were agreed upon unanimously.

The miners were then presented with the results of the District Board at a **FODMA** meeting at Cinderford Town Hall, Presided over by Mr Martin Perkins. Mr Rowlinson gave an exhaustive talk on the pros and cons of their previous deliberances and reiterated that the **Act** only referred to underground workers and that no man would be paid less than he did now. The agreed rates were then presented to the meeting and after another appeal by Mr Rowlinson for miners to join the Union, a vote of confidence in the District Board and to both Chairmen was carried unanimously. Other individual meetings were held in various villages around the Forest where Mr Rowlinson, with the help of other Association members helped to explain the new rating system.

On Sunday the 16th of June 1912, Mr Keir Hardie, MP for Merthyr Tydfil came to the Forest of Dean and made speeches at meetings at Cinderford Town Hall and Coleford Drill Hall. The meetings, conducted by Mr William Smith, President of the **FODMA,** advocated the election of a Labour Candidate for Parliament to fight their cause.

In one of his addresses Mr Hardie said; **'for my own part I am becoming more and more convinced that legislative action would produce quicker, more permanent and more satisfactory results than we could ever hope to win by strikes. A reform enacted by the State became permanent. On the other hand, an increase in wages and other advantages won by a strike in a period of good trade, could be taken away from you and you would have to lose it in a period of bad trade. We must now aim at securing not merely a minimum of subsistence but a maximum of life for every member of the community. An indispensable preliminary to this, however, is that every industrial constituency should be represented by a Labour member. The Forest of Dean is essentially such a place.'**

At the end of June 1912, Mr Rowlinson who had acted as the Union Agent for the previous 25 years sent in his resignation to the Council. He confessed this was mainly due to a difference of opinion between himself and one or two of the steam coal Lodges in West Dean.

At the **Miners' Annual Demonstration** held on Saturday the 13th of July 1912 at the Speech House field, there was much disappointment at the absence of the newly elected Liberal MP Mr Harry Webb on the platform. Many speakers were heckled by a faction of miners and unable to be heard for some time. A resolution urging all men and boys to join the Association and so take advantage of the **Minimum Wage Act** was proposed by Mr Henry Young and seconded by Mr David Organ but their appeal was drowned by heckling. The main invited speaker, Mr Albert Stanley MP was also unable to proceed but he came out fighting and said if they didn't wish to hear him, he would pack his bags and return to Staffordshire. He shouted that he had also fought for a Labour candidate and that he did not intend to compete with this continual interruption. That had the effect of quietening the crowd and he was then able to state his points. At the end of the meeting, the original resolution was then put and carried unanimously.

A Rival Union

By October 1912, Mr Rowlinson had been approached by representatives of 19 Lodges to withdraw his resignation. He promised to do so provided he got a favourable vote in the re-election which was being contested by two other candidates. One being the **FODMA** President Mr William Smith and the other, Mr Sims Banks Jenkins, a local Conservative Councillor and landowner from Bream.

On Saturday 26th October 1912, an acrimonious meeting of the **FODMA** Council at the Speech House came to a decision that one of the candidates for election to replace Mr Rowlinson, Mr Sims Banks Jenkins should not be put forward. It was generally accepted that his position was honorary and that he knew nothing about mining.

Mr Sims Banks Jenkins then called several meetings in West Dean and at an inaugural meeting at Bream had enough support to form an alternative Union with himself as honorary President and to act as Agent for 12 months without pay. The Union was to be known as **'Forest of Dean Miners' New Association'**. Other committee members were Messrs H. Beach, J. Jones and F. Philips with Mr Edwin Morgan as Secretary and Mr Charles John James as Treasurer. It was however stated by the **Miners' Federation of**

Great Britain that this Union was designed to break up the existing **FODMA** and that in no way could it have recognition within their Federation.

And so, in December 1912 the **FODMA** held their Annual meeting to elect a new Agent and other Officers of the Association for the forthcoming year. There were now two candidates for the position of Agent – Mr G. Rowlinson, the retiring Association Agent and Mr William Smith the existing President of the Association. Mr Rowlinson polled 1,276 votes and was elected with Mr Smith polling 423 votes.

For President, Mr Martin H. Perkins 700 (elected), Mr David R. Organ 620, Mr Henry Young 222. For Vice President, Mr William Taylor 499 (elected), Mr Richard Kear 306, Mr Philip Powell 266, Mr Joseph Holder 256, Mr Thomas Parker 181, Mr Samuel Rickards 102 and Mr George Rudge 37. For Treasurer, Mr James Baldwin 1247 (re-elected), Mr Stephen Howell 386. For Secretary, Mr Richard Buffrey 1305 (re-elected), Mr H. Watson 186 and Mr Harry Brookes 182.

Martin Perkins – 1858 to 1927

A very well known and respected member of the Forest of Dean mining community, Martin Perkins who was born in Cinderford and brought up in the Baptist religion, worked in the pits from the age of 14. As a strong Liberal supporter, Perkins was an ally of both Sir Charles Dilke and George Rowlinson but after WWI he became disillusioned with Liberal policies and switched to supporting the Labour Party. He was a family man who married Miss Elizabeth Knight in 1876 and they had eleven children.

Fig. 54 Mr Martin Perkins

Martin Perkins was elected checkweighman at Lightmoor colliery in 1893 and served on the Executive Committee of the Forest of Dean Miners' Association until his retirement in 1925. He also served on the Westbury Board of Guardians from 1893 to 1895.

He was elected President of the **FODMA** in 1913 and elected annually until 1918. He also served as Vice President for many years. He was also President of the Forest of Dean Freeminers from 1919 until just before his death.

Outside of colliery life Martin Perkins was also President of the Cinderford Co-operative Society for over 25 years and also President of the Forest of Dean Miners' Association General Accident and Health Insurance Society and the Cinderford Medical Aid Association. After WWI he became a Justice of the Peace (JP) and a member of the Forest of Dean Council of School Managers.

It was now clear that the mood of the Forest of Dean miners was changing. The new **Minimum Wages Act** left a lot to be desired and a feeling that their new MP was 'out of touch' with the grass roots of the industry and with the question of 'abnormal places' still not fully resolved. Still a future possibility was the choice of a political representative in the form of a Labour candidate more in tune with the miners' social standing and working conditions and so more forceful voices began to be heard. Their new Liberal MP was not to be trusted and Mr Rowlinson's loyalties began to be questioned.

A pamphlet called **'The Miners next step'** published by the Unofficial Reform Committee whose main author was a Welsh Trade Unionist Noah Ablett, was published nationally. In the light of past strikes in South Wales, particularly the Cambrian Combine dispute, it encouraged miners to think differently regarding trade Unionism and to adopt a more militant stance towards the Coal Owners. A new word had entered the British vocabulary in the form of **'Syndicalism'** which, as well as other demands, called for the elimination of the Employer, working slowly as to make collieries unprofitable and Nationalisation of the whole of the mining industry.

However, it is not to be suggested that the Forest of Dean miners had endorsed the Syndicalism philosophy but something had tilted the balance. The sad deaths of **FODMA** President George Barnard in 1910 and of Sir Charles Dilke in 1911 could have been the possible starting point as their successors were totally different characters. George Barnard was replaced by William Smith who often admitted his militancy while the new Liberal MP was considered a Capitalist who didn't support the **Minimum Wage Bill** as it was going through Parliament. He also failed to appear at the **Miners' Annual Demonstration** as Sir Charles Dilke had always done. Coupled with that was the fact that although desired by most Forest miners, a Labour candidate was not allowed to stand at the April Bye Election and differences between at least two West Dean steam coal Lodges and Mr Rowlinson, caused the latter to resign as Agent after 25 years' service – although he was later re-elected after an acrimonious campaign by his opponents, one of whom went on to form a rival Union.

Nationally

President of the **Miners' Federation of Great Britain** Mr Enoch Edwards MP who died in June 1912 was succeeded in October 1912 by Mr Robert Smillie who, up until then had been their Vice President. Smillie had been a staunch advocate of the Nationalisation of the Coal Mines since 1892 and after Edwards' death, and as Acting President, set in motion a draft Bill which was first put to the Annual Conference in October 1912. This was given unanimous approval and copies were sent to the Labour Party with a view to introducing it before Parliament.

The Forest of Dean was not the only District to find problems with the provisions of the **Minimum Wages Act** and their Joint District Boards. The Forest District was one of only three Districts to agree their rates within three weeks while others took somewhat longer and many failed to agree. In these cases, the Chairmen, who in many cases were lawyers, had a casting vote and the power to set rates and make all the decisions.

Inevitably, many of these forced decisions paid the miners less than a reasonable living wage and in the case of piece workers, their rates contravened certain paragraphs of the **Act.** The **MFGB** were aware of all this and wrote to Prime Minister Asquith requesting an interview but Asquith decided to wait until all Joint Boards had set their rates. When at last the Executive Committee met Asquith, they explained their concern that in many Districts miners were being paid considerably less than the 5 shillings minimum while some District Chairmen had fixed rates for coal getters far below the average wages. Asquith of course didn't want to get involved with the day to day running of the **Act** but suggested further legislation was possible if the Executive Committee could justify a case.

Accidents/Fatalities

On Monday the 22nd of January 1912 at the Wallsend Colliery, Mr Horace Brain from Pillowell was killed by a fall of earth while working underground. The Inquest at Pillowell Methodist Chapel heard that Mr Brain was working with Mr Frank Virgo for about half an hour when Mr Virgo shouted for him to get on one side so that he could throw some dirt away. Mr Brain did so but leaned up against one of the props which gave way bringing down two further props and a quantity of earth. He was pulled out as soon as possible but was found to be dead. It was stated that the spot had been examined before the men went to work and was found to be safe. The verdict recorded was accidental death with no blame attached to anyone.

On Wednesday the 3rd of April 1912 at the Peglars Drift mine near Coleford, a young workman by the name of Croat from Bream was killed by a fall of earth. Fellow workmen pulled him away from the fall but there was nothing to be done as extensive head injuries had caused instant death.

On the same day, again at the Wallsend Colliery, Mr Albert Smith, a married man with five children was severely injured while oiling an underground water pump. His shirt sleeve got caught in the machinery which badly lacerated his arm at the elbow. He was attended by a doctor and sent to Gloucester Royal Infirmary where it was found necessary to amputate the limb.

On the 18th of July 1912, an Inquest was held at Cinderford Town Hall into the death of Mr Henry Hemms aged 56, a collier of Forest Terrace, Cinderford who worked at Foxes Bridge Colliery. Dr Mitchell of Cinderford said that Hemms had consulted him on Monday evening the 8th of July 1912 saying that he had 'had a smack in the ear' that day when some earth had fallen on him. He examined his ears and eyes but could find no evidence of injury and advised that he go home and rest. On the Wednesday, Dr Mitchell received a message saying that Hemms had had a stroke and on visiting his house found him in convulsions and unconscious. A later Post Mortem conducted by Dr Beedle of Cinderford in the presence of Dr Mitchell and Dr Buchanan of Coleford found some blood in the left passage of the ear and a perforated eardrum but no skull fracture. On examination of the brain he came to the conclusion that the deceased had been suffering from meningitis. A fall of earth could have contributed to a perforated eardrum but no more. A verdict of death from meningitis was recorded and there was insufficient evidence to show whether the deceased had suffered from an accident or not.

On Tuesday morning the 20th of August 1912 at the Norchard Colliery near Lydney, 17 year old Charles Powell from Aylburton was killed by a fall of earth while working underground as a filler in the upper Trenchard seam. The first indication that something was wrong was when the workmen's candles were blown out and a cry for help from Powell. He was found pinned against the side and while rescuers were trying to pull him free, another more extensive fall drove the rescuers back and he was completely enveloped. Two fellow rescuers, brothers by the name of Norris from Viney Hill received minor injuries and because of the effect this accident had on the workforce, the afternoon shift was abandoned. At the Inquest, it was stated that the fall was 16 yards along one road and 20 yards along another and the question of using timbering instead of cogs was discussed. The verdict was of suffocation due to a fall of earth.

On Thursday the 12th of September 1912, Mr John Waite of Horsepool Bottom near Micheldean, died at home from injuries he had received from a fall of rock at the Crump Meadow Colliery on the 31st of October 1911. He had been in Gloucester Royal Hospital since then but was discharged on the 2nd of May 1912 as incurable and had lingered in great pain at home until his death. At an Inquiry at Plump Hill Council School it was said that the deceased had worked at the colliery nearly all his life and that he was a capable and experienced worker. He had left a widow and six children and Mr Joseph Hale the colliery manager said he would do what he could for them. A verdict of accidental death was recorded and that no one was to blame for the accident.

Chapter 17
East v West Dean

Trade Union Act – 1913

The previously mentioned **Osborne judgement of 1909** which prevented Unions collecting a levy for the benefit of the Labour Party was practically reversed by the introduction of the **1913 Trade Union Act.** The Osborne Judgement resulted in many Unions and the **MFGB** being taken to court for alleged breaches of that Judgement and the Asquith Liberal Government were coerced into supporting this **Act** because they needed the Labour support to remain in office. Specifically, the **Act,** introduced in March 1913, gave the Unions the right to divide their subscriptions into a political and a Social fund so that if a member objected to paying the political levy, he then had the right to contract out.

Starting early in the year, Mr Rowlinson, in an effort to suppress the strength of the new Union which threatened to split East and West Dean, held meetings at collieries throughout the District. He was warmly greeted at many of these and also congratulated for his recent re-election as Agent. He wasn't afraid either, of entering parts of the Forest where dissent was most popular. For instance, on Wednesday evening the 8th of January 1913 he held an outdoor meeting with the two shifts working at the Flour Mill colliery where only 145 miners were members of the **FODMA** out of a workforce of over 700. He received a respectful hearing which covered several topics of concern to the men. These included developments concerning Doctors proposed rates in relation to the 1911 National Insurance Act and the Compensation Act where there were differences on offer from the employers as opposed to the Government and the continuing argument over Saturday working hours. Regarding the latter he said he was pleased to announce an agreement with the Employers that work would stop at 2pm on Saturdays and that the lost hour would be deducted from the men's wages. Similar meetings were held at Yorkley Slade, Elwood and others where it was agreed and voted upon to accept the Saturday working arrangement and all meetings ended cordially.

Apart from the formation of the new Union which threatened to reduce the strength of the **FODMA** and split the District, there was a faction within the Association that thought that the Joint Wages Board should negotiate separate wages agreements between the steam coal colliers and the house coal colliers. In June, the Union, working on a mandate from the general body of men, decided to give notice to the Joint Wages Board to terminate their present agreement – giving the statutory three months notice – and to re-negotiate on the split system as suggested.

This subject was brought up at the **Miners' Annual Demonstration** which was again held at the Speech House field on Saturday the 12th of July 1913. The meeting was chaired by Mr Martin Perkins, President and was supported by Mr Harry Webb, MP, Mr Will Crooks MP, Mr John Robertson, Vice President of the Scottish Federation and others on the Committee.

In a resolution proposed by Mr William Taylor and seconded by Mr David Organ and carried unanimously, it stated once again the necessity for workmen to join the Union. Unless all workmen were in the Union, the proposal to split the Joint Wages Board into two sections, one for the steam coal men and one for the house coal men, they would not be able to negotiate a fair and reasonable rate for the lower seams and the case would be useless.

Both Mr Crooks and Mr Robertson supported that cause and urged all workers to join the Union. Mr Harry Webb MP came in for a certain amount of criticism after he made reference to an earlier heckler's remark that one guest, Mr Robert Smillie, President of the Miners Federation of Great Britain who could not make it to the event, should be the Member for the Forest of Dean. He said that if the people of the Forest of Dean wanted Mr Smillie as their candidate, then as a believer in democracy, he would not stand in his way but would support him against the Conservatives. **'That's all bluff'** said a voice in the crowd who was then invited onto the platform to explain himself – which he did. Mr Webb ended by saying that he hoped Mr Smillie would find some other constituency other than the Forest of Dean.

Fig. 55 Lightmoor Colliery,
courtesy of the DHC, Soudley, Cinderford.

In early September 1913, a Union meeting was held at the Higher Elementary School in Cinderford with Mr Martin Perkins acting as Chairman. Guests included the Rev. George Neighbour from Mountain Ash, formally a Baptist Minister at Ruardean Hill and Mr George Rowlinson. Satisfaction was expressed at the reported increase in Union membership after calls throughout the year and Mr Rowlinson said that where, six weeks previous there were only 50 members at one colliery, now there were 500 and in another, membership had risen from zero to 100. Over the last six weeks he said the membership had increased by over 700. Finally he touched on the proposal of splitting the wages board into two sections in order to negotiate separate agreements between steam and house coal collieries. He said that he believed that the idea was a lost cause.

Later in September 1913 it was announced that the Joint Wages Board had agreed to raise the cost of coal by one shilling per ton which meant, according to the agreement, that the miners would receive an advance of 5% on their current wages. The Union had been pressing the Employers for some months for an increase and the announcement was prompted by the Midland Federation granting an increase to their workers.

At a further meeting at the Rising Sun Inn, Ruspidge on the 18th of September 1913, Mr Rowlinson again referred to the East and West system and the forthcoming expiry of the current wages agreement. He said that although he was satisfied with the recent wage increase, the men were still dissatisfied with the small increase and expected more. He then alluded to the Dilke Memorial Hospital and the apparent apathy on the part of the miners to contribute to the cause and suggested that they put more energy into it. He said that he had done all he could to push the matter forward and that they were now awaiting the result of the ballot of the men. He hoped that by the spring of next year there would be better progress than at present.

In an October 1913 meeting at Bream, the speaker Mr David Organ said that he was now pleased with the current inflow of new members to the Union and that numbers mattered when it came to negotiating new wage agreements. He said that there was now a need to review the current arrangements due to the rapid development of the deep seams. Currently the arrangements were designed to suit the house coal colliers but now that the steam coal men outnumbered the house coal men, there was a need for change and re-negotiation. He said it was clear that if there was to be peace, then there must be two agreements.

However, the Joint Wages Board had been aware of the steam coal men's concern for separate wage agreements to the house coal men and had met to consider the matter. The independent Chairman, Mr Russell Kerr J.P. heard arguments both for and against the proposal to divide the Board but before coming to a decision, he wanted to see for himself the different working conditions in both house and steam coal collieries. Consequently he visited both Lightmoor colliery (house coal) and Flour Mill colliery (steam coal) with a proviso that a decision would be forthcoming in the near future.

On Friday the 28th of November 1913, a full meeting of the Joint Wages Board was held at the Speech House to hear the Chairman's decision with Mr T.H. Deakin in the Chair. The Independent Chairman's decision was read out, stating that having consulted the revisions of the **Minimum Wages Act**, he could see no way in which a second Board could be established within the same coalfield. This, in effect, ended the argument but in further discussions, the Board conceded on a number of points pushed forward by Mr Rowlinson and the men's representatives. One was to raise the minimum wage from 5 shillings and twopence halfpenny to 5 shillings and 5 pence per shift. Skilled timbermen also received a rise from their minimum of 4 shillings per shift.

Exploiting the Coleford High Delf steam coal seam.

Firstly, operations were going forward with a view to re-opening the Crown Colliery at Moseley Green. Fifteen years previous it was purchased by Mr Thomas Johnson who sank two shafts but abandoned the venture after spending a considerable amount of money on it. It was then sold to Messrs Lancaster who owned large collieries in South Wales and who subsequently sold it on to the British Red Ash Company, owners of collieries near Newport and Pontypool and a small concern in Lydbrook. Since its closure, the colliery had accumulated a large amount of water which had risen to a depth of six yards in the shafts. This was pumped out using winding operations and a 'bowk' which was able to raise 4,000 gallons an hour and as the whole of the workings were inundated, it would take some time before coal getting could begin. There was however considerable interest in the venture in the local villages of Parkend, Yorkley and Blakeney.

Two years previous, the old workings at the Howbeach colliery were purchased by a Company called Wallsend Ltd., which was owned by six Manchester men. They also purchased the area of the Pillowell Level Colliery, total area being in the region of 1,000 acres which contained the Yorkley, Whittington and the Coleford High Delf seams. New equipment was installed including electric and steam pumping plant estimated to raise 3,300 gallons of water per minute. The mine which was only 400 yards long but was planned to be extended to around 1,000 yards, produced around 60 tons of coal per day but was forecast to increase that to 400 tons. 120 colliers were working at the mine but at full capacity they anticipated the number would increase to 300.

In late December 1913 the **Forest of Dean Miners' Association** held their annual meeting for the election of Officers and Committee for the forthcoming year. For the second time, Mr Rowlinson's position as Agent was challenged by Mr William Smith but at the count, Mr Rowlinson was confirmed as Agent with 1,184 votes as against Mr Smith's 358. Mr Martin Perkins was confirmed as President with 915 votes as against Mr Tom Parkes' 479. Mr David Organ was confirmed as Vice President with 474 votes, Mr James Baldwin, Treasurer with 1058 votes, Mr Richard Buffrey, Secretary was returned unopposed. Auditors Messrs Ambrose Adams and George Baghurst were re-elected with 461 and 237 votes respectively. The

Finance Committee consisted of Messrs Enos Taylor 422 votes, Henry Beddinton 358 votes and Horace Jones 317 votes.

Accidents/Fatalities

On Friday the 21st of February 1913, labourer Mr Thomas Timbrell aged 17 from Howbeach near Blakeney was killed while working at the surface yard of the Wallsend Colliery. The inquest, held at Moseley Green heard that he and several other men were engaged in moving a one ton motor on a low trolley up an incline on an improvised set of rails. While on the incline, the motor toppled over and fell onto Mr Timbrell where his stomach took all the weight and he died within the hour. Asked whether he thought all precautions had been taken, Mr Peter Richardson the chief engineer at the colliery said that at the time he thought that they were but now had thought differently. The Jury recorded a verdict of accidental death with a rider that in future more effective steps should be taken when such work was in hand to prevent a recurrence.

On Sunday the 27th of April 1913, Mr Evan George Howells aged 39 and a collier from Broadwell, died as a result of a fall of earth while working underground at the Flour Mill Colliery that occurred on the 14th of August 1912. An Inquest at the Pisgah Primitive Methodist Chapel at Broadwell heard that Mr Howells had been working at the coal face with other colliers and they were clearing up the roadway before putting timbers up. Unfortunately, before they could do so, a fall of earth from above the coal fell onto the back of Mr Howells before glancing off onto the floor. He called for help and said that his back was broken. Eventually he was transported to Gloucester Royal Hospital where he remained until he was returned to his home on the 18th of December 1912. He was taken to his bed and remained there until his death on the 27th of April 1913. Dr McQuaide's evidence was that Mr Howells had fractured his spine which brought on paralysis and later blood poisoning due to bed sores. The primary cause of death was severe injuries to the spine and the Jury returned a verdict in accordance with the medical evidence.

On Monday the 28th of April 1913, Mr Ernest Toomey aged 22, a single man from Gloucester was killed while working underground at the Flour Mill Colliery near Bream. Mr Toomey had no previous experience of working in a mine and on this occasion was working with a group of colliers at the bottom of a steep incline, the last 50 yards being very steep. It was a double roadway where drams could ascend and descend and soon after the signal was given for the journey to begin, the rope/ cable gave a violent movement which the men surmised that an accident had happened. They made their way to the spot and found several drams off the rails and Mr Toomey pinned underneath. He was freed as soon as possible and taken to the surface where medical assistance was given and Dr Pugh attended. Mr Toomey died within three hours and Dr Pugh's evidence was that his right thigh was fractured in two places, the right leg broken below the knee, the bones of the left leg were also broken and sticking through the clothing and there was a cut on the head. Death was due to shock following extensive injuries. It came to light that there may have been a malfunction of the hook at the end of the drawbar which secured the haulage rope. When examined, it was discovered that the hook had been pulled apart, revealing a flaw that could not have been detected. Extreme force would have been necessary to pull the hook apart and it was assumed that something must have got in the way of the drams being drawn up the incline which put great strain on the engine and haulage rope. Mr Toomey was behind the drams and following them up the incline to get his food and drink when the accident occurred and the Inquest recorded a verdict in accordance with the medical evidence. The Company Directors expressed their extreme regret at this distressing accident and although he had only been at the colliery a short time, Mr Toomey had gained the confidence of those with whom he had worked and was regarded as a steady and careful young man.

On Tuesday the 20th of May 1913, Mr Arthur Wicks was killed by a fall of earth while working underground at the Lightmoor Colliery. He was rescued by fellow miners but before they could get him clear, another fall completely covered him and he died almost immediately. An inquest recorded a verdict of accidental death and that no blame should be attached to anyone.

On Wednesday the 15th of October 1913, Mr William Lea aged 29 and a single man living at Yorkley and who supported his widowed mother, was killed by the fall of earth while working underground at the Wallsend Colliery near Blakeney. At the Inquest held at Pillowell, it was recorded that Mr Lea and another collier Joseph Smith were working a stall in the High Delf seam and that morning they had both decided that the piece of clod in the roof was safe. Mr Smith then moved away when the 5 hundredweight clod fell onto Mr Lea crushing his head and killing him instantly. As a result, the rest of the shift left the colliery for the remainder of the turn. The fall brought down two pieces of timber but it was uncertain that the roof had been double timbered. According to the Deputy Mr Thomas Mudway, he judged that the roof was quite safe when he had examined it at the start of the shift. A verdict of accidental death was recorded.

On Tuesday the 21st of October 1913, Mr Ernest Willetts aged 42 was seriously injured while working at the Norchard Colliery near Lydney. The inquest, held at the Petty Sessional Courtroom at Lydney heard that at around 4.30pm, Mr Willetts was engaged in uncoupling four drams while they were in motion when he found himself entangled in the haulage rope. This in turn threw him onto the rails where the first dram passed over his right thigh which was badly fractured. He was transported to Lydney Cottage Hospital where he died later that night. It was discussed as to whether the drams should have been uncoupled while in motion or at a standstill and the Coroner suggested to the colliery manager that it appeared to be *'a sort of go-as-you-please'* system. The manager, Mr Hooper disagreed. A verdict of accidental death was recorded with a rider that the drams should always be at a standstill when being unhitched and notices to that effect to be posted at the colliery.

On Tuesday the 25th of November 1913, Mr George Hale aged 37, a collier, was injured in a fall while working at the Cannop Deep Pit. It transpired that he had tripped and fallen onto a wooden sleeper and injured his back. He had walked home from the pit but gradually his condition worsened and he died on Saturday the 29th. Dr McQuaide carried out a post mortem and found the heart, liver and kidneys in an advanced state of disease. But he said that the cause of death was Syncope, occasioned by the fall onto the sleeper, although he could have dropped dead at any time. The verdict was in accordance with the medical evidence and the fees were handed to the widow.

South Wales - Senghenydd – Again
On Tuesday the 14th of October 1913, the worst colliery disaster to happen in the United Kingdom happened at the Universal Colliery in Senghenydd near Caerphilly in South Wales. Universal was a steam coal colliery and unlike those in the Forest of Dean, suffered from high quantities of firedamp, an explosive gas containing mainly methane. At approximately 8am on that day, two explosions occurred in the colliery's west side workings eventually travelling up the Lancaster shaft, destroying the headframe and killing the engine man. The colliery was known to contain a large quantity of airborne coal dust that had been responsible for an earlier explosion on the 24th of May 1901 which killed 81 men and one horse.

In this current explosion, firedamp, ignited from a signalling spark was assumed to be responsible for the first explosion and the shockwave raised coal dust throughout other parts of the underground workings, so contributing to the second explosion. This disaster killed 440 men including one rescuer. Due to the fact that the colliery workings were divided into west and east workings, around 450 men from the east side were rescued relatively unharmed. Several men found by rescuers did survive the west side explosions and were brought to the surface as quickly as possible but the heat and damage caused by the explosions meant that the majority of the victims could only be located after an adequate supply of water was connected to a nearby reservoir. 432 miners died that day and seven others succumbed at home or in hospital. Men returned to work in the western workings by the end of November 1913 even though 11 men were still unaccounted for.

Fig. 56 Universal colliery, Senghenydd,
coffins being carried out

An enquiry in January 1914 criticised the management of the colliery for not carrying out ventilation changes in accordance with the **1911 Coal Mines Act** and other measures in relation to the control of coal dust considering that that had been the cause of the 1901 disaster. The lack of respirators and an inadequate water supply was further criticism. The colliery manager Mr Edward Shaw who was the first to enter the underground workings and who was criticised for not fixing the ventilation fan and not calling in more rescue teams earlier, was considered a hero within the local community. Fines were eventually imposed with Mr Shaw being fined £24 and the Company £10. The colliery continued to operate with Mr Shaw as manager until its closure in 1928.

This disaster is again, a striking reminder of the risks that miners took while trying to earn a decent living wage for their wives and families. Their demands for better working conditions, safety measures and a wage commensurate with the risks they took, were certainly justified by the terrible price they paid over many years. It also brings home to us today the heartache it must have brought to those families stricken by the loss of a husband, brother or son and what a brave set of workers this country has taken for granted for so long. They will always be remembered.

Chapter 18
1914 – 1918 - World War I

For years, many prominent European Nations had been building up their armed forces and foremost was the race to increase their Naval power. The arrival of the British Battleship HMS Dreadnought in 1906 was a turning point that made all other Nations' Battleships obsolete. Guns were larger, their range was longer and the armour plating was thicker and was overall so advanced that it precipitated a World-wide arms race.

Fig 57 HMS Dreadnought

Rumblings over the possibility of a European War were aired in 1907 when the International Socialist Congress met to formulate a policy to prevent such a happening. Affiliated members included the Labour Party and the Independent Labour Party and the resultant resolution was adopted *'If war threatens to break out it is the duty of the working classes in the Countries* concerned and their Parliamentary Representatives, with the International Socialist Bureau acting as coordinator, to use all efforts to prevent war by all means appropriate, having regard to the sharpness of the class war and to the general political situation.'

Two later Congresses were held, one in Copenhagen in 1910 and the other in Basel in 1912, both of which added further resolutions; *'Should war nevertheless break out, it is our duty to intervene to try to bring it to an end'* and *'to use their energies to use the political and economic crisis created by the war to rouse the people from their slumbers and to hasten the fall of capitalist domination'*.

The British miners were party to both the Copenhan and Basel resolutions due to the fact that the **MFGB** had joined the Labour Party in 1909.

There were also Alliances between various Nations such as between Britain, France and Belgium, France and Russia, Germany and Austria-Hungary, Russia and Serbia. After the assassination of the Austrian Archduke Franz Ferdinand and his wife in Sarajevo on the 28th of June 1914, Austria-Hungary declared war on Serbia. This was the catalyst that prompted each of the separate Alliances to declare war upon each other. In turn, when Germany invaded Belgium and an ultimatum issued on the 4th of August to withdraw was ignored, Britain declared war on Germany.

On the home front, the beginning of 1914 saw no particular change in priorities within the Forest of Dean although there was speculation that Army manoeuvres would begin in the Forest during the latter part of the year. Around 80,000 Army troops were expected to be involved in Gloucestershire, Herefordshire, Worcestershire and Monmouthshire and military officers had already been making enquiries as to accommodation for billeting and foraging. The only place in the Forest of Dean that showed any current military interest was Ruardean where there was a strong Company of Territorials but moves were afoot to establish another Company at Drybrook and certain moves were also being made to expand the home defence forces throughout the Forest.

Territorial and Regular rallies were held at Cinderford, Drybrook, Newnham and other venues throughout the Forest. At the Malt Shovel Inn in Ruardeen on Saturday the 2nd of May 1914, Captain L.B. Green Officer Commanding E Company of the 1st Battalion of the Hereford Regiment Territorials held a meeting and talked on various subjects that interested the men. Camp would be held near Cheltenham and each man completing the course would receive a sovereign. They would be able to drill at Drybrook and Littledean as well as Ruardeen and that numbers had now risen to 64, although he thought there were at least 1,000 eligible young men on this side of the Forest who could be recruited. He concluded by referring to the forthcoming Army manoeuvres where the King usually put in an attendance and said it could induce others to sharpen their interest in the movement.

At the Haie near Newnham, the home of Major R.J. Kerr of the 3rd Battalion of the Gloucestershire Regiment, a parade of the Forest of Dean District National Reserve was held on Saturday the 23rd of May 1914. Brigadier-General P.S. Marling VC inspected the parade and in his address said that those present should do their utmost to induce the present rising generation to join the Territorial Forces. In a later address he remarked on the strength of the Gloucestershire National Guard as being 2,675, of which the Forest of Dean's portion was 167men, 130 of which were there present.

As far as the Forest of Dean mining industry was concerned, there was good news regarding more development to access the Coleford High Delf steam coal seam. At the Park Gutter Colliery near Whitecroft, the shafts were being deepened to 220 yards, with electric power supplied from the Flour Mill Colliery at Bream, about one mile away. However, production wasn't anticipated to start until the beginning of 1915.

Forest of Dean coal output during the past year was 1,127,198 tons, an increase of 60,423 tons on the previous year, mainly due to the increased output from the steam coal collieries. Iron ore output however was down to only 6,300 tons. All this of course was in1913 but reductions in wages due to seasonal demands for house coal was still being made, and it caused some controversy with another possible rift between West and East Dean. At the beginning of May 1914 the Joint Wages Board agreed to reduce the men's wages at both the house and steam coal collieries by 5% with a similar reduction in the price of coal. However, an objection was raised by men at the steam coal collieries that their employers were acting highhandedly. By negotiation it was finally agreed that they would accept the reduction but to take effect two weeks after that of the house coal collieries.

This situation caused some controversy at the time because traditionally both steam and house coal miners' wages were either raised or lowered simultaneously regardless of the state of output. The steam coal men argued that because they had been unaffected by the drop in demand, they should not have to take a reduction. However, it was pointed out that in the event of a rise in wages, the steam coal men readily accepted that raise at the same time as the house coal men so that, with a reduction, the same principle should apply. This situation further emphasised the growing differences between East and West Dean where the new deep seam steam collieries were employing far more men than the house coal ones. It further added to the argument that there was a case for separate wage agreements as discussed in 1913 but thrown out by the Joint Wages Board as not legally possible within one coalfield District.

In June the **Forest of Dean Miners' Association** welcomed two Labour leaders from South Africa where a major flare-up of industrial unrest was happening in the mining Districts of the Witwatersrand. Labour Party and Union officials were being arrested, imprisoned or deported for allegedly being responsible for instigating strike action against poor pay, redundancies, short time working and general working conditions that affected both white and coloured workers. In response, their Government mobilised 10,000 troops to restore order. An incident occurred at a diamond mine where a white overseer had kicked a coloured worker to death and the mine manager refused to have him arrested. Fellow workers attempted a breakout and shots were fired which resulted in 11 deaths and 37 wounded. Union leaders Messrs A. Waterston and R.B. Watson were deported to Britain and found their way to be welcomed in the Forest of Dean.

An enthusiastic Miners meeting was held at the Speech House on Saturday the 30th of May 1914 chaired by Mr David Organ where both leaders were speakers. Mr Rowlinson proposed a resolution; *'welcoming their South African guests and entered a protest against the attempt by the South African Government to suppress Trade Unionism and the setting up of Martial Law in order to crush a perfectly legal strike. The arrest without warrant of Trade Union leaders, their imprisonment without crime or offence committed and their deportation or banishment without trial'*. The resolution was seconded by Mr William Smith and passed unanimously. Both Mr Waterston and Mr Watson were received enthusiastically and dealt at length with the situation in South Africa but hoped very shortly to return to their country despite further threats of re-arrest and re-banishment.

A similar meeting was held at Whitecroft on Saturday the 20th of June 1914 where again Mr David Organ, Vice President of the **FODMA** took the chair. Both South African Union leaders were present and spoke again of their struggle and suggested that when policemen shot at strikers, the strikers should shoot back and that they should be able to hold meetings in public squares without the danger of being shot down like dogs. They said that the Capitalists rule and that Smuts and Botha were better able to exploit the country under the Union Jack than they were under Kruger. Mr W.H. Smith proposed a motion that; *'the citizens of Whitecroft, Bream, Pillowell, Yorkley and Parkend strongly protest against the despotic action of the South African Government in declaring martial law in order to crush a perfectly constitutional strike'.* This was seconded by Mr T. Liddington.

The **Forest of Dean Miners' Association** again held their **Miners' Annual Demonstration** at the Speech House field on Saturday the 11th of July 1914 with Mr Martin Perkins, President of the Association in the Chair. Over 5,000 miners and their families attended and on the platform were two political figures of opposite persuasions. Mr Harry Webb M.P. for the Forest Division and Mr Vernon Hartshorn the Welsh Labour leader and member of the National Executive of the **MFGB.** Before they were called to speak, a resolution was moved by Mr David Organ Vice President, advising all non Unionists to become members of the Association in order that they might take part in the improvement question which would have to be considered and dealt with in the near future. This was seconded by Mr David Morgan and supported by Mr Vernon Hartshorn.

In his address, Mr Hartshorn praised the early leaders of the Labour Party and said that workers were now beginning to write a new chapter in the history of democratic development and he advised those present not only to organise industrially but politically as well. He said that he regarded the Labour Movement as being more hopeful today than it had ever been in the history of the country. Referring to the Minimum Wage Act, Mr Hartshorn said that when the original Bill was introduced, neither the Liberals or the Tories had treated it seriously but that in the future, the workers' battle would inevitably be fought on the floor of the House of Commons.

In his reply, Mr Webb said that on the whole he heartily agreed with almost everything that Mr Hartshorn had said except for one or two points. He disputed the accusation that Labour could not get its demands through the ruling Liberal Party because he and others were doing everything that was economically and reasonably possible for the welfare of the people of this country. He said that he would be regarded as a traitor if he didn't object to what had been said.

The meeting was then interrupted by the persistent shouts from a supposed Suffragette who herself was eventually shouted down with cries of **'Duck her'** and **'throw her out'**. When order was restored Mr Webb went on to say that he believed in a proper combination between the Liberal and Labour Parties and believed that they could work together and thought that Mr Hartshorn would agree. In his reply, Mr Hartshorn said that he was very much against being invited as a Labour representative to a Liberal meeting and poured cold water on the suggestion that both Parties could work together. He said that in Wales, at their **Annual Demonstration**, Politicians would appear on their platform to further their own ambitions so they had now kept them away. He advised that they should do the same in the Forest of Dean – it was a Labour Demonstration and should be kept that way and not to be used by a hostile Party policy.

During all this verbal sparring, the crowd were very active in shouting advice for both speakers but it all ended amicably with Chairman Mr Martin Perkins remarking that Mr Webb did not wish to reply to Mr Hartshorn for fear of hurting his feelings. The meeting concluded with addresses from the two deported South African Labour leaders who were also on the platform.

It had now become somewhat uncomfortable for the sitting Liberal M.P. occupying a platform with other guests ready to pour criticism or scorn on either his actions or those of the Liberal Party. Mr Hartshorn's comment that the **Annual Demonstration** was a Liberal meeting was partially true as both the President of the **FODMA** Mr Martin Perkins and the Agent Mr George Rowlinson were staunch Liberal Party supporters. However, some other members of the Executive Committee of the **FODMA** had already publicly declared their support for the Labour Party including Mr William Smith and Mr David Organ.

East and West Dean rivalries continued to drive a division between steam and house coal men and Mr Rowlinson's popularity tended to decline in the steam coal areas. He lived in Cinderford and had, over the years become a prominent local public figure. He was a County Councillor for East Dean Ward, he sat on the East Dean School Board, was on the Board of the Westbury Poor Law Guardians and had become a JP who sat as a Magistrate at the Littledean Petty Sessional Court. All this was in addition to his activities as Agent for the **FODMA** and so the West Dean men were more than concerned (rightly or wrongly) that his sympathies lay with the East Dean men.

As War with Germany had been declared on the 4th of August 1914, recruitment for Kitchiner's new army moved up a notch. An enthusiastic meeting was held at the Cinderford Town Hall on Wednesday the 2nd of September 1914 where the hall was so packed that many had to be accommodated outside. Many prominent members of the coal mining community and military men were on the platform and the meeting was Chaired by Mr Rowlinson, supported by Mr Harry Webb MP and many local Coal Owners.

Mr Rowlinson opened the meeting with a stirring speech and said that; **'such a great response as this shows that the Foresters now realise the very grave crisis with which this country is facing and that I feel sure that you will be as true and brave as you have always been proved to be in the past'.** Sir Francis Brain said that; **'the Germans have made up their minds for years past to conquer this country and it is now a question of annihilation or victory'.** He appealed to the men of the Royal Forest of Dean to come forward at their country's call. Captain Allan said that he required 11 stalwart Foresters to make up the 5th Gloucestershire Regiment. Mr Deakin and other Coal Owners made promises

Fig. 58 Government Recruitment Drive Poster

of supplying free coal to the families of those who volunteered and to keep their jobs open while they were away. It was suggested by Captain Atkinson that perhaps the villages in the Forest might be able to raise a Forest Battalion that would be attached to the Gloucestershire Regiment. Around 50 men volunteered at the end of the meeting. At a similar meeting held at Drybrook School on Monday the 7th of September 1914, another 11 recruits were enlisted.

October 1914 brought two groups of people to the Forest of Dean from Belgium – the first to arrive were around half a dozen wounded and invalided soldiers (our boys) returning from the Front to their homes to convalesce – their experiences being told to local audiences and the press – so helping somewhat with the slacking recruitment drive.

The others to arrive were a contingent of 15 Belgian refugees. Many people gathered at Cinderford town railway station on Saturday the 17th of October 1914 to welcome them when they arrived on the evening train. They had been subjected to the brutality of the invading German army and came from the towns of Antwerp, Louvain and Malines. Provision to accommodate many of them was made by the Cinderford Auxiliary Committee of the War Relief Fund who had secured a large house at Plump Hill near Micheldean. At Lydney, a subsidiary committee had also agreed to accommodate a further eight refugees at a house in Regent Street while in Blakeney, one Belgian family was promised further accommodation.

At a miners meeting at Two Bridges near Blakeney on Saturday the 24th of October 1914, Mr Rowlinson referred to the war levy that the Forest of Dean miners had contributed to voluntarily and was pleased that the Association was able to forward £300 to the cause. He mentioned the recent arrival of Belgian refugees and hoped the money would go to helping them in their distress as more could be expected to arrive in the near future.

The Joint Wages Board agreement on Forest of Dean miners' wages was due to be reviewed on the 31st of March 1915 when a further agreement would have to be negotiated. As a result of the War, the current agreement was extended until the 31st of December 1915.

Although there was a sharp demand for Forest coal during the early part of the War, there had been a drop-off in demand during October and November 1914. Nevertheless, the Joint Wages Board decided that from the 1st of December 1914, the price of coal would rise by one shilling per ton and correspondingly, miner's wages would rise by 5%. This rise in price was justified by the Coal Owners as necessary due to the increased cost in raw materials such as pit wood and horse feed.

Mr Harry Webb M.P., who was prominent in heading the local recruitment drive, was also trying to raise recruits for the Rhondda Battalion – the Welsh miners' battalion of the Welsh Regiment. Mr Webb had financial interests in some Welsh collieries especially the Ocean Colliery and he promised to lead 'A' Company made up of men employed at Ocean colliery.

Accidents/Fatalities

On Monday the 2nd of February 1914 at the Princess Royal's Flour Mill Colliery near Bream, Charles William Stanley Ellsmore aged 15 and from Ellwood near Coleford was injured while working as a labourer underground but died later the same day. He had been working at the bottom of the shaft doing odd jobs when at approximately 11.20am he was told by Thomas Brooks to take a message to a horse driver named Brice. This he did but while returning, was caught between drams being taken to the shaft bottom by another horse driver Aubrey Williams. Mr Williams noticed Ellsmore between the drams and shouted **'what are you doing there'** and having got no reply went back and found Ellsmore bleeding from the head. He was taken out of the colliery and attended to by Dr Steward and then taken home. He was further attended by Dr McQuaide but died later that day. At the Inquest, held at Ellwood, Dr McQuaide stated that death was due to haemorrhage, fracture of the skull and brain injury. A verdict of accidental death was recorded with no blame to anyone. Sympathy was expressed to the parents by the Coroner, the Jury and the Company.

On Thursday the 5th of February 1914 at the Eastern United Colliery near Ruspidge, Mr Henry Thomas Gwilliam aged 43 and Mr Hubert Leyshon aged 27 both from Littledean and married men with families, were killed by a fall of eight tons of earth and rock. The fall completely buried them and injured another man Mr Horace Evans of Ruspidge who was severely cut about the head. The Inquest at Littledean Courthouse heard that they were all working underground at the Walmers pit loading coal in the High Delf seam with another youth Mr William Morris. At around 6.30am there was a cracking noise and when William Morris looked round he saw that rock had fallen on two men and that Mr Horace Evans was injured on the shoulder and cheek. They both ran to get help but both Mr Gwilliam and Mr Leyshon were found to be dead at the scene. It was heard that the colliery was examined at 5 o'clock that morning by Mr William Ruck and declared to be safe. The fall was in the nature of a 'slip' and not a 'bell' and there was a difference of opinion on the method of timbering between Mr Rowlinson and the Owners Representative. The rock that fell was measured as 7 feet by 12 feet and 5 feet thick and it was declared that any amount of timbering could not have prevented its fall. Mr Horace Evans, the injured man was taken to Gloucester Royal Hospital where he received treatment for facial injuries that was still ongoing. The verdict was that the fall was an accidental one and that the deaths of the two men were caused by it. Sympathy for the families was expressed by the Coroner, the Jury and the Company.

On Friday the 20th of March 1914 at the Crump Meadow Colliery near Cinderford, Mr Fred Ward aged 31, a married man from Steam Mills was killed while entering a cage that had started to descend the pit shaft. An Inquest held at the Bethel Chapel in Steam Mills heard that at approximately 6.5am, Mr Ward and five other men were about to descend the shaft. Mr Ward was the last man to enter the cage but before he could get his body fully into it, the cage started to descend, trapping Mr Ward between the cage and the wall of the shaft. His head was in the cage but his feet were out. A shout **'hold'** was made and the engine was stopped. It was stated that no shout or signal was made for the engineman to start lowering the cage. Mr Walter Parsons the engineman said that he distinctly heard the shout **'down'** and started the engine and although the banksman would normally shout the signal, Mr Parsons said that on this occasion he didn't recognise the voice. Mr Parsons had been the engineman for 17 years and nothing like this had ever happened before. Since the accident the signal was made inside the engine-house. Safety measures were discussed and Mr Joseph Hale, Manager at the pit stated that there were no 'caps' at the top of the shaft as laid down by the **Coal Mines Act** but said that alterations would be made at once. He commented that the colliery had already spent thousands of pounds to meet the requirements of the **Coal Mines Act**. A post mortem examination of Mr Ward revealed that he had a broken spine and Dr Campbell of Drybrook concluded that Mr Ward's death was due to compression of the heart and lungs and subsequent collapse from shock. The Jury returned a verdict in accordance with the Doctor's report and said that death was due to being crushed between the cage and the shaft through the cage being lowered prematurely. There was insufficient evidence to indicate that the engineman had received the signal but that there was negligence on the part of the Company for not providing the necessary signals between the banksman and the engineman and also for not providing caps for the cage to stand on at the top of the shaft.

On Sunday the 3rd of May 1914 at the Arthur and Edward (Waterloo) Colliery in Lydbrook, Mr Henry Charles, a pumpman aged 42 and married with five children was killed while working underground. Mr Charles and three other workmen were in the process of removing disused pipe-work, a pump barrel and chains from the pit bottom by lifting them up the upcast shaft with the help of the engineman. One load had already been safely removed and at 10.30am a second load of a lesser tonnage was in the process of being lifted. When the lift had done only a few yards, a loose chain had pulled tight and the engineman knew that an accident had happened below. Mr Charles was at the bottom to see that the lift was clear of obstructions but rescuers who had descended the downcast shaft failed to find him. It was discovered that the load had broken free and dropped through the timbered planking and into the sump. Mr Charles's body was found underneath the submerged load the next day.

The Inquest, held in Lydbrook, it was stated that on examination by Mr Chew, a well known local engineer, that the teeth of the lifting winch were stripped. He estimated that the load would have been in the region of seven and a half tons and the load on the teeth would be around five tons. He said that in order to cause the teeth to strip, there must have been an obstruction in the shaft and the extra load on the winch caused the teeth to strip. As a consequence, the load broke free and crashed to the bottom of the shaft. Dr Bennett said that the cause of death was a fracture of the skull and the Jury returned a verdict of accidental death. Sympathy was expressed by all present with the family.

On Wednesday the 8th of July 1914 at the Norchard Colliery near Lydney, Mr Noel Walter Akers aged 33 from Pillowell and a married man with one child was injured while working underground. Both Mr Akers and another man named Rider were employed to fill drams with rubbish and convey them down an incline which varied from 1 in 18 to 1 in 12. As was usual in pits throughout the country, sprags were used to slow the descent of drams on a downward incline i.e. an iron bar that was inserted in the wheel spokes and wedged between the leading wheel and the underside of the dram. In this case, Mr Rider inserted the sprag in place and both he and Mr Akers pushed the dram down the 1 in 18 incline but on the steeper part only one man – Mr Rider - was needed. Mr Akers then ran forward to lift the canvas screen sheets that hung down to deflect the air but the dram suddenly went out of control. Mr Rider shouted a warning **'look out'** and heard Mr Akers shout back but the dram ran Mr Akers down just before the second screen. When help arrived, Mr Akers was found lying injured in the road with the dram nearby with its wheels off the rails. The Inquest, held at Gloucester Royal Infirmary heard that before starting the dram down the first part of the incline, it had to be jerked backwards a little to get it started. This action it was suggested could have dislodged the sprag and caused it to fall out because it was found just three or four yards from the starting point.

After the accident Mr Akers was put into a dram and taken to the surface and then transported to Gloucestershire Royal Infirmary. His injuries were a fracture of the pelvis, rupture of the urethra and bruises to the right side of his chest. He was in a very collapsed condition and died on the Friday night. The Inquest recorded a verdict of accidental death and expressed their sympathy with the widow and child.

Another Runaway dram

On Friday the 10th of July at the Eastern United Colliery near Ruspidge, Mr Ernest Tom Fenner aged 35, a colliery trammer from Brains Green near Blakeney was injured while working underground. He was working with another collier, William John Davis and was engaged in loading coal from the coal face into drams and sending them down an incline to the next level. The Incline was a 1 in 3 double acting as it had a down and return rail system whereby the returning empty drams were turned around and held in position for loading by a stop block. Seven or eight drams had already been sent down that morning and it was Mr Fenner's duty to insert the stop block. On this occasion, no stop block had been inserted and for some reason, Mr Fenner had walked in front of the dram when it started to run down the incline of its own accord and ran over him. The Inquest, held at the Gloucester Royal Infirmary heard that Mr Fenner had been working at this post for several months and that all employees working in that area had been warned not to walk in front of the drams. Stop blocks were provided by the Company and witnesses said that they could not account for Mr Fenner's actions. Mr Fenner was taken by ambulance to the Blakeney Doctor and then to the Gloucester Royal Hospital where the house surgeon Mr Rupert Haines said the patient was admitted with a compound fracture of the lower end of the thigh bone and the upper end of the leg bone. An operation was performed on the joint but Mr Fenner did not rally and died that same evening. The Jury returned a verdict of accidental death with sympathy expressed for the relatives.

On Friday the 11th of September, Mr Harold Valentine Bloxome aged 22 and married was killed by a fall of debris while working underground at a colliery at Ruspidge. An Inquest at Blakeney recorded a verdict of accidental death. No further details were available.

Yet another runaway dram

On Saturday the 24th of October 1914 at the Arthur and Edward Colliery near Lydbrook, Mr Leonard Jones, a collier living at the Pludds near Lydbrook was killed while working underground. He was engaged with another collier Mr Wallace Jones in filling drams with dirt and seeing them down an incline. As normally happens in this type of work, drams are required to be spragged in order to slow their descent and this was the responsibility of Mr Leonard Jones. On this particular occasion, the dram was not spragged and it careered down the incline with Leonard Jones holding on behind. The dram tipped up when it reached the bottom of the incline with Mr Jones still holding on. He was taken out of the colliery seriously injured and was seen by Dr Bennett who determined that Mr Jones had sustained a fractured skull and had died almost instantaneously. The Inquest held at the Masons Arms Inn, Hawsley near Lydbrook returned a verdict of accidental death.

1915

After recruitment meetings mainly in towns of East Dean, the much talked of Forest of Dean Battalion had now become a reality with their headquarters based at the Cinderford Institute. Their official designation was the 13th (Forest of Dean) Battalion, Gloucestershire Regiment. The full complement of men was to be 1,350 made up of carpenters, joiners, coopers and masons although other occupations would fill the ranks. They would all be trained to use a rifle and expected to take their place at the Front. Route marches to Coleford and Lydney where they were also billeted added to their prominence with volunteers from those areas making up the numbers. Their move to Malvern for the second stage of their training was by train from Cinderford station where large crowds saw them off while the rest of the Battalion from Coleford and Lydney joined them further down the line. The whole Battalion was commanded by Mr Harry Webb, MP for the Forest of Dean Division who had joined the colours and accepted a commission as Major. This was followed shortly by promotion to Lieutenant-Colonel and his second in command was Captain W.H. Drummond, prospective Unionist candidate for the Forest of Dean.

Of course, the intense round of recruitment drives had somewhat depleted the local collieries of many of its workforce and with the unprecedented demand for coal, had caused quite a problem for the Coal Owners. At one nameless colliery the whole office staff eligible for service and over 70 others had enlisted and many other young men who worked underground as hewers, trammers or hodders had joined the ranks. This problem was also exacerbated by the arrival at various collieries, of miners from South Wales canvassing to entice more Forest miners away to the Powell Duffryn and other collieries in the Aberdare valley. A significant number were tempted to accept their offer of over £3 per week in wages plus travel costs plus housing. Naturally the Coal Owners took exception to this practice and it was stopped in its tracks although replacing skilled workers was a problem. However, seeing that they were the main instigators in encouraging young men to enlist, the Coal Owners had to accept the situation with resignation.

Good news however for those still working in the Forest collieries as another increase in wages was agreed in April 1915 by the Joint Wages Board. Due to the increase in the price of coal in other competing Districts, the Owners had decided to raise the cost of their coal by 2 shillings per ton. This in turn meant that Forest miners wages increased by 10% and they were now at 60% above the 1888 Standard.

More Belgian refugees arrived in the Forest and Sir W. Gwynne-Evans at Oaklands Park between Blakeney and Newnham agreed to accommodate two families from Liege. They arrived at Awre station and were taken by motor car to their accommodation at the octagonal lodge at the western entrance to Oaklands Park. Mrs Gwynne-Evans had kindly furnished the Lodge and the **Forest of Dean Miners Association** agreed to maintain the refugees from the miners levy.

Pit Stop – South Wales
The Forest of Dean Coalfield's close neighbour, the South Wales Coalfield was coming to the end of their wages agreement with the Coal Owners. On the 1st of April 1915 the Executive Committee of the **South Wales Miners' Federation** submitted to the Coal Owners three months notice to terminate their current agreement when it came to an end on the 30th of June 1915. New terms were put forward that included a 20% wage rise plus other far reaching proposals agreed at a meeting of the Executive Committee in Cardiff in February 1915.

During the three month notice period, no progress had been made with the Coal Owners who flatly refused the miners demands despite the efforts of Mr Walter Runciman, the President of the Board of Trade to act as a mediary. The miners were determined to take strike action in order to get their demands met, despite their getting a War bonus. Meanwhile 1,700 men at the Ocean Collieries in the Rhondda valley had gone on strike as a result of the Company employing 100 non Union men. A further 600 men at a colliery at Tonyrefail tendered notices for the same reason.

The Government had let it be known that a strike at this time would not be tolerated as the Navy depended on South Wales for its coal supply. David Lloyd George, the Minister of Munitions interceded and at meetings held in Cardiff, was successful in resolving the dispute. At the eleventh hour it was announced by the **SWMF** that by a vote of 123 to 112, they would accept the Government's terms for agreement which included an 18.5% wage rise, but in the end both parties still had their differences which could not be resolved at that time.

Forest of Dean

As the only public gathering scheduled for 1915, the **Miners' Annual Demonstration** – or Gala as some would call it – was held again at the Speech House field on Saturday the 10th of July 1915. Regarded as one of the best yet, the event attracted an enormous crowd of miners with their families or girlfriends on a fine day with all the attractions that a fairground could offer. With surplus money in their pockets this year and accompanied by the Berry Hill Brass Band, families were able to enjoy the carousels, galloping horses, swing-boats, side shows, coconut shies, mechanical organ music, beer tent and much more, all provided by Messrs Studt and Co. and accompanied by the regular thump and toots of steam engines used to power the event. Early afternoon was given over to the mass meeting of miners and their guests in a large marquee with the platform occupied by the Executive of the **Forest of Dean Miners' Association** and guest Mr Robert Smillie, President of the **Miners' Federation of Great Britain.**

In consideration of the spectacle at the 1914 Annual Demonstration where politics disrupted the meeting, Mr Martin Perkins, President of the **FODMA** in his opening address said that the Executive Committee had decided that for the first time for many years, they would not have politics on the Platform and that in future only Labour leaders would be invited to speak. This brought cheers of agreement from the crowd and Vice President Mr David Organ in his usual appeal for more miners to join the Union proposed a resolution, seconded by Mr Edward Morgan that stated; *'That this meeting of miners fully believes that the best way to obtain fair wages and reasonable contracts and also our minimum wage is to become thoroughly organised to a man and we pledge ourselves to use our utmost endeavours* *to persuade all our fellow workers to at once join the Forest of Dean Miners Association'.*

Fig. 59 The legendary Speech House and adjoining field
Photo Author

This was supported by Mr Smillie who went on to say that; **'this country and the rest of Europe are now under a dark cloud and I have no desire to see the War last a moment longer. I detest this War and the methods of war show a terrible downfall for the teachings of Christ and Christianity. The recruitment campaign has depleted the mines of many of its men to the extent that some pits in other parts of this country are unable to operate. I urge you fellow miners to support the country and bring the War to an end by getting more coal to supply our Navy and manufacturing companies which are supplying the instruments of death.'** Asked from the floor about the situation in the Welsh Coalfields where strike action was threatened due to higher wage demands, Mr Smillie said that; **'I have to be very careful with my words on the matter but it is a fact that the Welsh Coal Owners are making untold fortunes and I can't see why the miners cannot get a decent** wage agreement. The miners have given way on some of their ideals and I believe that the Coal Owners should make similar concessions and conclude a lasting deal. In fact I have given my personal pledge to Lloyd George that the MFGB will willingly act as mediators should it be needed in order that nothing will impede the solidarity of the Nation.'

After being given a rapturous applause, the meeting concluded with Mr Rowlinson thanking Mr Smillie, the Chairman and the mover and seconder of the Resolution.

Pit Stop - South Wales continued.

The South Wales miners decided to take strike action as from Thursday the 15th of July 1915 and determined as he was to avoid a strike under wartime conditions, Lloyd George, acting as Minister of Munitions, invoked the **Munitions of War Act**. This effectively made strike action an offence and in the Valleys, this only made matters worse. So, on that Thursday, over 200,000 men went on strike. Although the **MFGB** opposed this strike action, it was also opposed to Lloyd George's **Munitions of War Act** aimed at the mining community.

However, how did you prosecute that many individual men from the Valleys? Lloyd George had his back to the wall and his only escape was to strike a deal with the Coal Owners to accept all the miners' demands. Meetings took place at Cardiff between Lloyd George and his Ministerial colleagues, the Coal Owners and the **SWMF** and on Tuesday the 20th of July 1915, an agreement had been reached. This had to go before the Delegate Conference on the 21st but was foreseen as a foregone conclusion. One of the Owners' representatives was brave enough to express his opinion on the deal by saying; **'we are thoroughly sick-wounded and we have given in simply because of our loyalty to the country's interest. There is not the slightest likelihood of the terms being rejected for the men have come out trumps all round'.**

The Delegate Conference, as predicted, adopted the terms of the settlement and the men were recommended to return to work – which many did on that same day with the rest returning on the Thursday. The Terms of the agreement are complicated to describe here but as a result, the South Wales miners, having used the War as a lever against the Coal Owners had achieved concessions they could not have dreamed about.

On a National basis, it was acknowledged that the rate of voluntary recruitment had slowed but Prime Minister Asquith was reluctant to introduce Conscription. However, in July 1915 the Government did pass the **National Registration Act** which required compulsory registration for all men between the ages of 18 and 65. This was seen as a prelude to Compulsory Conscription but voluntary recruitment continued with Lord Derby as Director General in control.

In the Forest, it was muted at several local meetings that some form of Conscription was necessary. One of the prominent colliery managers Mr Percy Moore remarked at a meeting in Lydney that due to the inefficiencies of the recruitment campaign, he would urge the Government to adopt Conscription at an early date.

It became known through Lodge meetings that the finances of the **FODMA** were still in a very poor state, especially after the 1912 strike where they had to borrow £800 from the Old Age Pension Fund to pay miners their strike pay. Around £400 had already been paid back and unless the balance could be settled soon, there was the possibility that the Union could be wound up. This crisis prompted yet another round of Union recruitment with the arrival of Mr James Winstone, President of the **SWMF** on his tour of the local district intent on persuading Forest miners to use tactics currently in use in some of the mining Districts in South Wales. These involved waylaying miners on their way to work and asking them to show their Union Card before clocking on their shift. It was widely thought that eventually this would lead to strike action at a number of local pits where miners would not work with non Union men. These Welsh tactics were generally viewed with distaste as relationships between men and Employers in the Forest had been good for many years despite the 1912 strike. By mid October 1915 however, the Union ranks had swelled by over 1,000 so it was supposed that Mr Winstone's methods of persuasion must have had some effect.

Whatever may have been the woes of the **FODMA,** Forest miners were still contributing liberally to the War Fund and Mr Rowlinson's reports showed that they were regularly contributing around £300 monthly to the cause. He also reported that the Forest collieries had contributed between 600 and 700 men to the Army and although numbers working in local collieries had, over many years averaged 5,600, he was surprised to learn that the figure had increased to over 6,000.

Military recruitment had taken a downturn in numbers during this period and it didn't help matters when Col. H. Webb, commander of the Forest of Dean Battalion, suddenly resigned his position, leaving Major Boulton in command. During his many appearances at recruitment drives, Col. Webb had repeated his dedication to the Battalion and said that he would train with them and go into battle with them. Many local men therefore refused to join the colours quoting Col. Webb as being dishonest in not carrying out his promise to the men. This local attitude was relayed to Col. Webb who was, at that time involved in the recruitment of the 14th Battalion of the Worcestershire Regiment, the Severn Valley Pioneers.

In October 1915 he published a very strongly worded critical letter in the Dean Forest Mercury in answer to his critics; *'It has come to my notice that the young men of the Forest who are in large numbers, in my judgement, refusing without any justification whatever to enlist, are making as their excuse that I, as Commanding Officer of the 13th Gloucesters, have not carried out the promise made at the time I was engaged in raising the Battalion, namely, to go out with the Battalion. I should not have thought it necessary to write this letter had not the information come to me from a brother Officer of the 13th Gloucesters, now engaged in recruiting in the Forest of Dean, that he is actually hindered in his work by the absence of any information from me as to my reasons for leaving the Forest of Dean Battalion. The fact is I am not today commanding the 13th Gloucesters because the War Office directed me to relinquish the command to another and an elementary regulation of military discipline is that a soldier does as he is told. The order to relinquish the command did not contain any reasons for the step taken, and it was not for me to question my orders. The whole thing was a bitter disappointment to me but I had no option in the matter. Subsequently, the War Office invited me to raise another Pioneer Battalion and I am now engaged in this task at Worcester. I sincerely hope that after this word from me we shall hear no more of these absurd excuses, which appear to be the feeble response which too many young Foresters are content to make when Lieutenant Larder and others point out to them which way their duty lies. I hope you support me when I say that after this brief explanation I do not think it necessary to further pursue a matter so distasteful to me and so unworthy of the best traditions of the Forest and of its residents'*

At the end of November 1915, Mr Rowlinson joined a party of representatives of Labour civilians who made a visit to the Western Front near to Loos in France. Just two months earlier, the great push, known as the Battle of Loos against German defences using chlorine gas, had failed, leaving a mind boggling 59,000 British casualties. However, Mr Rowlinson's party were given every facility for viewing operations going on there but were also subjected to constant shellfire with a * 'Jack Johnson' exploding quite close, although he described his experiences as 'exciting'. Mud was the great problem in the trenches and he had to extricate himself more than once from the morass but he confessed that he was greatly impressed by the Army's organisation and their efforts to promote the comfort of the troops. He was satisfied that everyone engaged on the allied side in Flanders was doing their bit and that those at home should do their part to support them.

* A 'Jack Johnson' was the British nickname used to describe the impact of a heavy, black German 15-cm artillery shell.

Accidents/Fatalities

On Friday the 5th of February 1915, Mr James Herbert Nash aged 57 of Marsh Lane, Ellwood, was killed while working underground at the Flour Mill Colliery, Bream. On the Thursday evening, Mr Nash was working with Mr Albert Powell blasting rock in order that double timbering could be installed on a roadway. A shot was fired early on the Friday morning and after about half an hour when it was considered to be safe, Mr Nash returned to the spot and started work. A large rock suddenly fell onto Mr Nash's leg causing such severe injuries that he died shortly afterwards. An Inquest held at the Primitive Methodist Chapel at Ellwood returned a verdict of accidental death.

On Thursday the 11th of March 1915, Mr Benjamin Joseph Ensor aged 22, a haulage contractor of Church Road, St John's, Cinderford, was killed while working underground at the Foxes Bridge Colliery. Mr Ensor was working in the pit bottom with Mr Albert Merrett driving a horse and drams. Both men were riding in one of the drams when it became derailed and crashed into some timber supports which fell and brought down about a ton of earth onto Mr Ensor. Mr Merrett was miraculously unhurt. Mr Ensor was so severely injured that he died almost at once. He was brought out of the colliery and taken home. At the Inquest held at Cinderford, it was heard that the deceased knew the roadway well and that it was usual for the haulier to ride in the dram. The Jury recorded a verdict of accidental death and expressed their sympathy for the deceased man's relatives.

On Saturday the 20th of March 1915 Mr Alfred John Butt aged 42 of the Rocks was injured while working underground at the Lightmoor Colliery near Cinderford. Mr Butt had been working with Mr Charles Bowdler and Mr William Perks in the Churchway seam when there was a sudden fall of coal and clod which covered the three men. They were all released with help from other colliers but Mr Butt had received two broken legs, and another man had one broken leg. Mr Butt was able to speak after the accident and said that no one was to blame. Both men were taken to the surface and conveyed home. Mr Butt was seen by Dr Beadles but he did not rally and died the following Monday. The place of work had been examined that same morning without comment and the men had been employed removing 'clod' in order to put up some temporary supports.

At an Inquest held at Ruspidge, Mr Bowdler said he could not think of any other cause for the fall, other than a blind slip but there had been no evidence of it beforehand. Dr Beadles gave evidence that death was due to an embolism – a clot of blood on the brain. The Jury returned a verdict of accidental death and expressed their sympathy for the widow and family. Mr Treasure on behalf of the Owners said that Mr Butt had worked at the colliery for 12 years and was a competent and respected workman.

On Tuesday the 18th of May 1915, Mr Frank Bevan aged 34, a Butty collier and married with no children was killed while working underground at the Cannop Colliery near Parkend. Mr Bevan was working at the coal face and before holing was in the process of putting up props. Without warning, some four tons of coal fell onto him and he died instantly as his body had been terribly broken up. At the Inquest held at Lydbrook, it was heard that the scene of the fall was examined later and found that there were cross slips in the vein of coal that could not have been seen earlier. The Jury returned a verdict of accidental death due to injuries received by the fall. The Colliery proprietors expressed their sympathy with the widow and said that Mr Bevan had been a capable and steady man in whom they had had great faith.

On Friday the 25th of June 1915, Mr Charles Angel aged 60 a workman, died as a result of injuries he received while working at the Norchard Colliery, Lydney. Mr Angel had met with previous minor accidents and at some time had received two separate pinches to the small finger of his left hand. He was seen by Dr Thomas who dressed the wound but as it became very painful, he was admitted to Lydney Cottage Hospital suffering from septic poisoning. His condition appeared to improve for two or three days but he died on the morning of Friday the 25th of June 1915. At the Inquest held at the Lydney Police Station, Dr Thomas said that the cause of death was septicaemia and the Jury returned a verdict that death was due to septic poisoning as a result of an accident at the colliery and that no blame was attached to anyone. The colliery Directors expressed sympathy with relatives and their regret that so slight an accident should prove fatal.

On Friday the 16th of July 1915, Mr Edward Vaughan aged 29, a collier from Mill Hill, Bream, was killed while working underground at the Princess Royal Colliery, Bream. Mr Vaughan was working at the coal face with his brother Mr Arnold Vaughan aged 24 who had estimated that the timbering looked sound when they started their shift at 6.30am. Everything had gone well until at about 10.15am when he heard his brother shout **'Arnold'** and he looked around to find him completely covered in a great fall of coal. He said he shouted for help and two other colliers came and helped him get his brother out onto a stretcher and Dr Pugh was called but he had died almost immediately. At the Inquest held at the Primitive Methodist Schoolroom at Bream, the colliery Inspector said that he had inspected the place an hour before the accident and it had appeared perfectly safe. He estimated that about one and a half tons of coal and earth had fallen onto the deceased who was a very competent workman. The Jury returned a verdict of accidental death and together with the colliery Owners, expressed their sympathy to the family of the deceased.

On Thursday the 5th of August 1915, Mr John Henry Lodge aged 37, a collier from The Reddings, Lydbrook was injured while working underground at the Waterloo Colliery, Lydbrook. Mr Lodge was working with his brother Mr Frank Lodge at the coal face. Mr John Lodge was lying on his side holing the bottom of the face when, at about 11am, a large piece of coal fell from the top of the face. Mr Frank Lodge was loading drams about six feet away and heard his brother call for help and went to see what was the matter. He said he found him lying under the block of coal which had covered him except for his head. With the help of another collier Mr Joseph Hale, he managed to get his brother clear and took him up to the surface where Dr Bennett was waiting to examine him. He was then taken by motor car to Gloucester Royal Infirmary accompanied by Messrs Lodge and Hale. At the Inquest held at the Gloucester Royal Infirmary, the temporary House surgeon Dr Ernest John Crawshaw said that Mr Lodge was admitted at 3pm on Thursday the 5th of August 1915 with multiple injuries. He had a fractured pelvis, a broken collar bone, one or more fractured ribs that could have punctured the lungs and was suffering from extreme shock. He also said that his condition was such that he could not immediately perform an operation and that in the first twelve hours, he did improve a little. However, his condition deteriorated and he sank and died on the Saturday evening. Witness Mr Joseph Hale said that the roof near the spot where the coal fell was properly propped but not the coal itself as it hadn't yet been holed. Mr Joseph Kear, shot firer and overman said he walked down the road where the deceased had been working on the Thursday morning and noticed nothing remarkable about the spot where the coal fell. Mr Charlie Cooper, under manager said he was at the spot where the coal fell just before it happened and although the coal was overhanging, he considered the road to be in proper order. The Jury returned a verdict of accidental death and the colliery and Miners Agent's representatives expressed appreciation of the deceased and sympathy with his relatives.

1916

His Majesty the King saw fit to include Lieutenant Colonel Henry Webb MP for the Forest of Dean Division in his New Years' Honours List with an offer of a Baronetcy. He became Lieutenant-Colonel Sir Henry Webb, Bart., M.P. honoured in recognition of his War services.

The New Year in the Forest was greeted with strong winds and snow blizzards that took its toll on the transport system and industry. Several trains were held up due to snow drifts and roads became blocked with fallen trees, causing many collieries to either close for periods or go on short time. Telephone lines were down in many areas and homes became covered in drifts and it took several days before people could dig themselves clear. At a time when coal production had been on the increase, this came as a serious setback in the push to help the country supply its much needed resources. By April however, things were very much back to normal.

In January 1916, the Home Secretary established **Colliery District Special Recruiting Courts** directed especially to deal with the enlistment of miners. It was decided that miners working underground and those on the surface engaged as winding enginemen, pumpmen, weighmen, electricians, fitters or mechanics would not be enlisted without the consent of the Home Office. Other workers at the surface including officials and other staff would not be subject to these exemptions except under special circumstances decided by these courts. Forest of Dean Courts consisted of Mr G.H. Rowlinson, representing the workmen, Sir Francis Brain, representing the employers and Dr W.N. Atkinson, chief Inspector of Mines.

As the casualties of War continued to grow within the pages of the local press, especially many from local villages who joined the Gloucestershire Regiment, the poor recruitment record in the Forest came in for much criticism. It had been reported that some young miners were regularly absenting themselves from their workplace by either feigning illness for a day or two or taking time off to recover from either weekend excesses or extended holiday time. This did them no favours, either within their own community or with the authorities and they were regarded as delinquents. Collieries were bound by law to keep records of absenteeism and to make them available to the Special Recruiting Courts if requested. So they were treading a fine line. Mr Rowlinson made several appeals for these men to attend their employment regularly and to assist their fellow countrymen fighting in the trenches by maintaining the maximum output of coal.

Compulsory Conscription

The Military Service Bill was introduced to Parliament in January 1916 which advocated compulsory Conscription on sections of the male population. The **MFGB** organised a vote of all the coalfields as to their agreement or otherwise to this Government Policy.

Results were;

For Conscription	38,100,
Against Conscription	653,190,
Neutral	23,200,
Majority against Conscription	**615,090.**

The Forest of Dean Miners balloted 2,000 votes for Conscription.

And so, the **Military Service Act** came into force on the 10th of February 1916 with the 2nd of March 1916 being the last day for voluntary enlistment and the 3rd of March 1916 for compulsory enlistment to begin. Basically it imposed Conscription on a section of the male population of England, Wales and Scotland between the ages of 18 and 41 years. This was a controversial move by the Asquith coalition government, the Home Secretary John Simon resigning in protest and many Liberal Members voting against the Bill. However it did provide exemptions for certain marital states or a reserved occupation such as mining.

In accordance with the January legislation, miners were excused from enlistment unless they decided to join the colours of their own accord while underground workers were exempt anyway. If, for any reason a person objected to being conscripted, they, or their representative or employer were able to put their case before a Military Service Tribunal and an appeal before a County Appeal Tribunal (held at Lydney, Coleford and Cinderford). A second **Act** was introduced in May 1916 to include married men.

The **FODMA** were now boasting nearly a full membership of miners in the district with around 300 or so yet to join. Many collieries had no non Union men on their workforce and the threatened strike over this issue was averted by prompt negotiations between Union executives and Coal Owners. Furthermore, many felt that calling a strike at the time of National crisis was not in the interests of the workforce.

However, the generosity of the miners of the Forest of Dean could not be questioned. Apart from contributing generously to the War Levy, they were also making fortnightly contributions via the **FODMA** for the purchase of a motor ambulance to be presented to the Red Cross and St John's Ambulance Associations for use of our troops in France. With help from local concerts and social events and also contributions from the Coal Owners Association, £600 was raised and the Ambulance was handed over at Nottingham by Mr H. Deakin and Mr G. Rowlinson.

In early July 1916, wage increases of 10% were granted to Forest miners with permission from the Board of Trade, bringing the rate up to 70% above the 1888 Standard. Coal Owners however were disappointed that they could not at that time raise the price of coal despite the rising cost of materials and labour.

The **Miners' Annual Demonstration** was again held at the Speech House field on Saturday the 8th of July 1916 in fine weather. Much merrymaking was the order of the day with the usual attractions of the fairground attended by upwards of 3,000 people. At the afternoon public meeting, Mr Martin Perkins, President of the **FODMA** was in the Chair and the platform, as was decided in 1915, was devoid of any Political presence as the Member of Parliament for the Forest Division had not been invited. The main speaker was again Mr Robert Smillie, President of the **MFGB** who congratulated the Union for the direction they had made to complete organisation during the past 12 months and hoped that further progress to solid organisation within the next year. He also alluded to the hard work the miners of the country had put in to secure the maximum output of coal despite contributing 250,000 men to the Colours but criticised the weak link in the distribution system as the middle men. He said that although the price of coal for domestic consumers had been kept quite low, there was apparently no control over the middle men charging their own inflated price for coal on the home market where some small industrial consumers had to pay shameful prices for small quantities they were able to secure.

Following his speech, the Vice Chairman Mr David Organ moved a resolution which was seconded by Mr W.H. Smith and supported by Mr Smillie; *'That the Committee of the Forest of Dean Miners Association are pleased to report that since the last Demonstration, there had been a very large increase in the membership of the Association. Still, we urge all Lodge committees not to slacken their energies till every man and boy in and about the mines of this District are members of the Association. Also, that in view of the enormous increase in the cost of living which has taken place during the last two years, we strongly urge the Government to take over the mines, to take control of the prices of foodstuffs and other necessities of life of the people, and to prevent the exploitation which is at present going on.'* This resolution was carried unanimously.

In order to keep coal production at its maximum, both miners' representatives and Coal Owners came to an amicable and patriotic agreement not to disrupt production by taking leave on the August Bank Holiday. It was originally agreed that the house coal collieries would end their day at 2pm instead of the usual 3pm but get paid for the lost hour. But as the steam coal men had agreed to work the whole Monday, the rest of the Forest miners agreed to do likewise and work without stoppage. By contrast, the South Wales miners voted to take two days' holiday.

A further advance in the Forest miners' wages of 10% was made, starting in October 1916, bringing the rate up to 80% above the 1888 Standard. Similarly the Board of Trade gave the Coal Owners the authority to raise the price of Forest coal by 1 shilling and 6 pence per ton in consideration of increased costs of materials and the recent 20% increase in miners' wages.

Government Control in South Wales
In November 1916, the South Wales miners were involved in a dispute with their employers which resulted in the threat of another strike. The miners distrusted the Coal Owners in honestly keeping to the terms of the previous

agreement under which the rates of wages are fixed. The miners wanted an increase in wages of 15% to keep up with the continued rise in food prices but the Coal Owners wanted a decrease of 10%. This stalemate could easily have been resolved had the Coal Owners taken steps to clear themselves of the accusation and submitted to a Joint Audit, but they refused. Negotiations in London between both parties and the Board of Trade resulted in the Government taking control of the South Wales and Monmouthshire coalfields as from the 1st of December 1916 under Regulation 9G of the Defence of the Realm Act. The miners were also granted their 15% wage claim which brought their rate up to 40.83% above the new Standard and 111.25% above the old Standard plus their War Bonus of 17.5%. A Joint Audit with an independent auditor was also part of the deal and Viscount Alfred Milner was appointed as Coal Controller.

Dilke Memorial Hospital

Progress was made with the **'Dilke Memorial Hospital scheme'** and the sub-committee was of the opinion that a suitable site at Yew Tree Brake between Cinderford and Speech House was the best option. When built it would initially have 8 beds with a medical staff consisting of a Matron, a nurse and an assistant nurse. The amount of donations had reached £2,567 with a further promise of £1,000 from an anonymous donor plus £500 from Inglis Charitable Bequest. Local businesses promised another £200 and a further £500 was promised from the Crown if the Scheme is approved and they would also contribute £25 per year towards its maintenance.

The **FODMA** held their recent ballot of officials for the forthcoming year, the only change being at the top. Current President Mr Martin Perkins was defeated by Mr William Smith by a narrow majority – Mr Perkins receiving 1,121 votes and Mr Smith 1,164 votes.

As the course of the War became bogged down due to constant indecision at the top of Government, Prime Minister Herbert Asquith came under pressure from so-called coalition colleagues and was ultimately forced to

Fig. 60 David Lloyd George

resign on the 5th of December 1916. A new coalition Government was formed under the leadership of David Lloyd George, who it was accepted had a more positive and firm resolution as to the direction in which they were to fight the War and took charge of a slimmed down War Cabinet.

Accidents/Fatalities

On Friday the 21st of January 1916, Mr George Morgan aged 49, a married man with a family, was killed while working underground at the Arthur and Edward (Waterloo) Colliery near Lydbrook. The Inquest held at Joys Green heard that three men had been lowering loaded drams down an incline when the leading dram ran away. Mr Morgan was working at the bottom of the incline repairing the roadway and was unable to get clear in time and he was hit by the runaway dram. He suffered severe injuries to the base of his skull and died immediately. It was stated by the witnesses that the drams had been properly spragged but one must have either broken or fallen out accidentally. The Jury recorded a verdict of accidental death. Sympathy was extended to the widow and family of Mr Morgan from both the Jury and representatives of the colliery. Mr Joseph Hale, the colliery manager expressed his deep sorrow at losing such a valued workman and said that the Company had done all in its power to keep his workforce safe. Mr Rowlinson also said that he had known Mr Morgan for over 25 years and that a more capable workman would be impossible to find.

On Tuesday the 4th of July 1916, Mr Albert Edward Watts Treasure aged 17 and a single man, was killed while working underground at the Eastern United Colliery near Ruspidge. Mr Arthur Turner the engineman at the colliery had received a signal to wind up the dipple a train of drams but immediately after starting, he noticed that something was wrong and shut down the engine and applied the brake. Another workman Mr Oliver Grindle, a haulage contractor was sent down the dipple to see what was wrong and discovered Mr Treasure lying dead on his right side in front of the train and on top of the front dram which had been pulled over onto its side. Mr Treasure's job was to receive the 'bond' as it came down the road and attach it to the train and set them off towards the surface. He had been known to sometimes ride up the dipple on a train of drams but not improperly.

The Inquest, held at Ruspidge heard witness Mr Oliver Grindle say that he could see no obstruction that could have caused the accident but suggested that if the deceased had had his foot on the buffer when the train was started, this could have been the cause. This theory was corroborated by three other workmen. Dr Rigden said that death was instantaneous and was due to injuries to the head which was extensively fractured. There was also laceration to the brain on the right side behind the ear. The Jury returned a verdict of accidental death and together with the colliery Directors expressed their sympathy with the parents and family.

On Thursday the 7th of September 1916, Mr Thomas Webb aged 68, a married man from Brierley, was injured while working underground at the Trafalgar Colliery. Mr Webb had worked there for 40 years and on the day of the accident was seen walking up the incline with an acetylene lamp. The accident happened at 2.45pm when he was hit by some runaway drams and severely injured. The Inquest held at the Gloucester Royal Infirmary heard from Mr George Cutter of Edge End, a bogie driver who said that he had attached the clutch to the rope and also taken out four spraggs from the wheels and left six in before letting the train down the incline. He said that somehow or other the clutch must have slipped from the rope, so letting the drams free to start down on their own. He followed the drams down and came across the injured man. Mr Robert Pember said that he was in the road and heard the sound of the runaway drams and crouched in the side. Then a number of drams rushed passed him and stopped when they came off the rails. He then saw Mr Webb lying in the road but could not say how he met his death. Mr Thomas Townshend stated that he was waiting in a manhole for some empty drams to pass when he heard a crash and rushed to the scene which was about thirty yards away. He found Mr Webb lying on the side of the road but not quite clear of the rails with his head to the ground and bleeding from the head, face and nose. He was taken to the surface and transported to Gloucester Royal Infirmary.

The House Surgeon at the Infirmary stated that Mr Webb was brought to the Institution on Thursday suffering from a fractured skull, a scalp wound on the right side of his head and a small wound on the right eyelid. He was unconscious at that time but did not regain consciousness and died on the Friday. He said that in his opinion death was due to a fractured skull. The Jury returned a verdict that death was due to a fractured skull as a result of an accident. No blame was attached to anyone. Sympathy was expressed with the widow and family by both the Jury and the colliery representative.

Fig. 61 Foxes Bridge Colliery, courtesy of the DHC, Soudley, Cinderford.

1917
The Comb-out and Government Control

All Forest of Dean miners now had to appear at special centres set up by an order requiring all miners of military age to present themselves for medical examination. This included men who were already declared exempt and those who had received exemptions from the local appeal courts. However, a further development during January 1917 changed all that.

The Comb-Out
On Tuesday the 23rd of January 1917, every colliery in Great Britain received a Government directive aimed at culling 20,000 more men from the mines into the Military. The men to be combed out were divided into three classes;
1. Men who had entered the mines since August 14th 1915,
2. Surface workers or Officials supervising such workers
    (except enginemen, pumpmen, weighmen, electricians,
    fitters and mechanics),
3. Workers of military age employed in the mines who, during
    the previous three months had lost on average two or

more shifts during the week from avoidable causes. Volunteers would still be able to enlist.

The **MFGB** held urgent meetings with Sir George Cave the Home Secretary clarifying their position and demanding concessions on the three classes of men described. The outcome agreed between both parties was that Class 1 - only men who had entered the mines since August 14th 1915 were to be targeted with a few minor exceptions. Retrospective absenteeism was withdrawn but employers were urged to crack down on those who were considered persistent absentees. It was stressed that if that agreement failed to gain the 20,000 men needed, then the other options would be put into force.

Opposition to this came, not unexpectedly from the South Wales coalfield and the **SWMF**, at a meeting in Cardiff on Tuesday the 13th of February 1917 decided by an overwhelming

Fig.62 More men and Still More

majority to reject the arrangements arrived at between the **MFGB** and the Home Secretary.

Government Control
It was inevitable that Lloyd George's Coalition Government would eventually take control of all the remaining coalfields of Great Britain and this proposal was announced on the 14th of February 1917. The Board of Trade took charge of the mines under Regulation 9G of the Defence of the Realm Act on the 1st of March 1917 and Mr Guy Calthrop was appointed as Coal Controller, assisted by Sir Richard Redmayne, chief Inspector of Mines. An Advisory Committee was also set up consisting of seven Coal Owners and seven workers representatives. Sir Francis Brain was appointed as one of the Coal Owners on that Committee.

Over 25% of the country's coal industry workforce had now either voluntarily enlisted or been taken by Conscription with the result that coal production had been drastically reduced. Some of this workforce had been replaced with unskilled labour but as it was the young and efficient able bodied men who had been taken, it proved difficult to replace them. Coal was the Country's energy source but it was also necessary in order to fight the War. Both required large numbers of the country's workforce and it was recognised by Government that something must be done to re establish the Nation's coal supplies. The Coal Controller was looking into ways of solving this problem although it was announced that another 20,000 men were to be taken from the Nation's mines.

However, on Thursday the 8th of March 1917, the **MFGB** received notice from General Geddes, Director of Recruiting on behalf of the War Office, of a concession which would alleviate the problem. It stated that if through voluntary recruitment from the mines, 20,000 men could be found within two months from March the 8th 1917, then men who had received their notices but not yet enlisted, will not be called up. If, after two months, the 20,000 had not been raised then those men will be called to make up the number. This concession was agreed to by the Executive Council of the **MFGB.**

In the Forest of Dean, as War casualties continued to grow, Mr Rowlinson was still active in supporting the Military in their recruitment drive. However at several meetings, attendances were poor and at one such meeting in Cinderford Town Hall in April 1917, a small crowd gathered in the street and would not go into the Hall. Instead, the meeting was held in the street and speeches were addressed by both Mr Rowlinson and Mr Abel Evans who had come down from Gloucester. By way of contrast, a similar meeting held at the Picture House in Lydney four days later was well attended.

For a variety of reasons, the **Miners' Annual Demonstration,** usually held at the Speech House field in July, was cancelled for 1917. Besides the stirrings of discontent within the **FODMA** and Mr Rowlinson's position within it, it was also felt that an event of that nature during the ravages of War would have been inappropriate.

Mr Rowlinson's Exit
Mr Rowlinson's position was made clearer at an open air meeting at Speech House on Tuesday the 7th of August 1917 chaired by Mr Richard Kear. Three prominent South Wales miners' leaders Mr Victor Banks from

Abertillery and Messrs F. Marchant and F. Barry from Blaenavon were invited to speak, principally on resisting the **'comb-out'** and a demand for a negotiated peace. A Resolution was passed condemning the Agent (Mr Rowlinson) for committing the Forest of Dean miners to the **'comb-out'** scheme without consulting them and to oppose any future 'combing out' of miners. Another Resolution called for Trade Unions in all countries to take the necessary steps to negotiate an immediate and honorary peace.

Mr Martin Perkins the ex President of the **FODMA** was in the chair at another miners meeting at Cinderford on Monday the 20th of August 1917 and supported by Mr Rowlinson urged the miners to listen to reason regarding the **'comb-out'** and said that the Military would always have the last word. Mr Rowlinson said that because the miners Union was now strong, the men should not take advantage of the situation because they were numerous and organised. He said that as he gauged the feeling of the District, he would sooner drop out of existence altogether than be a bone of contention or the cause of the least quibble amongst them. He said that the Recruiting Authorities had been unable to get the 40,000 men asked for from the mines from those who had rushed to the mines to escape enlistment. They were either too old or physically unfit and only one third of them were capable of carrying arms. He urged his audience to abide by the decision of the **MFGB** as the Military ruled supreme and would always have the last word.

At this time the **MFGB** leaders met with the Coal Controller and submitted a request for a 25% increase in miners wages which, he said he would convey to the Government for consideration. All mining Districts were then sent forms by the Coal Controller asking for particulars of those who had entered the mines since August 1914 and who had not been called-up. And so the net appears to have widened to include another 40,000 men from the mines and backdated the order to August 1914, replacing the original 'August 1915' order.

At a meeting at the Speech House on Sunday the 25th of August 1917 in pouring rain Mr W. H. Smith, President of the **FODMA** spoke to over 2,000 men and women and defended Mr Rowlinson's actions in voting with the **MFGB** in favour of the **'comb-out'.** He said that Mr Rowlinson had held that voting power for years past without any recriminations from the men. Mr Rowlinson spoke of the Executive Council's decision to take no further part in the **'comb-out'** but said it would mean that they, (the **FODMA**) would have to come out of the Federation if they did. He said that he would do all he could to keep the Forest of Dean coalfield in the Federation.

In response to the **MFGB's** request for a 25% increase in miners' wages. the Coal Controller responded in September 1917 with an improved offer which the **MFGB** accepted unanimously. The improved offer was an extra 1 shilling and 6 pence per day for over 16 years of age and 9 pence per day for youths.

Another visitor from the South Wales coalfield, Mr W.S. Jones from Blackwood in Monmouthshire, addressed a meeting at Speech House on Sunday the 23rd of September 1917. Mr Reuben James from Pillowell took the chair and in his opening speech declared that the **FODMA** was in a funny state and wanted overhauling. He said that they should keep the Agent (Mr Rowlinson) and the Executive Committee but make all efforts to secure a Labour candidate to represent them in Parliament at the next General Election. Mr Jones however, didn't mince his words when he suggested the Association was in a deplorable state, behind the times and needed overhauling. He said that Forest of Dean wages rates were the lowest that he had ever seen and outlined his vision of what needed to be done to improve the situation but said that he didn't blame the Agent nor did he want to take his place.

Three Resolutions were passed
1. *'That this mass meeting of members considers that it would be to the general interest of all the members of the Association to adopt a scheme of reorganisation. We therefore request the Agent Mr G.H. Rowlinson and all other Officials of the local Association to immediately tender their resignations and place the same in the hands of the Secretary.*
2. *That we appoint the Agent pro.tem and the following persons to the Emergency Committee ---------. This Committee to have power to control and direct, along with the Agent, all business belonging to the Association.*
3. *That we appoint the new Agent to be the Inspector of Mines as per general rule and the following to act with him in his capacity as Inspector.*

As this meeting was deemed to be Unofficial, it was then considered that the resolutions were void and so it was decided to hold them over until the next official meeting and to invite the Agent to attend.

In December 1917, the **FODMA** carried out a ballot of all its members of a vote of no confidence in their Agent Mr G.H. Rowlinson for his support of the **'comb-out'** of miners for Military Service. Forest of Dean miners had been subject to some influence by several of the more militant South Wales activists who spoke against the **'comb-out'** at many local meetings. However they needed little convincing of their own opposition to the Agent's actions.

The votes cast were;
Against Mr Rowlinson 3,460,
For Mr Rowlinson 1,300,
Majority against .... 2,160.

This result effectively meant the end of Mr Rowlinson's 31 year career as Miners Agent for the Forest of Dean and his resignation was anticipated.

Pit Stop
The manager of the Norchard Colliery near Lydney, Mr J.A. Hooper brought a case to the Lydney Petty Sessional Court on Wednesday the 29th of November 1917 summoning one of his employees for breach of regulations. Collier Mr William Hoare appeared before the Court for disregarding Section 43 of the Coal Mines Regulation Act 1911 in that he crossed a haulage road in the mine while the haulage was in motion. He was found guilty, fined £3.00 and his Employers saw fit to sack him.

As a result, on Monday the 3rd of December 1917, 350 men walked out on unofficial strike claiming that Mr Hoare had been victimised and demanded his reinstatement. Negotiations at the colliery between management and Union officials failed to get Mr Hoare reinstated but at a mass meeting of strikers, the Agent of the Union pointed out that the men had acted contrary to their own Articles. He said that they should have consulted the Union and taken a ballot before calling a strike. In consequence, the men decided to return to work with the proviso that they were prepared to hand in their notices if they didn't get the satisfaction they sought. The men returned to work on Thursday the 6th of December 1917.

Accidents/Fatalities.
On Saturday the 17th of February 1917, Mr Arthur Harley Brain aged 24 and a single man living at Collafield, Littledean, died of injuries he received on the 26th of May 1916 while working underground at the Foxes Bridge Colliery. Mr Brain had been working at the coal face holing a piece of coal

when a quantity of earth fell on him, injuring his back. He was taken to the surface and conveyed to the Gloucester Royal Infirmary where he was treated for a fractured spine. After nine weeks treatment, he was sent home as incurable and he died on Saturday the 17th of February 1917. An Inquest held at St Stephens Mission Room, Littledean Hill heard that the usual precautions had been taken for testing the roadway roof and that it was well timbered. The earth which fell on Mr Brain was of a different kind to that of which the roof was generally composed and which no one could have foreseen. The Jury returned a verdict of Accidental Death.

A Sad Accident

On Tuesday the 15th of May 1917, Thomas Ivor Davis, a lad of 13 living at Brierley Hill, Ruardean, was severely injured while working on the screens at the Trafalgar Colliery. He was taken to the Gloucester Royal Infirmary where he died that same day. At the Inquest, held at the Hospital, House Surgeon Dr Rupert Haines said that the deceased was admitted in a dying condition and suffering from a compound dislocation of the hip joint, a fracture of the thigh bone with extensive lacerations to both legs and other minor injuries. He was also suffering from shock and an operation was considered unnecessary. His condition deteriorated and he died at 2.30pm that same afternoon.

There was a great deal of concern over why a boy of 13 should be working at the colliery and not at school. The boy's father stated that his boy was consumptive and his wife had told him that someone at the school had prescribed a little light work and fresh air. Asked if the doctor had prescribed that, he said that he didn't know. The boy had not attended school for two months previous to the accident. There was cross questioning as to who in particular had examined the boy and prescribed absence from school and light work and the father's response was that all the information came from his wife and that she organised his working at the colliery.

The lad's work colleague Frederick Hale said that he was working on the screens picking dirt from the coal on a conveyor belt 3ft wide and 40ft long that carried large lumps of coal to trucks further along. The deceased was working on the opposite side of the belt and it appeared that he tried to cross over the moving belt to his side. He had put his foot up onto the belt but his leg was dragged under the covering of the wheels. Mr Hale said that he ran to stop the engine but found it already stopped.

Mr Tom Woodhouse, a foreman at the colliery said that the boy had only been put on temporarily to light work and that no one was justified in crossing a moving belt. If they wished to cross to the other side, they should go round the proper way which would take about a minute but there was no rule saying you had to. He said that he himself had stepped over the belt but only at a safe place which was near the middle. At the end where the boy tried to cross there was guarded machinery and there were notices warning persons not to touch the machinery. The Inspector of Mines Mr Rowley said that due to this particular case, he had been in conference with the colliery managers and that certain protections would be made to prevent accidents such as this happening in the future.

The Coroner, in summing up said that boys aged 13 could be taken from school provided they had reached standard five or six but in this case, he didn't know how the deceased came to leave the school, although he understood from the father that he had only reached standard two. He also said that this case would be referred to the local Education Authority. Mr Treasure on behalf of the colliery said that it was out of sheer kindness that the boy had been taken on and that it was the first accident in the Forest this year and he hoped it would be the last. The Jury returned a verdict of accidental death.

On Tuesday the 5th of June 1917, Mr Lionel Lee aged 20 and a single man from Pillowell was killed while working underground at the Wallsend Colliery near Blakeney. Mr Lee had been working with Mr Edward Waite ripping down the roof of a roadway and on the day of the accident they had stripped for work when a large rock weighing around three tons fell onto Mr Lee, killing him instantly. At an Inquest held at Yorkley, it was heard from two pit Deputies that the roof had been inspected that day and deemed safe as they had sounded and tried it all ways. On inspection after the fall, it was discovered that there was a slip at the back of the rock which could not have been seen beforehand. Colliery manager Mr Wilson said that just before the fall, shots had been fired which could have led to the loosening of the rock. He promised to have the roof timbered in the future but thought the use of timber generally would be a waste of time and materials. The Jury returned a verdict of accidental death.

On Monday the 10th of September 1917, Mr Augustus Morgan from Lydbrook, aged 39 and married with four children, was killed while working underground at the Trafalgar Colliery. At about noon on that day, Mr Morgan was working with Mr Albert Lewis driving wedges underneath a 20 inch seam of coal about two yards from the roadway. Suddenly there was a cry of **'look out'** but Mr Morgan was caught in a large fall of earth while Mr Lewis had managed to step back out of harm's way. When help arrived and he was taken out of the fall, Mr Morgan was already dead and this was confirmed by Dr Watson who was waiting at the pit bank. The Inquest held at Lydbrook heard that the workmen's opinions were that the roof had been properly timbered and that no shots had been fired in that area for several days. Mr John Parsons, one of the colliery Examiners said that he had inspected the place of the accident only two hours previous and found it to be safe. They also heard that the deceased had been for some years with the Monmouth Royal Engineers and a trumpeter at the Monmouthshire Assizes. He had also been a member of the Lydbrook Church Choir and leader of the Lydbrook Excelsior Brass Band. The Jury returned a verdict of accidental death in accordance with the medical report.

On Tuesday the 11th of September 1917, Mr Henry Walter Vaughan, a married man aged 30 years from Lensbrook near Blakeney was injured while working underground at the Wallsend Colliery near Blakeney. At the time of the accident, Mr Vaughan was working with Mr Isaac James at a Stall picking at the coal. A large quantity of coal and earth suddenly fell on both men, partly burying them. When help arrived, both were extricated and Mr James' injuries were not serious but Mr Vaughan was badly hurt. He was taken to the surface where the Doctor ordered that he be taken to the Gloucester Royal Infirmary where he died two days later. An Inquest held at the Hospital heard Mr George Baghurst, a Deputy at the colliery, state that he examined that part of the mine on the morning of the accident and found the roof properly timbered up and everything in order. Mr Isaac James said that he could not account for the coal and earth falling. Dr Shand, the assistant House Surgeon at the Hospital said that when Mr Vaughan was admitted, he was suffering from a fractured spine and died two days later. The Jury returned a verdict of accidental death.

On Thursday the 13th of December, Mr William Mark Edmunds a single man aged 20 was killed while working underground at the Princess Royal Colliery, Bream. On the day of the accident Mr Edmunds was working with his father William Edmunds Snr. in number 7 dipple and after loading a dram with rock, walked together to a manhole a little distance away. The deceased then proceeded to walk to the top of the dipple and when the appropriate time had elapsed, Mr Edmunds Snr. gave the signal for the engine to start the haul. As the dram passed him he thought he heard someone shouting but couldn't hear clearly because of the noise of the pumps. He caused the engine to stop and when he got to the dram, found his son lying underneath with the greater part of the dram and its load on top of him. Help came and he was removed but he was already dead. Dr Mayne later examined the body and recorded that death was due to fracture of the base of the skull. The Jury returned a verdict of accidental death and the Company Directors wished to express their regret that the deceased should have met with a sad end. He was a smart and active youth and his father had been a trusted servant of the Company for many years.

Fig. 63 Waterloo Colliery (Arthur and Edward) - Courtesy of the DHC, Soudley, Cinderford.

Chapter 19
1918 – The end of the Great War

Following Mr George Rowlinson's resignation as Union Agent for the **Forest of Dean Miners' Association**, it was announced that King George V had conferred on him the honour of an **MBE** (Member of the British Empire) in the 1918 New Years' Honours List. The honour was granted in recognition of Mr Rowlinson's work as Miners Agent and in the Forest of Dean Recruiting Court.

In January the **FODMA** held a ballot for their Officers for the forthcoming year. There were four candidates for Presidency – Martin Perkins, William Smith, Richard Cook and George Anderson – Richard Cook came out top of the poll but had left the district. George Anderson was second but declined the position. The other two candidates considered that a second ballot should take place and that resulted in a surprising win for a fifth candidate, Mr Reubin James from Pillowell. Vice President was David Organ, Pillowell. Treasurer, Henry Watson, Berry Hill. Secretary, Richard Buffry, Cinderford. Auditors, Ambrose Adams, Ruspidge and John Blewitt, Parkend. Finance Committee, W.P. Buffry, Cinderford, Charles Luker, Whitecroft and Thornton Reeks, Whitecroft.

In March 1918, the **MFGB** held a ballot of members on whether they agreed or not for the **'comb-out'** of another 50,000 men from the mines for the army. 471,874 miners took part in the ballot and the result was;

For the comb-out 221,152,
Against the comb-out 250,722,
Majority against .... 29,570.

Of all the coalfields, only Northumberland, Durham and Kent voted for the **'comb-out'**. However due to an anomaly in the voting paper, the Executive Committee of the **MFGB** were forced to concede that because there wasn't a clear two thirds majority against, they recommended the miners not to resist the comb-out.

Meanwhile, at a meeting in Cinderford Town Hall of largely Liberal supporters on Thursday the 9th of May 1918, Mr George Rowlinson was presented with a publicly subscribed cheque for £622 14s 6d and an Illuminated Address designed by the Lydney Art Master Mr J.J. Purdy. The

Address read; *'To Mr G.H. Rowlinson M.B.E. J.P. Dear Sir, we, the undersigned, on behalf of a large body of your friends in the County of Gloucester, desire to express our congratulations upon the completion of 31 years' service as Miners' Agent of the Forest of Dean. At the same time, we wish to place on record, the respect which you have earned by your untiring public work both in the Forest of Dean and in County Affairs as County Councillor, Magistrate, District Councillor, Poor Law Guardian and Educationalist. In your respective positions you have always acted under a strong sense of duty and with unswerving fidelity to your high principles. While asking you to accept the cheque and letters of appreciation which accompany this Address and the silver flower stand on behalf of your wife, we express the hope that she and you may enjoy good health and a long, prosperous and happy life. We remain, dear sir, yours faithfully, - M.H. Perkins, Chairman of Committee; D.R. Campbell and W. Constance, members of Committee; W. Whitehouse, Treasurer; J.A. Emery and R. Powell, honorary secretaries'.*

Others at the ceremony were Lieutenant Colonel Sir Henry Webb MP who held the Chair, Alderman T.H. Deakin, Mr Russell J. Kerr, Mr M.H. Perkins, Mr W. Smith and Mr M.W. Colchester-Wemyss.

New Miners' Agent and Labour Candidate

There were over 30 candidates chasing the office of Agent for the Forest of Dean Miners, vacated by Mr Rowlinson's resignation. This number was eventually reduced to a final 6 who began to organise meetings throughout the forest and it was then up to the Association membership to ballot for the winning candidate. This resulted in a clear majority of 1,595 votes over all the other candidates for Mr Herbert Booth to be the next Agent to represent the Forest of Dean miners within the **MFGB.**

Herbert Booth – 1886-1978

Mr Herbert W. Booth was a former coal miner and a member of both the Nottinghamshire Miners Association and the Independent Labour Party. He was known to hold left wing views and was a strong supporter of the Miners Federation of Great Britain.

Fig. 64 Mr Herbert Booth. Photo Author

And so, the Liberal dominance of the Forest of Dean was at an end and steps were now being taken to adopt the first Labour candidate to represent the Forest of Dean constituency in Parliament. The Labour Party nationally was now on the march with over 300 candidates promised to stand at the next General Election. On Whit Monday in May 1918, the Forest of Dean Parliamentary Division Labour Representation Committee held a meeting at the Speech House where nearly 70 delegates met to decide on whom to adopt as the first Labour candidate. Mr Arthur Hicks acted as Chairman and there was a unanimous vote in favour of Mr James Wignall JP from Swansea and a representative of the Dockers Union. A mass meeting of electors, Presided over by Mr David Organ was then held in front of the Hotel under the shade of the Forest Oakes where speakers included Mr James Wignall, Mr George Brown from the Bristol N.U.R. and Mr J.R. Drinkwater from Stourbridge. A resolution was later passed congratulating the Selection Committee on having chosen Mr Wignall to be the Labour candidate for the constituency and pledged to do their utmost to secure his triumphant return. This was carried with applause after which Mr Wignall received a rousing reception and delivered a well received speech.

James Wignall – 1856-1925

James Wignall was born in Swansea on the 21st of July 1856 and whose father was killed in the Crimean war. He first went to work in the docks at Swansea and later in the copper sheet rolling industry. He became a Baptist lay preacher and in 1890 started his association with the Trade Union movement by becoming organiser of the Dock, Wharf, Riverside and General Workers' Union. In 1893 he was appointed their Union Secretary and in 1900 he became their National organiser – becoming their President from 1905 to 1908. Mr Wignall was warmly acknowledged as the 'Father' of the Trades Union movement in South Wales and became a Justice of the Peace for Swansea.

Fig. 65 Mr James Wignall

Dilke Memorial Hospital

At a meeting in Cinderford Town Hall, further details of the Dilke Memorial Hospital Scheme were discussed, Presided over by Mr George Rowlinson. Sir Henry Webb MP said that the Crown could not gift the site at Yew Tree Brake but that it may be bought cheaply. It was revealed that plans of the Hospital had already been drawn up and that the building would lend itself to future extension. Building costs had increased since pre war times by around 40%. A Trust Deed and Administrative rules were provisionally approved and the Trustees should be at least five in number but not more than eight.

The first Trustees were named as The Right Hon. Earl Beauchamp C.M.G., Sir Henry Webb Bart. M.P., Sir F.W.T. Brain, Alderman T.H. Deakin, Mr S.J. Elsom, Russell Kerr, Mr G.H. Rowlinson and Mr M.H. Perkins.

It was further resolved that control and government of the Hospital should be run by a Council of not less than eighteen members who were then elected. They were Mr Joseph Hale J.P., Mr H.K. Hudson, Colonel Marling C.B. V.C., Mr M.W. Colchester-Wemyss J.P. C.C., Mr B.H. Taylor, Mr E.W.

Morgan, Mr E.C. Taylor, Mr J.H. Fewings, Mr Ambrose Adams, Mr Horace Jones, Mr John Harper, Mr William Morgan, Mr M.S. James, Mr W. Penwarden, Mr H.W. Smith, Mr J.J. Joynes, Mr D. Walkley, Mr W.H. Smith, Mr Charles J. Harris, Mr William Bradley, Mr S. Jordan and Mr J.A. Emery. In addition, there were the following ex-officio members – the Trustees, the Hon. Treasurer, every consulting medical officer of the Hospital and the Hon. Solicitor.

It was revealed at the meeting that the secret donor of £3,000 was Sir Henry Webb who said when confronted on the matter that he **'thought the rumours were well founded'** – which brought loud and continued applause. He also said that he and Lady Webb were particularly keen to have a Hospital in the Forest of Dean and that his anonymity in the matter was how he had wanted it, rightly or wrongly. A resolution was then adopted giving the warmest thanks to Sir Henry Webb for his splendid gift to the Hospital Fund.

Of course, the progress of the War was uppermost in people's minds at this time with more casualties – killed and injured – filling the local newspaper columns with more and more families receiving the dreaded telegram. While there were continued reports of several gains on the Western Front, miners were still being selected for Military Service. At the Gloucester Guildhall on Wednesday the 22nd of May 1918, another **'comb-out'** of Forest of Dean miners took place in the form of a lottery draw under the auspices of the Ministry of National Service. Bishop Frodsham was selected to draw the lots and remarked before the draw that this was necessary for the defence of the realm and that the draw would be conducted with scrupulous care and impartiality. There were around 60 miners in the hall and the Bishop welcomed them and said that there could be no discussion after the draw and that those selected should regard it as a high privilege to stand side by side with the gallant defenders of England. The names of those chosen were not released.

The **Miners' Annual Demonstration** at Speech House took place once again on Saturday the 13th of July 1918, after the previous years' cancellation. New President Mr Reubin James was in the Chair and guests on the platform included Mr James Wignall prospective Labour candidate for the Forest of Dean Division, Mr Herbert Booth, miners Agent and Mr John Robertson of the Scottish miners. Vice President David Organ's message by way of a resolution stated; ' *That the time has arrived when to secure the further advancement of labour, more united action, industrially* *and politically is essential and this meeting pledges itself to its utmost to assist in bringing about the same'.* This was seconded by Mr Leonard Douglas and supported by Messrs Robertson and Booth. It was later carried unanimously.

Mr Robertson gave a lengthy speech praising Mr Wignall's virtues saying; **'I have known Mr Wignall for over 20 years and any miner that doesn't vote for him at the next General Election is a blackleg. There should be no class distinction as between miner and the factory hand. The worker earning a few shillings more than his fellow man has no right to look down upon him with an air of superiority. We must all act as one if we want to win the fight. Mr Wignall is a worker and a representative of the toiler and that in the House of Commons he will represent all classes of Labour – not the miners alone.'**

Mr Wignall, who was warmly applauded, gave support to the resolution and said that he thanked Mr Robertson for commending him to the voters of the Forest of Dean constituency and that if he was successful, he could assure them of the very best of his intelligence and interest and activities. There were many things that needed to be done and improvements were long overdue. He mentioned that the Compensation Act needed bringing up to date and the recent addition of five shillings compensation for injury would have been doubled if Labour had been adequately represented in Parliament. He said that at present they had 300 candidates for Labour seats but there was no reason why that figure should not reach 500 by the time of the next Election. A resolution of sympathy with Mr Wignall was then adopted in the recent loss of a son at the Front and the meeting concluded with thanks to the speakers, which was duly acknowledged.

Armistice

Reports were reaching Britain's shores of successes in Flanders during the summer months involving British, French, United States and Canadian forces. Since the Battle of Amiens, German forces had to withdraw from many previously held positions and a further Allied advance in late September, **'the Hundred Days Offensive'** led to the German Supreme Army Command admitting that their position was hopeless. Negotiations started between President Woodrow Wilson and the German Government on the 5th of October 1918 but Germany would not submit to Wilson's terms which included the abdication of Kaiser Wilhelm II. Meanwhile the Bulgarian Armistice was signed on the 29th of September 1918; the Turkey

Armistice was concluded on the 30th of October 1918 and the Italy – Austria Hungary Armistice on the 3rd of November 1918.

Morale within both the German civilian population and the armed forces was at an all time low with chronic food shortages and a war weary army. Their Navy at Wilhelmshaven went into open revolt on the 29th of October 1918 and spread rapidly throughout the country with Army soldiers deserting and others defying their Officers orders. This lead to what came to be known as the **German Revolution.**

On the 6th of November 1918 a German delegation left Berlin and arrived at Compiegne on the 8th of November 1918. They were escorted to a secret location in a forest where the Allied Supreme Commander, French Marshal Ferdinand Foch received them in his railway carriage. Foch led the negotiations which lasted 3 days and were based on President Wilson's fourteen point plan. The German Kaiser was forced by events to abdicate on the 9th of November 1918 and when the negotiating delegation was informed, they were forced to agree to Foch's strict terms. The proclamation of a Republic was declared on the 9th of November 1918 – **the Weimar Republic** or **the German Reich.** And so, at 5.45am on the 11th of November 1918 the Armistice was officially signed by both sides and came into force at 11am that same day when hostilities ceased. Unfortunately, during that intervening period, there were over 10,000 casualties, of which, 2,738 men lost their lives.

Fig. 66 Signing of the Armistice in Ferdinand Foch's own railway carriage in the Forest of Compiegne – Illustrated by Maurice Pillard Verneuil

In the Forest of Dean - Strike Threat – again

The dispute at the Norchard Colliery in December 1917 was yet to be resolved and with no settlement in sight, the workmen decided on strike action throughout the Forest of Dean coalfield. The problem surrounded the sacking of collier Mr William Hoare by the colliery Manager for breaching Regulations by walking across a roadway while it was active. The men and the Union, with the support of Herbert Booth the new Agent wanted reinstatement for Mr Hoare but the colliery refused. He had been offered employment at several other collieries on the western side of the Forest including Cannop and Trafalgar but had refused them all. This notice of the Union's intent was sent to all Colliery Owners by post;

'Forest of Dean Miners' Association,
Miners' Offices,
Cinderford,
October 18th 1918.
Dear Sir,
On behalf of the workmen in your employment, I am to give seven days notice to terminate all contracts.
Yours faithfully,
H.W. Booth, Agent'

At this time, strikes were illegal, coming under the **Munitions of War Act** and the situation was considered so serious that the Coal Controller Sir Guy Calthrop came to the Forest of Dean in a bid to avoid any disruption in country's coal supply. He held a meeting with the workmen's representatives, Coal Owners and managers in Cinderford Town Hall on Saturday morning the 26th October 1918 with Sir T.H. Deakin taking the Chair. Sir Guy explained the national coal supply situation and asked the miners to consider the coal face as another fighting front which, he said was less dangerous than the Flanders Front but asked the men to do their best. He said the Forest of Dean coal output was 3,000 tons a week less than a year ago and that the shortfall could be made up by each man producing 30 cwt per week more and by encouraging the regular absentees to pull their weight. He also said that nothing should be done to prevent a concentrated effort to win the war and appealed to the men not to fail on the last lap of this great race. He urged the miners to put their grievances aside so that they could all say at the finish that the British Miners had done their best and done it well.

After this pep talk, Herbert Booth suggested that the local question was of more importance to the miners than what they had just heard and that it ought to be settled first before tackling the output question. He said that this visit of the Coal Controller was a golden opportunity and to let it slip would be most unfortunate.

In the afternoon, Sir Guy held further talks with both Coal Owners and the Union Executives where the latter further expressed their resolve to get Mr Hoare reinstated at the Norchard Colliery. Sir Guy pointed out that Mr Hoare had already been offered employment at several collieries in his locality and the meeting offered more choices – but Mr Booth on behalf of the Union declined them all and wanted nothing less than reinstatement.

Sir Guy said that he could do no more and in his report to the **MFGB** hoped that wiser councils would prevail and that no stoppage would take place. The matter could be resolved by Mr Hoare accepting the offers at one of the three collieries that were still open to him. In response, the Colliery Owners Association posted this notice at all colliery entrances;

'Forest of Dean Colliery Owners' Association.
The Colliery Owners have received certain Notices which they do not consider are valid, and which they decline to accept. This colliery will therefore be open for work as usual on Monday next.
Manager,
October 31st 1918'

The **FODMA** held a mass meeting at the Speech House on Sunday morning the 3rd of November 1918 to decide on further action to be taken on the dispute at the Norchard Colliery. Mr Reubin James, President occupied the Chair and Herbert Booth spoke at length to the men and reported on the meetings held with Sir Guy Calthrop and the possible consequences of strike action. It was finally resolved that the strike threat be withdrawn and the men would return to work the next day, Monday morning the 4th of November 1918.

General Election
As a precursor to the next General Election, 1918 saw the introduction of the **Representation of the people Act 1918**, also known as the **Fourth Reform Act.** It received Royal Assent on the 6th of February 1918 and extended the franchise for men aged over 21 whether or not they were property owners and to women aged over 30 who lived in the constituency

or occupied land or premises above a rateable value of £5 or whose husbands did. Local Government extension of the franchise was to include women aged over 21 – the same as for men.

In the Forest of Dean, the standing M.P. Sir Henry Webb confirmed at a Liberal Council meeting in October 1918 that he would stand again at the next Election and the new Labour candidate Mr James Wignall confirmed his candidacy in a detailed open letter in the local press in November 1918. The Conservative and Unionist Association decided not to oppose their coalition partner Sir Henry Webb so it was to be a straight fight between Liberal and Labour. They did however promise to support Sir Henry Webb's campaign on certain conditions which, in the event, proved to be complicated.

The Prime Minister Lloyd George issued a letter to all Coalition candidates – known as a 'coupon' – endorsing them as the official representatives of the Coalition Government provided they all supported his manifesto. This included some controversial issues such as Irish Home Rule, Free Trade and the dis-endowment of the Church of Wales. The Conservative Association originally gave their support to Sir Henry on his acceptance of those principles and in a telegram to them on the 20th of November 1918, he said *'Endorse Prime Minister's assurances'.* Lieut.-Col. R.J. Kerr then promised to support Sir Henry personally and to advise all his Unionist friends to do the same. Then on the 28th of November 1918, they received a long letter from Sir Henry explaining that he had changed his mind and would withdraw his original assurances but would otherwise support the general Liberal cause. In response, the Conservatives called a meeting on Monday the 2nd of December 1918 at the Town Hall in Newnham and unanimously passed a resolution that refused to give Sir Henry Webb their active support. It was also discussed whether at that late stage, Lieut.-Col. Kerr could declare his candidacy in opposition to Sir Henry Webb but in the event, this was not sanctioned.

And so the first General Election to be held in Great Britain on one particular day, took place on Saturday the 14th of December 1918. Due to delays in receiving votes from soldiers serving abroad, the vote count took place after Christmas on Saturday the 28th of December.

Accidents/Fatalities

On Tuesday the 9th of April 1918, Mr Frederick Moses Brain aged 46, a collier from Hawkwell Row, Cinderford, was injured while working underground at the Trafalgar Colliery. He was taken to Gloucester Royal Infirmary where he died on Saturday the 13th of April 1918. An Inquest held at the Hospital on the 16th of April 1918 heard that Mr Brain was working at the coal face with Mr John Hale at around 7am on the 9th of April 1918. Mr Hale stated that everything seemed alright and the Inspector's mark was on the face of the seam. He said that he had left Mr Brain at the coal face and had gone to load some trucks when he heard a shout and rushed back to find Mr Brain in a kneeling position with a clod of earth, which he had meant to sprag up, had fallen on him. Mr Brain had sent a boy, Winfield Roberts aged 18 to fetch a sprag from a supply nearby and when he got back he found Mr Brain with a clod on him and called for help. Mr Brain said that he **'was smashed all to pieces'.** The clod of earth measured 4 feet by 18 inches. With help from other miners, Mr Brain was helped to the pit bank where a doctor ordered him to be taken to the Royal Infirmary.

The assistant house surgeon Dr Henry Grimshaw said that Mr Brain was brought in suffering from a fracture of the spine. He said that he examined him but no operation was performed. Mr Brain sank and died on Saturday the 13th of April 1918. A post mortem showed that the spine had been broken in two places and that death was due to a broken spine and shock. The Jury returned a verdict of Accidental Death.

On Friday the 26th of April 1918, Mr William Hale aged 76, from Woodside Street, Cinderford, died from injuries he received on the 12th of February 1918 while working as a fan engineman at the Foxes Bridge Colliery. An Inquiry held at Cinderford on Tuesday the 30th of April 1918 heard that on the 12th of February 1918 Mr Hale walked on a plank to watch Mr James Wright an engineer fix some lagging round a steam pipe. The engineer warned Mr Hale of the danger of his position but he seemed to ignore this and eventually the plank broke, sending both men fifteen feet to the ground below. Both men received multiple cuts and the colliery manager sent them to Dr Bangara. Mr Hale was then off work until 1st of April 1918 when he returned for 14 days. He then fell ill and was taken home where he died on Friday the 26th of April 1918. Dr Bangara reported that death was due to injuries to the brain as a result of the fall from the plank and the Jury returned a verdict to that effect.

On Tuesday the 8th of October 1918, Mr Edwin George Gambold, a mine timberman from Upper Lydbrook, died from injuries he received on the 24th of July 1918 while working at the Old Engine Colliery. The Inquest, held at the Gloucester Royal Infirmary on the Saturday the 12th of October 1918 heard that at around midday, fellow workman Mr Alfred Ward saw Mr Gambold put down an axe and came to him asking to go with him to his house as he had been chopping timber when he missed the wood and cut his knee. Mr Ward administered what first aid he could and with the help of another worker, helped Mr Gambold to his home. A Doctor saw him the same day and redressed the wound over many days. He grew worse and was taken to the Gloucester Royal Infirmary on the 3rd of August 1918. Dr Ignatius Cruchley the house surgeon said that the leg did not improve and it was amputated on the 6th of September 1918. Mr Gambold then gradually sank and died on the 8th of October 1918. He said death was due to heart failure and septicaemia. The Jury then returned a verdict of death from blood poisoning brought on by an accidental cut on the leg.

Chapter 20
1919 – The Sankey Commission

The result of the 'snap' General Election which took place on the 14th o December last was a resounding victory for Lloyd George's Coalition Government. It was also an upset for the Liberals in the Forest of Dean Division where the first Labour candidate Mr James Wignall scored a win over standing MP Sir Henry Webb.

National Results;
Coalition candidates... 484 seats,
Non Coalition Parties...................................,..... 222 seats,
Coalition Majority..,... 262 seats.

Forest of Dean Result;
Mr James Wignall (Labour) 9,731,
Sir Henry Webb (Coalition Liberal).................. 5,765,
Labour Majority... 3,966.

Mr Wignall's victory was announced at the Town Hall, Newnham but Sir Henry Webb was absent due to the serious state of Lady Webb's health. Mr Wignall went on to make rousing speeches at Cinderford and Coleford where he said how surprised he was at his victory. He praised the voters of the Forest for their loyal support and promised to do his bit to return that support when he was at Westminster.

Sir Henry Webb's defeat was attributed to his lack of support for Lloyd George's Coalition Programme which the Unionist Party supported. He at first agreed to support that programme but subsequently changed his mind which resulted in the local Unionist Party withdrawing their previously promised support. Local opinion however was not so polite, especially at a meeting held at Coleford during the Election campaign in December last when Sir Henry was heckled and confronted by questions as to why he hadn't kept his promise to take the Forest Battalion to France and go *'over the top'* with them. And when he got there and the War was over, he would go on to Berlin with them. Sir Henry responded angrily by saying; **'that is an unqualified lie; I never said such a thing.'** The response from the audience was; **'you did and there were hundreds who heard it'.**

As mentioned above, Lady Ellen Webb had been ill for some time and she sadly passed away on the 4th of January 1919 at home in Oswestry. It was said that she never recovered from the loss of their only son who was killed in action in December 1917. Lady Webb was involved in supporting the War effort by raising funds for charitable groups and for providing places of entertainment for troops returning on leave. After a memorial service at Oswestry parish church, her body was taken to Tunbridge Wells for burial in the same grave as her daughter. In her Will, she left £82,668 15s.

At a Liberal Council meeting of Executive members on the 23rd of January 1919 chaired by Mr George Rowlinson, there was a great outpouring of sympathy for Sir Henry Webb, for the loss of his son and heir and lately for his wife Lady Ellen. A letter from Sir Henry was read out by Mr S. Jordan the Agent in which he said *'Please inform the Liberal Council that I have definitely decided to sever my Political connection to the Forest'*. A resolution was then passed thanking Sir Henry for his services in and out of Parliament these past eight years.

The Forest of Dean Miners' Association met again to appoint their District officials for the forthcoming year by ballot. The new President was Mr David Organ, Pillowell. Vice President Mr Gilbert Jones, Yorkley (to 14/5/1919) then Mr Leonard Douglas, Lydbrook. Financial Secretary Mr Charles Luker, Whitecroft. Treasurer Mr Henry Watson, Berry Hill. Auditors Messrs Richard Kear and Ambrose Adams.

David Organ –1876 - 1954

David Richard Organ was born at Oldcroft near Lydney on the 4th of October 1876. He was the eldest son of James and Harriett Organ and started work in the local pit as a 13 year old door boy and hodder. Just a month short of his 20th birthday David married Kate Phipps and in 1897 they moved to Derby where David worked as a railway porter. In 1898 they moved to Rotherham but in 1900, the couple, now with a family of two children, moved back to the Forest of Dean and settled in Pillowell. David found work as a hewer at the Norchard colliery near Lydney and soon found himself elected as checkweighman. David had certain political leanings and joined the fledgling Forest of Dean Labour Party

Fig.67 David R. Organ, photo Author

where, for many years he was their Treasurer. He was a keen member of the **FODMA** and by 1912 was Chairing local miners' meetings and had become a member of the District Board that determined miners' wages under the terms of the Mines Minimum Wages Act 1912. He stood for President of the Association for the year 1913 but was narrowly beaten into second place by Martin Perkins but was elected Vice President for the following year, 1914. He continued serving the cause in that position throughout the War years and in 1919 was elected President of the **FODMA** – retaining that position until 1939.

As a committed Labour supporter, David was also a member of the team that was successful in getting Mr James Wignall elected as the first Labour M.P. for the Forest of Dean Division. Throughout the following turbulent years, David was at the forefront in fighting for the rights of miners to better wages and working conditions and in particular, Nationalisation of the coal industry. He worked closely with the **MFGB** Agents for the Forest of Dean, in particular with Mr Jack Williams who came to the Forest in 1922.

So at last the political bias in the Forest of Dean had finally moved to a more socialist system, in keeping with the miners long held wishes. The Liberals were out and Labour was in and this remained the status quo for the next thirteen years. Nevertheless, a Liberal Coalition was still in power at Westminster and they had problems on their hands. The Armistice, signed November last was no guarantee of a lasting peace and although peace negotiations were continuing in Paris, fighting was still going on in Europe. British troops were still fighting in Russia and there was civil war in Germany. Compounding all this was the critical position on the home front. There were riots, mutinies and strikes within all three British Services and social unrest within the general population was rife.

Miners were especially effected by demobilised soldiers returning home to hopefully take up their old jobs in the collieries, (this was a promise given by all the Forest Coal Owners to all those who took the King's shilling) but miners who had latterly filled their positions were reluctant to give their jobs up. Some were able to be absorbed into the local mining workforce because the mines were short of manpower and production levels had fallen sharply.

The miner's main concern now was that the Government would return ownership of the mines back to the Owners with the added concern that wages would be reduced. In January 1919 the **MFGB** Executive voted by a large majority to demand an immediate 30% increase in wages, 18 shillings per week war wages, full wages for miners displaced by ex-soldiers and for ex-soldiers not re-employed, a six hour day and Nationalisation of the mines and minerals. Not surprisingly, the Government response fell far short of these demands. They offered one shilling per day increase and no concessions regarding demobilised men. There was no mention of Nationalisation.

On the 6th of February 1919, the **MFGB** conference decided to take a strike ballot and the votes to be returnable by Saturday the 22nd of February 1919. Should the ballot be in favour of a strike, then notices would terminate on the 15th of March 1919. The Executive urged the men to vote for a national stoppage while the Railwaymen's and Transport workers Unions who had a long established agreement known as the **Triple Alliance**, were considering joint action to enforce their demands.

At this time, the long serving Secretary of the **MFGB** Mr Thomas Ashton resigned his position after 30 years loyal service. His position was taken by Mr Frank Hodges who, at that time was a Union representative in South Wales.

Frank Hodges – 1887 to 1947

Less mentioned but nevertheless an influential Union Leader, especially in the South Wales District was Frank Hodges. Hodges had a Forest of Dean link as he was born in Woolaston near Lydney, the son of a farm labourer who moved with his family to Abertillery at the turn of the Century. He started work in the local pit at the age of 14 but with a desire for learning, attended night school and at the age of 16 became a Methodist preacher. This in turn led him to further understand the plight of his fellow miners and so joined the Trade Union Movement and became a member of the Independent Labour

Fig. 68 Mr Frank Hodges

Party. Hodges was influenced by several socialist activists notably Noah Ablett, author of 'The Next Step'. At the age of 22, he secured a Scholarship to Ruskin College, Oxford that offered courses in Political economy, Sociology and the history of the Labour Movement to adults with no formal previous education.

After leaving College in 1909, Hodges was influenced by Marxist ideas but eventually returned to South Wales where in 1912 he was appointed Union Representative for the Garw District of the South Wales Miners Federation. In 1919 he became the Permanent Secretary of the **Miners' Federation of Great Britain** where he became influential in negotiations with Lloyd George's coalition Government, especially in the 1920 strike and the 1921 Lockout. However, his reputation took a knock in the latter dispute when he supposedly agreed a deal with the Coal Owners that led to the withdrawal of the Triple Alliance support and a day forever known as **'Black Friday'.** In the event, Hodges resigned his position but was persuaded to withdraw it and continued in his office but he lost the support of the miners.

In 1923, while still retaining his Secretaryship of the **MFGB**, he was elected as Labour M.P for Lichfield in Ramsay MacDonald's minority Government and was given the post as First Lord of the Admiralty. The rules of the **MFGB** insisted that the Secretary give his full time to the post but eventually in December 1923, he lost a vote for suspending the rules and he was forced to resign. His replacement was Arthur J. Cook. Frank Hodges ceased to voice his previous radical views and became friendly with his former opponents –Coal Owners and Industrialists and held an ambition to become a Cabinet Minister at the next Election, but that eventually eluded him. He also lost his seat as an M.P. in the 1924 General Election but was then elected as Secretary of the **International Miners' Federation**. In 1925 he gave evidence to a Parliamentary Commission and suggested that miners should work longer hours which didn't endear him to the mining community. In 1926 he was critical of the General Strike and subsequent Lock-out and made more enemies with most of the mining hierarchy. The **MFGB** asked for his resignation as Secretary of the **IMF** when the Government appointed him a member of the newly formed Central Electricity Board at yearly salary of £750. He contested that he could do two jobs but constant criticism caused him to resign in April 1927. He then held directorships in a number of other Companies including being Chairman of the Glasgow Iron and Steel Company. He also became a Justice of the Peace. He died in 1947 leaving £132,959.

Trafalgar Colliery closed

Over 450 men were thrown out of work because of serious flooding at the Trafalgar Colliery near Brierley. Heavy rain during January 1919 coupled with an electrical pump failure had caused a rise in the water level to an extent that it endangered the ventilation of the colliery. When the last shift left the colliery on Saturday evening the 11th of January 1919, the sump at the bottom of the shaft was empty but when the pump-man went down on the Sunday morning, he found it full of water and other places nearby flooded. Every effort was made during the Sunday to start the electric pump which had been in service for 30 years but by the end of the day it had become submerged and unworkable. The Norchard Colliery sent another pump and efforts to get it working was stopped by the inrush of black damp. Eventually that pump was also lost and the bad air made it too dangerous for the men to work, so on Wednesday afternoon the 15th of January 1919 they were all called out. On the Thursday, the bad air had extended to about half a mile underground and notices were issued that the pit had to be closed. Until the bad air could safely be removed it was considered that the pit would be closed for an indefinite time.

Pit Stop

Meanwhile, there was a strike in Forest of Dean in mid January 1919 when men walked out of the New Fancy Colliery in a dispute over the minimum wage. The colliery was at a standstill for a week while negotiations with the Coal Owners took place and the men eventually returned to work.

Further afield, men at many collieries in Yorkshire called a strike over 'snap time for surface workers. The miners' main demand was for a 20 minute mealtime break in every shift for surface workers and over 130,000 men walked out of the Yorkshire collieries at 6am on Thursday the 23rd of January 1919. Engineers and pump-men would follow by the Saturday unless there was a settlement. Intervention by the Coal Controller promptly conceded this demand and ended the strike after one day. Thousands of Nottinghamshire miners were on strike over the 'butty system' of working which was eventually settled by a day wage arrangement.

In Scotland, over 8,000 men in collieries of Kirkcaldy and Lothian Districts were on strike for over a week over working hours.

In South Wales, the miners demanded a six hour day, pensions at age 60 and a system for integrating demobilised soldiers and sailors back into the mines. All collieries in the Dowlais District were on strike awaiting a decision on their grievances and this had a knock-on effect on other industries in the local area and at the Newport Docks.

The result of the **MFGB's** strike ballot showed a majority of over 5 to 1 in favour of strike action. The overall national result was;

For strike action 615,164,
Against strike action 105,082,
A majority for a strike .... 510,082.

The Forest of Dean miners voted 4,260 for a strike and 160 against a strike.

The Sankey Commission
In view of the strike threat, the Prime Minister rushed to Parliament on the 24th of February 1919 and introduced the **Coal Industry Commission Bill** authorising a **'Royal Commission of Inquiry'** to be headed by Mr Justice Sankey. He was trusted by both sides in this dispute but said that as time was of the essence, he couldn't promise to complete his Inquiry until the 31st of March 1919 – the 15th of March 1919 being the start of the strike. A compromise was reached and the **MFGB** agreed to a week's adjournment of the strike date to the 22nd of March 1919 on a promise by Lloyd George that an interim report would be ready by the 20th of March 1919. The Commission's eventual 'Interim Report' was divided into 3 main reports and

four recommendations. This interim report was presented to Parliament on the 20th of March 1919 and was favourable to the miners' demands in the following recommendations;

1. Amendment of the 1908 Eight Hour Day Act to substitute 8 hour day with 7 hours so making a reduction in the working day from 8 to 7 hours for underground workers excluding meal time from the 16th of July 1919. By the end of 1920, a further amendment to introduce a 6 hour day, subject to the economic position of the Industry at that time;
2. The working hours for surface workers as from the 16th of July 1919 to be 46.5 hours per week excluding meal times;
3. An increase in wages of 2 shillings per shift or day and 1 shilling for workers under 16 years of age;
4. That the Government should adopt some form of Nationalisation.

That same day, Mr Bonar Law who spoke for the Cabinet in Parliament on behalf of the Prime Minister announced that the Government had adopted the 'Sankey Report **'in spirit and in letter'.**

On the 26th of March 1919, the **MFGB** called for a vote of members on whether or not to accept the **Sankey Report** with a strong recommendation that they do. Results were declared on the 15th of April 1919 and showed an overwhelming majority for acceptance.

Figures were;
For acceptance 693,084,
Against acceptance 76,992,
A majority for acceptance ....616,092.

The miners felt that at last the Government were now pledged to ending private ownership and that Nationalisation was a step nearer. And so the original strike notices were withdrawn.

The Commission started its second stage of meetings on the 24th of April 1919 and lasted until the 23d of June 1919. Its job was to basically define and recommend or otherwise the various forms of Nationalisation they thought could end the existing system of private ownership. This was a lengthy process involving the examination of 116 witnesses ranging from Peers of the Realm with mining interests to miners wives from England, Scotland and Wales. In addition, the **MFGB** submitted its own plans for Nationalisation that proposed a National Mining Council of 20 members – 10 from Government and ten from the **MFGB** – plus a Minister of Mines.

In all, four Reports were presented;
1. The Chairman's Report – this recommended State ownership of the mines but had several variations from that suggested by the **MFGB**
2. The Miners Report – this was in basic agreement with the Chairman's Report and although there were differences of opinion with the make-up of the administration of the new system, in the event, they did sign the agreement.
3. The Coal Owners' Report – came to the conclusion that any form of Nationalisation of the Coal Industry would be detrimental to the development of the Industry and to the economic life of the country.
4. Sir Arthur Duckham's Report – recommended against Nationalisation but suggested an alternative scheme. Complicated as it was, his suggestion of 'District Unification' would split the country up into many publicly controlled corporations.

In addition, all four groups were agreed on two principles;
1. State ownership of all coal seams and royalties,
2. Distribution of coal to be handled by Local Authorities.

The Government received this Report on the 20th of June 1919 and it was assumed that they were bound by the terms of the Interim Report as stated by Mr Bonar Law in the House of Commons that they had adopted it '**in spirit and in letter**'. Also, with the Chairman and seven of the Commissioners agreed on Nationalisation, it appeared that the principle would be adopted in some form. If not, it would be regarded as a breach of faith.

The Government stalled and time went by without a decision one way or the other. It became known that before the end of June 1919, a large number of MP's had been strongly lobbying the Prime Minister on behalf of large coal mining interests against any form of public ownership. Warnings were given of severe hostility to the scheme from influential capitalists which obviously contributed to the delay in a Government decision.

Pit Stop threat
Miners in the Forest of Dean had their own problems. An Award of 7 pence per day under the Minimum Wages Act to higher standard wage earners had caused some dissatisfaction with the men earning the lower wage. The men asked for 10 pence per day but the Coal Owners offered 3 pence. **FODMA** negotiations failed to settle the dispute and on Saturday the 10th of May 1919, Herbert Booth the Agent had instructions to give one weeks'

notice to withdraw contracts for nearly 5,000 miners in the District. Copies were duly served to the colliery managers that same day and at Speech House on Sunday, a large gathering of miners heard Mr Booth outline the dispute and what action had been taken. A resolution endorsing the action was then carried unanimously.

The Coalowners' Association held meetings during that week and offered to submit the dispute to a Board of Arbitration. Strike notices were then suspended for one week to enable the men to meet at the pitheads to consider the matter. It was then agreed that the Coal Controller should be the arbitrator and meetings were held by both sides in London during that week. On Sunday the 25th of May 1919, Herbert Booth addressed a mass meeting of miners at the Speech House and gave them the terms of agreement which had been negotiated on their behalf. He said it wasn't all that they had asked for but it was the best that they could get. There was some dissent among the gathering but it was put to a vote and the agreement was passed by a very large majority and strike notices were withdrawn.

Treaty of Versailles
Considering the varied and sometimes contradictory aims of the four victorious Nations, it is amazing that this Treaty was ever agreed. The four Nations, United States, Great Britain, France and Italy all had their own ideas as to how Germany should be treated after the peace and Russia didn't participate because its new Revolutionary Bolshevic Government had already signed a peace pact with Germany before the Armistice.

U.S. President Wilson had already set out his fourteen point plan but these were eventually watered down and became ineffective. Lloyd George wanted to rebuild Germany to become a strong trading partner. French leader Clemenceau wanted severe reparations from Germany so as to limit their recovery and so protect France from another attack. Italy's leader Orlando wanted to expand Italy's influence in Europe so that it could become a major power.

However, in the end, harsh terms were imposed on Germany including demilitarisation, occupation of the Rhineland, forbidding the formation of an Air Force, limiting the size of their army and navy, give up all overseas territories and lose 10% of its own and to conduct war crimes trials against the Kaiser and other German leaders. Furthermore, Germany was forced to accept full responsibility for starting the War and to pay large reparations for Allied War losses.

The Treaty of Versailles Peace Document was duly signed on the 28th of June 1919 between the Allied and associated powers and Germany in the Hall of Mirrors, Palace of Versailles, France. It was to come into force on the 10th of January 1920.

Fig. 69 Image of David Lloyd George signing the Treaty of Versailles in the Hall of Mirrors in the Palace of Versailles, Paris, France – 28th June 1919.

The **Miners' Annual Demonstration** was again held at the Speech House field on Saturday the 12th of July 1919. Many thousands attended that event which was Chaired by newly elected President of the **FODMA** David Organ. Speakers on the platform were Mr Duncan Graham MP and Mr James Wignall MP for the Forest of Dean. A resolution was carried demanding the withdrawal of British troops from Russia, calling on the Government to Nationalise the coal industry without delay, demanding the abolition of conscription, a reduction in the cost of living, better housing for the workers, proper provision for the care and maintenance of the soldiers and sailors disabled by the War, with ample pensions secured for widows and children of those killed. The meeting passed the following resolution; *'we pledge ourselves to use every effort to maintain the unity of this Association and of the Miners' Association in the full confidence that the benefits of the reforms already secured and our hopes for the future, can only be realised through the continued solidarity of our organisation'*

The following Saturday Forest of Dean miners' agent Herbert Booth attended a Conference of the **MFGB** held at Keswick and moved a resolution on behalf of Forest of Dean miners to secure time and a quarter wages per shift for afternoon and nightshift workers. He contended that these two shifts were detrimental to home and social life and prevented education and asked for compensation for those losses sustained by working those two shifts. This was seconded by Mr Tom Cape MP and the resolution was adopted.

An interesting change of life for Forest of Dean ex MP when it became known that Sir Henry Webb Bt., married Miss Helena Kate de Paula of Finchley on Tuesday July 22nd 1919 at St James Church, Piccadilly, London.

Pit Stop – Yorkshire

While the Sankey Report was still being considered, the Government was seen to be trying to provoke the miners by insisting on raising the price of coal by six shillings per ton in an attempt to turn public opinion against them. This was denied of course but their refusal to remove the increase threatened another dispute. In Yorkshire, the miners were already in conflict with the Coal Owners over the working of the new seven hour shift and the percentage to be paid as compensation to pieceworkers for their reduced hours. The men refused arbitration and an offer of 12% was made but the men contended that a promise was originally made to offer 14.3%. With this deadlock, coupled with the six shillings per ton increase in the price of coal, the Yorkshire Miners' Association decided to call an all-out strike at the end of the last shift on Tuesday the 15th of July 1919. Over 150,000 men and boys were laid idle and within a week when 50,000 pump and enginemen were also called out, over 200,000 men were on strike.

The Coal Controller decided to sanction the offer of 14.3% which the South Yorkshire Coal Owners had agreed to but the West Yorkshire Coal Owner's offer was only 12%. And so the strike continued with some collieries now becoming flooded. Three were completely flooded with twelve more likely to become flooded. The Government sent in Naval Ratings to help with the pumping and to avoid the total loss of some of the mines and by the end of July 1919 158 Ratings were actively at the pumps. In Nottinghamshire, six collieries were laid idle in protest at the six shillings per ton increase in the price of coal.

The strike spread to other Districts including 7,500 men in Lancashire 20,000 in Nottinghamshire and 11,000 in Monmouthshire and the Yorkshire textile industry was virtually at a standstill. Eventually, after the stoppage had cost the Yorkshire Miners Association over £300,000 of Union funds the South Yorkshire men were persuaded to return to work and the West Yorkshire men followed. The strike lasted five weeks but it was many more before some collieries were able to resume production due to flooding and collapsed roofs. The position of the **MFGB** was to stay out of the argument and let the local Associations handle their own affairs. Some say that it was an unnecessary strike over a few pence but caused mayhem for many Yorkshire industries and their workers.

The Sankey Commission Report – continued.

The Sankey Report had now been in Government hands since the 20th of June 1919 without any form of declaration throughout the month of July. By the third week in August however, Lloyd George stood up in the House of Commons in the evening of Monday the 18th of August 1919 and delivered his response to the Commission's Report. It was not what the miners wanted to hear. Broken down to its simplest form, he said;

For acceptance in the Sankey Report;
1. Government purchase of mineral rights.
2. A discount on that purchase to provide for the improvement of the social conditions of the miners and their housing and standard of living.

Not for acceptance in the Sankey Report;
1. Although the principle of re-organisation or unification was accepted as quoted in Bonar Law's **'in spirit and in letter'**, but not Judge Sankey's final interpretation of it.

Lloyd George admitted that the Nationalisation scheme would create greater harmony between employers and workers and that although the miners may strike against a private employer, they would not strike against the State. He said that the miners were asked not to strike while the various Councils considered the merits of Nationalisation but the **MFGB** could not give that assurance'. As recent events proved such as the Yorkshire miners' strike which was a strike against the State, the Government considers 'that **harmony would not be achieved by Nationalisation of the mines.'** In other words, the Yorkshire miners' strike was used as an excuse to effectively scupper Nationalisation.

As an alternative to direct Nationalisation, the Government agreed to divide the country into convenient areas, each area controlling the mines in that area for a suggested time of two years. Miners would have their own Directors on the body controlling the policy in each area. All subject to Government approval.

South Wales miners' leader and MP, Vernon Hartshorn questioned whether the whole business of having a Commission **'was a huge bluff'** and that the Government never intended the miners should have Nationalisation. He said **'we have been deceived, betrayed and duped'.**

Not surprisingly, the **MFGB** Executive rejected the Government's alternative but stopped short of recommending strike action. Instead they agreed with the Trade Union Congress to launch a propaganda programme in the hope of gaining public support should there be any future strike action. It was labelled **'The Mines for the Nation'.** Unfortunately, the general public outside of the mining areas took little notice of this campaign and by the end of the year, the **MFGB** were forced to consider their options. Many believed at the time that this bluff had always been Lloyd George's policy and that to offer a Royal Commission was his way of dealing with a potential strike. In time, he would come to regret his deception.

Meanwhile there was further unrest within the rail industry with individual strikes breaking out in most parts of the country. The main argument in these disputes was over pay – the Government planned to reduce wages to pre-war rates - and a national stoppage was called by the National Union of Railwaymen. The men stopped work at midnight on the 26th of September 1919 and returned after nine days when the Government agreed to maintain current wages for another two years. The strike caused havoc within the mining industry nationally and in the Forest of Dean 6,000 miners were thrown out of work, collieries closed down and the Lydney Tin works had to close.

Dilke Memorial Hospital Scheme

Good news for the Memorial Fund when, in September 1919 the Red Cross Surplus Scheme announced a £956,900 share out from the surplus funds of the Joint War Committee of the British Red Cross Society and the Order of St. John. These grants were only to be applied for the relief of sickness and suffering of the general population of England and Wales with a separate amount being applied to Ireland. Hospitals and Nursing Homes were considered a priority and in Gloucestershire a total of £34,750 was allocated to various Hospitals and Out Station Schemes. For the Forest of Dean, the Dilke Memorial Hospital Fund received a total of £4,000 which it was hoped would bring the schemes to maturity at a much faster rate.

Miner to Millionaire

In the Forest of Dean 58 year old Mr George Morgan was awarded extensive mineral rights on a plot of land near Coleford. His family had occupied the plot of common land for generations and 40 years previously he and five others had pegged their claim to the land. When he heard of his good fortune, Mr Morgan was working at the coal face at the Bute-Merthyr colliery in Treherbert but had lived for many years at Lane End, Coalway near Coleford. All his fellow claimants had died so he had become the sole surviving commoner. The Government acknowledged his claim and forwarded Mr Morgan the title deeds as a *'free miner with benefit of all mineral rights and turn out'*. The plot had access to the valued Trenchard steam coal seam which varied in thickness between 3ft and 17ft and was estimated to yield 2,000,000 tons of coal. The only stipulation was that he paid the usual Royalties of 2 pence per ton. The seam was easily accessed by Levels and an old Level was still on the plot. Mr Morgan, who had worked in some of the most important collieries in South Wales said; **'I will open up immediately with these Levels. I have six sons, also colliers who will assist me. They are all good men'.**

New Developments at Howbeach

Interesting developments were reported at the Howbeach Colliery near Blakeney where some years previous, a Manchester syndicate had taken over the colliery and had carried out considerable developments at great capital expense. That Company was sold for £6,000 to a new syndicate comprising Lord Bledisloe as Chairman, Mr Arthur J. Morgan J.P. as Deputy Chairman and Mr Percy Moore as Secretary. Their intention was to scrap the current Dipple workings and concentrate on the Blackpool shaft which was 100 yards deep with access to over 600 acres of coal measures. These included the Yorkley and Whittington house coal seams and the Coleford High Delf and Trenchard steam coal seams. A complete reorganisation of the colliery was planned and during that time, 200 men and boys would be discharged and integrated into other collieries locally. It was anticipated that the reconstruction would eventually be of benefit to those who lived and worked in the local area.

No beer on Sundays

Forest of Dean miners and other residents, having suffered the Liquor Control Board restrictions imposed during the War were now in a state of unrest because pubs were still closed on Sundays. Weekdays were also affected inasmuch as pre war Sunday opening times were imposed on those as well. When these restrictions were imposed, the Government promised to remove them once the War was over and this had not happened. Meetings on the matter were held in the Coleford Drill Hall and Speech House and a resolution was passed; *'we protest rigorously against the restrictions of our right to obtain reasonable refreshment at Public Houses on Sundays and also against the restricted and unsuitable hours for opening and closing on weekdays. We call upon the Government to restore pre-war liberties as promised by the Prime Minister when they were imposed.'* Copies were sent to Mr James Wignall MP, Prime Minister Lloyd George and the Chairman of the Control Board. In the event of a failure of a favourable response, it was considered that the workers in the district would 'down tools' until the matter was settled. They had also asked why these restrictions were ever imposed on the Forest of Dean in the first place and the only answer they received was that it was in consequence of the Government shipyards being built at Beachley. What had Beachley to do with the Forest? Beachley was not in the Forest of Dean and was miles away from the homes of the Forest miners who had loyally responded to the call of King and Country.

Forest of Dean MP Mr James Wignall himself stood up in the House of Commons and asked Lloyd George if he was aware of the unrest it was causing and why it applied only to the Forest of Dean. Of course, the matter was referred from one department to another without firm answers. It was however ironic that Mr Wignall should fight for liquor relaxation when he himself had declared before the Election that in the eyes of the people, he had committed an unpardonable offence - he was a total abstainer from any form of intoxicating drink and had been for nearly 38 years.

Coal Price Reduction

In a surprise move, the Board of Trade announced that the price of domestic coal would be reduced by 10 shillings per ton as from the 1st of December 1919. This was to include that used for the production of Gas and Electricity. While this was welcomed by the **MFGB**, they were suspicious that this was a political move on behalf of the Government and showed that the rise of 6 shillings per ton in July 1919 was completely unnecessary. Only a few days previous, the President of the Board of

Trade had stated that he would make no reduction in the price of coal and if they did, it would be by small amounts. The Government however, in qualifying the reduction said that it was due to the effect of coal prices worldwide in view of the United States strike. The price of export coal had subsequently increased which, on balance, allowed for the reduction in price to the domestic market.

Accidents/Fatalities

On Wednesday the 22nd of January 1919, Mr James Smith aged 27, a collier living at Nelson Green, Cinderford was killed while working underground at the Arthur and Edward Colliery near Lydbrook. The Inquest held at the Swan Inn, Brierley heard that Mr Smith had only recently returned from two and a half years' duty in the Army in France and had been working in the colliery for only ten days. He was an experienced collier and was working at the coal face with two other colliers, Mr George Turner and Mr Wilfred Ward. It was without any warning that several tons of rock fell on Mr Smith and just missed Mr Turner. When help arrived and Mr Smith was released, he was found to be already dead and Dr J. C. Watson of Lydbrook later confirmed that he had died from a broken neck. The Jury returned a verdict in accordance with the Doctor's report and sympathy was expressed to the widow and relatives of the deceased.

On Monday the 31st of March 1919, Mr Henry Evans aged 48, a collier, was killed while working underground at Lightmoor Colliery near Cinderford. At the Inquest it was said that Mr Evans was about to leave the stall in which he was working when half a ton of earth fell on him. He would have finished his shift within another half a minute. He died before he could be brought to the surface and the Jury returned a verdict of accidental death.

On Saturday the 22nd of November 1919, Mr Albert Webb aged 55 and a fettler living at Brierley, was killed while working at the Trafalgar Colliery near Brierley. Mr Webb with three other men, Mr James Rawlins, Mr William Hatch and Mr Ernest Meek were contracted to removing old water pipes from the 200 yard deep pit shaft. Both Mr Webb and Mr Rawlins were operating from the roof of the cage while the other two men were on the 'landing' at the colliery surface. Work to remove the pipes had gone on successfully for a number of weeks and signalling procedures were agreed between all the men. On the day of the accident Mr Webb and Mr Rawlins descended the shaft on the cage roof and successfully loaded and lashed a number of sections of the pipes onto the roof ready to be raised to the surface. The signal was given and the cage ascended. When it reached the top, Mr Rawlins stepped off the cage and with Messrs Hatch and Meek began unloading the pipes. A signal was then given to lower the cage about a foot and the cage suddenly gave way and plummeted to the bottom of the shaft carrying Mr Webb with it. An hour later when rescuers were able to reach the bottom of the shaft by way of a second shaft, they discovered the wreckage of the cage with the mangled body of Mr Webb underneath it. At the Inquest held at Lydbrook, it was heard that on examination, the winding rope had broken and had pulled through the coupling, so releasing the cage. Mr Rawlins emphatically declared that he had given no signal for the cage to be lowered and having realised what was happening, had called to the engineman to stop, But it was too late and the pipe being raised must have struck against some obstruction and caused the accident. The Jury returned a verdict of accidental death with fatal injuries caused as a result of a fall down the mine shaft due to the winding rope breaking and pulling through a coupling.

Chapter 21
1920 - Pit Stop
The Datum Line Strike

Good news for the Forest of Dean when it was announced that as part of the new Electricity Supply Act, the Gloucestershire County Council had taken steps to set up a joint electricity authority for this part of the West of England. The government owned electricity generating station at Beachley was considered for purchase and it was proposed that cables could be laid to the Forest of Dean coalfield should the purchase go ahead.

Good news also for the proposed new Dilke Memorial Hospital where public subscription funds had reached £10,000. Legal possession of the site of the hospital at Yew Tree Brake had taken place and was being pegged out ready for building work to start.

Mr George Morgan who was reported to have been granted extensive mineral rights near Coleford last autumn, had been having talks with a London coal syndicate with a view to selling his rights. A figure of £70,000 was offered to Mr Morgan with £50,000 being paid in cash and £20,000 being in shares. Mr Morgan admitted that he could not open up the seams without substantial capital and until the matter had been settled, he was not prepared to name the syndicate.

It wasn't until March 1920 that the **MFGB**, after several meetings with Lloyd George, failed to come to any agreement on the principle of Nationalisation. On Wednesday the 10th of March 1920, the day before the Trade Union Congress, the Executive revealed the results of a vote taken among the nation's miners, on the policy of direct action in relation to the Nationalisation of the mines. The votes received were;

For direct action 524,000,
Against 346,000,
A majority for direct action .... 178,000.
The Forest of Dean vote was For direct action.

At the Trade Union Congress the next day – 11th of March 1920, the **MFGB** demanded a vote be taken for direct action in the form of a National strike on the question of Nationalisation of the mines. This was firmly rejected by the Congress with persuasive speeches by both Mr J.H. Thomas M.P. who presided and Mr J.R. Clynes M.P. Both were of the opinion that a strike at the present moment would be welcome by Mr Lloyd George in the propaganda war against the miners. The Conference put it to the vote and the results were;

For Direct Action	1,050,000,
Against Direct Action	3,870,000,
Majority Against Direct Action	**2,820,000.**

For Political Action	3,732,000,
Against Political Action	1,015,000,
Majority for Political Action	**2,717,000.**

This result showed that the overwhelming majority were persuaded to adopt the policy of Political action and so Direct Action as proposed by the miners' leaders was defeated. And so the threat of strike action had been averted for the present.

It was therefore clear to the **MFGB** that Nationalisation was, for the time being to be put aside. During the early months of the year they had failed to convince the Government to reduce the price of coal due to inflation being at over 130% since July 1914, so some alternative policy was necessary. On Friday the 12th of March 1920 they passed a resolution calling for a wage increase of 3 shillings per shift and 1 shilling and 6 pence per shift for those under 16 years of age – this was to be backdated to the 1st of March 1920.

Negotiations with the Coal Controller broke down and day to day meetings eventually led to the Prime Minister making his final offer on the 29th of March 1920. This was for a 20% wage increase with a gross flat rate of 2 shillings per shift for persons aged 18 and upwards, 1 shilling per shift for persons between 16 and 18 and 9 pence per shift for persons below 16 years of age. This would be backdated to the 12th of March 1920.

A ballot vote on the Government's offer was taken during the next two weeks and the results were announced at the **MFGB** Conference on the 15th of April.

For acceptance of the Government's offer	442,704,
For a strike	377,569,
Majority for acceptance	**65,135.**

Only three Districts voted for a strike which included the Forest of Dean who voted;

For acceptance...	1,716,
For a strike..	3,508,
Strike majority of	**1,792**

Equalling 67.15% of votes recorded.

And so, the 15th of April 1920 became known as **'the Miners Peace Day'** with the agreement being backdated to the 12th of March 1920 and was signed on the 29th of April 1920 by the Coal Controller Mr A.R. Duncan and by the Executive members of the **MFGB.**

Princess Royal

While all this was going on, in the Forest of Dean it became known that the Princess Royal Colliery at Bream had been sold to a new and wealthy Company and that the new owners were taking over on the 1st of April 1920. This sale would include both the Princess Royal (Park Gutter) and Flour Mill collieries employing over 800 men and boys and would have over 2,000 acres of access to the Coleford High Delf steam coal seam. The Chairman of the new Company was Mr Percy Berrill.

Fig. 70 Photographic copy of a painting by Eric Rice of the Princess Royal Colliery – locally known as the Park Gutter

On the 12th of May 1920, the Government raised the price of household coal by 14 shillings and 2 pence per ton and for industrial coal 4 shillings and 2 pence per ton. This rise was qualified by the Coal Controller as a move in order to bring both household and industrial rates to the same level. It was stated that the 10 shillings per ton reduction in December last was only a temporary measure and now they had to be equalised.

This was seen by the **MFGB** as another move in the direction of de-control of the mines and coupled with the Coal Mines Emergency Bill then being debated, the Government appeared to have every intention of doing so. There was no deficit at the Exchequer, in fact the surplus profits from the mining industry in May 1920 were £3,800,000 so justification for the price rise appeared dubious.

The Coal Mines (emergency) Act

The Government were planning to introduce new legislation to control the mining industry in Great Britain. The first part was an emergency Bill that was given its first reading in Parliament in February 1920 and in March at its third reading, the Labour Party moved to reject the Bill on the grounds that it gave excess profits to the Coal Owners. Their motion was rejected by 163 votes to 43. Even in this, its early stages, it was seen by the **MFGB** as the first stage in the Government's plan of returning the mines back to its owners and an end to Government control. The Bill was given the Royal Assent on the 31st of March 1920 and became the **Coal Mines (emergency) Act 1920**. The Act dealt mainly with the control of profits and assets from mining operations and gave the Coal Controller power to make cash advances to maintain the output of a mine.

The **MFGB** met on the 10th of June 1920 to discuss what future steps to take as a consequence of the coal price rise. The continual and relentless rise in the cost of living had reached 150% since July 1914 and the Executive Committee saw no alternative than to seek either a substantial wage increase or to demand the removal of the recent coal price increase. This was to be put to a card vote at the Annual Conference on the 6th of July 1920 and was passed by 545 votes to 360 – each vote representing 1,000 members.

The Government response was received on Monday the 26th of July 1920 which was an emphatic NO. The President of the Board of Trade Sir Robert Horne was adamant that profits from the sale of coal should not be frittered away on wage increases but instead should go to the Exchequer. In response, another Special Conference of the **MFGB** took place on Thursday the 12th of August 1920 and decided to call a strike ballot of members during the following two weeks. Their resolution; *'That this Conference recommends the members of the **MFGB** to vote in favour of a stoppage in order to secure the demands which have been put forward'* .

The ballot paper asked the voters the following;

'In view of the refusal of the Government to concede the claims of the Miners' Federation of Great Britain for a reduction in the price of domestic coal by 14s. 2d. per ton and an advance in wages of 2s. per shift for members of 18 years and upwards, 1s. per shift for members from 16 to 18 years and 9d. per shift below 16 years of age, are you in favour of strike action to secure these claims?'

The Mining Industry Act

This was the second and main part of the legislation and on the 23rd of June 1920 more details emerged as to its content. The Bill which the new President of the Board of Trade Sir Robert Horne revealed, provided for a complicated tier of control headed by a Minister of Mines and a department set up to regulate the coal industry. The Minister would have powers to regulate the price of both export and pithead coal produced for home consumption, miners wages and the distribution of profits. The Board of Trade would refer to an Advisory Committee consisting of 24 members and a Chairman, there would be a National Board, an Area Board, a District Committee and a Pit Committee, all represented with equal numbers of workers and owners representatives. This was the overall plan and the finer details would be revealed when the Bill became law.

Back in the Forest of Dean, the **Miners' Annual Demonstration** took place on Saturday the 10th of July 1920, again at the Speech House field. It was somewhat marred by the inclement weather which made the field rather soggy but there was a good attendance in the marquee where the miners held their meeting in the afternoon. On the platform which was Chaired by the President of the **FODMA** Mr David Organ were Vice President Mr Albert Wildin, Mr Charles Luker, the Agent Mr Herbert Booth, Mr James Wignall M.P. for the Division and Secretary of the **MFGB** Mr Frank Hodges. In his opening remarks, Mr David Organ said that weather wise this was the worst meeting he had attended in the last 18 years but nevertheless welcomed the two distinguished guests, Mr Wignall and Mr Hodges to the meeting. He said that on these occasions they liked to take stock and reflect on what improvements their Association had made during the past 12 months. Although some had been made he said, they could not improve conditions under which the workers lived, under the present capitalist system. The whole system needed to be changed before any vital improvement could be effected. He concluded by saying; **'At present we toil in the mines, not for ourselves but for Capitalist enterprise and gain. We want to see to it that we risk our lives, not for those people but that we might have justice and in the interests of the community at large. Nothing would give more satisfaction to the miners of this country than to see the mines Nationalised. That is what we are out for and I contend that not only would that be a benefit to the miners themselves but it would be in the interests of every individual in the country. We also require to use every effort to turn out David** (Lloyd George) **and his crew and to return a Government to power that is fit to be entrusted with the reins of Government and who can see that this is a land fit for heroes to live in'.**

After great applause, Vice President Mr Albert Wildin proposed a resolution; *'That, in the opinion of this meeting the present Coal Mines Bill now before Parliament is unworkable and disastrous to the coal mining industry and we pledge ourselves to support the Miners Federation in any step they take to oppose this measure. It further records its conviction that this industry will never be placed upon a satisfactory basis, in the interests of the community until it is publicly owned and controlled by representatives of the State and the technical and manual workers engaged in it. We also call upon all the workpeople employed in and about coal mines to become members of the Federation'.*

Mr Wildin went on to confirm his opposition to the Coal Mines Bill and Mr Charles Luker who seconded the resolution went on to describe his thoughts on the unworkability of the Bill when it became law.

Mr Frank Hodges who was Secretary of the **MFGB** and who had recently taken a major part in the wage negotiations with the Government, was greeted with warm applause when he rose to speak in support of the resolution. He alluded to the fact that he was now back on home soil where his father had taken him when he was only six, little realising that in later years he would be a speaker on this platform. He said he liked to be back where he could hear the local dialect and often thought of the Forest of Dean while Secretary of the **MFGB** and hoped that they had made good progress since the days when his grandfather worked at the Norchard Colliery and his own father went with him as a boy aged nine.

Mr Hodges went on to express his concern over wages in the smaller Districts like the Forest of Dean where mining difficulties caused lower production figures than the larger Districts. He said that it was only within the last five or six years that Forest miners' wages had come up to nearer the average wage of the country and that was because they as a District had linked up with the mightiest organisation in the World, the Miners Federation which took care of the weak as well as the strong. He said that he believed that any man who produced a ton of coal no matter what the coalfield, should have the same wage as if he worked in the most favourable Districts. He said that the introduction of the latest Mines Act would see some Districts get a wage reduction which the Miners Federation would fight tooth and nail and could lead to a general strike if their demand for a wage increase was not met.

The Mining Industry Act
This was given the Royal Assent on the 16th of August 1920. It established a Mines Department within the Board of Trade administered by a Secretary for Mines with powers to regulate the Coal Industry. He would be able as from the 1st of September 1920 for one year to regulate the export of coal and the supply of coal for bunkering of vessels and also to regulate the price of pithead coal for home consumption, give directions as to the wages paid to miners and to regulate the distribution of profits.

The Board of Trade would be able to refer to an Advisory Committee consisting of 24 members and a Chairman, four would be workers representatives and four owners representatives, one would be a mining engineer, one would be a coal exporter, one would be a coal merchant, two would be agents or managers of coal mines with first class certificates and the rest would be drawn from other industries.

Each colliery would have a Pit Committee of 10 members, each District (26 in total) would have a District Committee. There would also be Area Boards (southern area to include Forest of Dean, Somerset, Bristol and Kent) and a National Board. All would have equal representation between workers and owners.

Speech House was again the venue on Sunday the 22nd of August 1920 when a large attendance of miners gathered to hear Mr Herbert Booth give a report on the Government's refusal of the application made by the **MFGB** for an increase in wages. Mr David Organ, President acting as Chairman said; **'The action of the Government has forced us to a position in which we have to prove what grit and what manhood we have in us and whether or not we are prepared to fight for the demands which have been put forward. Are you satisfied that those demands were just?** (Yes). **As miners, we cannot afford to allow the Government or any other body of men to bleed and exploit the mining industry to the extent of 60 or 70 million pounds a year. We are not acting from any selfish standpoint or we would have put in an application for the whole of the surplus but we have considered those who are engaged in other industries. I would advise you to be very careful where you put the cross when you get the ballot paper. I am asking for unity in this matter for if there should be a big division in our ranks, we will alienate the sympathy and assistance which we would otherwise receive from other bodies of workers'** (Hear, hear).

Mr Booth then explained the sequence of events that had led them to this position and went into depth on the reasons for the Government's rejection of the **MFGB's** demands and the counter arguments from their President Mr Robert Smillie. The whole question depended on which viewpoint was considered correct and both sides had opposing arguments in their own favour. The Federation had based their claim on the fact that the cost of living had increased out of all proportion to the miners' wages and figures proving this had been disputed by the Government. Winding up his speech, Mr Booth said that the challenge thrown to them by the Government could not go unchallenged and the man who failed to respond to the challenge was a traitor to his class and to his interests. He asked the men to forgo strike pay if they could as the Union purse was only so deep and to start preparing for that now. A resolution pledging those present to vote solidly for a strike was formally moved and seconded and carried unanimously. The ballot result was announced on the 2nd of September 1920 at another **MFGB** Special Conference;

For strike action 606,782,
Against strike action 238,865,
Majority for strike action .... 367,917.

The Forest of Dean vote was; For 5,132,
Against ....388.

It was agreed that all members hand in their notices in the normal way so that work would cease on the 25th of September 1920.

Meanwhile a Conference of the **Triple Industrial Alliance** took place on the 31st of August 1920 where the Railwaymen, Transport workers and Miners representatives agreed that the miners' claim was valid but were prepared to take part in further negotiations if necessary. And at the Trades Union Congress held at Portsmouth on the 8th of September 1920, an emergency resolution was passed confirming that; *'the miners' claim was reasonable and just'*. The news prompted Sir Robert Horne to offer to put the case to arbitration and invited the miners' leaders to London for further discussions.

These were not productive but a few days later after the Government had published financial figures for the mining industry, the **MFGB** modified their claim. There were seven points of note, two of which suggested a Tribunal to be set up to determine whether a reduction in the price of coal should take place based on the Industry's financial state and for the Government to adopt the Tribunal's recommendations.

Again, these proposals were rejected and were reported to another Special Conference of the **MFGB** on Tuesday the 21st of September 1920.

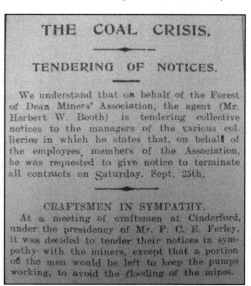

Fig. 71 Forest of Dean Mercury Notice.

That turned out to be a very busy week for all parties concerned. The National Union of Railwaymen and the Transport Workers Federation met and reaffirmed their support for the miners, subject to a **Triple Alliance** Conference on September the 22nd 1920. This meeting passed a resolution for further talks with the Government and that same evening met with Lloyd George, Bonar Law and Sir Robert Horne. The offer of arbitration still stood and at the **MFGB** Special Conference the next day, President Robert Smillie tried hard to persuade Conference to accept the offer. This was strongly opposed by numerous speakers and a vote of 545 to 360 against, meant that arbitration was off. This decision was reported to the **Triple Alliance** on September the 23rd 1920 where Railwaymen and Transport workers representatives were not happy. They argued that as they themselves had benefited through an arbitration process, they saw no reason to support a strike.

Several letters then passed between Mr Robert Smillie and Prime Minister Lloyd George and polite though they were, no further progress was made. Mr Smillie made an impassioned speech at the Triple Alliance Conference on September the 24th 1920 and said that the miners' Executive had decided that afternoon to suspend strike action on September the 25th 1920 for one week to allow further discussions with the Coal Owners. The vote in favour of this was 134 votes to 31.

They met on Saturday the 25th of September 1920 and miners leaders asked for an advance of 2 shillings per shift based on existing output and further advances dependent on an increase in output. This was rejected by the Coal Owners who put forward a counter proposal of 1 shilling per shift with smaller amounts for lower age groups all based on an increase in output during the first two weeks of October 1920. This was rejected by the miners' executive but a meeting between both sides and the Prime Minister eventually led to the **MFGB** deciding to take a ballot vote on suggestions put forward by the Coal Owners. The pending strike was again suspended until October the 16th 1920 to allow for the workers ballot which would be a free vote.

The Coal Owners offer on which they were voting was printed on the back of the ballot paper – an advance of 1 shilling per shift, 6 pence for youths and 4 and a half pence for boys – if output averaged a rate of 240 million tons per annum in the first two weeks of October. If the rate was 244 million tons per annum the rate would increase to 1 shilling and sixpence per shift and pro rata for youths and boys and progressing upwards at 6 pence per shift for each additional 4 million tons per annum.

The ballot was taken on October the 11th and 12th 1920 with the result being declared at a Special Conference on October the 14th 1920. The miners' verdict was a decisive NO to the offer;

For the Owners' offer 181,428,
Against the Owners' offer 635,098,
Majority against Owners' offer .... **453,670.**

Forest of Dean vote was For **718**
Against **4,514**

Strike notices were then issued to cease work after Saturday the 16th of October 1920 and the strike eventually began. However, arrangements had already been agreed in order to keep the collieries safe by allowing the minimum of maintenance workers to go about their work.

In the Forest of Dean the strike began after the morning shift on Saturday the 16th of October 1920 at 2 pm and a mass meeting of miners was held at the Speech House the next day – Sunday the 17th of October 1920 and again on Thursday the 21st of October 1920.

With over 86% of those who voted against accepting the Government's offer, the minority remained loyal to the Union and came out with the rest of the men, making over 5,000 striking miners in the Forest of Dean. At both meetings, Mr Booth the Agent stressed the importance of keeping the collieries going and to save them from the perils of destruction by flooding. He said that he had had reports of large numbers of men coming from the collieries and warned of the consequences of breaking the strike. It was agreed that certain collieries needed urgent repairs and so repair work and pumping could be carried out with agreement from the pit committees and management but not development work. He also said that strike pay would be paid out by the Lodges and if any worker was able to forego strike pay which they were entitled to, they would eventually get paid when the strike was over. Rates of strike pay were 1 pound per week for a full member, 10 shillings for a half member and 2 shillings for a child.

Reports on the behaviour of striking miners were favourable as they were taking the advice of the Union to keep in the *'Best of temper and humour'*. All were convinced they were taking the right steps and with the fine weather, many were taking up healthy activities such as football. In Cinderford the Baptist minister offered to open his schoolroom as a meeting place should the miners so desire and the Cinderford branch of the **NUR** passed a resolution to support the miners cause and recommended a 'down tools' policy as the quickest way of ending the dispute.

Further negotiations

After an exchange of letters between Mr Smillie and Lloyd George, Mr Smillie offered his resignation to the Federation due to his favouring arbitration and that strike action was a vote of no confidence in him. Strong voices were heard in support of Mr Smillie and he was eventually persuaded to withdraw his resignation and to support the strike.

A week went by before the National Union of Railwaymen agreed to support the miners with strike action themselves if the miners claims were not settled by October the 23rd 1920. This threat prompted Lloyd George to offer to negotiate further that weekend but at the same time was plotting to introduce to Parliament the **Emergency Powers Bill** which became an Act on October the 27th 1920. This flew in the face of the miners who thought they were supposedly negotiating with fair and honest men. Lloyd George's underhand move had created an Act that gave great powers of authority to both police and Ministers and to declare a state of emergency if necessary. It also declared that any action that threatened the supply and distribution of food, water, fuel or light or with the means of locomotion to deprive the community of the essentials of life would suffer imprisonment for three months or 100 pounds fine or both.

The **MFGB** decided to call another ballot of workmen on the latest Government offer which became known as the **'datum line proposal'** that accepted the 2 shillings per shift demand but with other modified output targets. The revised offer proposed an advance of 2 shillings per shift for persons over 18 years of age, 1 shilling per shift for persons between 16 and 18 years of age and 9 pence per shift for persons below 16 years of age. This was guaranteed until the 31st of December 1920 and from then on depended on the level of national output in relation to the datum line figures produced during the five weeks ending on the 18th of December 1920. If output increased, wages went up and if output fell, wages would also fall. The target output rates were calculated every four weeks and wages calculated in accordance with that and paid the following month. This was to continue until a National Wages Board could be set up by the end of March 1921.

The ballot result was declared at a Special Conference on Wednesday the 3rd of November 1920;

For the Government offer 338,045,
Against the Government offer 346,504,
Majority against .... 8,459.

Forest of Dean vote was; For the offer 1765
                        Against the offer 1961
Majority against 196

Total votes cast of 3726 was just over 2/3 of the previous ballot where 5232 votes were cast.

Under the rules of the Federation if a ballot is taken during a strike, a vote of two thirds of those taking part in the ballot shall be necessary to continue the strike. Therefore with great regret the delegate vote was;

For the rule 121,
Against the rule .... 46.

And so the strike ended with the workers being instructed to return to work the next day November the 4th 1920. It had lasted 18 days.

At the Speech House on Sunday the 7th of November 1920, a large gathering of miners from all parts of the district gathered to hear the Government's proposals for a settlement. The meeting was Chaired by the President of the **FODMA** Mr David Organ who stood on a large trolley in front of the hotel. In his opening remarks he said **'we are not very much 'in the know' apart from what we have learnt in the newspapers and I really confess that I don't fully understand the terms of the proposed settlement. The one thing that I do understand is that it will not give us what we started fighting for and that is the two shillings unconditionally and the datum line was also brought in'.**

Mr Herbert Booth the Agent tried to explain the terms of the agreement and that the **MFGB** had given it their blessing (laughter). He said that he himself was unable to explain the agreed terms because it was exceedingly difficult to understand and that he wished the **MFGB** had called a delegate conference of all the Districts so that the proposals could have been discussed and explained and made clear.

Norchard Colliery and Lord Bledisloe

Amid the turmoil of the miner's dispute, there were celebrations at Lord Bledisloe's residence at Lydney Park on Saturday the 2nd of October 1920. The occasion was the 'coming of age' (21) of his eldest son and heir Benjamin Ludlow Bathurst and proceedings continued throughout the day in very inclement weather. Lord Bledisloe was a major shareholder in the Norchard and other Forest of Dean collieries and also a major benefactor in his local area. His first duty that day was to dedicate a new swimming pool to the people of Lydney and Aylburton on a portion of his land opposite the gates to Lydney Park. He said that in conveying the property to the local public, he had adopted the useful modern expedient of vesting it in the Charity Commissioners who would hold it in trust for ever thereafter for the benefit of the inhabitants of the locality.

After tea at The Park there were a series of presentations, one of which was from the employees of the Norchard Colliery where over 400 workers were, at that time considering going on strike. Mr J.A. Hooper the colliery manager presented Mr Benjamin Bathurst with a Half Hunter 18 carat gold watch and an illuminated address on behalf of the workers at the Norchard Colliery, 98% of who had contributed towards the presentation. Following Mr Benjamin's heartfelt reply, Lord Bledisloe said that; **'of all the touching events which has marked this day's proceedings, there is absolutely none which has so deeply affected me as the gift which the men of the Norchard Colliery have made to my elder son on his 'coming of age'. I thought they were going to strike. I certainly never thought that either of us would receive at their hands such a striking and warm tribute of their friendly feelings towards us, not merely as their neighbours but as representing those who are employers in their industry, and against whom, if one were simply to judge from what one read in the newspapers, there is deadly hostility intended on the part of the mining population.'**

Beachley Power Station

There was a further move in November 1920 to get electricity cables into the Forest of Dean. The Government accepted a purchase price of £163,000 from the West of England Joint Electricity Authority for the purchase of the redundant Beachley Power Station.

Election of Officials - F.O.D.M.A.

In December, the ballot took place to re elect Officials for the forthcoming year 1921. President Mr David Organ, Vice President Mr Albert Wildin,

Financial Secretary Mr T.H. Etherington, Finance Committee Messrs Horace Jones, S. Cooke, G.L. Jones, Auditors Messrs. Richard Kear and Ambrose Adams, Political Committee Messrs. C.W. Luker, D.R. Organ Albert James, William Howells, Ivor Brain, Chas. Beach.

Accidents/Fatalities

In May 1920 it was reported that Mr Alfred Barnard aged 55 of Woodside Street, Cinderford, received severe injuries due to a fall of earth while working underground at the Lightmoor Colliery.

Also in May 1920 Mr George Fields aged 19 of Dockham road, Cinderford received head injuries due to a fall of earth while working underground at Foxes Bridge Colliery.

On Wednesday the 6th of October 1920, Mr Ernest Charles Whitson, a pit sinker, was killed by falling down a shaft while working at the Howbeach Colliery near Blakeney. The Inquest held in Blakeney on the 9th of October 1920 heard that Mr Whitson had been working with two other men engaged in widening the pit shaft from 8ft to 14ft. He was at the top of the shaft with banksman Mr Reuben Biddington who operated the engine that raised and closed the doors that covered the shaft. Mr William Hawkins operated the winding gear. Mr Whitson had climbed into the iron bowk (a large barrel) that was attached to the lowering rope by a patent hook attached to the bowk handle. Also in the bowk was a piece of loose timber. Mr Whitson was then heard to say 'right' and Mr Biddington then raised the doors causing the bowk to go up with them and tilt over. Another man Mr Denis Neese asked Mr Biddington to drop the doors again as he could see the precarious position the bowk was in. But before the doors could be lowered, the bowk toppled over and Mr Whitson said **'what are you doing'** before raising his arm and grabbing hold of the lip. This action unfortunately released the patent hook and the bowk then fell to the bottom of the shaft which was 116 feet deep and Mr Whitson was killed instantly.

Mr Harry Baker and Mr Sidney Hawkins the two pit sinkers already down the shaft said how they saw the doors opening above them and the bowk falling. They jumped clear as the bowk passed them 'in a flash'. They denied calling to Mr Biddinton for timber to be sent down. On examining Mr Whitson's body, Dr Hill said that his skull was terribly shattered and eleven ribs were broken.

The Coroner commented that quoting from safety rules; timber should have been lashed and should not be accompanied by workmen. Also, as Mr Biddington was 'captain of the ship', he should not have raised the doors until the winding gear had lifted the bowk clear of the doors. He concluded that the matter of the hook coming undone had nothing to do with it as that would not have happened if the bowk had not tilted. He said it was a clear case of one man causing the death of another and put the matter to the Jury. They found Mr Biddington in default and recorded a verdict of manslaughter against him. Sympathy was expressed to the widow and the Jury also gave her their fees.

On Monday the 18th of October 1920 at Littledean, Mr Reuben Biddington, ex publican and banksman was committed for trial at Gloucester Assizes on the charge of manslaughter of Ernest Charles Whitson of Blakeney. He was bailed on a surety from himself of £25.00 and the same from two other bondsmen – Mr Herbert Booth, miners Agent and Mr F. McAvoy the colliery manager.

At Gloucester Assizes on Monday the 25th of October 1920, the Jury heard the case of manslaughter against Mr Reuben Biddington aged 52, again in great detail with submissions from both prosecution and defence witnesses. The defence lawyer Mr Lort Williams M.P. submitted that the utmost the prisoner was guilty of was an honest error or inadvertence and that what he did was not the direct cause of the accident, which was due to Mr Whitsun releasing the safety catch. This was taken into account and the Jury agreed. Mr Biddington was found 'not guilty' and discharged. There were cheers and applause from the public gallery.

On Wednesday the 29th of December 1920, three workmen – Mr Albert Cole and Mr John Horlick from Cinderford and Mr Harold Collins from Blakeney were injured while working in the forge at the Howbeach Colliery near Blakeney. All three men were working on a piston and block which had been hoisted onto the blacksmith's forge in order to remove the piston rings. Heat was applied in an attempt to separate parts but the block exploded sending out debris which injured the men. Mr Collins was the most severely injured with bad cuts to his hands and thigh while the other two were less severely injured. It was later considered that the likely cause of the explosion was water in a cavity in the block which, when heated burst open.

Chapter 22
1921 – Pit Stop -The National Lockout – Black Friday

The end of 1920 saw Great Britain and other European countries entering a recession with a slump in foreign markets and unemployment on the rise. This situation continued into 1921 and as a consequence, the miners' planned target output of coal could not be realised as per the agreed settlement of November 1920 and consequently resulted in a corresponding fall in miners' wages.

There was also frantic activity on the part of the **MFGB** and Government to come to some agreement on another part of the November 1920 settlement, namely the setting up of a National Wages Board by the 31st of March 1921. To this end, the **MFGB** submitted their five point proposals to the Coal Owners, all of which were rejected. The Coal Owners were adamant that miners' wages should be settled by their Districts. This of course meant that Districts like the Forest of Dean which had comparatively low productivity levels due to geological problems such as water ingress and faults, would see a large decrease in their wages.

The first offer
During further negotiations, the **MFGB** insisted that wages should be distributed by the newly formed National Wages Board and that profits from the industry should be shared from a National Profits Pool. Both sides then submitted their respective proposals to Government during February 1921 and Sir Robert Horne, President of the Board of Trade invited the miners' representatives for further talks. In straight terms he announced that the Government had decided to decontrol the mines on the 31st of March 1921.

So this would mean that the Coal Owners were then at liberty to wipe away 50% of all the wage rises given during the War period – 3 shillings per shift war wage, the April 1920 20%, the Sankey wage of 2 shillings per shift and the November settlement, all in one swipe. As an example, a coal hewer's wage at the end March 1921 was 15 shillings and 3 pence per shift but if he accepted the Coal Owners' offer, in April his wage would be reduced to 8 shillings and 8 pence per shift.

The Coal Owners protested too, on their understanding that August the 31st 1921 was to be the date, as laid down in the **Coal Industry Act** – so both parties were thwarted by the betrayal of the word of the Government yet again. There was however, some compensation for the Coal Owners in that the accumulated Government profit surplus was paid back to them – but none for the miners.

The Coal Owners lost no time however and posted notices at the beginning of March in every colliery and pit in the country of their collective intention to terminate all existing contracts with the men as from the 31st of March 1921.

In the Forest of Dean

Miners again gathered in very wet weather at Speech House on Easter Monday the 28th of March 1921 to hear the latest news. Chairman David Organ was in fighting mood and said '**In my opinion if ever there was a time in our history when we ought to feel like getting our backs up, then it was this time** (hear, hear). **The Government which had betrayed and broken faith with us not for the first time, told us that a National Wages Board should be in existence by the end of March. Instead of giving us assistance in that direction, the intention is to drive us back to the District arrangements, practically the same as before the War. We as miners say that we ought to have our wages regulated nationally with a practically uniform rate as far as possible throughout Great Britain. Sooner or later we have got to make a more strenuous fight than ever and, if so, it should be this time** (hear, hear). **The Federation has instructed the Districts that no man should do any work whatever** (hear, hear)**, and let every man who received notice to come out, do so and let the owners and their collieries go where they choose** (hear, hear and applause). **I am of the opinion that it would be as well to go and have some fresh air and starve as to go and bury ourselves in the mine and starve there'.** (hear, hear).

It was unanimously agreed not to accept the Coal Owners' offer of a 50% reduction in wages and the men were advised not to attend their work from Friday morning the 1st of April 1921. The Coal Owners response was to impose a **National Lockout** which meant that over 6,000 men and boys in the Forest of Dean were out of work.

The Government immediately enacted the **Emergency Powers Act** which effectively declared a state of emergency in the country. Armed forces were mobilised and sent to the coal Districts and troops were recalled from abroad with all leave cancelled.

On the same day, at another Speech House mass meeting, the miners were in defiant mood. Both Mr Herbert Booth the Agent and President of the **FODMA** Mr David Organ were again united and *'to stand together shoulder to shoulder with the determination to fight on to the bitter end.'*

At this time there was grave concern as to the state of Forest collieries underground workings due to flooding. Members of the Craftsmen's Union who usually manned the pumps had also withdrawn their labour so that the collieries were left to flood and in some cases pit ponies were left underground. Colliery managers and office staff were called in to help save their collieries where it was possible.

At Howbeach and Wallsend, water was being kept in check by two relays of men doing 12 hour shifts. At New Fancy, director Carl Deakin and volunteer staff were keeping more boilers going than in normal times with staff doing eight hour shifts while at Cannop the situation led to the closure of the mine. Cannop was the most advanced and newest colliery in the Forest with vast amounts of money being invested in it. Water accumulated at the rate of 2,000 to 3,000 gallons per minute and without the means of pumping, the workings were lost. At Waterloo near Lydbrook, flooding was being kept in check by a sufficient number of workers manning the pumps and were going along quietly. At the collieries of Lightmoor, Foxes Bridge, Crump Meadow and Eastern United, the management were hopeful of keeping the workings in good order. At Norchard near Lydney there were sufficient staff and volunteers to man the pumps and to keep the boilers fired up. Flooding was kept in check and His Lordship, Lord Bledisloe also lent a hand with the boilers as did both his sons, a fellow director Mr R.R. Bowles JP and a shareholder Brigadier General Tyler of Clanna. Comment in the 'Daily Herald' newspaper suggested that the practice his Lordship was getting may prove useful when he had to earn a living.

Fig. 72 Lord Bledisloe helps with feeding the boilers at Norchard

Coal Owners and Government were putting pressure on the **MFGB** to save the mines by allowing men to attend the pumps and although they were open to negotiation with a view to a settlement, their insistence on saving the mines was the first priority. Lloyd George made it clear in several letters that the condition of the mines must come first and also to rescuing the 'poor dumb animals' still underground. The **MFGB** were insistent on having negotiations free of pre-conditions, the withholding of pumpmen being their trump card - and so stalemate prevailed.

The Forest of Dean Craftsmen's Union leader Mr J.B. Allen read out a letter at a Speech House meeting on the 14th of April 1921 that he had received from the Crawshay colliery managers. It read; '*In the event of the necessary assistance for the safety of Lightmoor, Trafalgar, Foxes Bridge, Howbeach and Eastern United collieries not being immediately forthcoming, we shall call a meeting of shareholders at the earliest possible moment and advise the abandonment of these collieries and the realisation of assets. – signed J.W. Brosier Creagh, Arthur Morgan.*'

The meeting however decided to ignore this threat and instead declared a resolution to stick to their original decision that none of the Craftsmen or Miners Union members should go to work during the period of the dispute

The Triple Alliance

The miners Executive had already met the Triple Alliance Executives before the lockout and had asked for their assistance by taking strike action in support of the miners. This request was discussed at separate meetings of the National Union of Railwaymen and the Transport Union on the 5th and 6th of April 1921 respectively. On the 8th of April 1921, the Triple Alliance had made their decision to support the miners and to take strike action as from the 12th of April 1921.

However, there were misgivings among some Triple Alliance members who preferred negotiations to start straight away. Fearful that they might lose support, the miners Executive agreed to concede the Government's insistence on saving the mines and issued a directive which urged their members to stop all actions that interfered with securing the safety of the mines.

Negotiations started at the Board of Trade on Monday the 11th of April 1921 with Federation Secretary Frank Hodges leading the miners Executive Committee's cause. The proposed Triple Alliance strike action was postponed pending the result of negotiations but after two days, they ended in failure. On Wednesday the 13th of April 1921 the Triple Alliance again called for their members to take strike action starting on Friday the 15th of April 1921 and was amply supported by other smaller Unions and the Parliamentary Labour Party.

The next day, Thursday the 14th of April 1921, further meetings were held in the Committee rooms of the House of Commons where Members of Parliament met with representatives of both miners and owners. It was a question and answer session where some sought to trick the miners into accepting a temporary settlement on a District basis. For the miners, Frank Hodges answered as truthfully as he could but he was misunderstood by some who were only too keen to see an end to the dispute. The Prime Minister was informed of this supposedly change of policy by the miners and promptly invited them for talks the next day. On that day, Friday the 15th of April 1921, the miners Executive received that letter from Lloyd George and refused his invitation stating their original claim of a National Wages Board and a National Pool was the only basis for negotiation.

At this decision, Frank Hodges resigned his position of Secretary but was later persuaded to withhold it. The decision not to agree to Lloyd George's invitation was sent to the Triple Alliance who tried to persuade the **MFGB** to change its mind and agree to further talks. This they refused to do and fully expected their allies to come out on strike that evening as promised. Mr J.H. Thomas, leader of the Transport Union expressed his opinion that if the miners refused further talks with Government, the strike probably wouldn't take place. This provoked panic within other Unions, especially the National Union of Railwaymen who became concerned for the consequences of supporting the miners and defying the Government. The result of all this was that Mr Thomas announced to the Press that the Triple Alliance strike was cancelled. And so Friday the 15th of April 1921 went down in history as **'BLACK FRIDAY'.**

In the Forest of Dean many local railwaymen and others came out and said they deplored their leaders' decision and would have willingly supported the miners cause. However there was little or no animosity within the community and on Monday the 18th of April 1921, another mass meeting of miners gathered at the Speech House enclosure. A large crowd of West Dean miners and their wives and girlfriends marched up the road, headed by the Pillowell brass band. Someone in the crowd shouted **'are we downhearted?'** 'No' came the reply. The mood was as firm as ever for continuing the strike alone and President Mr David Organ said; **'we are disappointed with the attitude of the railwaymen and transport workers. Our expectation that our friends were coming out at 10 o'clock last Friday night, has been dispelled – it did not come off'.** A voice in the crowd said; **'it was the leaders who let us down'.** Mr Organ replied **'Yes I agree, it was not the rank and file. Although there are changes being made, it cannot be said that the rank and file of the miners are showing signs of weakening'.** Another voice in the crowd said; **'the only change on our side is that we are firmer and more bitter'.** Carrying on, Mr Organ said; **'I regard the action of the railwaymen and their friends as downright rotten. If there is going to be all this jibbing every time joint action is taken, the sooner the Triple Alliance was done with, the better. What is the use of going with them up to a certain point and then turning their backs and leaving us? In spite of this however, I take it that we are not deterred and that we mean to stick to our guns'.** (hear, hear). **'We will at any rate stick it and see this business through, even if we are upset at the last ditch. We will not bend until we are starved into submission'.** (applause). 'Then how much better would the country be? Despite the expense we have gone to, the discontent that has been caused and the names we have been called of 'Rebels, Bolshevists and a lot of other ists and isms, let us stick to it'. (hear, hear). 'let us not be led astray'. (hear, hear). 'Under the proposals that have been made, we cannot possibly live, and seeing that we cannot live while at work, we might as well enjoy God's sunshine and not descend and get coal and let someone else live on our backs all the time'. (applause).

Mr Herbert Booth said; **'The Triple Alliance has been made out to be our gateway to Heaven, but we have been disillusioned,** (laughter). **'The railwaymen's turn will come so let them be on their guard. This is a more critical time than this country has experienced since 1836 and if the miners go down, then so will the railwaymen. The Triple Alliance is as dead as a doornail but don't be downhearted. Dean Forest has fought months at a time against a 10% reduction and this time it is 50% the owners are after'.** (applause).

Eventually a resolution was adopted to support the actions of the **MFGB** and to suspend judgement on Mr Hodges until he had spoken.

Strike pay had been paid out by the local Lodges at the rate of 10 shillings for men, 5 shillings for youths and 1 shilling for boys but by the third week in April 1921, the **FODMA** coffers were empty. On Monday the 25th of April 1921, both they and the Craftsmen's Association held a meeting at Speech House to offer a credit note scheme to their members and invited local traders and shopkeepers to participate. It was understood that the **FODMA** would guarantee the scheme and that eventually, everyone taking part would get reimbursed. In addition, the Association struck up a deal with the local Cooperative Society allowing credit to be given to miners and their families while local religious organisations began raising funds to feed those that were destitute and to make sure the children were fed.

On Sunday the 24th of April 1921, the Forest of Dean Labour Party held a meeting at Lydney Picture House where Mr C.T. Cramp, General Secretary of the National Union of Railwaymen was invited to speak. Although the then situation was mildly hostile towards the Triple Alliance members, Mr Cramp had apparently been invited to the venue a month previous and was now likened to Daniel being thrown into the lion's den – although he did receive a warm welcome from a packed audience made up mainly of miners.

His speech was mainly concerned with an explanation of the failure of the Triple Alliance to support the miners at the eleventh hour but said that the following day, the National Union of Railwaymen had issued instructions to its members not to touch or transport coal from any colliery sidings until the dispute had been settled – a sort of compromise from an all out strike. He said they had also been informed that the Dockers Union had instructed their members not to handle any imported coal and to refuse to part bunker any ships leaving port. He pointed out that these instructions also applied to the Forest of Dean coalfield and if any railwayman took part in it, it would be considered as blacklegging his own Union. A voice in the audience shouted **'it has been done and it is being done every day here in the Forest. 40 trucks were moved yesterday.'** Mr Cramp ended by saying that there was much sympathy for the miners and asked them not to become divided among themselves.

There was a question and answer session and afterwards Mr Rennolds, a National Union of Railwaymen member and engine driver moved a vote of thanks to Mr Cramp and said that 98% of Forest railwaymen were ready then and were ready now to come out to the aid of the miners. He said that as he was a local engine driver, he would now refuse to take his engine into a colliery yard.

David Organ who rose to support the vote of thanks commended Mr Cramp for coming to Lydney but a member of the audience called; **'you are standing where you ought not to be'.** Mr Organ replied; **'I am not taking this present action because I am satisfied with the position in which we find ourselves. I confess that I am disappointed with a lot of things. In the first place I am disappointed with Frank Hodges and I am doubly disappointed with the action of the Triple Alliance. But while that is so, I admire any man who has the courage and the manhood to face an audience, irrespective as to whether his views coincide with ours or whether they were right in the opposite direction'.** applause)

On Monday the 25th of April 1921, another meeting of miners was called at the Speech House and three Forest bands – Cinderford Town, Yorkley Onward and Pillowell Brass – all converged on the now famous meeting place followed by large processions of miners and their wives - with the Yorkley Women's Labour Party waving their red flag. This turned out to be the biggest meeting yet and the mood was of a determination to stick it out with no weakening of the spirit. In the Chair was Mr C.C. Cox of the Craftsmen's Association supported by Mr J. B. Allen, (Agent), Mr David

Organ, President of the **FODMA**, and Mr W. Vedmore, member of the **FODMA** Executive. The Chairman's opening remarks praised the number of ladies present which he thought was a good sign and apologised for the absence of Mr Herbert Booth who was attending a Conference of the **MFGB** in London that day.

Mr Vedmore reported back from his attendance of the previous Conference on Friday the 22nd of April 1921 and said the District reports from the whole of the country's rank and file were as firm as ever in sticking to their original demands. He also reported on Frank Hodges' explanation of what happened at the House of Commons meeting on Thursday the 14th of April 1921 which caused the Triple Alliance to call off their support. He said that Mr Hodges was in a question and answer session and one of his answers had been misinterpreted as a statement of the miners' willingness to accept a temporary settlement. Mr Hodges said that no such statement had been made and that his answer was that any proposal put forward by the owners or Government would be given full consideration by the **MFGB**. He said that the Government and newspapers had twisted Mr Hodges words about

Mr David Organ said that he was pleased that the country's rank and file were standing firm, and he did hope that there would be no change as far as the Forest of Dean miners were concerned. **'let us stick to our guns and continue to fight and not bend the knee to anything put forward to sidetrack us so that in six, nine or twelve months or perhaps in two or three years we would have to fight again and make the same sacrifice again. I want the ladies to stick with us as it is their business as well and if their men get downhearted, let their womenfolk put some grit in them.'**

Mr Organ also mentioned that he had attended a meeting the previous day at Lydney and heard the leader of the National Union of Railwaymen Mr Cramp, explain their position as regards the strike. He said he was pleased that Mr Cramp's Union had instructed their members not to move coal from any colliery in the country (applause).

Mr Organ concluded; **'I hope that you, as miners are as determined as ever and are not prepared to move one iota until Lloyd George and his good wife are prepared to accept 8 shillings and 8 pence a day and work under the same conditions as the miners and the miners' wives** (hear, hear). **This, we as miners and miners' wives are not**

prepared to accept and will continue the struggle right out to the last ditch.'

The second offer

And so, on a National basis, the miners were as one – they demanded a National Wages Board and a National pool while the Coal Owners favoured District settlements. During the last week in April 1921, the Coal Owners met daily with the Government in the hope of coming to some agreement to put forward to the miners Delegate Conference. On Thursday April the 28th 1921 the Government made their offer in the form of a subsidy. The Government called it a *'grant of £10,000,000'* which was intended to compensate the miners for their drop in wages from May until the end of August 1921. From then on, there would be District settlements which would last until November the 30th 1922. The idea of a National Pool was rejected. On the same day, the Conference rejected this offer with a Delegate card vote of 890,000 votes to 42,000.

Despite the miners' strike, Labour Day or May Day was celebrated in the Forest of Dean with a mass gathering at the Speech House on Monday the 2nd of May 1921. The Berry Hill brass band led a large contingent of families from the Coleford area onto the field. Mr David Organ again Presided over the meeting and was supported by Mr James Wignall M.P., Mr Herbert Booth, Agent, Mr J.B. Allen, Craftsmens Agent and Mr F.H. Yeatman, Treasurer. Mr Organ's opening remarks were to reiterate the solidarity of the working class movement and the power they had within them to overthrow the Capitalist system and to be able to live a free, full and nobler life (applause).

Mr Booth remarked on the publicity campaign in the newspapers regarding the Government's offer of £10,000,000 and how it would be distributed with favour given to the Coal Owners or Government side of the argument. He said that the Government had nothing to do with it so the Coal Owners must have been responsible. If they accepted the present offer, the money would certainly be exhausted before the end of August and they would be in the same situation then, as they are now with District agreements.

The crisis continued throughout May 1921 and another joint miners and craftmens' Union meeting was held at the Speech House on Monday the 23rd of May 1921 accompanied by the Pillowell Brass Band. Attendance was lower than expected. Mr David Organ said that the present situation was shrouded in mystery but he hoped that whatever happened, the rank and file were still going strong although they had now entered the eighth week of the strike. He said that he hoped there was no weakness in the ranks.

This theme was repeated often during those weeks but there were often reports that men were still getting coal. Mr Herbert Booth was questioned about this and particularly with regard to activity at the Eastern United Colliery. It was discovered that the men who were working there were non Union men – they were not in either the Craftsmen's Union or the **FODMA** The colliery manager assured the Unions that if any non Union man could be found working there, they would be stopped immediately.

Mr Organ then referred to a letter in a local newspaper signed *'Wife of a Forest of Dean miner'* and said he was pleased with the number of miners wives present that day and to the fact that they were prepared to support the miners in their struggle to the bitter end (hear, hear). He asked the ladies present to vote by a show of hands if they were prepared to support the miners in their struggle in which they were engaged, right through to the end? A woman called out **'we will do our best'**, followed by a unanimous holding up of the right hand (applause).

The third offer

Another Government and Coal Owners' proposal was received by the Executive Committee of the **MFGB** on the 27th of May 1921 and it was decided to send it to the Districts and for them to report their views by the 3rd of June 1921. These proposals were on similar lines to the previous offer except for introducing the suggestion of arbitration should both sides not agree.

On Monday the 30th of May 1921, the Forest of Dean miners met again at the Speech House. Mr David Organ and Mr Herbert Booth were present but it was explained that Mr J.B. Allen the Craftsmen's Agent was otherwise engaged. Mr Organ spoke about the length of time they had now been on 'holiday' and that the latest Government proposals would be put before the men for their decision of whether or not to accept them. A further meeting in three days time would be arranged for their decision to be made and sent to the Miners Executive of the **MFGB**. He said that this was now a serious matter and hoped that it would receive their best consideration. He said **'As far as I am personally concerned, I am not prepared to move one iota from the original demands of the MFGB and I believe there are a considerable number of workers, not only in the Forest of Dean but**

right up and down the country who are prepared to stand until those demands are conceded'(applause).

Mr Booth then explained the Government's latest offer which contained a proviso that if the miners and Coal Owners could not agree on a durable settlement, it should go to arbitration. Mr Organ said that if this latest offer is rejected and the Federation stood in the future as it had done for the last eight and a half weeks, he felt sure that with a little more suffering, they would yet win through to a better state of affairs than they had had in the past. A lady in the crowd interrupted and called out; **'we will have them Mr Organ',** to which he replied; **'are you prepared to go on then Mrs Jones?'.** The lady replied; **'Ah that I be'** to some laughter. Mr Organ continued to say that he hoped the latest proposals would be turned down and so a proposition rejecting the proposals and adhering to their original demands of the **MFGB** was carried unanimously.

Cracks appearing

Even before the result was known, there were signs that the miners' resolve was weakening. In Derbyshire, the Swanwich collieries which employed around one thousand men were re-opening for work with the miners accepting a reduction of 2 shillings and 6 pence per shift.

In the Forest of Dean, the local Craftsmen's Agent Mr J.B. Allen had been conspicuous by his absence at **FODMA** meetings, especially at Speech House on the 30th of May 1921. It became known that he had been to meetings with certain colliery managers, under pressure to get his men back to work. The Crawshay collieries were using imported blackleg labour to man the pumps and the craftsmen were threatened with losing their jobs. So far, the Craftsmen's Association had given the **FODMA** their full support and had even mentioned the possibility of affiliating with them and the **MFGB.** Mr Booth was made aware of these events and confronted Mr Allen at a meeting of miners at Speech House on Monday the 6th of June 1921. Mr Allen defended his position but agreed that if any of his members were attempting to return to work, the **FODMA** would be informed first and he was grateful that the **FODMA** had provided strike pay for his members. He admitted meeting with colliery managers but denied he was in negotiations with them. He further hoped that this situation would not cause disunity between the men. The meeting ended with a vote of confidence for Mr Allen.

In contrast, four members of the **N.U.R.** (National Union of Railwaymen) at Sharpness docks who were supporting the miners' strike were suspended for refusing to unload imported coal from Belgium. One Gloucester man and three Sharpness men alleged that blackleg labour was being used to unload the cargo and on communication with their local railwaymen's Union, they were instructed to refuse to handle the coal. Other men later refused to move the train and were also suspended. By the 3rd of June 1921, the miners' response to the latest offer was rejection from all Districts.

The Ballot

In response to the refusal of the **MFGB** to accept their latest offer, Lloyd George saw fit to keep the offer of £10,000,000 open for another two weeks only. This prompted a meeting between the miners Executive and the Coal Owners Association, the result of which was the suggestion of a nationwide ballot. On the 10th of June 1921 the **MFGB** agreed to take a ballot vote during the following week and made ready the ballot papers. Two questions were on that ballot paper;

1. *Are you in favour of fighting on for the principles of the National Wages Board and National Pool, with loss of Government subsidy of ten million pounds for wages if no settlement by June 18th 1921?*
2. *Are you in favour of accepting the Government and Owners' terms as set forth on the back of this ballot paper?*

Please place your 'X' in the space provided for the purpose, June 10th 1921. Signed, Frank Hodges, General Secretary.

The back of the ballot paper stated in short;

1. That they totally rejected the call for a National Wages Board and a National Pool,
2. The Temporary Period. To use the offer of £10,000,000 to prevent large reductions in wages. The first reductions not to exceed 2 shillings per shift for all workers of 16 years and upwards and 1 shilling per shift for workers below 16 years. No further reductions until August the 1st. Further reductions after that date to be agreed mutually until the grant is exhausted.
3. The Permanent Scheme after the temporary period of £10,000,000 was exhausted to set up a National Board for fixing principles for guidance of District Boards. These District Boards to fix the percentage of profits to

wages using the audited ascertainment of Coal Owners profits from each District.

4. To put a time limit on the cash offer of the 18th of June 1921.

The ballot results were published on the 17th of June 1921 and showed an overwhelming majority for rejecting the terms.

For rejecting the Government's offer 434,614
For accepting the Government's offer 180,724
Majority for continuing the fight.................... 253,890

Forest of Dean vote was;
Against the Government's offer 5,222
For the Government's offer 659
Majority against offer 4563

The Final offer

Lloyd George was swift to condemn the result and was prepared to withdraw the subsidy offer as stated – i.e. the 18th of June 1921 unless an agreement could be reached. The **MFGB** Executive Committee asked other Unions to support their cause but none were forthcoming. They were then forced to come to some accommodation with the Government and a meeting between parties was convened for Monday, the 27th of June 1921. The result of that meeting was a complicated compromise which the Executive Committee accepted with the proviso that the £10,000,000 subsidy was still available. The **MFGB** decided to consult all Districts on the terms agreed and the results to be in by the 1st of July 1921.

Results were in;
For acceptance 832,840
Against acceptance 105,820
Majority for acceptance 727,020

The Forest of Dean District voted against accepting the offer as did Lancashire, Bristol, Somerset and Kent Districts.

And so the lockout ended and the miners were instructed to return to work by Monday the 11th of July 1921.

Miners' Annual Demonstration

On Saturday the 9th of July 1921 - just after the Settlement and the miners returned to work - **the Miners' Annual Demonstration** at Speech House took place in gloriously hot and dry weather, in contrast to the previous years' event which was blighted by rain and lots of mud. As can be seen from the accompanying poster, this annual event was not just for the "Meeting". It was also a time for letting one's hair down with both children and adults enjoying the attractions and fairground supplied by Mr Jacob Studt - all supported by the Pillowell Prize Band.

FOREST OF DEAN MINERS' ASSOCIATION

THE ANNUAL DEMONSTRATION

Of the above Association will be held on

SATURDAY, JULY 9th, 1921

AT THE

SPEECH HOUSE GROUNDS

(Kindly lent for the occasion by Mr. Pritchard, proprietor).

A GREAT MEETING

ADDRESSED BY

MR. ERNEST BEVIN

THE DO KERS' K.C.:

Mr. James Wignall, M.P.

MR. H. W. BOOTH (Agent), and others.

Chair to be taken at 2.30 p.m. by MR. DAVID ORGAN, President.

The CELEBRATED PILLOWELL PRIZE BAND

Will give Selections during the day. DANCING after 6 p.m.

AMUSEMENTS will be provided by MR. JACOB STUDT.

ADMISSION TO FIELD, 6d. Children under 14, 3d. Gates open 10 a.m.

NOTE.—All noise of roundabouts, etc., must cease during the meeting.

Applications f r stalls, etc., to be made to Mr. A. Adams, Ruspidge.

Fence breaking strictly forbidden. No Stalls, etc., must stand outside grounds on July 9th.

1391

Fig.73 Miners' Annual Demonstration poster for July the 9th 1921,

Within the shade of a large tent, David Organ Chaired the meeting in the early afternoon and among those present were Mr Albert Wildin, Vice President of the Association, the local M.P. Mr James Wignall, Mr Herbert Booth the miners' Agent and Mr Ernest Bevin the Dockers K.C.. As Chairman and President of the Association, David Organ's opening remarks fairly summed up the feelings of those present when he said that **'since our last demonstration, we have had many ups and downs and unfortunately we've had more downs than ups, with the result that every workman, wife and child will have to suffer. At the end of this recent struggle, the spirit of the men is not broken even though we have not obtained the pool. I don't want you to be disheartened by the recent setbacks and you will gain nothing by taking individual and selfish courses of action – let us be more and more prepared to keep ourselves organised'**(applause).

Fig. 74 Group photo taken at that meeting – those identified are; Back row 3ʳᵈ from right is Herbert Booth, front row from right are David Organ, Ernest Bevin, James Wignall M.P.

Photo courtesy of Author.

Mr Ernest Bevin was warmly applauded by those present and gave a very eloquent address and said he was glad to be here and to meet with the miners who had been involved in the recent titanic struggle. He outlined what he believed to be the failure of that struggle and suggested that Mr Frank Hodges had made the discovery that the working class movement was divided into trade unions that were operating in compartments and not acting as one body.

He also said that the present situation was a farce and concluded his speech with the words; '**I say, let us drop our personalities and for God's sake get together and be united in a common unity and common strength. That way we can remedy the mistakes of the past and that the disappointments of the past will lead to victory in the future'.**

The Aftermath

The Forest of Dean miners suffered great hardships during the thirteen weeks of the lock-out and starvation was not too strong a word to describe it for many miners and their families. Even after the lock-out had ended many were still poverty stricken and unable to buy food or to pay their rent. It is hard to believe that many miners ended up in the Courts as many were in arrears with their rent and landlords applied for repossession of their homes. As the collieries started reopening, most were unable to get coal until underground roadways were repaired and electrical power systems such as pumps and lighting could be restored to working order.

Of course it was argued by many that the miners were victims of their own actions and it was estimated that less than half were able to be employed during that repair period. Some collieries were up and running fairly quickly but others took up to five weeks to become productive. Cannop Colliery which was originally doomed to closure was, in the event, brought back into use within a short time but it took almost a year to achieve full production.

As for miners' wages, during the temporary period the Government subsidy helped to cushion the fall. The months concerned were July, August and September starting with the established rates for March 1921 plus the March percentage of 33% plus the sliding scale of reductions each month from the subsidy. In the Forest of Dean these reductions had the effect of reducing a typical hewers' wage from 16 shillings per shift to 12 shillings per shift – other workers such as trammers or surface workers received lesser amounts.

This reduction in wages couldn't have come at a worse time for the miners as the demand for coal was declining fast due to the deepening worldwide depression. Many Forest collieries could only offer work for three or sometimes only two shifts per week which lessened the take-home pay even further. Unemployment benefit was denied to miners who were out of work due to industrial disputes as did both the Westbury and Monmouth Guardians. It is not difficult to understand the level of destitution and starvation that many families in the Forest were then facing as even short time working didn't give them the minimum basics to survive.

Under the terms of the Coal Trade Settlement, District Boards were set up to determine the rate of wages to be paid in that District from October 1st 1921. The Forest of Dean District Board was constituted and held their first meeting in mid September 1921. Mr Montague Maclean of Cannop was elected Chairman and David Organ the Vice Chairman. Theirs wasn't an easy or pleasant job especially for David Organ who, with others who had fought and lost, now had to determine the level of a miner's wage under the terms of the Settlement. A major factor in that decision was the calculation of the District Coal Owners' audited ascertained profits for that particular month. To make things more difficult, the price of coal nationally had fallen and some collieries were only working two shifts a week so the eventual rate for a hewer, determined by the District Board for October 1921 was 9 shillings and 10 pence a shift.

Resistance to the Settlement also came from Coal Owners Henry Crawshay & Co. who owned Lightmoor, Foxes Bridge, Eastern United and Trafalgar collieries. They refused to take part in the joint Audit or to pay wages fixed by the District Board – due they said to the falling price of coal and the fact that they were making no profit, despite offering their shareholders a guaranteed 10% on their investments. For October 1921 they were offering to pay 7 shillings and 5 pence per shift for a coal hewer compared to 9 shillings and 10 pence agreed by the District Board. A meeting of miners at Bilson Green, Cinderford on the 20th of October 1921 voted to oppose the Company's independent offer but in view of their recent hardships with the lockout, decided to keep working but continue to try and negotiate a settlement. During the following few days Herbert Booth and Enos Taylor of the **FODMA** had negotiated an agreement with Crawshays who had eventually agreed to pay the rates set by the District Board. They relayed this information to the men at another meeting at Bilson Green on the 24th of October 1921. However, it wasn't to be a permanent agreement but *'until further notice'* and so without any funds to support a strike, the men decided to continue to work under protest. In November 1921, the District Board had to consider another wage adjustment based on the auditors report of the District Coal Owners' profits for September 1921. The rate for November was subsequently adjusted downwards to 7 shillings and 5 pence per shift for a coal hewer – as compared to 18 shillings and 9 pence before the 1st of April 1921. This meant that the Forest of Dean Miners were the worst paid in the country.

The **FODMA** were having troubles of their own as they had run out of funds during the first three weeks of the stoppage. As work in the collieries resumed, the **FODMA** found itself in debt to the tune of £27,000. As a consequence they were forced to raise their weekly subscription rates to 1 shilling and 6 pence after promising to pay off their debts to the Cooperative Society and local traders. By mid November the **FODMA** had paid off £1,035 of their debt to the Cooperative Society, while the Craftsmen's Association had paid off £52.

Association membership also suffered as miners became disillusioned and felt betrayed by their Union for accepting a poor agreement with the Government and the abandonment of their demands for National Wages Board and a Pool. As a consequence, membership dropped sharply from over 5,000 to less than 2,000 by the start of 1922.

Unlike the Crawshays, some colliery owners such as Lord Bledisloe – besides being a generous local benefactor, also had a considerable interest in the welfare of his workers. He invited his employees at the Norchard Colliery to attend a meeting at the Lydney Picture House on Saturday morning the 26th of November 1921 to discuss the affairs of his colliery – which, he said was; **"far from being satisfactory, either to the owners or the men".** The meeting was attended by all colliery directors - others invited were David Organ as President of the Forest of Dean Miners Association and Mr H.W. Booth as Miners' Agent. The local and national press were excluded from this gathering but the Daily Telegraph got wind of it and printed what it thought was the theme of the meeting. After the event, Lord Bledisloe issued a statement that was telegraphed to the local 'Observer' office which read; *'Meeting quite private; confined to Norchard men, except Miners' Agent; held to consider best means of avoiding permanent closing of colliery; proceedings entirely friendly throughout. Endeavours will be made to carry on for present. Reporters purposely excluded'.*

Howbeach Colliery

In March 1921 the Howbeach Colliery Company Ltd. and its owners were summoned to appear before the Divisional Inspector of Mines for several breaches of the **Coal Mines Regulations Act** which related to the fatal accident at Howbeach on Wednesday the 6th of October 1920, which was reported on previously. The charges were;

1. Failure to provide signalling apparatus in the colliery,
2. Negligently omitting to arrange the transmission of signals between engineman and banksman,
3. Failing to arrange transmission signals to persons stationed at the top of the shaft.

Similar offences were charged against Mr Frederick McAvoy, the colliery manager. In the event, Mr McAvoy was found guilty of two technical offences and was fined £3 for each offence while the charges against the Company were withdrawn.

The Howbeach Colliery had suffered several incidents in its recent past, notably a fatality in October 1920 where an employee fell down the mine shaft. This was reported on previously and eventually ended up in two court cases (one against an employee at Gloucester Assizes and another earlier this year where the Company was summoned for a breach of the **Coal Mines Regulations Act,** also in relation to the October fatality). The other incident included an explosion at the Company's forge in December 1920 where three men were injured, one seriously.

In 1919 as reported earlier, Howbeach Colliery was sold for £6,000 to a local consortium consisting of Lord Bledisloe, Mr Robert Bowles, Mr Arthur Morgan Mr Brasier Creagh, Mr Tudor Crawshay, Mr William Jones and Mr Percy Moore with promises of opening up the Blackpool shaft to access over 600 acres of coal measures. This reconstruction meant that around 200 employees were laid off and integrated into other working collieries.

On the 18th of May 1921 at a shareholders meeting, a resolution was moved by Lord Bledislow to the following effect; *'That, seeing that the present industrial crisis has finally destroyed all hope of obtaining from outside sources the large amount of capital still required for completing the new development work at Howbeach Colliery, and that the local colliery companies financially interested therein are unable to provide further capital for this purpose without imperilling their own future existence and the employment of labour which they normally provide, immediate steps be taken for winding up Howbeach Collieries Limited and a liquidator forthwith appointed with that object'.*

It appeared that this colliery was purchased, not as originally implied for further coal exploration but to prevent flooding in other major adjacent collieries. Howbeach was reported as being the most heavily watered colliery in the Forest of Dean with 25% of its original coal output being expended on boiler furnaces to keep the pumps going, extracting 1,200 gallons of water per minute.

The follow-on during the continued lockout dispute was a request from Lord Bledisloe to the **FODMA** that twelve men be detailed to work on dismantling the colliery as desired by the Directors. The request was voted on and turned down and so it was resolved by the miners Executive that they could not advise consent.

However, there was some criticism from the miners that this entire move to close the colliery was just a threat in view of the ongoing dispute. Lord Bledisloe was quick to dispel this theory by these words;

'Why use the word threat in reference to my proposal (which I deeply deplore having to make) to wind up Howbeach Collieries, Ltd.? There is no threat about it. As Chairman of the Park Colliery Company Ltd., I have now to make the simple choice between closing permanently the Norchard Colliery, as the result of applying the remainder of the little Reserve Fund set apart for its development in the vain attempt to find its quota of at least £40,000 still required for the completion of the Howbeach developments, and a further £20,000 required for its working capital, and keeping the former open for several years in the future as a source both of coal and of employment in my own neighbourhood. My first duty is to save Norchard, and this alone dictates the proposal which is erroneously described as a "threat." The estimate of the cost of developing and equipping Howbeach, formed 18 months ago, has already been more than doubled, and the time then estimated for carrying the work to completion is bound to be more than trebled. The facts and figures are all quite well known to the leaders of the Forest of Dean Miners' Union, whose sympathy and co-operation in approaching the Government for financial assistance prior to the coal crisis were very valuable. The stoppage of the last few weeks has not materially affected the problem, except to render it impracticable to obtain from outside sources (other than the Government) any fresh capital to enable the development of Howbeach to be carried through to

completion, and there is no present prospect of the Government *providing what is required, even if they are given (as we are willing to give them) a first charge upon all the assets and prospective income of the Company. The winding up of this Company does not necessarily mean the abandonment the mine. I may mention, incidentally, that the Howbeach Company has never made any profits, and in the case of Norchard the small amount of profits distributed among the shareholders has not for several years equalled in amount even the value of the men's "allowance coal," not to mention their wages. Neither of these Companies has anything that it desires to conceal from its employees, nor has it or its Chairman anything to gain from uttering threats.'*

Yours faithfully, Bledisloe, May 24th 1921.

Although this was the end of mining at Howbeach for the time being, this was not the end of the Howbeach colliery.

A Grand Scheme

In April 1927, Howbeach Collieries Ltd. was sold to Morris Collieries Ltd., the major shareholder being none other than Mr William Morris of Morris Motors Ltd., of Oxford, later to become Lord Nuffield. He had grand ideas of creating a Combine with five other large collieries in the Forest of Dean to produce cheap coal, providing miners with model villages and creating an old age pension scheme and a sick fund for his work-force. The managing director of the colliery was to be Mr Sydney Taylor, a colliery proprietor of Old Dean Hall near Speech House. By January 1929, things hadn't planned out as Mr Morris had hoped and the scheme was abandoned, Mr Morris having disposed of his interest in the project.

Fig.75 Morris's Scheme as advertised.

Accidents/Fatalities

On Tuesday the 8th of February 1921, Mr James Taylor aged 56, married with 10 children and a pit fettler was killed by falling down the mineshaft while working at the Crump Meadow Colliery near Cinderford. The inquest held in Cinderford on the 11th of February 1921 heard from the engineman and banksman that repairs to pumpwork was being carried out in the shaft and appropriate methods of signalling were being observed. They said that all was going well until a fettler came up from the bottom and said that Mr Taylor had fallen the 120 feet from half way down the shaft and had been killed. Mr Hicks, another worker said that he and Mr Taylor were together putting down a length of 3" piping and were working on the top of the cage and that ten yards below them was another cage. He said that he was standing on a piece of timber fixed to the side of the shaft and had just handed Mr Taylor a hammer when he heard a thud. He believed that was caused by Mr Taylor falling.

Mr Hicks was questioned by the Coroner and the Inspector about the wearing of safety belts and admitted that if Mr Taylor had been wearing such a belt, his life would probably have been saved. He contended however, that a belt could sometimes be a hindrance and that he preferred not to wear one as it was cumbersome. The colliery officials stated that years ago when the belts were available, no one would wear them but since the accident, the belts had been used. The Jury returned a verdict of accidental death and that no one was to blame.

On Thursday the 8th of December 1921, Mr Victor Jones aged 30 was killed while working underground at the Hopewell in Wimberrry Level. He was engaged in erecting timber to support a suspected dangerous roof when approximately two tons of stone suddenly fell on him, killing him instantly.

On Saturday the 10th of December 1921, Mr Joseph Carpenter aged 68 of The Branch, Drybrook died in Hospital as a result of an accident on Friday the 9th of December 1921 while working underground at the Crump Meadow Colliery near Cinderford. An Inquiry held at the Gloucester Royal Hospital on Wednesday the 14th of December heard from Mrs Annie Carpenter that her husband was brought home at about 1.30pm on Friday afternoon and attended by Dr Beadles who advised he be taken to the Royal Infirmary. She said that he was conscious when he was brought home and he said that he had received a nasty blow to the bowels when lifting timber in the pit but that he didn't blame anyone. Mr Herbert Booth the miners' agent asked if he had ever complained of abdominal pains before and she said **'no'**. Mr Josiah Toombs who lived at Bilson Green said that he was working with Mr Carpenter timbering a horse road. He had asked him for help to remove a pit prop weighing about a hundredweight that was lying in the road so that a horse and wagon could pass. They each took an end and Mr Carpenter had to move backwards carrying the heavy end and they put it down when clear of the waggonway. Straight away Mr Carpenter said that he had hurt his bowels and asked for some water. Mr Carpenter then left the pit just before 1pm and Mr Toombs said that he didn't see him struck in any way and thought that the injury could have been cause by lifting the timber. On being questioned further, Mr Toombs said that he didn't think Mr Carpenter collided with a post behind him when carrying the prop but acknowledged that if that had happened, it could have caused the injury. Mrs Carpenter said that when her husband was brought home he had told her that he had been crushed between the post he was carrying and a post behind him. Mr John Parsons the colliery winding engineman from Church Road, Cinderford said that he had attended to Mr Carpenter who had told him that a stick had knocked him in the bowels and that he was in great pain. Dr Rufus Harris, House Surgeon at the

Gloucester Royal Infirmary stated that Mr Carpenter was admitted to the hospital on the Saturday and operated on by himself and Dr Knight. He died while under the anaesthetic. The post mortem revealed a long standing rupture and a puncture of the intestines. Dr Harris said that Mr Carpenter had said to him that he had been crushed by a piece of timber and that his injuries supported that statement. He didn't think the injuries had been caused by lifting and that in his opinion, death was due to shock and peritonitis. The Coroner in his summing up stated that it was not suggested that anything to do with the anaesthetic could account for the death and a verdict was recorded of death from shock and peritonitis resulting from injuries accidentally sustained under circumstances explained by the witnesses. The Coroner expressed his sympathy with the widow, as did other officials including Mr Booth.

Chapter 23
The Aftermath - 1922, 1923, 1924
Opening of the Dilke Memorial Hospital
Opening of the Lydney Power Station

As the depression deepened, coal prices continued to fall which, in turn led to the Coal Owners reducing miners shifts even further – some collieries in the Forest of Dean were down to two shifts per week. Take home pay for those unfortunate miners and their families was not sufficient to sustain them and those that met the six day qualifying period for unemployment benefit were paid 2s. 6d. per day. Those who had paid up unemployment insurance were entitled to 15s. per week. The Board of Guardians were short of funds and could only offer loans of up to 25s. per week to those who could afford the repayments.

Under those circumstances and with the cost of living at 80% above the 1914 level, unemployment continued to rise, not only within mining communities but in most industrial areas nationally with poverty and hardship affecting everyone. In January 1922, the total number of people registered as wholly unemployed reached 1,933,000 with 316,000 workers on short time – this represented just under 18% of the total workforce.

Government funded schemes provided work for over 33,000 men on new arterial road-making with a further 15,000 on repair and maintenance. Land drainage schemes provided work for 3,500 men and the Forestry Commission employed 4,000 men. Combined with other schemes, those directly employed were 126,000 but with those indirectly employed in the schemes, it was assumed to be much higher. Although this total figure represents a small proportion of the total unemployed, there was an overall downward trend in unemployment during the following months.

In the Forest of Dean several schemes were discussed or being operated by both West and East Dean Councils. The Forestry Commission were already employing men for widening and repairing forestry tracks while Mr Rowlinson, chairman of East Dean District Council was pushing for a loan to cover the cost of extending their water supply. He said the cost would be £27,000 of which £10,000 would be funded by a loan, payable at 5% interest spread over 30 years. Also on their agenda was the prospect of building 10 A class new houses.

West Dean were also considering the local housing needs and provision for the construction of several 2,000 gallon reservoirs to support them. Criticism however was levied at the Forestry Commission for spending £40,000 on 'useless' roadways that were only 9 feet wide and would test the driving skills of the owner of a three horse wagon. It was said that that amount of money could have been used more effectively on local water schemes.

Fig. 76 Pillowell recreation ground workforce during the 1921 Lockout.
Courtesy Author

The local Councils also favourably considered the construction of a road bridge across the river Severn at Newnham and Mr Rowlinson said that he could see the advantages of it and thought that the idea should be further ventilated to the County Council.

A plan was also in place for the construction of a Recreation Ground at Viney Hill as a 6 acre plot had been secured from the Office of Woods opposite the local school while the one at Pillowell on land bequeathed by Lord Bledisloe was well under way to being completed.

Surprise was expressed when the miners' Agent Mr Herbert Booth resigned his post and returned to his home County of Nottinghamshire. He was considered part of the local Forest of Dean community and held positions with several organisations including the Lydney and District Hospital management Committee and the Forest of Dean Labour Party, of which he was President. They were also taken by surprise.

The Forest of Dean Parliamentary Labour Party held their Annual meeting at the Onward Hall, Yorkley on the 27th of April 1922 to elect their officials. Mr Frank Yeatman was elected as the new President to replace Mr H Booth and the two Vice Presidents were Messrs Frank Ashmead and Mr J.L. Jones. Secretary was Mr J.C. Birt and Treasurer was Mr David Organ. Messrs Charles Luker and George Powell were the Auditors. Mrs P. Tawny was chosen as delegate to attend the Women's Conference at Leamington Spa. Resolutions were passed and speeches made, including an amusing speech from Mr Wignall in which he criticised the words he had heard expressed by the new prospective Liberal Candidate Mrs Coombe-Tennant. She was reported as saying that she was appealing for support because she was a woman. He said that she had no more right to that than he had to ask for support because he was a man (Laughter and cheers).

Mr John (Jack) Williams 1888 – 1968

The Forest of Dean Miners' Association were busy selecting their replacement of Mr Herbert Booth as Miners' Agent from a list of 58 applications. There was a shortlist of four, from which Mr John Williams was the successful candidate. Mr Williams aged 34 was born in 1888 at Kenfig Hill near the Garw valley where both his father and grandfather worked in the pits. He started work in the International Colliery at Blaengarw in 1901 at the age of 13 earning 1s. 6d. a shift, rising to 2s. a shift. Aged 14, he was injured in a small explosion and had to remain bathed in oil for six weeks. At the age of 17 he joined the Socialist Movement and attended Women's Suffrage meetings in London, taking part in marches and witnessing the arrest of Sylvia Pankhurst.

Fig.77 Mr John/Jack Williams.
From 'The Miners' by R. Page Arnot.

He became the wage agent for the International Colliery and was on the Executive of the Mid-Glamorgan Labour Party. He was also Chairman of the Blaengarw Workmen's Institute and Secretary of the Garw District of the South Wales Miners Federation.

Mr Williams was a man of drive and ability and had no illusions as to the task ahead of him, having seen for himself the deplorable state of affairs locally. He set about rebuilding the **FODMA** whose membership was less than one third of the 7,000 miners in the Forest of Dean and was saddled with a debt of £24,000. And also to improve the deplorable working conditions and local wages which he acknowledged were the lowest in the country.

Drama played its part in the **Miners' Annual Demonstration,** held unusually this year at Bilson Recreation Ground, Cinderford on Saturday the 8th of July 1922. Many were prevented from attending the event due to the bad weather which started the day with heavy rain followed by hurricane force winds which eventually snapped the post of the marquee and blew it over during a speech by Mr James Wignall M.P.. Fortunately, no one was injured and after impromptu repairs, the speeches continued. On the platform were President David Organ who Chaired the meeting, Mr James Wignall M.P., Vice President Mr Albert Wildin, Mr Martin Perkins, Mr John Williams the new miners' Agent and Mr Gwilym Richards, South Wales miners' leader.

Opening the proceedings, Chairman David Organ said; **'During this last year there have been many more downs than ups and after the last strike, many of you who were anxious to get back to work, were still in want of it. I regret the very short time that is being worked now and the prospect is still forbidding. We had to take the settlement that was offered in spite of ourselves and all sorts of things are being imposed on us. There is the Profit Sharing Scheme of Crawshay and Co. and in another direction, a certain number of colliery owners are seeking to impose an extra 20% off wages. It is all calculated to affect our loyalty to this Association.'**

A resolution, moved by Albert Wildin and seconded by Martin Perkins was unanimously carried; *'That this demonstration of the Forest of Dean miners calls upon all working men in and about the mines to immediately join the Federation as the only means of combating low wages and bad conditions; that mines of this and other Districts call upon the owners to fix minimum prices of coal and that the workmen have a voice in the fixing of prices, thus preventing in some measure, the miners working for starvation wages, that we deplore the actions of a few of the owners in this coalfield in attempting to introduce an independent profit sharing scheme in contravention of the National Wages Agreement and that we shall offer the utmost opposition to such unwarrantable departure'*

In his address, Mr Martin Perkins said; **'I deplore the state we are gradually drifting into. In two or three months the agreement set up a year ago will expire and seeing that two thirds of the men are unorganised, I ask what prospect is there of a new agreement which would be of any value to us being arranged? I hold that the Government and not the Owners should fix the minimum price of coal for I am one of those who think that the minerals the earth contains are a national asset'.**

Mr Gwilym Richards said that he fully supported the resolution and questioned whether they could increase their wages without an Organisation and asked if they thought the Owners loved them so much that they would volunteer them a rise at the end of the term. No, he said they could not expect to fight with any success with a weak Organisation and that their only hope was to give their own Organisation the backing it was entitled to.

Mr Wignall was introduced by David Organ as the man that Mrs Coombe-Tenant, the next prospective Liberal candidate wasn't going to replace. Mr Wignall said that he wasn't in favour of strikes or lockouts and preferred to solve those problems by other means but urged his audience to concern themselves with their own matters as no one else would. The meeting was wound up by a short address by Mr John Williams, the new miners' Agent who thanked the speakers for attending in such atrocious conditions.

As can be discerned from this transcript, the mood of the Forest miners since their defeat twelve months previous, was very low and that the message from the platform was that the only way to improve their wages and conditions was to unite within the **FODMA** and hence the **MFGB.**

At a later meeting of the Council of the **FODMA**, Mr Williams urged that the time had come to decide whether Union members should work alongside non-Union members. Although he was pleased that membership had now improved from less than 1,000 to 3,800, there were still around 3,000 non-

Unionists working in the pits. This, he said was unacceptable and that members adopt a 'show cards' policy and that notices be tendered. But he warned that if they did adopt 'show cards', it was imperative that they carry the matter through and that there would be no turning back. The final decision was then left to the Executive committee.

There was some good news in August however as export sales of both steam and house coal showed signs of improvement when large orders for South Wales coal came from the United States. This in turn had a knock-on effect for Forest coal where customers with small orders were diverted to the Forest coalfield for their supplies and this had the effect of increasing the number of shifts worked. As wages were dependent on output two months in arrears – as agreed in the 1921 Settlement - it was considered a possibility that miners might see some improvement from their present low wage position. The Joint Wages Board settlement for September wages based on the July output figures was to stay as they were at 20% above the 1921 Standard.

Lloyd George resigns
The political situation nationally was a complicated one with splits between both Liberal and Conservative M.P's in Parliament. The Liberal Party had already split following the 1918 'coupon' Election with many Liberal M.P's setting up their own Liberal Parliamentary Party. Lloyd George continued to hold the coalition together but by January 1922 he decided to set up his own Party – the National Liberal Council but remained Prime Minister of a failing coalition.

The Conservative arm of the coalition, now conscious of the fact that as a coalition they might lose the next General Election, voted to end their association and fight the next Election as an independent Party. So the split was complete and Lloyd George's resignation was submitted to the King on the 19th of October 1922.

General Election
The General Election of 1922 took place on Wednesday the 15th of November 1922 with the result that turned the political perspective blue. The Conservatives, led by Mr Andrew Bonar-Law won 344 seats; Labour came second with 142 seats; the Liberal vote collapsed with only 62 seats and Lloyd George's National Liberal Council 53 seats. Overall, the seats gained or lost were; Conservatives -35, Labour +85, Liberal +23, National Liberal -71.

In the Forest of Dean the results were;

Mr James Wignall – Lab. 10,820,
Mr Augustus Dinnick – Ind. Con. 5,976,
Mrs Coombe-Tennant – Nat. Lib. ....3,861.
Labour Majority of .... **4,844.**

As was the custom, results were announced at the Town Hall, Newnham on Thursday the 16th of November 1922 after an unusually prolonged count. The count started at 10.30am and went on for 9 hours until 7.30pm when the result was eventually announced. Mr Wignall gave a vote of thanks to officials and also thanked the electorate for their loyalty in returning him to Parliament. He said that he had had no doubts about the result. The other two candidates gave similar votes of thanks with Mr Dinnick remarking that he was so pleased with the reception he had received in the Forest of Dean that he would seriously consider returning to fight another day. Mrs Coombe-Tennant said that she was disappointed with the result but with the late entry of Mr Dinnick, she thought had spoiled her chances.

Dilke Memorial Hospital

With the site at Yew Tree Brake already cleared and foundations and footings built, the official laying of two Foundation Stones were carried out at a very special event on the 29th of June 1922 where many dignitaries, subscribers and local people attended. The assembly was Chaired by Major J. Penberthy who opened proceedings by saying; **'We are assembled here today to honour the man that the Foresters chose to be their leader and that no better memorial to him could have been thought of. It is equally fitting that the memorial should be erected in the middle of the district in which he had spent so much time'.**

Major Penberthy also thanked all those who had subscribed including Sir Henry Webb and Sir Francis Colchester-Wemyss who represented the Red Cross Society.

Sir Henry Webb laid the first stone and stated that the Hospital would be a suitable memorial to Sir Charles Dilke who, he said had devoted his life to public service. The second stone was laid by Mr M.W. Colchester-Wemyss who was standing in for his son Sir Francis Colchester-Wemyss. After the stone laying ceremonies, Mr George Rowlinson the Hon. Secretary spoke of the generosity of all the subscribers, giving details of the amounts given by individuals and organisations within the district. He said the total raised so far was £11,000 and he hoped that the final figure could be raised to complete the Hospital without going into debt.

The plan for the Hospital at that time was in the plan-form of a letter 'H' representing 'HOSPITAL' with the centre section devoted to the main entrance, out-patients waiting room and staff quarters which would contain three nurses bedrooms, a sitting room and accommodation for the Matron. The two wings were for the wards which were to accommodate eight beds and an operating theatre with a sterilising room and X-ray room and provision for a single bed ward alongside. The building would also contain a kitchen, offices and a dispensary and there would be an outbuilding to house an ambulance, mortuary and disinfector. The whole building would have a hot water heating system and lit by electric light.

Electricity Power Station

As was mentioned earlier, the West of England Joint Electricity Authority had made an offer to the Government for the purchase of the redundant Beachley Power Station. This was intended to supply electricity to the Forest of Dean and beyond but the logistics of supplying the plant with Forest coal and a clean water supply plus other provisions, estimated at a cost of £813,000 made the project <u>untenable.</u>

Much later, an offer was made by Lord Bledisloe to provide an area of land next to the Norchard Colliery near Lydney for the erection of a new Power Station which would supply electric power to the whole of the Forest of Dean and the Stroud Valleys via a cable across the Severn Railway Bridge. At a lively inquiry of the Electriciy Commissioners at the Town Hall, Lydney at the end of March 1922, arguments for and against using the Beachley Station was put forward by interested parties but the Lydney scheme, financed by a London syndicate, found more favour. It was estimated the total cost of the build and to erect the infrastructure of high tension cables would cost £500,000 and the output was estimated to eventually reach 33,000 volts with a total horsepower of 30,000. Lord Bledisloe had earlier stated that he had no connection with the London syndicate and that his interest lay in providing the necessary coal for feeding the boilers.

By August 1922, plans had been drawn up and preliminary work had started on the Norchard site by The Foundation Company Ltd. of Windsor House, Kingsway, London, WC2. They started preparations for laying the foundations on the 18th of December 1922 which required over 15,000 cubic yards of excavation.

Accidents/fatalities

On Tuesday the 14th of March 1922, Mr Cornelius Drew aged 54 and living at 32 Newerne Street, Lydney, died while working on the screens at the Norchard Colliery near Lydney. An Inquiry held at the Police Court, Lydney heard that on the day of the accident, Mr Drew was oiling bearings at the tippler while it was in use. Two young colliers who were pushing the next dram towards the tippler gave a warning shout but Mr Drew did not hear and was struck on the right ear and head. It was said that Mr Drew had been suffering from influenza and indigestion and a post mortem found that the cause of death was the rupture of an artery in the stomach which caused acute dilation of the stomach. The Jury's verdict was in accordance with the medical evidence.

On Wednesday the 12th of April 1922, Mr Thomas Henry Macey aged 43 a colliery underground Deputy living at Glenholme, Whitecroft Road, Bream suffered injuries to his legs while working underground at the Flour Mill Colliery, Bream, part of the Princess Royal Colliery Company Ltd. An inquest held at the Gloucester Royal Infirmary heard that at about 4 o'clock Mr Macey had been working at the coal face with Mr Matthew Jones and Mr Percy Thomas using a coal cutter. The cutter was being operated by Mr Thomas who said that when he started it up, it was rotating the wrong way. Mr Macey came back and changed the switch over and gave the order to start the cutter. As it was placed against the coal face, it suddenly jumped backwards and there were several shouts to stop the machine. It was then found that Mr Macey had suffered severe injuries to both legs with the right foot only hanging by a thread. A tourniquet was applied and he was brought to the surface. He was then attended to by Dr Pugh from Bream who said Mr Macey was suffering from shock and loss of blood. He had made him comfortable and put him on a stretcher and into an ambulance and followed it to Gloucester in his own motor car.

Unfortunately, the ambulance broke down at the Bird in Hand pub near Churcham and Dr Pugh saw that two men were attending to the engine. He entered the ambulance and found Mr Macey in a worse condition so continued on into Gloucester to find another ambulance. A policeman at The Cross said that their ambulance had also broken down so Dr Pugh made his way the hospital where Dr Rufus Harris tried to find an ambulance.

The broken down ambulance was eventually towed in by a passing lorry and Dr Harris said that the injured man was admitted at 7.30pm but that he had died at 8.00pm. Under questioning, Dr Harris was asked whether the delay in getting to the hospital had contributed to Mr Macey's death to which he replied; **'possibly'**, whereas Dr Pugh replied; **'yes, every moment was of importance.'** It transpired during questioning that Dr Pugh had said that Mr Macey had recently been away from work for seven weeks suffering from Influenza and pleurisy and that he was not a strong and healthy man. He said Mr Macey may not have survived an operation although, had he arrived in time, he would have stood a better chance.

The ambulance driver Mr William John Burdess, the under manager said that he had driven the ambulance which belonged to the Forest of Dean Coal Owners Association to save time as the official driver hadn't arrived. Further discussion tried to discover how much time had been lost due to the breakdown and Mr Burdess said that he thought they had left the colliery around 5.00pm and going via Newnham. The fault with the ambulance was eventually found to be a fracture in a cable of the Delco Ignition system that was discovered by Mr F. Gale, a foreman mechanic from the Watts garage, Lydney and which took three hours to repair. In a lengthy summing up the Coroner admitted that the evidence could not establish whether the delay caused by the ambulance breakdown had contributed to Mr Macey's death but was more than convinced that his previous illness of Influenza and pleurisy had some part to play as he could not have survived the shock of so severe injuries as could a robust and healthy man. The Coroner praised the colliery Company for retaining an ambulance for such emergencies and said that he attached no blame to the colliery for Mr Macey's death. He recorded a verdict that Mr Macey had died from shock and haemorrhage due to injuries accidentally sustained. Sympathy for the family was expressed by the Colliery Company who also said that he was a most valuable employee.

On Tuesday the 1st of August 1922, Mr Rowland Adams aged 40 and married with six children, was killed while working underground at the New Fancy Colliery near Parkend. His son aged 15 who had just started working at the colliery witnessed the accident. An inquest held at Littledean Hill heard that Mr Adams was working overtime clearing coal from the coal face when what was estimated to be 15cwt of earth fell on his head, knocking it against the side of a dram, killing him instantly. A verdict of accidental death was recorded due to a fall of earth thought to have been caused by an invisible 'well'. The Coroner expressed sympathy with the widow and her family.

On Saturday the 18th of November 1922, Mr Oswald John Taylor aged 44 and a collier from Lydbrook was injured by a runaway dram while working underground at the Cannop Colliery. An inquest held at the Gloucester Royal Infirmary heard from Mr Taylor's brother that his brother was in good health but suffered from defective hearing. Mr Oswald Taylor had been working with fellow collier Mr George Smith clearing a roadway of debris so that the drams could run smoothly on the rails. They were working on an incline with Mr Smith at the upper end and Mr Taylor below. When cleared, the drams were given a test run and one of them jammed at the top of the incline but this was put right. The test running continued and one empty dram became derailed but Mr Smith held the brake while another collier heaved it back onto the rails. The test run continued while Mr Taylor was standing in the roadway when an empty dram hit some timber and became uncoupled. It ran free down the incline and shouts were made while Mr Taylor was still standing in the roadway but no one seemed to have seen him struck by the dram. He was then found lying in the roadway bleeding badly and was helped to the surface by Mr Smith and others who all said that the incident had happened all too quickly.

Dr Rufus Harris the senior house surgeon at the Gloucester Royal Infirmary said that Mr Taylor had been admitted the same day suffering from scalp wounds and a suspected fracture at the base of the skull. He never regained consciousness and died the following midday. Dr Harris said he performed a post mortem which confirmed a fracture of the base of the skull which, in his opinion was the cause of death. A verdict of accidental death was recorded in accordance with the medical evidence, injuries being accidentally sustained. Sympathy with the relatives was expressed by the colliery representatives who said that Mr Taylor was a good workman who had been at the colliery for twelve years. Every precaution had been taken to avoid accidents in the mine.

1923

First task for the **FODMA** was to elect their officers for the forthcoming year which resulted in the following officials; President Mr David Organ, Vice President Mr Martin Perkins, Auditors Messrs J. Burnett and R. Kear, Finance Committee Messrs Ambrose Adams, Horace Jones and C. Taylor, Political Committee Messrs J. Brain, Harold Craddock, Joseph Holder, Reuben James, David Organ and William Morgan.

It had been the case for many years that miners' wages were dependent on coal output and this in turn was depended on demand. This demand had variations as to whether it applied to house or steam coal and each had had its ups and downs at various periods of time. House coal for example had a high demand during wintertime whereas steam coal usually had a constant year long demand for the likes of Industry and the Royal Navy. This is a simplistic view as many variations came into play in each and every District. Both however had an important role to play in the export trade and this was dependent usually on the political situation worldwide. Post war Europe was still in disarray with German war reparations to the allies not being met in accordance with the Versailles Treaty of 1919. Coal reparations had to be paid for ten years but it went into default in January 1923 which resulted in French and Belgian troops occupying German territory of the Ruhr. The Ruhr miners went on strike and the knock-on effect was that their coal exports stopped and the British coal industry enjoyed an export boom.

However, although coal export prices rose considerably, the miners' wages were slow to react, even considering the two month delay due to the audit of accounts ascertainment that determine the rate of wages. Forest of Dean miners were gradually returning to full time employment and rightfully anticipated an improvement in wages. Indeed, mining engineer Mr Ivor Baldwin J.P. with 30 years of local mining experience behind him, while opening a bazaar at Ruardean Woodside, was eager to let the miners know that they would be looking forward to a better time. He said; **'I am going to offer you some hope of the future because in the industry in which we are all interested there is great improvement, observable today compared with, say a year ago. I know from my own work that there is a big improvement all the way round. Miners' wages have been very low and the owners have also done very badly, but you can now think, with every confidence to look forward to a much better time with conditions much better, both regards work and remuneration for work because there has been a big increase in the price of the commodity in which we are all interested – in the house coal trade as well as in the steam coal trade'.** The Joint Wages Board saw things slightly differently and by July 1923 there had still not been any movement of Forest of Dean miners' wages from the minimum.

The Miners' Annual Demonstration took place on Saturday the 14th of July 1923, again at the Bilson Recreation Ground, in much better weather than in 1922. In the Chair was President of the **FODMA** Mr David Organ who was accompanied on the platform by Mr George Lansbury M.P., Mr W.H. Mainwaring, lecturer at the Central Labour College, Mr John Williams miners' Agent and other members of the Executive Committee.

After a minute's silence for Capt. Ted Gill who should have been on the platform but had recently died, the Chairman said that he wished that he could report progress on a much larger scale than had been achieved to date. However, some progress had been made with certain compensation cases and after efforts made by the Association, some individuals could say that they had derived certain benefits. Mr Organ continued with praise for Mr James Wignall M.P. who they had placed in the House of Commons and hoped that every constituency in the country would do the same so that they could change the state of affairs that existed at that time. Concluding his speech, Mr Organ said; '**I want to urge all the men and women of this District to do all you can to improve your position and for those of you outside the Association to come in. You will remember that two years ago we entered into a contract and we were indebted to the Cooperative Society and tradesmen of the Forest to the extent of thousands of pounds and we said that we would pay as an Organisation. Let us be honourable and do this, and further, to pay into this Association in order that we may be prepared for the next struggle.**' ('Hear, hear' and applause.)

A resolution was moved by Mr Harold Craddock and seconded by Mr Thomas Brain; '*That this meeting views with profound satisfaction, the status of the Labour Party, the official opposition of his Majesty's Government; that whilst this meeting is pleased with the position of the Labour Party as the official opposition to his Majesty's Government, it will be content only when the Labour Party becomes the Government of this country. This meeting regards the National Wage Agreement as wholly unsatisfactory and incapable of giving the miners of the Forest of Dean sufficient to enable them to obtain the bare necessities of life. It views any agreement which has been in operation for two years and has failed to provide the miners with a living wage, as immoral. This meeting deplores the Government's refusal to support the Labour Party's new minimum wage Bill for miners, but are not surprised, for the Government of this country comprises so many Colliery Owners and other owners*'. Mr Craddock concluded by saying that he was more optimistic than the Chairman because in the colliery where he worked, they had signed on fifty new members recently. In supporting the resolution, Mr Mainwaring pointed out that the men had weakened themselves by forsaking the Union and that their first task was to renew their lost strength and pursue a policy to persuade every miner to join the Union.

Mr Lansbury referred to the radicalism of Sir Charles Dilke and said it was revolutionary in its time and that the local people had stuck by him. He urged that more radicalism in the form of Political power should be concentrated on the evolution of the working classes to power and to use their Political power for the benefit of the people and especially the promotion of peace, without which there could be no improvement in social conditions or reform.

The resolution having been carried, Mr John William the miners' Agent moved a vote of thanks to the speakers and said; **'That this Organisation in the Forest has never been in more fighting fettle than it is now and we have put the employers into court more times in the last twelve months than has ever been the case before. There is a campaign being followed at the Princess Royal colliery which I want to see followed in all parts of the Forest. Nearly 70% of the workmen in the Princess Royal collieries have tendered notices against non-unionism and as far as I am concerned, no man would go to work eventually if there was a single man out of the Federation in the Forest of Dean** (applause). **We have to learn the lesson that Unionism is the real thing and that only by Unionism can we succeed. Notwithstanding the statement disseminated by evil minded people who wished that the Association should not succeed, I am not ashamed of its work during the past twelve months'.**

The Princess Royal Collieries that comprise the Flour Mill and Park Gutter Collieries employed around 1,200 men and boys and the 450 working at the Park Gutter Colliery had indeed tendered their one week notices against non-unionism on the 15th of July 1923. All men already in the Union had submitted their names which left around 100 who were still outside the Union. The Colliery Owners posted notices at the pithead that all those whose notices to terminate had come into effect, should remove their tools. The notices terminated on the 22rd of July 1923.

During the week, the Owners put up notices stating that the men would be allowed to continue working if they signed on afresh. Mr John Williams the Agent decided the notices to terminate should not go ahead as there had been an accession of new members to the Union. Work resumed the following Monday morning.

At their Annual Conference at Folkestone on the 9th of July 1923, the **MFGB** President Mr Herbert Smith said that the **MFGB** were not going to seek the abandonment of the National Wage Agreement but to request some modifications from the Coal Owners. He said that in six Districts, miners were receiving wages well above the minimum but there were seven Districts involving 210,000 men who were still on the minimum. To terminate the agreement would be a disaster to these men so we will ask the National Wages Board for certain modifications. So Conference instructed the Executive to meet with them with three main proposals for amending the current Agreement to provide better wages for the miners. The Coal Owners, in reply said that in view of the importance of these proposals, they would have to consult their own District Associations before a reply could be given. This was promised to be sometime in September 1923.

Meanwhile back in the Forest, at last there was some good news for the 7,000 plus miners with an increase in their rates, effective in September 1923 and calculated from previous audited accounts in accordance with the National Wage Agreement. Coal hewers who were on 7s. 5d. per shift were to get an increase of 10d. per shift with other grades getting a proportionate advance but no one to get less than 6d. per shift. For the time being at least, it meant that the Forest of Dean miners' wages were slightly lifted from the bottom of the pile.

However, this became a short term rise as it was later to be predicted, the November and December 1923 rates were calculated to fall again, but not quite down to the minimum. Rates were calculated at 22.5% above the 1921 Standard, whereas a hewer now on 8s. 3d. per shift would see his rate fall to 7s. 7d. per shift.

General Election
On the political front, the United Kingdom was heading for another General Election. The Conservative Government had lost its Prime Minister Andrew Bonar Law in May 1923 when he resigned due to ill health. He was replaced by Mr Stanley Baldwin. Likewise, the Labour Party lost its leader Mr John Clynes in a leadership battle with Mr Ramsay MacDonald less than a month after the 1922 General Election.

Prime Minister Baldwin wanted to introduce tariffs on imported goods in the hope of reducing unemployment levels here but he was opposed, not only by Opposition Parties but factions within his own Conservative Party. He wanted a mandate from the people so that he could carry out his reforms and so Parliament was dissolved on the 16th of November 1923.

In the Forest of Dean, the election campaigns of both candidates were under way with Mr Augustus Dinnick, standing as a Conservative candidate as he did at the previous election and Mr James Wignall M.P., the sitting member who was standing again as a Labour candidate. Mr Dinnick's campaign was organised from the Conservative headquarters in Commercial Street, Cinderford by his Agent Mr Manley Power, ably helped by Mr H. Cooper,

On the other hand however, the Labour candidate happened to be away in Australia on behalf of the British Emigration Delegation and was presumed not to be able to return in time for the Election. However, the local Labour Party appeared quite capable of organising their own campaign on behalf of Mr Wignall. Their major coupe was the arrival in Lydney of none other than Mr Ramsay MacDonald, Leader of the Parliamentary Labour Party in the House of Commons, He was received with great ceremony and musical accompaniment with over 1,000 miners gathered to hear him speak. Mr Yeatman, Chairman of the Forest of Dean Labour Party said in his opening remarks that the Labour Leader wasn't there in the Forest of Dean because he had any misgivings about Mr Wignall's prospects. He said that there need be no qualms about Mr Wignall, whose position, whatever the attacks on him, was safe although he wouldn't be home in time to fight. Mr MacDonald spoke of the current topic in Parliament, emigration and the pros and cons of losing skilled workers to the Dominions. At the end of the speeches, Mr Charles Luker the local Agent proposed and Mr David Organ seconded a motion of support to the Labour Party programme and pledging themselves to secure Mr Wignall's return.

The Election was held on Thursday the 6th of December 1923 and the result was;

Mr James Wignall – Labour 11,486,
Mr Augustus Dinnick - Conservative 7,383,
Labour majority .... 4,103.

Mr Wignall eventually arrived at Southampton aboard the liner Euripides on the 12th of December 1923 and immediately toured the Forest to thank his constituents and election team for all their efforts in returning him to Parliament.

National Ballot

In reply to the **MFGB** demands for modifications to the National Wages Agreement placed before the Coal Owners in August, the Coal Owners conference in late September rejected those demands. They had received replies from all their Districts which were unfavourable to the demands and said that if they had accepted them, they themselves would have had to make counter demands in their own favour.

Consequently, the **MFGB** delegate conference in December 1923 decided to hold a National Ballot with a view to terminating the Agreement by giving three months notice. The Ballot was to be held on Thursday the 10th of January 1924 with a recommendation on the ballot paper that the vote should be for termination of the Wages Agreement.

Dilke Memorial Hospital

As work continued on the new hospital being built at Yew Tree Brake and it was announced by Mr Rowlinson that building work had been completed during February 1923. Mr Rowlinson revealed at a meeting of the British Schools at Coleford that subscriptions received were £11,943 1s 9d while expenditure so far was £9,960. He said there would be a need for a maintenance fund but thought that it wouldn't be less than £2,000 per annum.

Fig.78 The original Dilke Memorial Hospital – Photo Author.

The grand opening of the new Hospital took place on the 28th of June 1923 on a fine afternoon with a large crowd of people and mainly Liberal dignitaries assembled. During proceedings, renderings were given by the Cinderford Male Voice Choir, the Cinderford Excelcior Brass Band and the Ruardean Hill and District Choral Society. It was unfortunate that Sir Henry Webb who was to open the Hospital and who had made the single highest private contribution to the Hospital fund was unable to attend through illness. His place was taken by Major J. Penberthy. The event was opened with a hymn and readings from the Bible with the dedication being conducted by Dr A.C. Headlam the Lord Bishop of Gloucester. He was accompanied by his chaplain and with prayers, led a procession through the building and continued the dedication on a stone platform in front of the south ward.

Fig.79 Dignitaries and staff at the opening ceremony. Those identified so far are; Top row extreme right, Dr Bengara, Front row second from left, Mr George Rowlinson.

Speeches were made by the Chairman of the Committee Mr J.J. Joynes who said that he regretted the absence of Sir Henry Webb but read a moving letter from Lady Webb who explained that Sir Henry was suffering from sciatica and gout and confined to bed. She said that he was bitterly disappointed that he couldn't be with them on that special day but it was fitting that in the Forest of Dean an Institution should bear the name of Sir Charles Dilke.

Mr George Rowlinson the Hon. Secretary of the Committee said that the Hospital was up-to-date and free from debt and went on to give some of the financial details of his campaign to raise the funds. He said that last March he had asked 50 of Sir Charles Dilke's friends to give £5 each, and he got 51 sums of £5. He also asked 100 people to give him a guinea each and he got 200 guineas and so he managed to raise £8 short of £500 instead of the target £350, most of which he said, came from men within the Forest. Other contributors were £3,000 from Sir Harry Webb, £4,000 from the Red Cross Fund, £1,000 from the Forest of Dean miners, £500 from the Commissioner of Woods and Forests, £500 from an estate in Bournemouth, £200 from the Miners Welfare Fund with another £200 promised soon.

Mr Rowlinson concluded by saying that the total fund including bank interest, was £12,800 14s. 1d. and the total cost, including furnishing had been £10,800. This left a £2,000 balance in hand which had been invested in war loans. He appealed for people of the Forest to contribute what they could for the upkeep of the Hospital and encouraged one penny per week be paid by working people. A promise was made by Mr Joynes to pay £25 per year for five years, which he encouraged other gentlemen to do likewise.

The official opening was made at the main entrance door by Major J. Penberthy who said that he regretted that Sir Henry Webb couldn't be there that day but he was honoured to be invited to take his place. He said that the Institution was a splendid one and an honour to the Forest and the Foresters and that he hoped it would for ages remind people of the great man in whose memory it had been raised.

Sir Charles Dilke's niece Miss Gertrude Tuckwell received the Hospital on behalf of the people of the Forest of Dean and in a passionate address, praised Mr Rowlinson for his role in raising funds to make that occasion possible and for his consideration in inviting her to receive the Hospital. She then described her visits to the Forest when she accompanied Sir Charles on his duties and said that she had many fond memories of those times. But both she and her uncle were well aware of the dangers the miners themselves were faced with and the fact that their nearest Hospital was in Gloucester and so she had never felt so honoured to receive this

Hospital on behalf of the brave, courageous and loyal people of the Forest of Dean.

Tea was then served in a large marquee and the public were allowed to look round the Hospital. There was a presentation by Mr Sidney Dykins on behalf of the Cinderford Momento Fund to the Hospital of specialist X-ray apparatus which was received with thanks by Mr Joynes on behalf of the Committee.

Lydney Power Station

Work continued during January 1923 on the Lydney site and it was anticipated that the enterprise would be up and running within six months. The whole scheme involved a lot of infrastructure that included an outdoor substation and three overhead transmission cables suspended on 40 foot high pylons. Two of them would form a ring around the Forest of Dean and the third would lead to a river Severn crossing to feed the Stroud and Dursley districts.

Technically, there were three Stirling boilers, each with an evaporating capacity of 35,000 lbs of water per hour at a pressure of 260 lbs/square inch at a temperature of 650 degrees Fahrenheit. These boilers were fed by coal on an electrically driven wide conveyor belt from the Norchard Colliery about 250 yards away and after weighing, the coal was deposited into the storage hoppers above the boilers. From there it was automatically fed into the boilers down chutes and onto a chain grate travelling stoker. Ashes and clinkers were sent down chutes to a lower floor where a large vacuum removed the soot with the residue being carried via an overhead cable to a dump to the east of the Lydney/ Whitecroft road. Water for the boilers came direct from the river Lyd through a filtering system of screens and two electrically driven centrifugal pumps.

Steam under pressure fed the two turbo alternators – one Bellis and Morcom and one C.A. Parsons which rotated up to 3,000 rpm and together produced 10,000kw. of electrical power. 6,600 volts was then fed by three underground cables to the outdoor sub-station where it was transformed to 33,000 volts by three Ferranti transformers. Water drawn from the river Lyd was used for cooling the condensers via two cooling towers.

Fig. 80 Lydney or Norchard Power Station.

Whereas the overhead cable ring around the Forest was reasonably straightforward, the cable carrying current across the Severn provided certain problems. It was originally planned to feed the cable across the Severn railway bridge but it was later decided to lay it in the bed of the river at a point between Lydney and Berkeley Pill. This was the most difficult part of the whole scheme with weather and tides to contend with during the laying process. The 33,000 volt cable itself was 4 inches in diameter and contained 3 insulated copper cores encased in a thick lead covering. This was again covered by 2 layers of steel armouring wires which were again covered with 4 layers of waterproof tape. The cable was over a mile and a quarter long and weighed 49 tons.

It was laid in 3 sections with 2 midstream joints and the longest section was 800 yards long. The drums containing the cable were loaded on to a barge and towed to the starting point near Berkeley Pill. The cable was then drawn ashore and lashed securely. The barge was then lashed to a paddle tug which was intended to keep the barge on the correct course. Two tugs were then attached, one to the barge and the other to the paddle tug and they towed both boats across the river. When it was necessary to join two cables together, the barge platform was especially set up as a workshop but the joining operation took 48 hours to complete. During this period, the tugs were in a constant fight with tides and cross currents and it took 9 anchors to keep the barge on station during this process. Eventually the cable was brought ashore on the Lydney side and secured – connection to the overhead cable being carried out later.

Fig. 81 Power Station view showing two cooling towers

As a precaution against accidental snagging by ships anchors, it was necessary to dig a trench in the gravelly bed of the river into which the cable was laid. It was then covered in bags of concrete which safely protected the cable from any risk of interference. A second relief cable of the same size was also laid about 300 yards upstream of the first cable.

On the 18th of June 1923, the first turbine was producing electricity and supplying power to the Trafalgar Colliery ten miles away. The Foundation Company had confounded their critics and had kept their vision of supplying electric power within six months of the start of the enterprise.

Accidents/Fatalities

On Tuesday the 16th of January 1923, Mr Thomas Ivor Baldwin, a collier aged 26, a married man with two children and living at Littledean Hill was injured while working underground at the Crump Meadow Colliery near Cinderford. He consequently died of his injuries at the Gloucester Royal Infirmary on Monday the 22nd of January 1923. An Inquest held at the Infirmary heard from Mr Baldwin's brother Mr Harold Baldwin that at 7.30am on the morning of the accident, they had both met and chatted for a minute near to the coal face before his brother went under the roof to the coal face. The working height was 2ft and 7ins and when he joined his brother, he was trying the roof with his pick to see whether it was safe. He was satisfied that it was safe and started picking at the coal face when, after only about half a dozen blows, the roof collapsed with rock falling on his brother's head and shoulders. With help, Mr Baldwin was taken to the surface and attended by Dr Beadles who advised he be taken to the Royal Infirmary in an ambulance. Mr Harold Baldwin continued to describe the fall of rock and said that at the time he could see no crack. There was a prop under the roof and plenty of timber around if needed. He said that he had later examined the fall and found that there was a crack at the back with a 'slip' which extended back over the coal face. Mr Alfred Williams, the colliery Examiner said that he had inspected the roof about two hours previous and had found no cracks or anything unusual.

Mr John Williams the miners' Agent said that the miners were not satisfied with the medical attendance and that he would like to ask a few questions as to the actions of Dr Campbell. The Coroner said that he did not think the question relevant as the deceased had died from a broken neck and no medical man in the four Kingdoms could do anything for him. He asked; **'did he come?'.** The answer; **'no sir'.**

The Hospital's assistant medical officer Dr Michael Pezaro said that Mr Baldwin was admitted to the Infirmary at 11.30am on the 16th of January with a broken neck. It was seen that there was no hope of recovery and pneumonia supervened and he died on the 22nd of January 1923. The post mortem confirmed a fracture and laceration of the spinal column.

The Coroner returned a verdict of accidental death and that there was no fault on behalf of the colliery Company. He also added with reference to Mr Williams remarks about the doctor, that it would not be fair to attack him in his absence but if they (the miners' Federation) had any complaint against Dr Campbell then they had another more potent weapon they might use.

Mr Treasure on behalf of the colliery Company expressed their deepest regret and said the deceased's father and both sons had worked in the colliery for many years and the family was highly respected by both the employers and men. Sympathy was offered to the widow and her family by all concerned.

On Friday the 16th of February 1923, Mr Edward Watkins aged 56 who lived at Pettycroft, Ruardean, was killed while working underground at the Arthur and Edward (Waterloo) Colliery near Lydbrook. The Inquiry at the Bell Hotel club room in Ruardean heard that Mr Watkins was a most trusted and careful workman. At 5.00pm on the Friday, Mr Watkins was engaged with a buttyman in holing coal at the coal face when suddenly and without any warning a fall of coal estimated at between 10 and 15 cwt fell on him. His vertebral column was fractured in two places. It was reported that the coal had been spragged with one short spragg whereas it was usual to be supported by two long spraggs which would have been in accordance with the rules of the Mines Act. However, it was seen that the fall was quite unexpected and the first intimation was a loud report caused by the coal breaking away. The Jury found that Mr Watkins had died from injuries sustained by a fall of coal that was insufficiently spragged.

On Thursday the 22nd of February 1923, Mr Alfred William Adams aged 68, died while working at the Foxes Bridge Colliery near Cinderford. Mr Adams was allocated to light work and was working with some pumping equipment and had just had his lunch on that morning when he collapsed and died. The Inquiry held at Cinderford heard that the post mortem had showed that Mr Adam's heart weighed 24 ounces instead of the normal 11 ounces. A verdict of heart failure was recorded, the heart valves acting incompetently.

Not strictly a coal mining accident but nevertheless a mining accident.

On Thursday the 10th of May 1923, Mr Charles Rosser aged 61 and living at The Cross, Clearwell, was killed while working in a sandpit at the New Dunn Iron Mine. An Inquest held at the Wyndham Arms, Clearwell heard from Mr Fred Watkins, the owner of the mine who said that Mr Rosser had been employed as a sandgetter for the past six or eight weeks but didn't know whether he had had any previous experience in that job. The sandpit was at the surface and was 13ft 6" deep at the time of the accident and Mr Rosser had been instructed to get the sand down from the top and screen it. Mr Watkins agreed that in future, a different method would have to be used in order to make the workings completely safe. At the time of the accident, shouting could be heard and when Mr Watkins arrived at the sandpit, he could see that Mr Rosser was buried under six or seven tons of sand. When he had been pulled out after 6 to 8 minutes, he was found to be dead. Sand quarrying wasn't covered by the Metaliferous Mines Act but Mr Watkins said that he had no reason to think the pit unsafe but in future they would work it in terraces. Dr Payne who examined Mr Rosser's body said that there were several abrasions on the face and a bad one on the forehead. However he said that he was of the opinion that death was due to compression of the vertebral cord. The Jury recorded a verdict of accidental death and recommended that in order to ensure the safety of workers, the method suggested by Mr Watkins should be adopted in future.

On Monday the 25th of June 1923, Mr James Walter Hillman aged 55 and a collier died while working underground at the Eastern United Colliery near Ruspidge. An Inquiry held at the Baptist schoolroom heard that Mr Hillman who was a well known and much respected townsman was working at the coal face when, without any warning there was a fall of rock caused by an unsuspected 'slip'. This 'slip' caused a fall of timber supports which caused a second fall of rock which fell on Mr Hillman's right leg. The leg was broken in two places and Mr Hillman suffered severe shock and died on the spot. The Jury returned a verdict to this effect and expressed their sympathy for the widow and her family.

In August 1923, Mr Harry Morgan aged 21 and who lived at Sling was injured while working as a trammer at Mr Peglar's Shutcastle Colliery. Mr Morgan was looking after some drams that were being towed up an incline when one came off the rails. Mr Morgan attempted to drag the dram back onto the rails when the rope went suddenly taut and threw him up against the roof. He suffered injuries to his leg and spine and was attended by Dr Buchanan from Coleford who escorted him home. It was found that no bones had been broken but there was a suspicion of internal injury.

On Thursday the 6th of September 1923, Mr Charles Smith aged 43, a married man with two children living at Whitecroft was killed while working underground at the Flour Mill Colliery near Bream. An Inquest heard that Mr Smith who had seen 21 years service in the Navy was working the Whittington seam with a team under the direction of Mr John Elsmore. He was cutting coal at the coal face when a fall of rock and earth, estimated at around five tons, suddenly fell on him without warning and crushed him. Help was at hand but when he was pulled out, he was found to have been severely crushed and had died instantly. It was said that the roof had been tested twice during that particular shift and that timbering regulations had been complied with. There was nothing to show what caused the fall. The verdict was that Mr Smith had died as a result of injuries caused by a fall of the roof.

On Tuesday the 20th of November 1923, Mr George Miles aged 68, a colliery road repairer from Ruardean was injured while working underground on the nightshift at the Trafalgar Colliery near Brierley. An Inquest heard that during his work, Mr Miles sustained two injuries, one to his knee and the other a lacerated bruise above the left cheek. As a result, Mr Miles did not return to work and on Sunday the 2nd of December 1923 he went to bed. He was seen by Dr Stanger but his condition worsened and he died on Thursday the 6th of December 1923. A post mortem examination was carried out by Dr Wharmby- Battle of Coleford which showed indications in the lungs that Mr Miles was suffering from tuberculosis of the adrenal glands, producing a condition known as Addisons Disease, which was the cause of death. The Coroner's verdict was death from the cause stated. The Company expressed their sorrow for the loss of an old and faithful servant.

1924

In January 1924 the **Forest of Dean Miners' Association** held their annual ballot of members to elect their District Officials for the forthcoming year. Results were; President, Mr David Organ – returned unopposed. Vice President Mr Martin Perkins J.P. Financial Secretary Mr Tom Etheridge. Auditors Messrs Charles Luker and Charles Buffry. Finance Committee Messrs Ambrose Adams, Horace Jones, Enos Taylor. Political Committee Messrs Tom Brain, Joseph Holder, Reubin James, Charles Mason, David Organ. Agent, Mr John (Jack) Williams.

The **MFGB** ballot for termination of the current wages agreement took place on Thursday the 10th of January 1924 and the results were in by the following Monday.

The final results were;
For termination 510,303,
Against termination 114,558,
Majority for termination.................................... 395,745.

Forest of Dean vote was;

For termination 3,429,
Against termination 626,
Majority for termination .... 2,803.

The miners Executive then met with the Coal Owners on the 18ᵗʰ of January 1924 and Mr Frank Hodges handed them three months notice to terminate the current wage agreement. Their new proposals were for an increase in the minimum wage from 20% to 40% above the 1921 Standard and a reduction of owners' profits with a larger percentage allocated to wages. Mr Herbert Smith the **MFGB** President asked that negotiations for a new agreement should be started straight away but the Owners said that they would need time to consult with their District Associations before making any further proposals. Mr Frank Hodges was later forced into resigning his position as Secretary due to his being elected an M.P. and by his appointment as Civil Lord of the Admiralty – all in accordance with the rules of the **MFGB.**

Following Mr Hodges' resignation, the **MFGB** held a ballot of members in April 1924 to decide who was to be the next Secretary of the Federation. There were seven applicants on the ballot paper and the results were;

Mr J. Jones, Yorkshire, ... 202,297.
Mr W.P. Richardson, Durham, ... 117,693.
Mr E. Edwards, Northumberland,........................... 69,440.
Mr F.B. Varley, Nottinghamshire,........................... 57,595.
Mr J. McGurk, Lancashire and Cheshire,............... 48,832.
Mr A.J. Cook, South Wales,............................... 217,664.
Mr W.B. Small, Scotland, ... 31,978.

And so Mr Arthur J. Cook became the new General Secretary of the **Miners' Federation of Great Britain** and started his new post on Monday the 14ᵗʰ of April 1924.

Arthur J. Cook - 1883 - 1931

Arthur James Cook, better known as A.J. Cook, was a Trade Union leader who was born in Wookey, Somerset and raised in the Baptist religion. He developed an early gift for oratory and by his teenage years Arthur was known as 'the boy preacher'. Due to difficulties with family life, he moved to Porth in the Rhondda Valley, South Wales when he was just 17, looking for work. His first job was as a labourer in a nearby colliery and a rock fall on his first day, killed a fellow worker standing next to him. However, Cook kept his head down and worked his way up, first becoming a haulier and then to skilled collier – eventually spending 21 years underground. At that time he was

Fig. 82 Arthur J. Cook

still a devout Baptist and preached in the local Baptist chapel, even becoming a Sunday School Teacher and Deacon.

However, Cook became more interested in political and Trade Union matters and joined the Independent Labour Party in 1905. He also became a member of the South Wales Miners' Federation. He conducted Union meetings in his own house and eventually resigned from the Baptist Chapel to concentrate on Union activities. In 1911 he was awarded a two year scholarship by the **SWMF** to the Central Labour College where he came under the influence of Karl Marx. On returning to South Wales, Cook took an interest in Syndicalism which promoted the overthrow of the Capitalist system and replaced with worker control. In the aftermath of the 1912 strike, he helped Noah Ablett write the pamphlet 'The Miners Next Step'.

Cook was outspoken about his opposition to the First World War and at one point was sacked by his employers and evicted from his rented home. The Union threatened to strike and Cook was reinstated. He opposed conscription and obstructed the military when they required 20,000 miners for the army. He only avoided prosecution by the threat of a Union strike. In March 1919, Cook was arrested and imprisoned for 3 months for sedition under the Defence of the Realm Act. He was released after another strike threat and served only 2 months.

In November 1919, Cook was elected miners Agent for the area and in 1920 became a founder member of the Communist Party of Great Britain but later resigned. In 1921 he was elected to the Executive of the **MFGB** and was a prominent agitator during the Lockout in that year. He was arrested again and jailed for 2 months hard labour for incitement and unlawful assembly.

In April 1924 Arthur Cook was elected General Secretary of the **MFGB** which caused alarm among many of the Union leaders who referred to him as a 'raving, tearing Communist' but he was acknowledged as a *'breath of fresh air'* and *'an agitator'* – and some said *'a time for new ideas',* just what the **MFGB** needed said some. He took to touring the country at weekends giving up to four speeches a day and mesmerising his audiences to tears in many cases. He visited the Forest in 1926 during the miners' lockout and people flocked to the Speech House field to hear him speak. In December 1926 he went to Russia to personally thank the miners who had supported the British miners during the lockout.

After the events of 1926, Cook's health deteriorated and in January 1931 he had a leg amputated due to an untreated injury which had been aggravated by a kick from a demonstrator. Cook persevered on a cork leg and crutches but later that year he was diagnosed with lung cancer and he died on the 2nd of November 1931.

As can be understood from the miners' standpoint, the constant fluctuation in wages, a system introduced after the 1921 lockout was far from satisfactory, hence this latest ballot. Local wages were at or near the minimum with many families on the breadline so there was little or no chance of a decent living wage under the rules of 1921. It is small wonder that the miners of the Forest of Dean voted for a change.

To emphasise this, the January/February ascertainment of wages saw a slight improvement of 3 pence per shift but the March/April figure saw a similar fall. So there was no standard wage which could be relied upon to support miners' families. These rock bottom wages were earned in an industry where death and injury were considered part and parcel of the risks involved. The terrible casualty list for the year 1922 showed that 1,105 men were killed in the British coalfields and 4,822 were seriously injured. This was the price the miners paid to produce coal coupled with the fact that wages were lower in real terms than they were in 1914.

Another Ballot

In early March the Coal Owners came forward with their counter proposals for modifying the 1921 wages agreement. They were prepared to offer 30% above the 1921 Standard with the lowest paid daymen's wage being raised to 40%. These were given consideration by a conference of the **MFGB** but were considered insufficient and rejected. Another ballot was called to consider the owners proposals, voting taking place on Tuesday the 8th of April 1924.

The results were;
For acceptance 322,392,
Against acceptance 338,650
Majority against 16,258

The Forest of Dean vote was;
For acceptance 1,991,
Against acceptance 2,511,
Majority against .... 520.

This small majority was insufficient for calling for strike action and the **MFGB** put wheels in motion to establish a Court of Enquiry to investigate and report on the question of wages in the mining industry. This began on the 24th of April 1924 and lasted for five days – much of which time was devoted to understanding the wages system then in use. Once fully understood, the Court's report was published on the 8th of May 1924 and favoured the miners cause. It recommended certain modifications to the 1921 agreement which were to be open for negotiation between the miners and Coal Owners. A settlement was finally agreed on the 15th of May which basically lowered the profits percentage for the Coal Owners and raised the minimum wage from 20% to 33.33% above the 1921 Standard. It was also agreed that the day-wage worker's rate should not fall below 40% above the 1921 Standard. On the 29th of May, the **MFGB** Conference called for a delegate vote on the new settlement and this was accepted by 473,000 to 311,000.

In the Forest of Dean, Coal Owners refused to honour the new wage agreement saying that the District was a poor one and that if they agreed to pay the new advance, the collieries would close down. Mr Jack Williams saw this as a ruse and openly declared that they had heard this before and that they were bluffing. At a mass meeting of miners held at the Speech House, Mr Williams said that he had met with Mr Percy Moore, Chairman of the Forest of Dean Owners who said that the owners were not prepared to pay any retrospective money. Mr Williams contended that they had not declared that officially by way of Notices at pitheads so therefore they were compelled to pay up. The owners did however suggest a compromise in the form of an offer which was outside the terms of the national agreement. This was to pay the lowest paid workers 5s. 11d. per shift instead of the current 5s. 3d. per shift.

This offer was firmly rejected by the **FODMA** executive and it was announced at the **MFGB** Conference that there should be no negotiations where the owners refused to comply with the latest National Wages Agreement. Other small Districts were similarly affected such as Kent, Somerset and Bristol. They also asked the Coal Owners' Association to put pressure on the owners in those four rebel Districts to encourage them to accept the new agreement.

Amid all this, in the Forest of Dean, heavy rain in June 1924 caused flooding in many collieries. Around 30 tons of water was being pumped out per ton of coal produced and at the Foxes Bridge Colliery near Cinderford, a burst of water half way down the shaft caused the colliery to close, throwing 700 miners out of work.

The **Miners' Annual Demonstration** took place once again at Bilson Green near Cinderford on Saturday the 5th of July 1924. Mr David Organ, President of the **FODMA** was in the Chair and the main speakers on the platform were Mr Frank Hodges, ex-Secretary of the **MFGB** and now First Lord of the Admiralty and Mr James Wignall M.P. for the Forest Division. Firstly a resolution was moved by Mr Harold Craddock and seconded by Mr Richard Kear; *'protesting against the continued resistance of the Forest of Dean Coal Owners to the National Wages Agreement and reaffirming the resolve to press the demand and, if necessary, take industrial action to enforce it.'*

In his address, Mr Hodges said; **'I have come to the conclusion that there are no 'poor Districts' and that there was no justification for requiring any District to take less than the National Agreement meted out to us. If we lost this point then I imagine no other national agreement would be made. The Forest of Dean Coal Owners could pay the national wage and it was up to the National Federation to compel them to do so.'** Mr Hodges also referred to the Labour Party's private members Bill for the Nationalisation of the Mines and declared that it was the only possible satisfactory solution of the problem.

Mr Wignall commented that with regard to the local trouble, he hoped that the Conference would support the local view and that a strike could be avoided. President Mr David Organ then put the resolution which was carried enthusiastically.

Mr Jack Williams then thanked the speakers for their addresses and said that he protested strongly against the action of the local Coal Owners in posting up the wages for July and August without first consulting the Forest of Dean Miners' Association, who were after all, partners in the business and had a right to know the basis on which the wages were paid.

Pit Stop

By August 1924 no progress had been made to resolve the dispute and the **FODMA** asked the **MFGB** for permission to tender notices to 'down tools' in order to enforce their demands for wages in accordance with the new agreement. This permission was given subject to further negotiations failing to resolve the matter. As these negotiations subsequently failed, the **FODMA** executive gave notice of termination of contracts from Monday the 29th of September 1924 and a strike to start the following Monday. The **MFGB** had agreed to finance the strike pay in view of the financial situation within the **FODMA.**

And so, on Monday the 6th of October 1924, over 6,000 miners were on strike in the Forest of Dean including safety men and craftsmen. There was a report that 130 men had gone to work at the Lightmoor Colliery and at a meeting near the Cinderford Town Hall, Mr Jack Williams urged the men to act as gentlemen. Consequently, around 1,000 men, headed by the Excelcior Brass Band marched in drizzling rain to the Speech House. There they divided into groups and walked the roadways stopping the men returning home from Lightmoor and persuading them not to go to work the next day. There was some hustling but no unpleasantness and the groups eventually broke up and returned to their homes in drenching rain.

On Tuesday afternoon the 7th of October 1924 at a meeting of miners at the Speech House, Mr Jack Williams gave a report on progress made with regard to the strike. He said that progress was being made in negotiations with several collieries and was pleased to report that some had now agreed to the new wages agreement and that the men at those collieries had returned to work. President of the **FODMA** Mr David Organ said; '**I understand that progress had been made in various parts of the District, a fact of which I am proud. It only goes to prove that the Agent and others had been right that there was now a possibility and a probability of fighting this fight and winning through.** (applause). **I trust it will only be for days but if the necessity arises, I hope that for weeks we can remain solid and see the whole of the business through'.**(applause).

Mr Williams who was optimistic said; '**I am sure that the instrument that we are adopting of persuading men who are inclined to go to work to stay at home is the correct and proper one so long as you do not abuse it and do not lose your tempers, which I have no doubt you will not do.** (applause). **With regard to the general position, we are winning** (applause). **I hope that at the end of this week we will be able to say that we have cleared the board.** (applause). **If there are still cases where they haven't settled, I am going to ask the men who are working to help to find the money to keep the men out,**(hear, hear) **and we intend to go on until things are put right'.**

President Mr David Organ said that congratulations were due on what they had already accomplished and that his sincere hope was that all the men in the Forest would come into the ranks of the Association and that they might henceforth have a hundred percent membership. Whatever steps they took with regard to the Craftsmen or any others, let them try to do everything peaceably.

By Wednesday morning the 8th of October 1924 Cannop, Parkend Deep Navigation, Lydney and Crump Meadow, Flour Mill and Park Gutter and the Lydney Norchard Collieries had all capitulated and signed to accept the new wages agreement. The Crawshay group which included Eastern United, Lightmoor, Foxes Bridge and Trafalgar still held out. They didn't recognise the 1921 wage agreement and instead introduced their own profit sharing scheme whereby the men were paid the minimum wage but shared in any profits the Company made. By the Friday however, they had conceded to abide by the new wage agreement and also to allow an audit of their books to enable the calculation of wages. **The one week strike then came to an end with all Forest miners back at work by Monday the 13th of October 1924.**

By this time, the **FODMA** were still in debt to local traders and the Cooperative Society to the tune of £4,585. The Craftsmen's Union had disintegrated, leaving a debt of £667. Mr Martin Perkins who presided over a meeting of the Cinderford Cooperative Society said that both debts were being written off by two and a half percent each quarter.

In a bid to free the Union from this debt and at the same time to strengthen their hand in future negotiations, Jack Williams started a vigorous campaign for a one Union membership within the Forest of Dean collieries which was wholly supported by the **FODMA.** At a meeting in Broadwell Mr Williams said that their greatest achievement during the recent dispute was that the Crawshay Company had fallen in line with the rest of the Forest collieries in accepting the new wages agreement. He also gave the news that miners back pay from the 1st of May 1924 had been agreed with the Coal Owners. He also said; **'We have been loyal to the non-Unionists and had got them strike pay. While victory is ours, we cannot go on indefinitely without a militant and progressive organisation. During the next three months a campaign is going to be started in the Forest by which every man will be driven into the Union. We propose to refuse to work with non-union men after the General Election and will adopt compulsory methods by strike action'.**

Another General Election
The minority Labour Government of Mr Ramsay MacDonald was dissolved after a vote of no confidence was called for by Liberal M.P. Sir John Simon, which was carried by a large majority. Parliament was dissolved on the 9th of October 1924.

In the Forest of Dean the candidates for the forthcoming election were;
Labour .... Mr James Wignall,
Conservative .... Mr Michael Wentworth-Beaumont.

Mr Wignall was again unable to attend his election campaign, this time due to his wife's serious illness but he had strong support from the local labour party led by his eldest son Mr Trevor C. Wignall. He did however start his campaign by making rousing speeches at Lydney, Alvington, Woolaston and Woodcroft before having to rush off to attend his wife.

The new Conservative candidate Mr Michael Wentworth-Beaumont, a cousin of Viscound Allandale, was educated at Eton and became a Lieutenant in the Coldstream Guards. His home was at Wotton near

Aylesbury in Buckinghamshire. He led a very strong campaign from the Conservative headquarters in Newnham, visiting many villages including Redbrook, Elwood, Clearwell, St Briavels, Berry Hill, Broadwell Lane End Staunton and Coleford. He had great support from his wife Faith who appealed for the vote of the women of the District.

Mr Wignall's wife passed away on Saturday the 18th of October 1924 at their home in Dulwich after a long illness. Mr Wignall was told of his wife's relapse on the Friday evening and managed to reach his home just before she passed. Formerly Mary Rees from Carmarthen in West Wales, they married in 1875 and had three sons and one daughter. Mrs Wignall was always fully supportive of her husband's political activities and was well known in the Labour movement.

Mr Wentworth-Beaumont suffered from an illness during the last week of campaigning but was recovered enough to attend the announcement of the results at Newnham.

The General Election took place on Wednesday the 29th of October 1924 and the results were;

Conservatives .... 412 seats,
Labour .... 151 seats,
Liberal .... 40 seats,
Others .... 12 seats.

The Conservatives net gain 154 seats, Labour net loss 40 seats, Liberals net loss 118 seats. Mr Stanley Baldwin became the Conservative Prime Minister with an overall majority of 209.

In the Forest of Dean, the results were;

Mr James Wignall (Labour) 11,048,
Mr Michael Wentworth-Beaumont
 (Conservative) 9,739,
Labour majority .... **1,309.**

The result was announced outside the Newnham Town Hall where Mr and Mrs Wentworth-Beaumont were greeted by the crowd. Mr Wentworth-Beaumont gave the usual vote of thanks which was seconded by Mr Trevor

Wignall in the absence of his father. Mr Wentworth-Beaumont received a telegram from the new Prime Minister Stanley Baldwin which read; *'Many thanks for a gallant fight. Better luck next time but still the fray goes on'.*

This was undoubtedly a disappointing result for Labour and was reflected in the National results but under the circumstances it was not unexpected especially in view of Mr Wentworth-Beaumont's very strong and popular campaign. Nevertheless, Mr James Wignall was still the Labour M.P. for the Forest of Dean District.

On Saturday the 6th of December 1924, notices to terminate contracts with employers were due to be served at those collieries where non Unionists were employed and would expire on Monday the 15th of December 1924. The aim was to include the 750 men from the defunct Craftsmen's Union so that come another dispute, they could act as one instead of having two Unions where differences could occur. Men were being wooed to join the National Winding and General Engineers' Association and Jack Williams issued strong words that; **'there is only room for one Union here'**.

At meetings at both Cinderford and Ruspidge on Wednesday the 3rd of December 1924 which were both attended by the new Secretary of the **MFGB** Mr A.J. Cook, strong appeals were made for non Unionists to join the Union and Jack Williams said that he hoped the men would enter this struggle with the same determination as they did in their recent one. Remarking on the subject of the Craftsmen, he said; **'It has been said that if I included these men in this campaign, then I would have more on my plate than I could tackle – I do not think so** (applause). **It is an absolute necessity that they should join. Let it be understood that it is going to be war to the knife as far as the Craftsmen are concerned. I do not want to scream 'strike' every five minutes and I shall only engage in a strike that I know I can win and I believe that I can win on this occasion. This is going to be my Leadership 'One man out of the Forest of Dean miners' Association – no work',** (applause). **Every man must be made to join. Notices are going in on Saturday and every single man must join. There will be no strike if those men had any sense at all'.** Mr Cook also said that there was a revival of spirit among the miners and appealed to the men of the Forest to be as loyal in this campaign as they were in the recent struggle which they had won.

Negotiations between Craftsmen and the **FODMA** ended in failure to agree and a meeting was held in Coleford on the 9th of December 1924 between the Craftsmen and representatives of the National Winding and Engineers Association. It was stated by Mr E. Healey, the chief organising Agent of the **NWEA** that the Craftsmen were in crisis with the owners in the Forest of Dean. He said; **'It is a very serious matter. The organisation represent is a new organisation in the Forest of Dean but we have a membership of 350 and not 90 as claimed by Mr Jack Williams, the miners Agent.'** As regards the threatened strike by the miners he said **'The miners Agent is going to have the biggest let down ever known in the history of Trade Unionism. The miners will not absent themselves on Monday next and it will be the biggest fiasco the Forest of Dean miners have ever indulged in. The Craftsmen are prepared to work alongside the miners but not with them. We are going to be an independent Union and in June 1925 it is intended to legislate for the Craftsmen.'**

Strong words indeed from both sides of the argument but by the Saturday it was announced that the strike had been postponed. A mix-up over the original posting of notices meant that there was a delay in all collieries receiving them at the same time. They were all registered and posted on Saturday the 6th of December 1924 but some collieries didn't receive them until the following mid week.

Mr Williams said that he had been away in London at the time and had no knowledge of the delay with the postal service and the Miners Association would be making enquiries into what was the cause. He also said; **'It is still our intention to fight the issue and we shall take the matter up again after Christmas'.** The **FODMA** stated that they now had 98% membership of the Forest miners which included a large proportion of Craftsmen. At that time there were only 40 Craftsmen working at four collieries that were still outside the Union.

During the week when the notices had supposedly been delivered, Mounted Police were seen in the District. This, the miners saw as an unnecessary provocation and Jack Williams was quick to criticise this action at a meeting in Cinderford Town Hall on Thursday the 11th of December 1924. He said; **'The drafting of Mounted Police into this district was the greatest insult the Forest of Dean had ever experienced** (applause). **Why did the police stay when it was generally known on Saturday that the strike was off? Whoever asked for the police to be imported into this district should be ashamed of themselves. Who was to pay them? the ratepayers?** (No, No). **I wrote**

to Mr Wignall that night, giving him the facts (applause) **and asked him to put several questions in the House of Commons** (loud applause). **There was considerable and widespread indignation among the miners of this District when they heard of this business but I am however pleased to hear that the police who had come, had a very pleasant time while they were here and had enjoyed themselves.'**

Mr Williams also backed this statement up by publishing a letter in the local press; ' *Sir, will you kindly grant me a little space to protest against the action of those responsible for drafting mounted police into the Forest of Dean? Is it the practice of the authorities to draft police into a district when a strike is impending and especially when it is only a strike against non-unionism? Why should police be drafted into the district before the strike takes place? Why should they come at all for that matter? The police were here three days before the strike was due to take place. The whole thing was a farce because on the very day on which the police came to the district, namely Friday December the 12th, the Executive of the Forest of Dean Miners' Association decided to postpone the strike. The presence of these mounted police caused bitter feeling among the public of the Forest of Dean and the miners in particular. I communicated with the collieries of the district early on Saturday morning, withdrawing the notices. I also issued an official statement to the press announcing that there was to be no strike, yet the mounted police remained in the district until the following Monday. The miners will want to know who asked the police to come here. Who is going to meet the cost of it? As far as the miners are concerned, they will expect those who brought the police here to foot the bill. The matter is not going to rest where it stands at present; much more will be heard of it in the near future.' Yours truly, John Williams, Agent, Forest of Dean Miners' Association, Cinderford. December 16th 1924.*

Accidents/Fatalities

On Wednesday the 10th of July 1924, Mr Tom Parry aged 36 and a collier from Yorkley was killed while working underground at the Oldcroft Colliery near Lydney. An Inquest at Yorkley heard that Mr Parry who had just recently married a widow with several children was working at the coal face when approximately two tons of rock and earth fell and crusthed him. He died instantly. The cause of the fall was suggested as being a hidden slip. A post mortem revealed that Mr Parry had died from a fractured skull and a crushed pelvis and a verdict of accidental death was recorded.

On Tuesday the 6th of August 1924, Mr Arthur Male aged 23, a collier and a married man living in Newerne, Lydney was injured while working underground at the Norchard Colliery near Lydney. An Inquiry held at the Lydney Police Station heard that Mr Male was working the morning shift which was just coming to an end when the engineman felt a violent jerk on the haulage rope. He stopped the haul at once and went to investigate and found Mr Male in the middle of the roadway being held by several other workmen. He said that he then looked around and found a broken pinion wheel on a motion shaft and the cable was also broken. It was stated that just before the accident, Mr Male was engaged in pushing a dram of coal to the roadway. He was taken to Lydney Cottage Hospital and seen by D Earson who attended his injuries. Mr Male died at 5 am the following morning, Wednesday the 7th of August 1924 and a verdict was recorded that death was caused by shock, multiple injuries and haemorrhage after being struck by a broken cable.

On Monday the 11th of August 1924, Mr Joseph Matthews aged 30 died while working at the coal face at the Norchard Colliery near Lydney. An Inquiry into his death heard that Mr Matthews had been injured at the colliery some time previous and had also had a nasty fall from his bicycle, both incidents resulting in head injuries. Mr Matthews' widow said that her husband had spoken to her and to other neighbours about his suffering from dizziness which he blamed on the head injuries he had received in those accidents. He had started work on the Monday morning and after a few minutes, he fell forward and died without saying a word. The Coroner, sitting without a jury, heard that the post mortem showed signs of brain injury but there was no sign of a fracture of the skull. There were also signs of a weakness of the heart. The Coroner expressed his difficulty at arriving at a verdict but said that the only conclusion that he could come to was that Mr Matthews' death was due to cerebral haemorrhage and rupture of the affected vein, the result of a blow or blows to the head sustained by the deceased. The Company expressed their sympathy with the widow in her bereavement and testament to the deceased qualities as a workman.

On Thursday the 16th of October 1924, Mr George Short aged 40 and from Five Acres near Coleford, was killed while working at the coal face in the Cannop Colliery. An inquest was held at the Berry Hill Red Triangle Hut where the Coroner heard that Mr Short was working with Mr Frank Edwards at the coal face in the Coleford High Delf seam. At just after 8 am without any warning, the roof gave way and four to five tons of rock fell onto Mr Short. When he was pulled free by several other colliers, Mr Short was found to be dead. It was said that the place had been examined by the Company Examiner and by both Mr Short and Mr Edwards before they started work, and everything appeared to be safe and well timbered. The part that had fallen was known as a 'Bell' which was said to be unusual. The body of Mr Short was examined by Dr Buchanan at the colliery surface who found that his left thigh was badly shattered with extensive bruising about the body and severe abrasions to the chest. When found under the roof fall, Mr Short was in a sitting position with his head crushed into his chest. The Coroner returned a verdict that death was due to being crushed by a fall of four to five tons of rock in the High Delf Seam at the Cannop Colliery.

Chapter 24
1925 – The Subsidy

Political Overview
The export boom of 1923 had come to an end with the inevitable effects of pits closing and miners becoming part of the long list of unemployed. The boom was initiated by the stopping of war reparations by Germany and the Ruhr being occupied by France and Belgium (as mentioned earlier). This situation led to a strike by German miners and galloping inflation where at one time the German mark, which was equal to the British shilling had become virtually worthless.

The German state was close to revolution and allied Governments were concerned to reinstate reparations and to stabilise the economy. A committee of bankers, headed by Charles Dawes, an American, was appointed to arrive at a plan to resolve the situation. Their conclusions were put into operation with French and Belgium troops being withdrawn and severe war reparations re-imposed on Germany. **'The Dawes Plan'** as it became known was signed in Paris on the 16th of August 1924.

And so, German coal reparations to the allied countries resumed as the Ruhr returned to work. As a direct result, coal exports from Great Britain, which had been subsidising the loss caused by the Ruhr stoppage, suddenly took a downward turn and we were once again suffering the yo-yo effect of boom and bust. Other industries were similarly affected so adding to the unemployment situation and unrest was rife in many industrial districts throughout the country.

International Trade Unions
As was seen during 1924, Trade Union activity in Great Britain took on a more aggressive role and at a Trades Union Congress in Hull, it was agreed that unity between Great Britain's Unions and the international Trade Unions was essential in the fight against Capitalism. In Europe, there were two Trade Unions – the **Red International of Labour Unions** consisting of Soviet Trade Unions and some East European ones and the **International Federation of Trade Unions** consisting of British, German and many other West European countries. The latter had a chequered history especially during the war years with some countries dropping out and others becoming affiliated. By 1924 after the German Ruhr crisis had

been settled, the **IFTU** became more stabilised but there were still differences concerning the Soviet influence. However, British Trade Union Congress Chairman Mr A.A. Purcell pursued his desire for unity within Europe by passing a resolution for the matter to be raised with the **IFTU**. They raised objections to this but ironically, at the June 1924 Vienna Conference, Mr Purcell was elected their President and continued his desire for unity with the Soviets.

However, efforts continued to reach out to the Red International and in November and December 1924, a delegation of seven members of the **TUC** visited the Soviet Union. On their return, they issued a detailed report which resulted in the formation of an Anglo-Russian Trade Union Committee in 1925.

In the Forest of Dean

The **Forest of Dean Miners' Association** met once again to elect officials for the forthcoming year. Ballot results were; President David Organ. Vice President Martin Perkins to May 1925, then Richard Kear. Financial Secretary Tom Etheridge. Finance Committee Horace Jones, Ambrose Adams, Enos Taylor.

As was the case elsewhere, severe rainfall in late December 1924 and early January 1925 caused much flooding, not only in the towns and low lying areas of Gloucestershire but in some collieries in the Forest. The Norchard at Lydney and both the Flour Mill and Park Gutter Collieries in Bream had to close temporarily, affecting over 1,000 miners.

Lord Bledisloe became involved in a conflict with the press who allegedly stated that the Norchard would close permanently. It later became clear that that was not the case and the Lord was forced into reassuring his employees of that fact. However, the colliery survived with around £16,000 being spent on new equipment and Lord Bledisloe declared that the pit stayed operational solely in the interests of his employees. At the same time, an agreement had been made with Jack Williams the miners Agent that there would be co-operation in every way to ensure harmonious working at the pit with discussions taking place through a Pit Committee. On the strength of this assurance, Lord Bledisloe offered the men two places on the Board of Directors with a share of the profits and also erected a large room for drying the men's clothes and for their recreation.

Mounted Police

There were serious accusations regarding the use of mounted police in the District in December last. The Chief Constable, Major F.L. Stanley-Clarke was forced to account for his actions at a meeting of the Gloucestershire Standard Joint Committee, held in the Shire Hall in January 1925. He said that during the first half of December last, it was reported to him that a strike was pending in the Forest of Dean owing to a dispute between two Unions. He said that after taking advice and carefully considering the matter he had no alternative but to draft in extra police to the area. Two police sergeants and 20 policemen were each sent to Lydney, Coleford and Cinderford and 20 mounted men were billeted at Cinderford and Speech House. He was glad to say that the strike did not take place and the men were recalled as soon as possible. There was however strong opposition to the Chief Constable's actions and several questions were put regarding the necessity of such a decision and of who would bear the cost. Several Forest of Dean members voiced their objections and emphasised how much resentment had been caused by the Chief Constable's actions. In reply, the Chief Constable said that from his point of view there was a possibility of a breach of the peace where strong feelings existed between the men of the two Unions involved. It was revealed that the cost of the operation was £385 which would be borne by the County generally. The Committee agreed that the Chief Constable's actions were reasonable, considering the circumstances and asked the objectors to withdraw their accusations - which they refused to do.

The Miners Wage Agreement came under fire in January 1925 when the **MFGB** Secretary Mr Arthur Cook declared that three courses of action were open to the miners when their existing agreement came to an end on the 31st of July 1925.
1. To continue with the present agreement,
2. Amend the present agreement,
3. Ending the present agreement.

Both the **MFGB** and the Coal Owners had agreed to meet at the end of January 1925 to discuss a new wage agreement and the **MFGB** asked each District to send them their own proposals before that meeting took place.

The Forest of Dean proposals were;
1. That the necessary notice be given to terminate the present National Wage Agreement,

2. That negotiations be entered into with the Coal Owners' Association of Great Britain to effect an agreement on the cost of living basis,
3. That in the new Agreement, such a percentage be arrived at as will give the miners a minimum wage equal to the cost of living,
4. That steps be taken to re-institute the operation of Mr Justice Sankey's award of two shillings per shift, given for the raising of the standard of living of miners,
5. That we submit, that the above proposals can be achieved by obtaining a subsidy from the Government and that steps be taken to effect the immediate subsidising of the mining industry,
6. That the title of individual workmen in the industry to the provisions of the Agreement shall be proof of continuous financial membership of the **MFGB,**
7. That we demand a guaranteed weekly wage,
8. That one and a fifth shifts or 20% be paid for all afternoon and night work.

In the event, the Coal Owners' response was to stall any counter proposals and instead asked for a Joint Committee of Inquiry to investigate the causes of the depression in the coal industry with a possible remedy. This Joint Committee met for the first time in London on Wednesday the 18th of March 1925 with eight representatives from each side. By Thursday the 18th of April 1925, no progress had been made and the meeting was adjourned until the 13th of May 1925.

Suspicious that the Coal Owners were again stalling and with pressure for a decision from some of the larger Districts, the **MFGB** decided to call a Delegate Conference in Blackpool on the 20th of May 1925. This resulted in no decision at all except to await the result of the Joint Committee. Mr Arthur Cook was firmly against this decision and said that he differed from some of his colleagues who had their heads in the sand and that the miners' problems were not going to be solved without a fight. But, he said that they could not fight the fight alone and a conference of other Unions in June 1925 would give them a chance to cooperate with the miners. They would tell the other Unions that they wanted solidarity translated into action – they wanted no more paper alliances.

The Gold Standard
Meanwhile, the recently elected Conservative Government led by Prime Minister Stanley Baldwin were able to govern with confidence due to their now considerable majority in the House of Commons. Before the War,

European currency was freely traded in gold and in general, the economy remained relatively stable. However, during the War and up to this time the Government suspended the export of gold coin and gold bullion and restrictions were enforced. By the end of 1925, these restrictions would either have had to be renewed or allowed to relapse. Due to a decline in this country's economy, the Government decided to allow them to relapse and return to the Gold Standard, which it was hoped would provide monetary stability and a step towards economic recovery.

And so, on the 28th of April 1925, the Chancellor of the Exchequer Mr Winston Churchill announced a return to the gold standard. Although gold could not be exported until the 31st of December 1925, the Bank of England was given a special licence to export gold bullion straight away. This had the effect of raising the value of sterling and made British exports more difficult to sell abroad but made imports cheaper to buy. This also had consequences in the coal mining industry where exports were calculated to be 10% more expensive than before.

Death of Mr James Wignall M.P.

The Forest of Dean was sad to learn of the death of their Labour M.P. Mr James Wignall who passed away in Westminster hospital on Wednesday the 10th of June 1925 after collapsing in the House of Commons that same day. Mr Wignall was a very popular and well liked man in Parliament and of course in the Forest of Dean where he became the Forest's first Labour M.P. at the December 1918 election after defeating Liberal M.P. Sir Harry Webb, the sitting member. Mr Wignall was warmly acknowledged as the 'Father' of the Trades Union movement in South Wales and became a Justice of the Peace for Swansea. Mr Wignall's last words to his son just before he died were **'Well, this is the end but I'm going as I want to – in harness. I'm quite ready'.**

Among the many tributes was one from Lord Bledisloe;

'It was not altogether a surprise – although with the most profound regret – that I heard this morning of the death of my friend James Wignall. For, during the long conversations I had with him at Whitsuntide, I felt that his interests were already in another world with the wife whom he loved so devotedly and whom he hoped and expected soon to join. Among the many politicians of different creeds whom I have known during the last 20 years, I can remember none whose honesty of purpose, whose uprightness and simplicity of character and whose deep human sympathy were so

conspicuously combined. He was justly respected by men and women of all parties in the House of Commons and not least by those who still believe in the beneficent influence of religion upon human character'.

Many other tributes followed including from the Press – the Westminster Gazette and the Daily Chronicle. Also from the Home Secretary and locally from Mr J. Johnson of the Blakeney Sub Committee of the Dilke Memorial Hospital. Memorial Services were held at St Margaret's, Westminster and at the Cinderford Baptist Church.

The funeral took place on Saturday the 13th of June 1925 with a service at the Mount Zion Chapel in Swansea followed by an internment at the Mumbles cemetery.

Bye-Election

The question was who could effectively replace James Wignall as the Labour candidate? Both the Cinderford branch of the local Labour Party and the **Forest of Dean Miners' Association** had proposed that their choice was the miners Agent Mr John (Jack) Williams. Others were Miss Margaret Bondfield and Mr Oswald Mosley. Jack Williams eventually declined the invitation citing a probable forthcoming conflict with the Coal Owners over a revision of the wages agreement and said that he wanted to play his full part in those negotiations.

Miss Margaret Bondfield, a prominent campaigner for women's rights and Chairman of the TUC Council was proposed by the Labour Party central office. She also served as an M.P. in Ramsey MacDonald's short lived previous Government. She declined the invitation.

Mr Oswald Mosley was invited by the Forest of Dean Labour Party and Secretary Mr Charles Luker announced that a telegram said that Mr Mosley *'cheerfully and readily'* accepts the Foresters invitation to contest the seat and would arrive immediately. However, a later message said that there had been a misinterpretation and that Mr Mosley had no intention of accepting the invitation and was instead, standing for the Ladywood Division in Birmingham.

Eventually the Executive Committee of the Forest of Dean Labour Council met at Lydney and unanimously invited Mr A.A. Purcell, Chairman of the Trades Union Congress, to stand as the Labour candidate. Mr Purcell accepted the invitation and started his campaign from the Cinderford office. Many considered Mr Purcell to be a Communist after being instrumental in forming the Communist Party of Great Britain **(CPGB)** in 1920 and as part of a T.U.C. delegation that visited Russia in December 1924. It was also the Communist Party's policy to infiltrate the British Labour Party by getting their endorsement of Communist members to stand for Parliament. In this way, several were successful and so there were some reservations as to whether Mr Purcell was the right choice for the Forest of Dean.

The other candidates contesting the vacancy were Mr Michael Wentworth-Beaumont (Conservative) who was defeated at the last election and Mr Harry West (Liberal).

The Bye Election took place on Tuesday the 14th of July 1925 and polling was extended until 9 pm.

The results were;
Mr A.A. Purcell – Labour 11,629,
Mr M. Wentworth-Beaumont – Conservative 8,607,
Mr H. West – Liberal .... 3,774.
Labour majority .... 3,022.

This result was announced at just after 3pm on Wednesday the 15th of July 1925 at the Comrades Hall, Newnham in front of an excited crowd estimated at over 1,000. After the result was made, Mr Purcell was carried shoulder high along the high street for about 500 yards where he was put into a motor car and asked to speak to his audience. Mr Purcell said; **'I am very glad that we are associated together in such a way that we have been able to secure a 3,000 majority. What we have to do now is to keep that 3,000 as a starting point for other thousands. After all the efforts that my opponents put forward and all the mean things they did and said, Labour thrashed them over and above all. I am now going to the House of Commons for the purpose of representing the working class and the Internationale because they require more representation and consideration.'**

Mr Wentworth-Beaumont was also carried shoulder high by his supporters and said afterwards that he wasn't going to make any excuses and he knew that they were beaten. Mr West made no comment. In Parliament when the result was announced, Mr Lansbury shouted from the Labour benches **'three thousand majority'** to loud cheering.

Coal Owners Proposals

On the 30th of June 1925, the Coal Owners issued their proposals for a new wage agreement after the 31st of July 1925 and issued notices to all employees terminating the 1924 National Wages Agreement to take effect from August 1st 1925 The notices indicated that the mines would be open for work on that date on the terms and conditions set by the Owners.

Their proposals were generally no surprise to the **MFGB** as it was anticipated that the Owners wanted to reinstate the eight hour day. Failing that, the proposals recommended doing away with the minimum wage which at the time was the 1921 Standard plus 33% but to continue with a profit sharing scheme with revised limitations. Each District would set its own minimum rates and if there was an insufficient surplus to pay this minimum, then deductions would have to be made from the wages of the better paid men. The **MFGB** had calculated that the reduction in average wages in the Forest of Dean would be 1s. 8d. per shift.

Miners' Annual Demonstration

In the Forest of Dean, the miners held their Annual Demonstration on Saturday the 11th of July 1925 – the first back at the Speech House for three years (circumstances had forced a change of venue and the previous three years' events being held at Bilson Green, Cinderford). While the sun blazed down, motor vehicles and char-a-bancs came from all over the Forest and as far afield as South Wales, discharging their occupants. While many were content with the amusements, there was much interest in the political meeting being held in the centre of the field and due to the present crisis in the mining industry, the attendance was the largest on record, estimated at around 10,000. Notables on the platform included the new prospective Labour M.P. for the Forest of Dean, Mr A.A. Purcell and his wife, Mr G. Shinwell M.P., Mr Robert Smillie M.P. and Mr John Williams the miners Agent. Chairman David R. Organ opened the meeting and remarked on the large attendance and the fact that they had outgrown the original tent in which previous meetings had been held. He said; '**The Forest of Dean miners have been under a cloud this past year and are struggling hard to obtain the arrears they are due under the national wage agreement. We have now got those arrears but clouds are still hanging over us and unless the mine Owners make very different proposals to those already offered, I can see nothing but a bitter struggle in front of us. The Owners proposals were absolutely ridiculous.'**

This was the theme throughout the meeting which the other speakers wholeheartedly endorsed. Mr A.A. Purcell was introduced by David Organ as the 'winning Candidate' in the forthcoming Forest of Dean Constituency by-election and was given a rousing reception as he rose to speak. There was laughter when he said that he wholeheartedly supported the remarks relating to his own election but then seriously referred to the coming struggle as a struggle for the whole of the working classes. Mr G. Shinwell M.P. said that the Mining industry was in a very perilous state and that one of the authors of that situation was at this very moment attending a political meeting being held at Cinderford. This was a reference to Mr David Lloyd George whose Government of 1919 failed to take account of the recommendations of the then Sankey Commission. He called him **'Ali Baba, the leader of 40 Liberals in the House of Commons, the 40 thieves'** which prompted laughter and applause.

The Meeting ended with a resolution to reject the Coal Owners' proposals and would resist further attacks on wages to the bitter end. They would also support the cause for wages equal to the cost of living and would be content with nothing less. Mr Purcell was given a pledge of whole-hearted support for the forthcoming by-election.

On the same day, the Rt. Hon. David Lloyd George M.P. was speaking at a Liberal meeting at the Recreation Ground, Cinderford, in support of the Liberal candidate Mr Harry West. The main theme of his speech after a rousing reception was to pour scorn on Mr A.A. Purcell, the Labour candidate and the other guests at the Speech House Demonstration. He said that Mr Purcell belonged to the other wing of the Party to that of the late James Wignall – not the Red wing he said, but the Scarlet wing. The other guests he said were tame politicians who were there to smooth the way for extremist Mr Purcell. On the mining industry he said that the trouble was that extremists had infiltrated both the Coal Owners Association and the **MFGB** and swept away the moderate men. He referred to Mr Frank Hodges who he said was a cool headed and most moderate and best of men that the miners had had to fight their cause. He was swept away by the extremists such as Mr Purcell. Lloyd George was an eloquent speaker and touched on many other subjects such as Unification of the mines, the result of the return to the Gold Standard and the current unemployment situation. He ended by decrying the record of the current Government on various issues and also the Labour Party when they were the short term Government in 1924.

The Power of the Triple Alliance

Moves were already afoot by the **MFGB** to consider forming of an **Industrial Alliance** between the miners, railwaymen, transport workers and engineers. A sub committee was formed to consider the basis of such an Alliance and to form a constitution that was agreeable to all the other Unions. The General Council of the T.U.C. could see that this attack on the miners could eventually lead to further demands on other groups of workers and so threatened an embargo on coal movement from the 1st of August 1925. The Triple Alliance was back in business.

Meanwhile, the **MFGB** issued instructions to all Districts to cease work on the 31st of July 1925 and that arrangements would be made for the minimum of workmen to continue working to secure the safety of the mines and care for the pit ponies. Included in that instruction was that no District should take instruction other than through the National Executive. The **MFGB** had also put their case in the hands of the General Council of the Trades Union Congress and called on the Government to take action to bring about an unconditional conference between both sides in the dispute in a step towards reaching an amicable agreement.

In the Forest of Dean, the **FODMA** issued a statement to the miners that the Owners intended to serve notice on Friday the 24th of July 1925 to terminate the operation of the 1924 National Wages Agreement as from Friday the 31st of July 1925. The notices indicated that the mines would be open for work on the 1st of August 1925 on the terms and conditions set by the Owners. They said that their terms for the renewal of contracts would be posted later that week. The Coal Owners asked for a meeting of the parties involved but Mr Jack Williams was away in London and unavailable.

Last minute agreement

The Prime Minister Stanley Baldwin held talks on Wednesday the 29th of July 1925 with both the miners and Coal Owners' representatives. Also present were Mr Bridgeman, Sir Arthur Steel-Maitland and Mr Lane-Fox. The Coal Owners insisted on reducing the minimum wage but said that this could be raised if the miners went back to an eight hour day. These were rejected by the miners' leaders who refused to discuss the hour's question. The Prime Minister also refused to grant a subsidy. However, the talks continued on the Thursday which was a crucial day in the discussions. Neither party would give way on their demands until late that day when the miners and the T.U.C. Committee reported to the Trade Union Executives. Their decision empowered the T.U.C. to issue strike orders and to put into force the embargo on coal movements. This news forced the Prime Minister's hand and he had no alternative but to go back on his word and to grant a nine month subsidy. The Coal Owners would withdraw their notices and a full enquiry into the mining industry would take place.

This settlement, which had been agreed between all parties, was announced by the Prime Minister in the House of Commons on Friday the 31st of July 1925. Word was sent via telegrams by the **MFGB** to all the mining Districts to continue working while the Triple Alliance partners including the railwaymen and Transport Workers Union officials cancelled instructions to put an embargo on the transport of coal. Apart from the details of the new settlement, this was considered a victory for the Triple Alliance and the 31st of July 1925 became known as **'Red Friday'.**

The settlement involved offering a subsidy to the Coal Owners to support wages for a nine month period to the 1st of May 1926 and to set up a Royal Commission to look into the coal industry's problems. Wages would continue to be paid on the 1924 agreement but in any month where the calculation of wages fell below the minimum, the deficiency would be made up by the subsidy. This subsidy was estimated to cost around £12,000,000 with the Forest of Dean receiving its fair share.

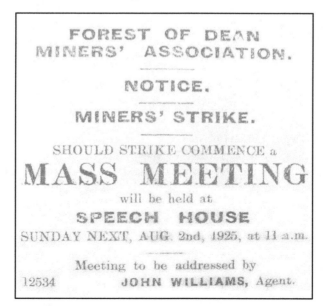

Fig. 83 Notice issued by the FODMA to discuss the settlement

The Forest of Dean Miners' Association had already called for a mass meeting the following Sunday morning to discuss the crisis. The Chairman, David Organ in his opening remarks said that; **'in my opinion it is a victory up to a point and if the country's workers hadn't stood by us, then we would probably have been defeated'.** He also remarked; **'I think we could have had a much better settlement than we have'.** Jack Williams the Miners' Agent supported this view and said; **'never in the history of the Trades Union Movement have the workers of the country displayed such solidarity but the result is far short of what we have been fighting for and it should not be considered a victory. The coal owners will have more profits than they have had before but the miners will not receive one brass farthing more than we have had before – it is a triumph not for the miners but for the coal owners'.** The meeting closed with a resolution that the settlement was totally unsatisfactory and expressed disappointment that the Miners' Executive did not stand by its demands for wages equal to the cost of living.

This dissatisfaction with the new settlement was expressed at an **MFGB** Delegate conference on the 19th of August 1925 where the Chairman said that the settlement was not a victory – it was only an armistice. Several Delegates expressed their doubts and raised the question of what would happen after the 1st of May 1926.

Rumblings of discontent continued through the following months and both John Williams and Arthur Cook, Secretary of the Miners Federation made public statements as to the position the miners would be in come May 1926, when the subsidy expired. Neither was happy with the situation and both urged miners to stand against any reduction in wages or increases in hours worked. Unity within the Unions was also strongly recommended with a view to the complete Nationalisation of the Coal Industry. The Forest of Dean portion of the current subsidy was £100,000 which was later increased to £130,000 – this going, not to supplement miners' wages but to the Owners to make coal cheaper and hence to increase demand.

Mr Arthur J. Cook warned; **'Next May we shall be faced with the greatest struggle there ever has been. We are going to prepare, not only the machinery but also the commissariat. I am going to get a friend in London if I can, that will buy grub, so that when the struggle comes, and indeed, before it comes, we can have grub distributed in the homes of the people. We have not got a living wage yet; we are going to get it. We warn the Government not to tempt the army and navy too** much. Numbers have gone there because they were unemployed. have enough faith in our own lads to believe they will not turn on their own kith and kin'.

Mr Jack Williams said; 'I say that this settlement is a rotten one. You can say what you like and you can think what you like but I think this is a rotten settlement. We have been told that this is a great victory. would ask in which respect is this a great victory? You are to work for nine more months with wages about 15% below the cost of living on the basis of 1914. Is that a victory? That is not a victory that is defeat The only people who have gained a victory in this struggle are the Coal Owners. Are you going to have a brass farthing increase in wages? The Coal Owners are going to have what they have never had before, an amount of profits they have never had before. You will not receive a brass farthing more than you have had since the operation of the last agreement. It is a triumph, not for the miners, but for the Coal Owners.'

Preparations for a forthcoming struggle.
The Royal Commission.

The Commission was initiated by Royal Warrant on the 5th of September 1925 and became known as the Samuel Commission after its Chairman Sir Herbert Samuel. Other Commissioners were General Sir Herbert Lawrence, Sir William Beveridge and Mr Kenneth Lee. There were no representatives from either the Miners' Federation or the Miners' Association but it was obvious that although regarded as an impartial body, these Commissioners represented the Capitalist class and so the miners didn't hold out much hope of a fair outcome. The Commission's terms of reference were simply; *'to inquire into and report upon the economic position of the coal industry and the conditions affecting it and to make any recommendations for the improvement thereof'*. The Commission started to take evidence in public on the 15th of October 1925.

Maintenance of Supplies
While the Royal Commission started their deliberations, another group of private individuals began to think ahead to a time of possible industrial unrest which could bring the country into anarchy. They formed an organisation called the Organisation for the Maintenance of Supplies (O.M.S.) which, should a General Strike take place, they could call on citizens throughout the country who would be willing to volunteer to help

maintain supplies and vital services. This was claimed to be a non-political organisation, more concerned with the welfare of the population than carrying out the Government's responsibilities. They also claimed not to be opposed to the legitimate use of Trade Union activity to bring about better conditions of employment for their members and to improve social and economic conditions. In response to the forming of this organisation, the Home Secretary Sir William Joynson-Hicks said that he was aware of its existence and although in the event of an emergency, the Government would discharge their own responsibilities, it would welcome private assistance from well meaning citizens from all parts of the country.

Emergency Powers Act

In parallel with this, the Government could also see the consequences of when the subsidy ended in April 1926. They accordingly put plans in motion to reactivate **the Emergency Powers Act** whereby England and Wales would be divided into ten regional areas. Each area was to be administered by a Local Authority which would maintain law and order and provide essential services such as road transport, food and fuel supplies. As an example, the **Forest of Dean** would form part of the South Western Division which would be sub-divided into four areas – Gloucester, Bristol, Exeter and Plymouth - with the Forest of Dean coming under the administration of Gloucester. They would also encourage volunteer help from Organisations and public spirited individuals who would be willing to help maintain vital services. Industrial Organisations and mine owners were also encouraged to stockpile coal.

Much of this was carried out secretly but in December 1925 Winston Churchill made a speech which made it clear publicly that the Government were preparing for a possible confrontation with the Unions. **'Therefore, should such a struggle be found to be inevitable at the very last moment, it was of supreme importance that it should only be undertaken under conditions which would not expose the Nation needlessly or wantonly to perils, the gravity of which cannot possibly be overestimated'.**

Industrial Alliance

On the Union side, as a follow-up to **'Red Friday',** the Industrial Alliance was beginning to form as many individual Unions began pledging their support. A draft constitution was accepted at a **MFGB** Delegate Conference on the 5th of November 1925 and was adopted on the 25th of November 1925. However, before it could be ratified, a ballot was needed from several Unions and this meant a delay before further progress could be made.

Pit Stop – Norchard Colliery

Frustration boiled over at one pit in the Forest – a strike of over 400 miners was called on Monday the 19th of October 1925 at the Norchard Colliery near Lydney – because 4 men were alleged to be in the wrong Union. Both Miners' Agent Jack Williams and David Organ, President of the **FODMA** were held responsible for calling out the men, in what was described at the time as **'a strike without rhyme or reason over a triviality'**. Two Unions were dominant at the pit – the **Forest of Dean Miners' Association** and the Craftsmen's Union (the National Winding and General Engineers Society) – both vying for maximum membership at this critical time. The four men, who were surface workers at the pit, had joined the Craftsmen's National Winding Union but the Miners' Association declared that as the men were not craftsmen, they should by right, be members of their Association. On the Monday morning an agreement was reached regarding one of the men – the other three stood out for their right to belong to the Union of their choice.

Lord Bledisloe, the virtual owner of the Norchard declared that if the men went on strike, he would be compelled to close the pit for good. When the pit suffered serious flooding at the beginning of the year, about £16,000 had been spent on new equipment and although not an economic decision, his Lordship decided to reopen the pit solely in the interests of his employees. At the same time, an agreement had been made with the Miners Agent that there would be co-operation in every way to ensure harmonious working at the pit with discussions taking place through a Pit Committee. On the strength of this assurance, Lord Bledisloe offered the men two places on the Board of Directors with a share of the profits and also erected a large room for drying the men's clothes and for their recreation (as mentioned earlier).

Fig. 84 Charles Bathurst , 1st Viscount Bledisloe

Nevertheless, for whatever the politics, the men were called out regardless of the threat of the pit closing permanently. On Wednesday evening the 21st of October 1925, the **FODMA** held a meeting at Lydney, presided over by David Organ. He reaffirmed the men's determination to carry on the strike and asked Agent Jack Williams whether the owners' threat to close the colliery should dominate the dispute. Mr Williams said that he didn't attach the slightest importance to those statements emanating either from Lord Bledisloe or the pit manager Mr Hooper.

As leader of the Miners' Association and also check weighman at the Norchard Colliery, David Organ was at the forefront of this dispute and consequently came in for much criticism from the press. To this end, Lord Bledisloe published the following two letters in the local papers, both addressed to David Organ;

1.

"I have just heard of the decision of your meeting at Norchard Colliery this morning. I am much grieved about it all. I am certain it will never be worth our while to open the colliery again after your strike has closed it. Our decision to do so after it was flooded last January (following a period of serious financial losses) was arrived at solely in the interests of the colliery employees, and due to the fervent assurance of yourself and Mr William, the miners' Agent, that you would (if the colliery were unwatered), co-operate in every way to ensure its harmonious working and augment its output, which had previously been deplorably low. On the strength of this assurance, the Company, after offering the employees through your Pit Committee, two seats on the Board of Directors and a substantial share in any profits which it might make thereafter, invited (and have taken) the advice of your Pit Committee as to methods of underground working, and at considerable cost have erected a large room for drying workmen's clothes and for their recreation.

I may remind you further that because you and some of our other employees live at Pillowell, I recently gave the village in perpetuity, a large public recreation ground in the hope of adding to the happiness and contentment of your lives and those of your children. That you should force the permanent closing of a colliery which gives settled employment to 450 men and boys in the district and which has been for several generations one of our leading local industries, because three men (while belonging to a trades union), are not members of the particular trades union that you and your miners' Agent favour, is to take a step involving the gravest responsibility. I feel it to be my duty to acquaint the public, either through the Press or through the Royal Commission, with the whole recent history of the Norchard Colliery. The employers at least have nothing to hide.

2.
By way of supplement to my letter of yesterday, I ought to remind you that your action in closing Norchard Colliery may seriously affect the whole future of the West Gloucestershire Power Station and its employees. It was for the sake of obtaining an outlet for the small coal of the colliery, which had become a glut on the market (and thus ensuring continuous employment at the colliery in bad times), that I persuaded the West Gloucestershire Power Company (with some difficulty) three years ago, to abandon their Chepstow scheme and erect their large power station on the site of our colliery. The widespread ultimate results of your decision seem indeed difficult to forecast.

In reply to this statement, the West Gloucestershire Power Company issued the following announcement; *'It has come to our notice that statements are being circulated to the effect that the unfortunate dispute among the employees of the Norchard Colliery may, by stopping supplies of coal from that source, seriously affect the future of the West Gloucestershire Power Company. Such statements are entirely incorrect. Neither the present nor the future position of the West Gloucestershire Power Company is in any way affected by the closing temporarily or permanently of the Norchard colliery. The West Gloucestershire Power Company is surrounded by collieries, and has always possessed facilities for taking coal supplies from the colliery offering the most advantageous terms'.*

To try to resolve their differences, a meeting of the two Unions took place at the Feathers Hotel in Lydney on the evening of Thursday the 5th of November 1925. Among those present were Mr Edwin Healey and Mr H. Hanman of the National Winding and General Engineers' Association together with some Norchard Colliery employees including the three men at the centre of the dispute. For the Forest of Dean Miners' Association were Mr Jack Williams miners' Agent, Mr David Organ President of the Association and other members of the pit committee. The Miners Association said that they attended the meeting prepared to give ground but the Craftsmen's Association conceded nothing other than vowing to keep the colliery closed for up to six months if necessary. No conclusions were reached and the negotiations eventually broke down.

In spite of this, the strike continued and at a mass meeting of Norchard miners on Saturday the 7th of November, a resolution was unanimously passed asking Mr Jack Williams the miners' Agent to take the necessary steps to bring out the whole District, estimated at around 6,000 men.

On Thursday the 12th of November 1925 Jack Williams, David Organ and an executive member of the Norchard colliery Mr Brown attended a meeting in London with the **MFGB.** It was agreed to put the matter to arbitration and proceedings were set in motion by Mr Arthur Cook, Secretary of the Federation.

And so, after a miners' meeting in Lydney Town Hall on the morning of Saturday the 14th of November 1925 where the current situation was explained by Jack Williams, the strike was suddenly called off. Mr Jack Williams informed Mr J. Hooper, the colliery manager, that his men were prepared to go back to work on the following Monday, the 16th of Novembe 1925. Mr Hooper promptly called for a meeting of all employees on the Sunday afternoon at the colliery where he questioned the men as to their loyalty and the pledge given by their own Pit Committee as to the continued working of the Norchard Colliery following the flooding of the colliery in January 1925. He said that £16,000 had been spent repairing the colliery providing the miners with facilities for drying their clothes and a substantia share in future profits. In response the Pit Committee had made a pledge to keep the colliery running and make it profitable. Jack Williams was present and constantly interrupted Mr Hooper, questioning the truth of his statements. Mr Hooper responded by saying that it was his meeting and Mr Williams could have his say at their own meeting later that day.

The Miners' Association's meeting was held on the Sunday evening at the Lydney Picture House. David Organ as President and Chairman opened the meeting referring to the dispute in general and that afternoon's meeting at the colliery and said that the men had now had time to peruse the issues involved and were now able to form their own conclusions. He said the meeting with the Craftsmen's Union had reached a stalemate and that there was no possibility of reaching an agreement with them. The question was then transferred to the Miners' Federation of Great Britain for arbitration and as a result of Saturday's decision, the employers were informed that the men were prepared to resume work on the Monday morning the 16th of November 1925. The strike had lasted for four weeks but the closure of the colliery was thus avoided and many were of the opinion that the threat of closure was something they had all heard before.

Dilke Memorial Hospital

Good news for the new Dilke Memorial Hospital which had been so successful since it was commissioned in 1923 that it became clear that more space was needed to meet the needs of the district. As a consequence it was decided to extend the building by adding a new administrative block which would include a Board room, operating theatre, casualty ward, nursing and domestic staff quarters. The building would include an extensive ground floor balcony and a caretaker's cottage would also be constructed. Part of the original building would be converted into a children's ward.

Fig. 85 Current view of Forest of Dean Miners Welfare Fund Foundation Stone – photo Author

The cost was estimated to be £5,500 with £3,000 already subscribed including £1,000 from the Forest of Dean Miners' Welfare Fund. On Thursday the 15th of October 1925 with Mr George Rowlinson presiding at the ceremony, the first foundation stone was laid by Miss Lisa Crawshay who was a donor of £1,000, in memory of her brother Mr Edwin Crawshay and another was laid by Mr C.A.J. Hale on behalf of the Forest of Dean Miners' Welfare Fund. It was estimated that the buildings would be completed during the next nine months.

Accidents/Fatalities

On Thursday the 29th of January 1925, Mr Samuel Fred Evans aged 24 was killed by a fall of rock while working underground at the Eastern United Colliery, Ruspidge, part of the Henry Crawshay group of collieries. An Inquiry held at the Ruspidge Memorial Hall heard that Mr Evans had been working at the coal face on the Coleford High Delf seam when he was struck by a sudden fall of the roof weighing around two tons of rock. The area had been examined shortly before the accident and was found to be a little breaking but nothing to indicate that it was unsafe and it was believed to be solid rock above. Timbering was compliant with regulations and more was available if required and the Coroner confirmed that there was a good understanding at the colliery and that more timbering could be used beyond the regulation measurements. The Coroner recorded a verdict of accidental death.

On Sunday the 1st of February 1925, Mr James Morris aged 53 and a collier from Harrow Hill near Drybrook, died in the Gloucestershire Royal Infirmary after suffering injuries while working underground at the Steam Mills Colliery near Cinderford. An Inquiry held at the Infirmary heard that on the morning of the 15th of December 1924, Mr Morris was working with M Wilfred Simmonds in the 'W' road where they were running trucks of dirt At around 9.30am Mr Morris's truck had come off the rails and he called for help to replace it. A man named Pritchard helped but afterwards Mr Morris complained of pains in his stomach and a lump that had come up in his groin. He said that the pain was bad and Mr Simmonds told him to report it to the manager. Mr William Pritchard agreed with that statement and also advised Mr Morris to go out of the pit which, after resting he did but appeared to be in pain. Mrs Maud Pritchard, Mr Morris's daughter said that on the 15th of December 1924 her father had told her that he had hurt himself while lifting a dram of dirt back on the rails. He had seen a doctor who had said that he had ruptured himself and advised him to go to the Royal Infirmary. He did this on the 20th of December 1924 but could not get admission because all the beds were full. He was admitted on the 12th of January 1925.

Senior House Surgeon at the hospital Dr A.L. Bernstein confirmed his admission on the 12th of January 1925 as he had been on the waiting list since December last. Mr Morris was operated on for the hernia on the 13th of January 1925 which was successful and he was making good progress. On the 18th of January 1925, Mr Morris complained of pains in the right side of his chest. He was examined and it was suspected he had pneumonia at the base of the lung. He was treated accordingly and by the 22nd of January 1925 he appeared to be completely recovered but was kept in hospital for post operative treatment. However, on the 31st of January 1925 his temperature rose and he complained of more pains in the right side of his chest. There was no sign of lung trouble and his temperature went down but then said there was pain in his left chest. After eating a good lunch and tea a nurse found Mr Morris in a state of collapse. He was treated but his condition deteriorated and he died at 5.25pm. A post mortem revealed no external injuries except for the hernia scar and all internal organs were consistent with a healthy man except for congested lungs. There was an embolism of the pulmonary artery and in the doctor's opinion, that was the cause of death. He thought that the previous chest pains could have been attributed to the embolism. The Coroner recorded a verdict in accordance with the medical evidence and expressed sympathy with the relatives. Representatives of the employers also expressed sympathy and were sorry to lose such a sober and steady workman. Mr Jack Williams, **FODMA** Agent responded on behalf of the relatives.

On Monday the 23rd of February 1925, Mr John Worgan aged 55 and a collier, was killed while working underground at the Park Gutter Colliery, Bream, one of the Princess Royal Company's pits. An Inquiry held at Bream heard that Mr Worgan was killed instantly by a sudden fall of stone estimated to be three tons while working at the coal face. Mr Reubin James who was working within three or four yards of where Mr Worgan was working said that he heard the fall and found him in a crouching position with his head forward. He was immediately taken out of the colliery but there was nothing to be done. Mr William Vaughan said that he had previously tested the roof where the fall had been and had found it safe. He said that there was a fault nearby and that all the workmen were aware of it. Dr Davidson from Parkend said that Mr Worgan had died from shock due to the dislocation of the spine and asphyxia caused by a fall of stone. The Coroner returned a verdict in accordance with the medical evidence.

On Tuesday the 10th of March 1925, Mr Francis Thomas aged 60 and a collier, was killed while working underground at Lightmoor Colliery near Cinderford. An Inquiry held at the Police Station in Cinderford heard that Mr Thomas was working with a fellow collier 'ripping' in a stall road when, not following the usual practice, he started moving timber. Half a ton of dirt then fell through a hidden 'slip' and partially buried him. He called out to a mate; **'Dick, I'm killed'**. Mr Thomas received severe injuries to his head and back with probable internal haemorrhage and died soon afterwards. The Coroner returned a verdict in accordance with the evidence and the Directors of Henry Crawshay and Company expressed their sympathy on the death of an old and valued workman.

Chapter 25
1926 – Pit Stop – The General Strike

In the Forest of Dean Mr Alf Purcell M.P. and past President of the Trade Union Congress made a speech at Broadwell in January 1926 where he said that the Coal Owners' way of getting out of their difficulties was to reduce the miners' wages and to work longer hours – which he thought was an idiotic remedy. He said that policy would throw 100,000 miners out of work but he was sure that when this matter came before the Trades Union Congress, they would support the miners.

And so the miners took great comfort from the joint decision by the **Industrial Committee** and the **MFGB** in February 1926 that the whole of the Trade Union movement would stand firmly and united behind the miners in their demands for a better standard of life. Their joint declaration was that there was to be no reduction in wages, no increase in working hours and no interference with the principle of National Agreements.

In the Forest of Dean
The Forest of Dean Miners' Association met in January to elect officials for the current year 1926. The result of the ballot was; President David Organ. Vice President Harold Craddock. Financial Secretary Tom Etheridge. Financial Committee Horace Jones, Ambrose Adams, Enos Taylor.

The Royal Commission
The long awaited **Royal Commission's report** was delayed because both the Coal Owners and the Miners Federation had not submitted their own proposals to remedy the problems of the coal industry. It was felt by both parties that due to fresh evidence being provided to the Commission, they needed more time to consider their options.

The Commission resumed its inquiry during the first week of January 1926 and produced its 300 page report on the 10th of March 1926. During its deliberations, the Commission visited 25 collieries, 42 others were inspected by the Mines Inspectorate and it had 33 public sittings interviewing 76 witnesses.

The Report's recommendations were broadly for the reorganisation of the mining industry at some future date but rejected Nationalisation. There was to be no continuation of the subsidy when its current term expired and a wage reduction for miners was to take place immediately.

An agreement was made between the **MFGB, the T.U.C. Industrial Committee** and the **Prime Minister** that no pronouncement should be made until both sides had had time to examine the Report and make their own decisions.

On the 24th of March, representatives from the **MFGB,** the Coal Owners Association and the Prime Minister met to discuss the Report. The Prime Minister acknowledged that parts of that Report were opposed by the Government but he said for the sake of a settlement, they would be prepared to accept the measures, provided the other parties agreed to accept the Report's recommendations.

To this end, the miners and Coal Owners' representatives met on the 25th and the 31st of March 1926 to try and reach some sort of common ground for agreement. The Coal Owners were adamant that there should be a reduction in wages and/or a longer working week and District Agreements. The miners were opposed to all of them. A further meeting of the two parties took place on the 1st of April 1926 but again, ended in deadlock.

Forest miners' position
In the Forest of Dean the **FODMA** held a special meeting at their offices in Cinderford on Wednesday the 7th of April 1926 with Mr David Organ acting as Chairman. It was resolved that Mr Jack Williams should, on behalf of the Association at the National Conference in London, put forward their proposition;

'That this Conference having considered the proposals of the Coal Owners regarding the Report of the Royal Commission resolves to reject them, as their acceptance means a reduction in wages, district agreements and a longer working day.

The Conference unequivocally demands a wage equal to the cost of living, a National Agreement which would embody a uniform percentage on basis rates and no interference with the hours of the present working day.

This Conference further resolves that the National Executive shall immediately formulate a programme setting out in detail the Terms of a National Agreement and fixing a percentage on basis rates which shall be approved by this Conference and which shall form the basis of any negotiations either with the Government or the Coal Owners, and in the meanwhile a statement of our demands to be communicated to the General Council of the Trade Union Congress'.

That Conference took place on Friday the 9th of April 1926 and unanimously passed a resolution to be distributed to the Districts for their consideration and decision. That resolution had three clauses broadly based on the **FODMA's** proposals;

1. No increase in the working day,
2. A National Wage Agreement with a National minimum wage,
3. No reduction in wages.

A miners meeting was called at Cinderford Town Hall on Sunday the 12th of April 1926, Mr Enos Taylor Presiding with Mr Alf Purcell in attendance. Mr Jack Williams explained at length the result of the Conference resolution and the deliberations in the meetings between both sides of the dispute. He said that the Owners were determined to reduce wages but had not yet released any details of the proposed District rates. He said that at the Conference he had put forward a proposal that instead of agreeing to a National Wage Agreement, they should demand a living wage, but that was turned down. As for wages and hours worked he said that the Owners' suggestion was to lengthen the working day to 8 hours and 24 minutes for 5 days per week as compared with the present 7 hours for 6 days. The average working week in the Forest of Dean was 4.5 days so the owners had nothing to lose. He urged the men to accept the recommendations of the Conference.

On the 13th of April 1926 a fourth meeting of representatives of miners and Coal Owners took place where the Coal Owners suggested they would meet with each District to consider the minimum rates. In view of their three clauses above, this was rejected by the miners. The meeting ended once again in deadlock. Further meetings took place on April the 22nd and 23rd 1926 but the Coal Owners refused to budge on their demands.

Coal Owners' move

The Coal Owners then delivered their ultimatum and on the weekend of the 24th of April 1926, all Forest of Dean miners received a letter terminating their present contracts as from the 30th of April 1926. It read; *'As the Coal Owners' agreement with the Government dated August 6th 1925 will come to an end on April 30th 1926, notice is hereby given to you that your contract of service with this Company will terminate on the same date, namely April 30th 1926. This colliery will be open for work on and after May 1st 1926 on terms and conditions which will be posted up before that date.'*

On Monday the 26th of April 1926, notices were posted up at all Forest of Dean collieries, setting out the new terms and conditions to be implemented as from the 1st of May 1926 and that all collieries would be open for those that agreed to those terms. The terms were prepared by each District Owners' Association and varied from District to District. So the Coal Owners' wishes for District Agreements had already been put into action.

Without going into detail of the complicated method of calculating rates, the new proposed rates would mean;

1. A colliers minimum wage would be reduced from 8s. 3d. to 7s. 1.5d. for a 7 hour shift,
2. From 8s. 3d. to 7s. 8.5d. for a 7.5 hour shift,
3. No reduction for an 8 hour shift.

If the miners claim that the 7 hour shift should be retained, the drop in wages in the Forest of Dean for a collier would be 1s. 1.5d. per shift or 5s. 1d. per week (4.5 days). In the cold light of day, one could plainly see why the miners objected so much to this idea but the Coal Owners were adamant that to make the mines profitable without the support of the Government subsidy, a reduction in wages was the only solution.

Mr Arthur Cook, the **MFGB** Secretary, speaking at a meeting of miners in York said; **'You might well have to fight for your existence when last month 300,000 of you took home less than £2 a week. We have reached the limit of human endurance. The fresh proposals of the Coal Owners mean reductions of up to 8 shillings a week in the miner's pay. No leader would recommend acceptance of those proposals which are impossible. The old rank and file of the miners' Union persisted in their slogan 'Not a penny off the pay, not a second on the day'. The labourers' holy trinity is the political movement, the industrial movement and the co-operative movement. It is the duty of the railwaymen to help us in the most fateful struggle in the history of the labour movement. I believe that the whole trade union movement will stand by the miners as they did last July'.** It was later confirmed by the President of the National Union of Railwaymen that in the present crisis the railwaymen would stand by the miners just as they did last July.

Last Minute Offer

The Unions were solidly behind the miners but continued to support further negotiations. They asked for more Government financial support and that the Contract Notices be suspended pending further talks even though they could see that the Coal Owners were sticking to their terms. On Friday the 30th of April 1926, last minute negotiations were still ongoing from the previous day and Prime Minister Baldwin wrote to Mr Herbert Smith President of the **MFGB** with a further offer from the Coal Owners. They proposed a National minimum rate of 20% on the 1914 Standard on an 8 hour day with the Government offering legislation promising that the 8 hour day be temporary and that another Commission be set up by 1929. To understand the implications of this offer, the cost of living index showed that prices were 70% above the 1914 level and the words of Mr Arthur Cook aptly described the situation the miners were in; **'It is quite evident that the Coal Owners, on posting their new wages proposals at the pit heads and in giving notice to the men, mean to force a conflict. No miner will be safe. In every District, reductions are to take place. Even the lowest paid men, whose wages have been a scandal, are to be reduced'.**

Although discussions are still proceeding, in view of the action of the T.U.C., the country must be prepared for a General Strike in many Industries and Public Services on Monday night.

The Government has taken all steps to maintain the supply of food, fuel, light and power, the protection of all engaged in these services and for the preservation of Law and Order. Recruiting stations for volunteers will be opened tomorrow. All loyal citizens should hold themselves in readiness to assist the Government. Full information will be issued tomorrow but in the event of any difficulty occurring in finding the right office on Tuesday, enquiries should be made at the nearest Police Station.

Fig. 86 Notice issued by the Home Secretary, Mr William Joynson-Hicks on Sunday the 2nd of May 1926

The Unions continued with negotiations. The **MFGB's** reply to Prime Minister Baldwin's letter was predictably in the negative but fairly worded and offered to continue negotiations on the reorganisation of the coal industry as recommended by the Royal Commission. On May Day the 1st of May 1926, the Conference of Executives of Trade Unions asked for a mandate of members to call for a General Strike. The votes from Trade Unionists were 3,653,527 in favour and 49,911 against and so the strike was to come into effect as from midnight on Monday the 3rd of May 1926.

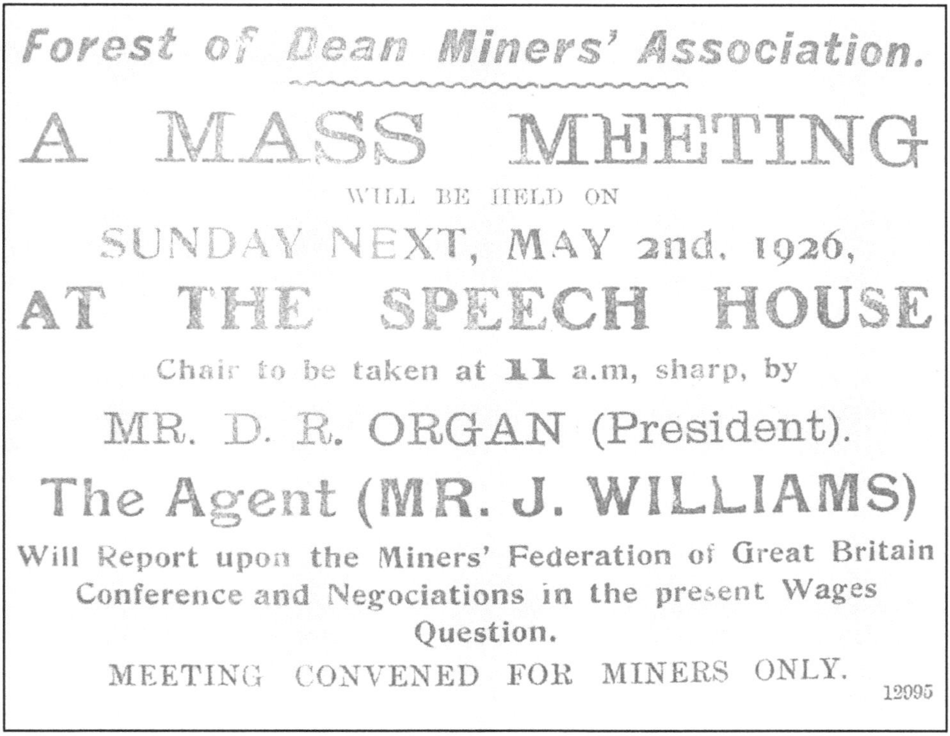

Forest of Dean Miners' Association.

A MASS MEETING

WILL BE HELD ON

SUNDAY NEXT, MAY 2nd. 1926,

AT THE SPEECH HOUSE

Chair to be taken at **11** a.m, sharp, by

MR. D. R. ORGAN (President).

The Agent (MR. J. WILLIAMS)

Will Report upon the Miners' Federation of Great Britain Conference and Negociations in the present Wages Question.

MEETING CONVENED FOR MINERS ONLY.

12095

Fig.87 **FODMA** *poster advertising the Speech House Mass meeting.*

At Speech House
On Sunday morning the 2nd of May 1926, a large crowd of miners attended a mass meeting at the Speech House, called by the **Forest of Dean Miners' Association** to discuss the critical situation.

President of the Association Mr David Organ said in his opening remarks **'as one of the smaller Districts, the Forest of Dean is one of the wors paid in the Federation and had the district wage agreements come into operation, we would have been the ones who would have suffered the most. I am glad to know that we now have the same solidarity among the British working classes as we were promised last July and the whole of the Trade Union movement are now prepared to support us in our desire for a wage that we can at least exist upon'.**(applause).

The agent, Mr Jack Williams then described at length the Coal Owners latest offers and the efforts being made in London on their behalf to avoid conflict. He detailed how the strike was to be conducted and who were able to be employed to help keep the pits from flooding. Regarding unemployment benefit, David Organ said he had had a meeting with the Labour Exchange manager who expressed concern if all miners descended on his offices at once. He desired that a representative number from each colliery from each grade of work should make an application and a test case could be made. David Organ also said; **'A great factor in a struggle like this is to keep our heads – do not lose your heads – do not get excited. It would not be won by muscle, but by brains and by remaining as quiet as possible throughout. I hope you all appreciate the seriousness of the position we are now in and our best way of carrying out the strike is to quietly take instructions from time to time as meetings were called and abide by them'.** The meeting ended cheerfully, all singing 'lead kindly light' and 'the Red Flag'.

State of Emergency Declared

Regardless of the strike threat, negotiations continued with the General Council asking for further talks with the Prime Minister. These last minute negotiations were conducted at 10 Downing Street in the evening of Sunday the 2nd of May 1926. Later that evening they were interrupted by news of the refusal of the Daily Mail machinists to print a Government propaganda leading article for Monday's issue and had gone on strike. This was the last straw for the Prime Minister who asked the Council to withdraw the threat of a General Strike and condemn the actions of the Daily Mail workers. By the time the Council was able to draft a reply, the Prime Minister was unavailable – he had gone to bed.

The next day, Monday the 3rd of May 1926 in the House of Commons the Prime Minister announced the receipt of a message he had received from

King George V 'Signed by his own hand' and asked the Speaker to read it out.

'Whereas by the Emergency Powers Act 1920, it is enacted that if it appears to us that any action has been taken or is immediately threatened by any persons or body of persons of such a nature and on so extensive a scale as to be calculated, by interfering with the supply and distribution of food, water, fuel, or light, or with the means of locomotion, to deprive the community or any substantial portion of the community, of the essentials of life, we may, by Proclamation, declare that a state of emergency exists: And whereas the present immediate threat of cessation of work in Coal Mines does, in our opinion, constitute a state of emergency within the meaning of the said Act: Now, therefore, in pursuance of the said Act, We do, by and with the advice of Our Privy Council, hereby declare that a State of Emergency exists.

Given at Our Court at Buckingham Palace, this Thirtieth day of April, in the year of our Lord one thousand nine hundred and twenty-six, and in the Sixteenth year of Our Reign.

This **'State of Emergency'** gave the Government powers to take any necessary steps it wished without consultation with Parliament. New regulations could be created, new types of offences and penalties and new powers to the Police and Armed Forces – Mr Churchill also made it known that the Government would commandeer the British Broadcasting Company but consultations between Mr Baldwin and Sir John Reith quashed that idea.

The General Strike

The T.U.C. set in motion their plan to initiate the General Strike which officially began at midnight on Monday 3rd of May 1926 – Tuesday the 4th being the first day of the Strike. Industry was called out in sections but essential services like health and food and sanitation were unaffected. By the end of the first day, over 2 million workers had been called out. The Forest of Dean saw solid support for the miners with all railway stations closed and the Lydney Tinplate workers also out in support. Power suppliers (regarded as essential services) had previously been encouraged to stockpile coal to cope with the intended strike and the Cinderford Gas Works had a three week supply while the recently opened Lydney Power Station had a three month supply.

GENERAL STRIKE!

All Railwaymen to cease work TO-NIGHT.

Transport Workers, Printers and Metal Workers to follow.

General Council's arrangements for General Stoppage.

Fig 88 Front page of the General Strike Bulletin on the 4th of May 1926

As the major printing Unions supported the strike, local newspaper staff were obliged to leave their jobs, leaving the Editor alone to assemble and print abbreviated editions. He also came under pressure from the local M.P. Mr Alf Purcell and Mr Jack Williams the miners' Agent. Initially, in order to give his readers a fair report on what the miners' leaders had to say, the Editor was given an assurance by Mr Williams that a newspaper representative could be present and report on local miners meetings – the two in question being at the Cinderford Palace cinema on Saturday the 8th of May 1926 and at the Speech House on Sunday the 9th of May 1926. However, when Mr Purcell heard about this, he said if newspapers were being published in breach of the T.U.C's instructions, then they were the products of blacklegs and he would not agree to their request. When Jack Williams was approached at another miners meeting with regard to his earlier assurance he said; **'In view of Mr Purcell's statement, certainly not. Personally I have nothing to say about it'.**

On Wednesday the 5th of May 1926, Mr Churchill commandeered the offices and equipment of the Morning Post and published a Strike bulletin **"The British Gazette".** In retaliation, the T.U.C. took over the Daily Herald offices and equipment and published their version called the **"British Worker".**

Fig. 89 Thursday the 6th of May 1926, Mounted Police in a baton charge at the Elephant and Castle, London where a bus had been set on fire – National Press.

On Thursday the 6th of May 1926, in the House of Commons, Sir John Simon, a highly respected Barrister, made a speech declaring that the General Strike was an **'unlawful act'.** He said that every striker had broken the law and could be sued in the Courts and that every Trade Union leader could be liable in Damages *'to the uttermost farthing of his personal possessions.'*

To Members of Trades Unions.

Work Stoppage by Trades Union Council.

Sir John SIMON, Attorney General under Mr. Asquith, said in the HOUSE of COMMONS, on Thursday, the 6th May, 1926:—

The decision of the Council of the **TRADES UNIONS** Executive to call out **EVERYBODY** regardless of the Contracts which these Workmen had made was not a lawful Act, and every Workman who had come out voluntarily or otherwise had broken the Law.

Every **MAN** who was out in disregard of his Contract was **PERSONALLY** liable to be sued in the County Court.

Every Trade Union Leader who had advised that course of action was liable in **DAMAGES** to the uttermost farthing of his **PERSONAL POSSESSIONS**.

Any Rule laying down that a **TRADE UNIONIST** forfeited his benefits if he did not obey the orders of his Executive meant that he would so forfeit those benefits if the order was lawful.

IT SHOULD BE PLAINLY KNOWN THAT THERE WAS NO COURT IN THIS COUNTRY THAT WOULD UPHOLD A RULE THAT A PERSON WOULD FORFEIT HIS BENEFITS IF HE WAS FORCED TO DO THAT WHICH WAS ILLEGAL.

TO ALL WORKERS IN ALL TRADES
OFFICIAL.

The BRITISH CONSTITUTIONAL GOVERNMENT state that effectual measures will be taken to prevent the Victimization by TRADE UNIONS of any Man who remains at work, either now or in the future, and no man will be left unprotected by the STATE from reprisals.

EDWARD A IND, PRINTER, 101 NORTHGATE, GLOUCESTER

Fig. 90 Sir John Simon's Declaration in the National Press.

Albert Arthur Purcell 1872 – 1935

On Friday evening the 7th of May 1926, Mr Alf Purcell, Forest of Dean M.P. and leader of the Strike Organisation Committee of the General Council, addressed a public meeting at the Gloucester Shire Hall, in which he covered developments on the strike to date including the ongoing negotiations still taking place in London. There was, he said, the possibility that the power workers would join the strike if it was thought necessary and he had heard that the Government had called out the military in London with machine guns mounted on the backs of Lorries. He said he was pleased with the cooperation of the various industries, especially in Gloucester for their support in this dispute and nationally, the numbers now out on strike was 2,750,000 and that by the following Monday, that could increase by another million. Support for the cause, he said, had come from many other countries around the world and that Russia had offered £25,000 and food ships if they could be unloaded by the strikers.

Fig. 91 Forest of Dean M.P. Mr Alf Purcell

Fig. 92 Armoured cars on the streets of London.

Prime Minister Baldwin made the Government's position clear in an article
published in the 'British Gazette' that the strike was the work of anarchists

MESSAGE FROM THE PRIME MINISTER

Constitutional Government is being attacked.

Let all good citizens whose livelihood and labour have thus been put in peril, bear with fortitude and patience the hardships with which they have been so suddenly confronted. Stand behind the Government who are doing their part, confident that you will co-operate in the measures they have undertaken to preserve the liberties and privileges of the people of these islands. The laws of England are the people's birthright. The laws are in your keeping. You have made Parliament their guardian. The General Strike is a challenge to Parliament and is the road to anarchy and ruin.

STANLEY BALDWIN

Fig. 93 Prime Minister Baldwin's Declaration.

In answer to this, the T.U.C. General Council published the following reply in the 'British Worker' on Friday the 7th of May 1926.

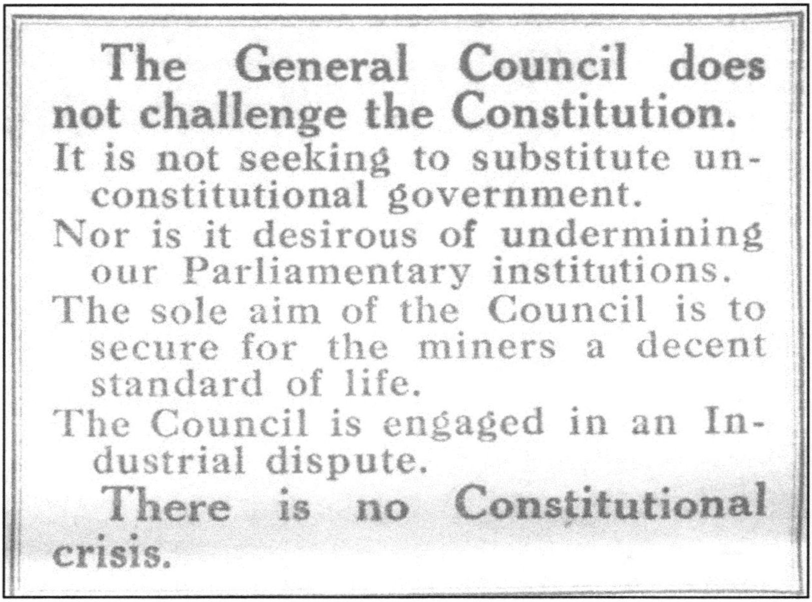

The General Council does not challenge the Constitution.
It is not seeking to substitute un-constitutional government.
Nor is it desirous of undermining our Parliamentary institutions.
The sole aim of the Council is to secure for the miners a decent standard of life.
The Council is engaged in an In-dustrial dispute.
There is no Constitutional crisis.

Fig. 94 The T.U.C. General Council's response.

Sir Herbert Samuel (of the Samuel Commission) hurriedly returned from his holiday in Italy on Thursday the 6th of May 1926 and the next day (7th of May 1926) he had talks with the T.U.C. General Council in which he offered his own personal proposals for a settlement. Copies were also sent to the Government. These became known as the Samuel Memorandum and contained the following proposals;

1. That the General Strike be called off,
2. The subsidy to be renewed while negotiations continued,
3. A National Wages Board with an independent Chairman,
4. No revision of wages without assurance that the Commission's recommendation of reorganisation of the Industry is adopted.

Sir Herbert offered to mediate but insisted that he had acted on his own initiative and had received no authority from the Government and could give no assurances on their behalf. Discussions continued through the weekend of the 8th and 9th of May 1926 and on Monday the 10th of May 1926, a draft of the Samuel Memorandum was put to the Miners' Executive for consideration.

The Miners' Executive of the **MFGB** rejected it making it clear that they would not accept wage cuts and that the Wages Board did not promise to fix wages on a National basis but indicated they were to be fixed on a District basis.

The T.U.C. General Council replied that the miners should consider making some concessions considering that their own members had come out on strike in their support. They emphasised the point by saying that the miners should not ask workers to support them indefinitely without submitting to further negotiations.

By this time, many strike leaders, their wives and Communists in cities and towns up and down the country were being arrested and imprisoned for sedition or riotous behaviour. Members of Organising Committees were also targets for arrest as were prominent members of the **MFGB** such as Mr Noel Ablett, co-author of 'The Miners next Step'. Mr Alf Purcell and Ernest Bevin were also in the firing line as warrants for their arrest were issued. Trains driven by volunteers were involved in accidents killing 4 people at Edinburgh and Bishops Stortford and the Flying Scotsman was derailed near Newcastle due to sabotage.

Fig. 95 Volunteer engine drivers and firemen study the map before setting off with their train.

Meanwhile, the strike began to take firmer hold as more workers joined the stoppage. Textile workers in Paisley, Lancashire and the Midlands came out on strike as their factories closed for the lack of fuel. The T.U.C. General Council issued a strike order to all shipbuilding and engineering workers to be effective from midnight on Tuesday the 11th of May 1926. On the 10th of May 1926 the 'British Worker' announced that; *'All's Well'* and the General Council published a long congratulatory message to all Trade Unionists which ended by saying; *'Stand firm. Be loyal to instructions and trust your leaders'*

General Strike terminated

However, it later became apparent that a different scenario had taken place behind closed doors. On Tuesday the 11th of May 1926 the negotiating Committee of the T.U.C. submitted their final draft of the Samuel Memorandum to their General Council, who agreed with it. Some suggested that the Council members had lost their nerve due to their concern for their own safety from arrest and imprisonment as threatened in Sir John Simon's declaration. At the same time, the **MFGB** Executive Committee by resolution had finally rejected the Memorandum.

And so, the T.U.C. General Council's acceptance of the Memorandum resulted in a decision to sue for peace and asked for a meeting with Prime Minister Baldwin. On Wednesday the 12th of May 1926 at 10 am at No. 10 Downing Street, a delegation including Messrs Pugh, Thomas, Bevin and Citrine from the General Council met with Prime Minister Baldwin and Messrs Worthington, Evans and Birkenhead.

Part of Mr Pugh's opening statement to the Prime Minister read; **'As a result of developments in that direction and the possibilities that we see in getting back to negotiations, and your assurance, speaking for the general community of citizens as a whole, that no stone should be left unturned to get back to negotiations, we are here today, sir, to say that this General Strike is to be terminated forthwith in order that negotiations may proceed, and, we can only hope, may proceed in a manner which will bring about a satisfactory settlement. That is the announcement which my General Council is empowered to make'.**

The Prime Minister responded; **'That is, the General Strike is to be called off forthwith?'** Mr Pugh's reply; **'Forthwith. That means immediately'.**

Fig.96 Pugh, Citrine and Baldwin after calling off the General Strike.

The other members of the Council made conciliatory remarks and clarifications but to all intents and purposes, the Strike was off and the miners were left to carry on the fight on their own. There was no mention of the Samuel Memorandum at that meeting.

A stunned public then heard the noon bulletin from the BBC that declared *'General Strike ceases today'* and confirmation was given by the reading of a message from the King. *'The Nation has just passed through a period of extreme anxiety. It was today announced that the General Strike had been brought to an end. At such a moment it is supremely important to bring together all my people to confront the difficult situation which still remains. This task requires the co-operation of all able bodied and well disposed men in the country. Even with such help, it will be difficult but it will not be impossible.*

Let us forget whatever elements of bitterness the events of the past few days may have created, only remembering how steady and how orderly the country has remained, though severely tested, and forthwith address ourselves to the task of bringing into being a peace which will be lasting because, forgetting the past, it looks only to the future with the hopefulness of a united people'.

Chapter 26
The Lockout - The miners fight on alone

The news of the end of the General Strike came as a shock to the Trade Union movement at a time when the Strike was solid. An explanation was demanded by loyal Unionists who had supported the miners and who were prepared to carry on the fight for justice. The General Council were forced to respond and issued a statement, the first paragraph read; *'The General Council, through the magnificent support and solidarity of the Trade Union Movement, has obtained assurances that a settlement of the mining problem can be secured which justifies them in bringing the general stoppage to an end. Conversations have been proceeding between the General Council representatives and Sir Herbert Samuel, Chairman of the Coal Commission, who returned from Italy for the express purpose of offering his services to try to effect a settlement of the differences in the coal mining industry.'*

On hearing the news that the General Strike had been called off Arthur Cook said; **'so far as the miners are concerned, we stand where we are. We are summoning a Delegate conference for Friday and shall then submit to them a full report of the situation. It will be for the Delegate conference to decide what our future action will be.'**

And so, the miners were left to fight on alone but the expected return to work of their supporting colleagues didn't happen straight away. Apart from the fact that many industries couldn't restart due to the shortage of coal, many employers tried to impose new working conditions such as lower wages and longer working hours on strikers before they returned to work. So they remained on strike – this also applied to the railwaymen who were dismissed by their employers and who would only be taken back with renewed contracts. By Friday the 14th of May 1926, there was no general return to work.

At their Special Conference on Friday the 14th of May 1926 the **MFGB's** response was to query why there were no Samuel Memorandum recommendations included which were the Trade Union's basis for ending the General Strike. Surprisingly the Conference were very magnanimous in spite of the 'let down' by the General Council and expressed their appreciation for the loyalty of the other Unions that had stood by them during the struggle and offered assistance where possible to those who still had difficulties as a result of the Strike. They also learned from the International Miners' Federation that agreement had been reached with each country that no coal would be imported from the Continent.

Another Offer

Prime Minister Baldwin was however quick to bring forward further Government proposals for a settlement and sent a document dated the 14th of May 1926 to the Executive Committee which was received on the Saturday morning the 15th of May 1926. The document contained proposals which the Government considered a basis for a settlement. It included;

1. A £3,000,000 short term subsidy,
2. A wage cut of 10% followed by a further cut after three weeks,
3. No National minimum rate,
4. Settlement by Districts.

The **MFGB's** Executive Committee considered the Baldwin proposals which, in their opinion failed totally to meet their long standing three basic demands. Their reply was predictable and by resolution of the Executive Committee, was delivered to Downing Street on Thursday the 20th of May 1926.

These proposals were also rejected by the Coal Owners who were insistent on the miners working an eight hour day and wage reductions of 10%. They also demanded freedom from political interference.

Meanwhile, Arthur Cook toured the coalfields desperate to keep the men from returning to the pits. His speeches attracted large crowds of striking miners – even some who had already gone back to work. He said; **'We still continue, believing that the whole rank and file will help us all they can. We appeal for financial help wherever possible, and that comrades will still refuse to handle coal so that we may yet secure victory for the miners' wives and children who will live to thank the rank and file of the unions of Great Britain.'** He was in particular praise of the miners' wives and said; **'I put my faith to the women of these coalfields. I cannot pay them too high a tribute. They are canvassing from door to door in the villages where some of the men have signed on. The police take the blacklegs to the pits but the women bring them home. The women shame these men out of scabbing. The women of Nottingham and Derby have broken the Coal Owners. Every worker owes them a debt of fraternal gratitude'.**

Fig.97 Arthur Cook speaking in Sunderland.

Cook, who was a self declared Bolshevik, appealed to the President and Secretary of the Russian Miners' Union for further financial help for the British miners. Later, this effort bore fruit when they launched an appeal on their behalf.

Reaction in the Forest of Dean

The Forest of Dean Miners' Association called another mass meeting at the Speech House on the Sunday morning of the 16th of May when the local press were allowed to be present. As usual, David Organ, President of the Association was in the Chair, supported by the agent Mr Jack Williams. In his opening remarks, David Organ said that; '**the reason for this meeting is to report fully on proceedings that have taken place since our last meeting a week ago and we have found now that there has been a big "let down". No one could say but that those in authority** had had the fullest support of the whole rank and file of the Trade Union movement of this country behind them. The men were solid there was no note of weakness anywhere and nothing so far as disturbance, or showing weakness was concerned. While we were going strong, we find that we have suddenly been let down by those people that hold the reins'.

He went on; 'When we got to the Miners' Conference on Friday, we learnt something more, though I want to say that our own officials did everything they could to bring about a successful issue and while others were pulling the strings, our own people were not directly responsible. It would appear from the remarks of our Federation's President Mr Herbert Smith, that the other fellows had got the "wind up"- they had a fright and the result is that they have called off the General Strike – it is a rotten agreement and we should have an explanation of that. The Prime Minister has placed certain proposals in the hands of the Miners' Conference and the Executive Committee will consider them and meet again next Thursday with their decisions. My contention is that victory, as far as I could see, was in sight and it was only for others to stand firm for a short time longer and they would have had the miners' demands met. I don't know what the ultimate position might be – we might get better terms or we might get worse but in order to hold our own, we have to stiffen in the fight to be put up, especially seeing that other grades of workers are going back, leaving us miners on our own'.

The following Sunday morning, the 23rd of May, they met again in the woods at Speech House and David Organ opened proceedings by saying they were not there to pick over the decisions made by the T.U.C. General Council last week – they all knew where they stood. 'We all deplore the fact that there had been no settlement in our fight, a fight we had never sought. It has not only been imposed upon us by the Coal Owners and the Government combined but as a result of certain action taken by the Trades Union Congress, through which us, as miners are left to fight the war on our own. It might be that we have a long, bitter struggle before us – if we have, we must tighten our belts and endure it. We now have the opportunity of enjoying some of God's fresh air and sunshine and you can go to the 'Guardians'. If any of you is in need, it is your place to swallow your poverty pride and go to the 'Guardians' rather than suffer starvation'.

Continuing his speech, David Organ went on to state; **'We should stick the battle through and if we go down, at least we go down fighting. We must continue the fight in order to obtain the best terms on offer. There are certain rumours that one or two of you think you ought to be back at work and that certain employers are bringing some influence to bear. I want to make an appeal to all you men to stand firm and that no one might go to work at any Colliery throughout the Forest of Dean'.**(hear, hear)

Mr Jack Williams said; **'The General Council of the Trades Union Congress are maintaining silence with regard to their cowardly decision to end the General Strike unconditionally. The silence will however soon be broken by a storm of protest and indignation expressed by the great mass of disgusted workers. There are two facts which the General Council of the T.U.C. will not be able to elude. They have said and continue to say that the Samuel Proposals formed a basis of negotiations with the Government. That was an excuse made by the General Council to cover up their inglorious decision to call off the strike. The miners have it on the authority of Mr Baldwin himself that the Samuel Proposals had no Government authority of any kind and that they were made by Sir Herbert Samuel on his own authority. How could the Samuel Proposals form a basis for negotiation since they were not made by the Government or by a representative of the Government?'**

'The other fact was that in calling off the strike unconditionally, they did something which they can never justify after the many professions they made during the period of the strike. They were told repeatedly that there would be no return to work unless guarantees were given that the strikers would be re-instated. Not a single guarantee have they secured from the Prime Minister or the Employers. The result has been widespread disaffection and disintegration of the workers. The Trades Union Congress has decided to convene a special conference of the Executives of the various Unions to explain away their actions. That again, is not going to satisfy the mass of the workers. They know that the Executives will support the General Council, as many of those comprising the Executives are in the same boat as the General Council itself. What the workers must demand is a special Trades Union Congress where the mass of the workers can express their views'.

He also referred to the money, or lack of it, that was available from the Miners' Association in the form of strike pay. He said; **'the reason why we have no strike pay is because during the 1921 strike, the Association incurred a debt of £23,000, only £8,000 of which has been repaid – so we have a coupon debt. When I became your agent in 1922, your Union membership was 1,300 out of a possible membership of between 6 and 7,000 and has never, on average reached 50% - this means that every other man working in the mines was not paying his Union. How can you now expect to be paid 10 shillings a week and so much per child if you have only been paying 6 pence per week? Thank goodness there are heaps of men in the Forest of Dean who are good Unionists and I glory in them. So don't let us hear any more as to where the money of the Forest of Dean Union has gone because you have had your money's worth every time'.**

He went on **'I now want to ask you to decide how you can spend £1,500 that is coming into the District next week. I am pleased to inform you that the Russian miners have given to the British miners a sum of no less than £270,000, a gift unexampled in the history of Trade Unions. Your Executive Committee have met to consider this but have made no recommendations. There are two ways in which the money can be distributed. We can pay about 5 shillings a man or more just to those who were paying members. It has now been agreed to pay every man whether in the Union or not. This is because the gift is generally intended to help all British miners in their present distress'.**

Russian Money

In fact, Russian money accounted for nearly £400,000 according to Arthur Cook who said **'Thank God for Russia'.** He said that he had received cheques for £270,000 and the Cooperative Societies in Russia had sent £40,000 and the Central Russian Union £70,000. He said that; **'it is a test of sincerity and I have never been ashamed to deal with those who are trying to make the World better'.**

The Government took a dim view of Russian money coming into the country as they said; **'for the purposes of the General Strike'.** In fact they sent a letter to the Soviet Government protesting against the transmission of money to the British Trade Unions – this money was later referred to as **'Russian Gold'.**

However, some strike pay was available from the National Federation – 5 shillings for a miner, 1 shilling for a wife and each child and 2s. 6d. for a youth. Poor law relief was available from the Boards of Guardians at the three offices that served the Forest - Westbury on Severn, Ross on Wye and Monmouth but if work was available for an able bodied applicant, he would not be entitled – he could only qualify if he was physically unfit for work and could produce a Doctors' certificate to prove it. If his dependants were destitute, they at least, could get help. During the month of May 1926, the Guardians were handing out over £500 each week in the form of food vouchers and were concerned as to how long they could continue to pay out. The standard pay out was 10 shillings a week for a wife, 4 shillings for the first child and 2s. 6d. for subsequent children. If the wife's husband was a miner getting either strike pay, "Russian Money" or had a little savings in the bank, this was taken into account before calculating benefit. Relief funds were set up throughout most areas of the Forest and were fully supported by those directly unaffected by the stoppage, the County Education Authority helping by providing school children with free meals 7 days a week.

Alf Purcell Muzzles the Press

Mr Alf Purcell, a prominent member of the General Council of the T.U.C. had been reluctant to explain away the Council's decision to call off the General Strike – as Jack Williams had called; **'a cowardly decision'.** He did however attend a meeting of miners held on Friday the 28th of May 1926 at the Cinderford Palace. This meeting and others were convened by Jack Williams to explain away the recent Government's settlement proposals and was chaired by Mr J. Harris. Jack Williams dealt with those proposals but had to dash off to a meeting at Eastern United concerning blacklegging. Before leaving he did make strong comments over the calling off of the General Strike and the Press were asked to leave before Mr Alf Purcell was called upon to address the meeting. It was stated that Mr Purcell wished his statement to be a private one and so his views on the matter were never recorded.

However, at a similar meeting the next day, a press representative was present but was requested not to take notes. He heard Mr Purcell say that more money in the form of £1,000,000 would shortly be coming from various sources on the Continent and that he totally agreed with money coming from Russia. He said; **'I will go to Timbuctoo for it or down to Hades if there was any possibility of getting some. If the miners are**

confident of receiving a sound backing, I am sure they will never give in to the Coal Owners'.

The meeting then adopted a resolution of confidence in Mr Purcell which was passed unanimously. Jack Williams was nevertheless adamant that calling off the General Strike was a decision taken unanimously by the Council, of which Mr Purcell was one. In view of the difficult circumstances some miners and their families had found themselves in, it was understandable that with the pressures of hunger and despair, some men could be persuaded to go back to the mines.

The Drift back to work

Many had already gone back to work, mainly in the smaller pits such as the Thornton Reekes Colliery at Oldcroft, the Fryers Level at Whitecroft and the Hopewell Drift mine, but there was little sign of a return at the larger ones. Feelings against these men (known as blackleggers) were high but, in keeping with the Union advice, there was little or no violence.

LIVELY SCENES AT A WHITECROFT LEVEL.

◆

EXTRA POLICE IN THE DISTRICT.

As reported below a number of smaller pits on the western side of the Forest continue to work, and although this fact has considerably incensed many of the miners of the district who follow the behest of their Trades Union leaders, until Tuesday nothing of an untoward character occurred. True on occasions large bodies of men have congregated near the pits where the so-called "blacklegs" have been engaged and have remonstrated with them, but the demonstrations have been such that there was no violation of the law.

On Tuesday, however, there were some ugly incidents in the vicinity of Fryer's Level at Saunder's Green, Whitecroft, at which a small number of hands are employed. At 2 o'clock in the afternoon, at which time the men who had been working on the day shift ceased operations, they were met by an angry crowd of men, women and children, estimated to number 200, and were given a very hostile reception. Many of the demonstrators had possessed themselves of old kettles, tins and other "instruments," and as they accompanied the men in the direction of their homes these were vigorously rattled and banged, the din being almost indescribable. Our information is that some distance from the level one of the workmen was assaulted by a portion of the crowd, who followed him right to his home.

There was a repetition of these proceedings when the next shift left at 9 p.m., the opposition on this occasion being even more numerous, and their hostility was again unmistakable. The marked men were booed at, and pieces of turf and other missiles were thrown, one, if not two, of the men being struck.

In consequence of these happenings, together with the fact that much damage has been done to some of the small concerns on the western side of the Forest and particularly in the Coleford area, a number of extra police were drafted into the district on Wednesday morning to assist the local officers in their efforts to afford protection to the pits and to the men employed.

Fig. 98 Report in the Lydney Observer of the Fryers Level incidents.

Some were heckled as they went to or returned from work and there were also some isolated incidents such as the Fryers Level mine near Whitecroft where a crowd of around 200 men, women and children jeered and banged tins when the working men emerged from the pit after a shift. This was repeated for about three days when the police stepped in and escorted the blacklegs to and from the pit. Several protesters were arrested, taken to court and found guilty of public order offences. Other incidents happened near Cinderford and at the True Blue Colliery at Ruardean where stones were thrown and insults shouted at three men leaving the pit. But the police and the courts acted swiftly against those involved.

Jack Williams – Charged

Rumour had it that men were also returning to work at Cannop Colliery for the purpose of getting coal to keep the furnaces fired and the engines going. Jack Williams called a meeting at the Speech House on Wednesday the 16th of June 1926 to discuss the matter and what action to take. Mr Harold Craddock Chaired the meeting in the absence through illness of their President Mr David Organ and who was wished a speedy recovery. Jack Williams firstly said that he was only going to remark briefly on the previous days' procedures in the House of Commons but his main concern was over blacklegging. He was supported on the platform by Mr Arthur Horner an executive member of the South Wales Miners' Federation and a committed Communist. He had just been released from prison for dodging his call-up in WWI and although he was asked to address the meeting, Jack Williams was clear that they should both prevail on the men not to hold a demonstration at Cannop.

However, over 2,000 men voted to march to Cannop and demonstrate against the blacklegs and Jack Williams was obliged to lead the way. They entered the premises and reached that part of the colliery where the blacklegs would come out but were confronted by a Police Inspector from Coleford. He said; **'Mr Williams, this is an unlawful assembly'** to which Jack Williams replied; **'I know it is and I am prepared to take the consequences'** to which the Inspector said; **'I charge you with an unlawful assembly'.**

Jack Williams then addressed the men and asked them to permit him to speak to each blackleg as he came out. He said that he had breached the law and could face imprisonment. The men agreed and he approached each blackleg and asked them to stop work. Serious trouble was thus avoided.

That evening at home in Belle Vue Road, Cinderford, Jack Williams and his wife awaited the knock on the door to take him to prison. But luckily, at the Speech House meeting, a police inspector had been there and had taken notes. It was therefore noted that the Inspector had heard Mr Williams and Mr Horner appeal to the men not to demonstrate and that saved them both from prison.

As was to be expected, there was much acrimony between the **MFGB** and the General Council of the T.U.C. over their termination of the strike. A Conference of Trade Union Executives was arranged for on Friday the 25th of June 1926 in order to try and settle their differences. However, the Government had set wheels in motion to lengthen the miners' working day to eight hours which was eventually wrapped up within the **Coal Mines Act** that received the Royal Assent on the 8th of July 1926. This move which effectively suspended the seven hour day for five years and made permissible the eight hour day, shocked the Unions. Consequently, they immediately decided to delay their differences and to *'bury the hatchet'* for the time being and form a united front to fight the Governments actions.

Miners' Annual Demonstration

On Saturday the 3rd of July 1926, the Forest of Dean miners again held their **Annual Demonstration** at the Speech House field. Although rain threatened the event around midday, the sun eventually shone and the usual attractions of the fun of the fair was accompanied by various selections by the Bream Brass Band. In the afternoon, the meeting was held and due to the size of the crowd, one end of the marquee had to be opened up so that the crowd could see and hear the speakers. On the platform were President Mr David Organ, Mr Alf Purcell M.P., Mr Jack Williams, miners' Agent and Mr S.O. Davies, vice President of the South Wales Miners' Federation and a member of the Executive of the **MFGB**. Other members of the **FODMA** Executive were also present.

In his opening remarks, the President of the **FODMA** David Organ said; **'It is the intention of this beautiful Tory Government to starve us into submission. If they do, they might depend upon it that it would not be for very long because there can be no lengthy settlement until something was done that would give us and every District a decent standard of living and comfort'**(hear, hear). **'There is one point about** it, this is some of the medicine they asked for at the General Election. They put these people into power and gave them a whip to whip us with. I hope that whenever the opportunity presents itself again, we will chuck the lot out and have somebody who understood the needs and aspirations of the working class movement'. (applause).

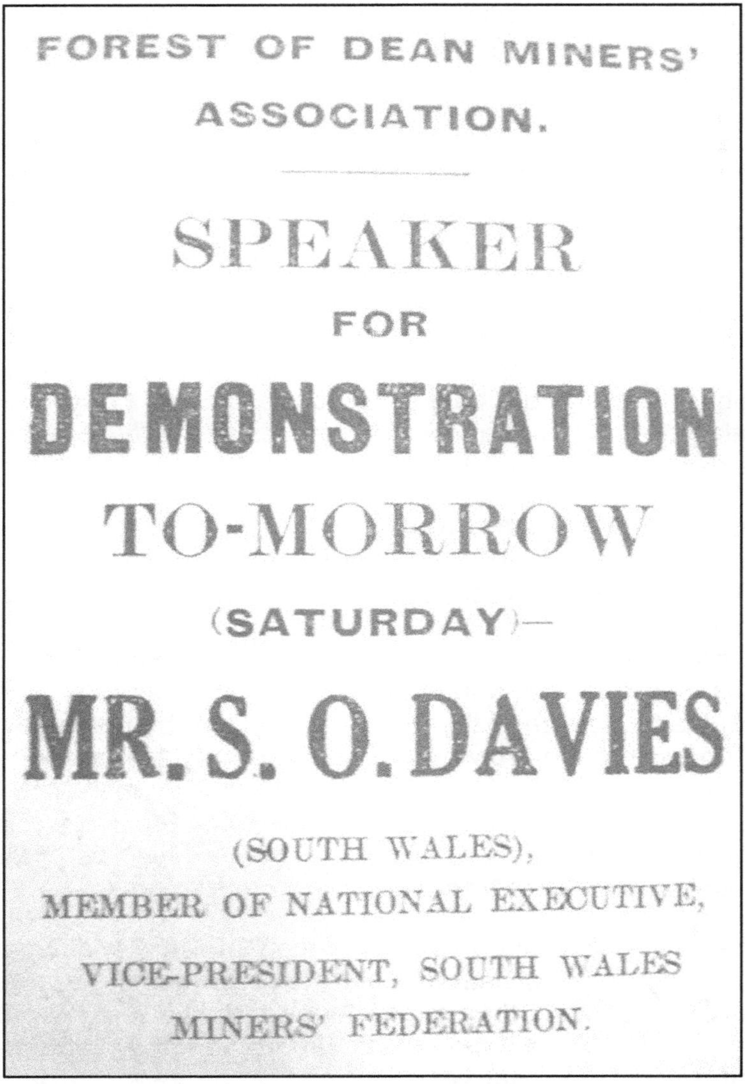

FOREST OF DEAN MINERS'
ASSOCIATION.

SPEAKER

FOR

DEMONSTRATION

TO-MORROW

(SATURDAY)—

MR. S. O. DAVIES

(SOUTH WALES),

MEMBER OF NATIONAL EXECUTIVE,

VICE-PRESIDENT, SOUTH WALES

MINERS' FEDERATION.

Fig. 99 July 1926 Demonstration Poster

Eating Grass

Vice President Mr Harold Craddock, moved the resolution '**That this mass meeting of the Miners of the Forest of Dean adheres to the original demands of the Miners' Federation of Great Britain, namely, no reduction in wages, no District agreements and no increase in hours. This meeting further pledges itself to stand united behind the MFGB in its endeavours to realise the above demands'.** Mr William Hoare from Bream seconded the resolution remarking; '<u>**we will eat the grass off the field rather than submit to 8 hours.'**</u>

This last remark seems to have been taken up by many prominent officials but its origin is still unknown. At another recent meeting, a Miss Hancock of Worcester said that she had been working among the women of Derbyshire who were bravely bearing the hardships of these times. They had said to her; '<u>**Tell the women in the Forest of Dean that we will eat grass before our men shall go back under such conditions'.**</u>

In another incident, Mr Percy Moore, Managing Director of the Princess Royal Colliery asked his driver to stop his car by a group of striking miners on the way down Whitecroft road from Bream. He asked Alan Beverstock when he was going to return to work and Alan replied; '**when you pay us a living wage'.** Mr Moore replied; '<u>**I'll see you all eat grass first'**</u>

Continuing with the **Annual Demonstration**, Mr Davies gave a speech in which he denied there was any division between the **MFGB** National Executives and that the resolution adopted by them last week was passed absolutely unanimously. He said that every member was against both any increase in hours or a reduction in wages. Reports which the Executives received made it perfectly clear that the men were standing absolutely solid. He also remarked that the Executive had discussed the possibility of withdrawing the safety men but no decision on that point had yet been reached.

A New Offer

On Monday the 5th of July 1926, the Coal Owners emboldened by the forthcoming legislation within the **Coal Mines Act,** posted notices informing the men that the collieries would be open under the new terms and conditions. These were an increase from a seven to an eight hour shift (in reality it was eight and a half hours), plus a seven on Saturdays on broadly the same rates of pay – 8 shillings and 3 pence a day - as previous to the strike.

Forest of Dean Miners' Association.

Local Colliery Owners' Proposals.

AN EMERGENCY MASS MEETING

WILL BE HELD ON

SUNDAY NEXT, JULY 11th, 1926,

AT

THE SPEECH HOUSE.

MR. JOHN WILLIAMS (Agent)

Will ADDRESS the Meeting upon the Question of the FOREST OF DEAN COLLIERY OWNERS' PROPOSALS as Posted at the Pit Head.

Chair to be taken at 11 a.m. by MR. D. R. ORGAN.

No Man must sign Contracts as asked by the Employers.

Every Miner is urgently requested to attend.

Fig.100 Notice of the 11ᵗʰ of July 1926 meeting

The **Forest of Dean Miners' Association** called a meeting at the Speech House on Sunday the 11ᵗʰ of July 1926 to discuss these new terms and how to address the issue of blacklegging. On this occasion, President David Organ in his opening address stated that; **'I want you to say that you will not accept the new proposals – we have now suffered 10 weeks of this business and if you are as firm now as you were at the start, we will not accept them'.** (applause). **'We have to make still further sacrifices and win our objective or give up the sponge and**

accept a permanent sacrifice'. Referring to rumours of men   returning to work, he said; **'we know that there are rumours that certain men have signed on at certain Collieries'.** Mr Jack Williams commented; **'you said Mr Chairman that there were certain men – they're not men.'**(applause). David Organ replied **'well, what we call men or what we have called men** (hear, hear). **This is not the first mistake I have made and it won't be the last. These men are endeavouring to sell not only themselves but their wives and families and you and me. All I want to say is that we don't return to work and don't sign any contracts and that we as Forest of Dean miners will be as loyal as any other body of miners in the Federation of Great Britain.'** (applause).

Help for the miners was not forthcoming from the T.U.C. General Council and financial assistance was desperately needed for the starving families. Arthur Cook took the decision with William Richardson and approached the Russian Miners' Union for more help and succeeded in setting up a financial appeal from the Russian miners. At the same time the Labour Women's Fund was making collections on the miners' behalf and contributors were given miniature miners lamps to wear as badges as a token of their loyalty.

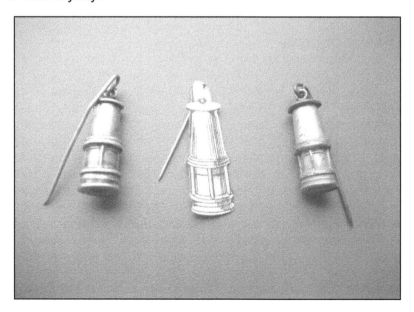

Fig. 101 Miniature miners' lamps worn as a badge by contributors.
Courtesy of Mr Mark Organ

By the end of July 1926, it had become clear that men were returning to work. Figures for the Forest of Dean estimated that about 275 had returned in addition to the safety men already there for maintenance reasons. A Eastern United and Lightmoor 206 returned, at Norchard 47, at New Fancy 20, while Mr Thornton Reekes' Colliery at Oldcroft was fully manned but working the old rate of 7 hours and not eight. The Forest of Dean was not alone as this trend was reflected in other Districts around the country especially in Warwickshire where some miners had also returned to work.

Further mediation in the dispute came from the Archbishop of Canterbury who approached the **MFGB** with proposals based broadly on the Samuel Memorandum. With approval from the **MFGB,** the Church approached the Prime Minister who rejected them out of hand. When some of the mining Districts heard of this approach they were far from happy and requested a Special Conference to debate the matter. At this Conference on the 30th of July 1926, it was decided to put the proposals of the Archbishop to a District vote, the results of which were not made public until mid August. The results showed a small majority for rejection of what became known as 'The Bishops' Memorandum' in which the votes in favour were 333,036 and against were 367,650 – a majority against of 34,614. The Forest of Dean vote of 5,000 was against the Memorandum.

In the Forest of Dean
The Bishops' Memorandum didn't sit well with some Bishops who were not consulted on its contents. The Bishop of Gloucester Dr A.C. Headlam writing a letter in 'The Times' was particularly scathing when he wrote *'MINERS' POSITION INDEFENSIBLE – to many of us the position of the coal miners and their leaders appears to be indefensible, alike economically and morally, and to buy them off with another subsidy is to encourage the worst forms of selfish profiteering. The wages of the miners are among the highest in the country and their hours the shortest. The economic position demands some reduction in wages or lengthening of hours or both. Almost every class of worker in the country has had to submit to a similar reduction. Why then, should not the miners submit to a reduction like other working men, and why should they receive a subsidy which must ultimately come out of the pockets of their fellow workers? What the many people who approach this dispute from a philanthropic and sentimental point of view, fail apparently to see is that the standard of living of the miners is being kept up at the expense of other workers whose standard is already lower.'*

On Sunday the 1st of August 1926, the Forest of Dean Miners' Association held another mass meeting at the Speech House to discuss the Bishop of Gloucester's views. In his opening remarks, the President David Organ said; **'I know that there are some - who we call men - who have returned to work at various places in the Forest of Dean. It is the ambition of the Coal Owners, not only in the Forest of Dean but in the rest of the Districts of the Federation to split up the men into as many sections as possible. Our attitude as miners should be to stand and resist every demand that they make and to stand to the very last ditch before we are prepared to give up** (applause). **If we act in haste, we will repent at our leisure. We see that the Bishop – a poor and solitary man,** (laughter) **said that the miners are a class of people whose hours of work are as short as any and their pay as good** (Oh). **Yet he was a chap in receipt of something like £85 a week. He wants to know why the country should be subsidised to find a decent standard of living for minerals. What I want to know is why the Bishop gets as much in a week as many of us get in 12 months.'** (hear, hear, applause).

Mr Alf Purcell M.P. said; **'While we may regard the situation in the mining industry as black, I don't think that it is anywhere nearly as black as it is painted. In the first place, a fourteen weeks' stand is no mean achievement, and on the statement of the Government itself, not more than 10,000 people in the country up to July the 20th have resumed work out of a million. That is a pretty fair example of solidarity. I ask you all to stand firm and whatever agreement is arrived at, to be a united army. With regard to the Bishop's proposals, if they are not always friendly to us as a working class, I think that they ought to give us the credit for having interested them. The Russians are arranging for a further contribution and I think it is up to everyone to do what they can to help the miners in their continued struggle'.** (applause).

Fig. 102 Eastern United Colliery. Courtesy of the DHC, Soudley, Cinderford.

March against blacklegging

On Wednesday the 4th of August 1926, a march was held in Cinderford to protest against the returning miners at Lightmoor and Eastern United Collieries. Headed by President of the **FODMA** David Organ, Alf Purcell M.P. Jack Williams the miners' Agent, Mr T.H. Etheridge the Association Secretary and Cinderford Town Band, a gathering of around 500 set off from the Town Hall at 5.00 p.m. down Market Street in the direction of Ruspidge. The route was lined with policemen keen to keep the peace but there were no incidents as the procession crossed St White's road and into Ruspidge road where they assembled just beyond the Memorial Hall overlooking the workings of the Eastern United Colliery. There, the road was blocked by policemen so the "Red Flag" was sung, cries of **'are we downhearted'** were made and the assembly turned round and headed back towards Cinderford. They were again met by an enthusiastic crowd in the Triangle and the procession ended in the Cooperative Society's field in Dockham road. The meeting there lasted about two hours and in his opening remarks, David Organ said; **'I am delighted to be here to take part in this demonstration and meeting in protest against those black scabs who are working in some of our mines. It is a thundering shame that there are men who are prepared to assist the employers and the**

Government and the enemy class so far as the working class is concerned and so help to deprive the latter of a decent standard of living and to cripple us through the ages to come' (hear, hear). **'I ask you men who are still with us to stick it out as I am prepared to do to the last and I do not think that we are prepared to allow a small minority to dictate terms to the majority of workmen or we might as well give in'**.(applause). **'I sincerely hope that after this demonstration today, nobody will go to work at Eastern United or Lightmoor Collieries tomorrow morning'.** (applause)

Mr Jack Williams assured the meeting that other demonstrations were going to be held and said; **'I have done my best to stop blacklegging in this District, so much so that I am bordering on shattered nerves. However, be that as it may, every endeavour will be made to stop the vilest thing we can conceive of, namely blacklegging. I am going to ask you all this question 'If men are going to work on an eight hour day, as they are doing in this District and on a reduction in wages, if the Miners' Federation succeeds in securing a seven hour day on a National Agreement and minimum percentage, where does the Forest of Dean District stand?'** ('on its own legs' said a voice from the crowd). **'Do those who are going to work realise that fact? Even if the Federation are defeated in their attempts – and they will not be defeated, I am going to surmise that while there is weakness exhibited in the Forest of Dean, in most other Districts they are solid. If we are going to struggle back to work on an eight hour day on local percentage and local agreement, we would rue the day when we permitted blacklegging.'** (hear, hear). **'It will be better to go back as one army than be completely routed and so be unable to resist any injustice the employers might inflict on us. I want to warn this meeting that you will have a similar or perhaps worse state of things unless you are prepared to show courage and to stick it to the end'.**

The Emergency Powers Act was still in force and many miners were still being arrested and charged for minor offences with either a hefty fine or imprisonment as a result. Many had resorted to poaching or scavenging for coal (outcropping) where coal seams breached the surface or from coal waste tips. Hunger was now an additional enemy and with the three Forest of Dean Guardians having run out of money, families were becoming desperate. So much so that at Westbury on Severn a crowd of around 500 men and women gathered outside the Workhouse in protest. In spite of their hardships, the gathering was good humoured with the singing of hymns such as *'Bread of Heaven'* and *'Guide me o thou great Jehovah'* followed by *'The Red Flag'.*

The Westbury Protest

This loud demonstration however didn't change the minds of the Board of Guardians. At the instigation of Jack Williams and Charlie Mason, a member of the Guardians, at 5 o'clock on Friday afternoon the 7th of August 1926, miners wives and children not getting out-relief were encouraged to assemble at the Town Hall in Cinderford and proceed in an orderly fashion to the Poor Law Institution (the workhouse) at Westbury on Severn, with a view to being admitted as inmates. A scene unprecedented in the Forest of Dean was witnessed when 296 women and children from Cinderford and Ruardean Hill boarded buses that left the Triangle at 5.00p.m.. Arriving at the workhouse, they were met by the Master and Matron Mr and Mrs Scriven who had made every possible arrangement for their accommodation.

Mothers were allowed to stay with their children but they had to submit to the rules and dietary code of the Institution. Although some were not prepared for this, they did admit to being given a good dinner on the Saturday. On the Saturday morning they were paid a visit by the Chairman of the Board of Guardians – none other than Mr George Rowlinson – the ex-miners' Agent who was concerned for their welfare.

Difficulties arose when dealing with so many people at once and it was decided that they leave the Institution during Saturday afternoon and early evening – some walked back to Cinderford while the majority were bussed back. All were received at the Town Hall by a cheering crowd that had gathered to see them safely back and tea was laid on for them.

By mid August 1926, the local press published what they believed was the true number of miners returning to work in the Forest of Dean;

Eastern United 260,
Lightmoor 272
Norchard 75,
Waterloo (Arthur and Edward) 28,
New Regulator, Cinderford 14,
Slope, Drybrook 13,
New Fancy, Parkend 15,

Oldcroft -Thornton Reekes 43
Total .... 720.

While the strike continued, more men returned to the pits in the following weeks and by the end of August 1926 the number had gone up to 850. It was now obvious that the strike was gradually collapsing – due largely to the lack of money to buy essentials, like food. The national press carried large notices to the miners, sponsored by the Coal Owners' Association, pointing out the financial situation and the losses they have incurred. The notices were obviously an attempt to drive a wedge between the men and their Union, urging a return to work and pointing out the futility of struggling on.

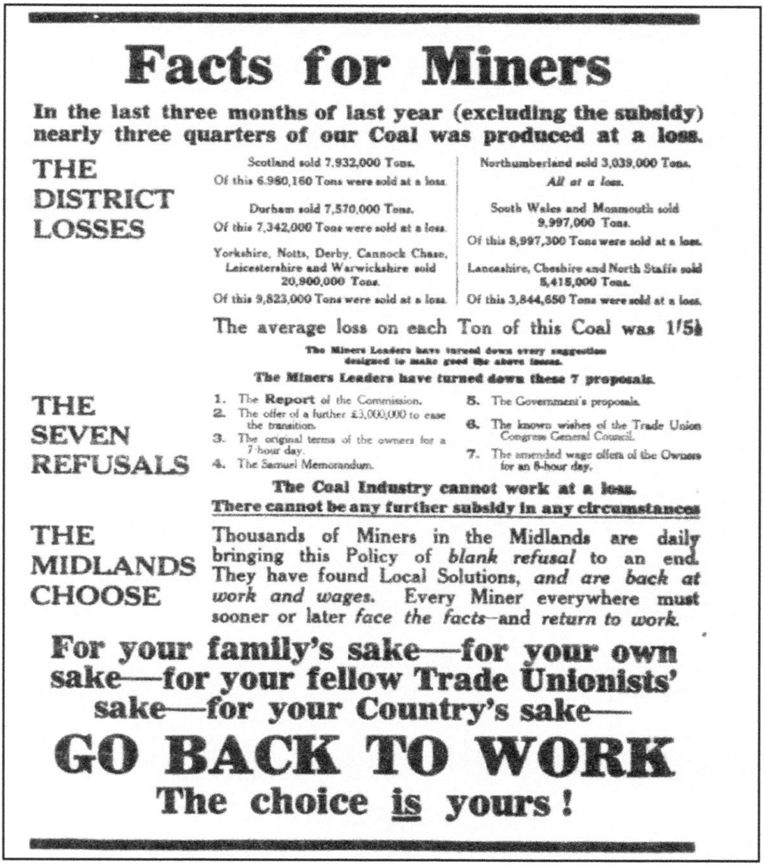

Facts for Miners

In the last three months of last year (excluding the subsidy) nearly three quarters of our Coal was produced at a loss.

THE DISTRICT LOSSES

Scotland sold 7,932,000 Tons.
Of this 6,980,160 Tons were sold at a loss.

Durham sold 7,570,000 Tons.
Of this 7,342,000 Tons were sold at a loss.

Yorkshire, Notts, Derby, Cannock Chase, Leicestershire and Warwickshire sold 20,900,000 Tons.
Of this 9,823,000 Tons were sold at a loss.

Northumberland sold 3,039,000 Tons.
All at a loss.

South Wales and Monmouth sold 9,997,000 Tons.
Of this 8,997,300 Tons were sold at a loss.

Lancashire, Cheshire and North Staffs sold 5,415,000 Tons.
Of this 3,844,650 Tons were sold at a loss.

The average loss on each Ton of this Coal was 1/5½

The Miners Leaders have turned down every suggestion designed to make good the above losses.

The Miners Leaders have turned down these 7 proposals.

THE SEVEN REFUSALS

1. The **Report** of the Commission.
2. The offer of a further £3,000,000 to ease the transition.
3. The original terms of the owners for a 7-hour day.
4. The Samuel Memorandum.
5. The Government's proposals.
6. The known wishes of the Trade Union Congress General Council.
7. The amended wage offers of the Owners for an 8-hour day.

The Coal Industry cannot work at a loss.
There cannot be any further subsidy in any circumstances

THE MIDLANDS CHOOSE

Thousands of Miners in the Midlands are daily bringing this Policy of *blank refusal* to an end. They have found Local Solutions, *and are back at work and wages.* Every Miner everywhere must sooner or later *face the facts*—and *return to work.*

For your family's sake—for your own sake—for your fellow Trade Unionists' sake—for your Country's sake—

GO BACK TO WORK

The choice is yours!

Fig.103 Coal Owners' propaganda notice.

Delegation to Russia

With strike funds drying up, Delegations from the **MFGB** were sent to the United States, Europe and the Soviet Union to appeal for their help in raising much needed relief funds. On hearing this, Prime Minister Baldwin published a message in the United States press declaring that there was no hardship or destitution among the miners – obviously aimed at scuttling the fund raising Delegation. It was rumoured that Mr Alf Purcell would be among the Delegation to the United States but this was emphatically denied by his wife.

The Delegation to the Soviet Union consisted of 10 men and 8 women, one from each of several mining Districts – including Mrs Cook, wife of Mr Arthur Cook - the Forest of Dean District being represented by the President of the Forest of Dean Miners' Association Mr David Organ. They set off by ship from Stepney, London on Friday the 27th of August 1926 and arrived via the Kiel Canal at Leningrad on the following Thursday morning the 2nd of September 1926. There, the party were shipped ashore from the main ship by small open boats. From there they travelled by train to Moscow where they were enthusiastically welcomed by representatives of the Russian Miners' Union.

Fig. 104 Delegates arriving at Moscow railway station

Their campaign took them on to several cities including Tutla, Kharkov, Artemovsk, Krasnogorsk, Shterovka, Gorlovka, Skakhta, Rostov, Kislovodsk, Grosny and Baku. Before the Delegation sailed for home, the Miners' Union of the U.S.S.R. presented each member with an album of photographs as a memento of their visit to Russia – some of which are reproduced here.

Fig. 105 Moscow – meeting at the Miners Executive

During this mission the Presidium of the U.S.S.R. Central Committee of the Trade Unions passed a proposal on the 31st of August 1926 to contribute 1% from the wages of all Trade Unionists towards the British miners struggle.

Fig. 106 Vlassovka Anthracite Pit – Shakhta (Donbas)

On the 4th of September 1926 the Presidium also resolved to transfer to the Executive Committee of the **MFGB**, money that was then on hand of ⁏ million rubles. In total, the overall contribution from Russia to the British miners was £986,000 – a colossal amount of money at that time and more than half the overall total amount received during the struggle.

Dilke Memorial Hospital
Building work on the new hospital extension had been going on for two years and during that time subscriptions had poured in from many local institutions and voluntary work carried out by an army of dedicated men and women – Friends of the Hospital.

As reported on earlier, a ceremony to lay two foundation stones was held in October 1925 where Miss Lisa Crawshay laid the first stone in memory of her brother Mr Edwin Crawshay and the second was laid by Mr C.A.J. Hale on behalf of the Forest of Dean Miners Welfare Fund.

By March 1926, work had advanced to the stage where it was predicted that the new extension could be ready for an official opening on the third anniversary of the original building, which would be at the end of June 1926.

However, there were certain delays but the buildings were eventually completed and the official opening ceremony was carried out on a rather wet Thursday afternoon the 2nd of September 1926. The weather didn't prevent a large number of people attending the special event which was preceded by prayers, a bible reading and a hymn.

Fig. 107 The new extension to the Dilke Memorial Hospital

The Chairman Mr J.J. Joynes in his opening remarks thanked the Committee for all their hard work in making the day possible and said that they originally thought that the hospital would be of main benefit to the mining community but it had been found that it had appealed to a much wider community and had subsequently outgrown its original buildings. The new extension provided for an additional 13 beds – from the original 18 to 31.

Mr George Rowlinson the Committee's Hon. Secretary who admitted that he was in poor health gave details of the finances and said he was pleased that they had raised £23,000 and thought that with the combined beds at Dilke, Gloucester, Lydney, Ross and Monmouth, that they now had sufficient beds to meet the needs of the district for some time to come. He said that they had originally hoped to complete the extension for around £5,000 but found later that it needed to be £6,300. They were £15 in dep but there were more bills to come in and that by the end of the year they could be around £850 in debt. He said that had it not been for the industria trouble where they had lost around £500, they would not now be in debt He appealed to those who could contribute to do so and suggested that the miners' weekly contributions could be raised by half a penny for a matter of six or twelve months. Mr Rowlinson went on to praise those who had already made contributions and mentioned Miss Crawshay who had contributed £1,000 and the Miners Welfare Fund for £2,500.

Miss Lisa Crawshaw then gave a speech and proceeded to open the new building. Miss Gerturde Tuckwell, neice of Sir Charles Dilke then accepted the extension and made a speech. Other dignitaries also made speeches and tea was then served in a large marquee where stalls were selling articles and a motor car was sold which raised £65. Also attending were the Ruspidge Male Voice Choir and the Cinderford Excelcior Band, both of which offered renditions during the afternoon.

The extension, which was joined to the original building by a covered corridor, comprised an additional 13 beds making a total of 31, a children's ward, an X-ray operating room with its necessary equipment for developing, improved casualty ward, additional private wards, accommodation for out-patients, bedroom accommodation for nurses and maids, a Board Room and a Porters Lodge for the Porter and machinery attendant. Electric light was supplied to all buildings. Builders for the project were Messrs Powell and Giles and the plans were drawn up by Mr W. Whitehouse of Cinderford.

Fig. 108 *View of 'The Dilke' today – c. 2023 – Photo Author*

Nationally – Prime Minister Baldwin's Proposals

The same day that the Russian Delegation reached Leningrad (2nd of September 1926), the **MFGB** held a Conference to decide their next step. August meetings between the Union, Coal Owners and Government had proved negative with each side sticking rigidly to their demands. Union funds were now running low and it had been calculated that at that time they were only able to pay out 1s. 8d. per head per week. Income had so far totalled £879,578 11s. 8d with over half, £517,000, coming from Soviet Russia.

Men were also returning to work but the numbers varied from District to District. Figures showed that 36,785 – less than 5% of the Federation membership – had returned. In the Forest of Dean the number of men returning was 850 out of a workforce of over 6,000 – around 14%.

The Conference agreed to pursue further negotiations and wrote to Winston Churchill, who was standing in for the Prime Minister who was abroad. Their letter stated; *'I beg to inform you that the Executive Committee and the Special Delegate Conference of the Miners Federation, having again carefully considered the present deadlock in the mining dispute, have resolved to ask you to convene and attend a Conference of the Mining Association and the Federation. We are prepared to enter into negotiations for a new National Agreement with a view to a reduction i labour costs to meet the immediate necessities of the Industry'* signe 'Yours faithfully, A.J. Cook, Secretary.'

Winston Churchill approached the Coal Owners' Association with thi initiative from the miners but they refused to discuss the matter. Churchi tried hard to bring both sides together but when Prime Minister Baldwir returned from holiday in mid September, the Churchill initiative wa dropped. Instead, on the 17th of September, Prime Minister Baldwin laid ou his own proposals in the form of a Memorandum offering three mair provisions;

1. A National Arbitration Tribunal to consider and make decisions or terms set out by District settlements.
2. Any provisional settlement involving working more than the ol hours may be referred to the Tribunal for review.
3. The Tribunal shall confirm or modify a provisional settlement whicl would entitle every man affected and working more than the ol hours to be entitled by law to receive wages in accordance with the Tribunal's decision.

Again, the **MFGB** Executive committee turned down these proposals bu on the evening of the 21st of September 1926 they again met with Prime Minister Baldwin and offered to return to work if their own modifiec proposals were accepted. These were;

1. Return to work at wages prevailing under the 1921 Agreement,
2. The terms of a National Wage Agreement to be referred to ar Independent Tribunal,
3. Tribunal to consider putting into effect the recommendations of the Samuel Commission.

It took three days for the Prime Minister to reply and to dismiss these proposals.

Forest of Dean

Early September 1926 saw a gradual return to work in several of the Cinderford area collieries but more specifically at Eastern United, Lightmoor and Foxes Bridge. None, apart from safety men had returned to Crump Meadow, Waterloo, New Fancy and Norchard.

Around 166 men had signed on to resume work at Cannop Colliery and by Monday the 6th of September 1926, the Colliery officially reopened as 238 men were now signed on to work including safety men. Reports said that there was no picketing and apart from the patrolling mounted police, there was little to indicate that anything unusual was happening. On the road to Broadwell, groups of men and women had gathered as a bus, loaded with miners returning to their homes, climbed the hill. However, there was no disorder and the men walked to their homes without trouble.

By the 21st of September 1926, the situation had changed and it was reported that 1,754 men were working on the Owners' terms of no reduction in wages for working an 8 hour day. A few days later the number had gone up to 2,355 with men returning to work at Norchard. Jack Williams, desperate to halt the collapse of the strike and stem the flow of a return to work in the Forest of Dean, held meetings in Bream, Ruardean and Cinderford where he was always enthusiastically received. Those miners who had already signed on also attended the meetings and there appeared to be no bitterness or animosity between the two parties. It was now obvious that the strike was gradually collapsing – due largely to the lack of money to buy food and other essentials – and that allegiance to the Federation came way down the list of priorities.

Outcropping

During those hard times, a practice known as outcropping was proving very popular. At many points in the Forest where coal seams were just under or even breached the surface, many families took advantage of this gift and free coal was there for those who wished to collect it. Other sites such as slag heaps where a mixture of earth, clay and coal had been dumped due to contamination were a rich source of the black gold. The Deputy Gaveller decreed that no royalties need be paid if the coal got was used for home consumption only. Some of the open excavations proved somewhat dangerous and risks were taken as to the degree of timbering needed - at least two persons were killed while outcropping.

At an outcropping site to the south of Speech House at what was known as the Oaken and Churchway Gale in Russell's Wood locally known as the 'Wet 'ood' near to the New Fancy Colliery, one Welsh miner was killed by a fall of earth which caused him to suffocate. The Gale had been transferred by Mr Sidney Taylor and Mr Gerald Thompson on the 7th of January 1924 to a London registered syndicate known as the 'O and C'

Syndicate Ltd. The outcroppers were striking Welsh miners who were operating independently until the O and C made them an offer of between 18 and 20 shillings per ton of coal – far above the rate offered by the Coal Owners. According to the Deputy Gaveller, as the men were working for Company, royalties were owed and so there was a contravention of the **Mines Act of 1841**. At the Inquiry into the man's death, 'O and C' were found liable, owing to their neglect in not complying with the rules and regulations of the said **Mines Act of 1841.**

At another site near Steam Mills, Cinderford where men were cutting down trees to support their excavations, several young children were with them collecting firewood. When two boys dropped a log they were carrying, a six and a half year old lad who had been walking unseen underneath the log was struck on the head. He died later that same day from injuries to the base of the skull.

Arthur Cook's visit to the Forest

The **FODMA** made a request to the Federation for Arthur Cook to visit the area and meet with the men. This was arranged and Mr Cook arrived at the Speech House on Sunday afternoon the 26th of September 1926. Vice President Mr Harold Craddock presided and with him were Mr Alf Purcell M.P. and Mr Jack Williams the miners' Agent. In a thunderstorm accompanied by hail and snow and where lightning felled a nearby tree, Mr Cook gave an inspiring speech to around 3,000 miners. Among other topics, he said; **'The stand that the miners are taking is a necessary one. We are attacked and self preservation is the first law of life. I want peace and no man has counselled the miners to keep cool more than I have. The Eight Hour Act has been a great hindrance to peace in the Industry. We have had to fight all the powers of the State and we cannot underestimate that. If private Capitalism were to retain the coal industry, wages would have to be reduced and hours extended.'** He also declared that his views could change but if he felt that he could not carry out the decision of the majority, he would clear out.

Fig. 109 Mr Arthur Cook speaking at the Speech House

He said; 'The men are going back to work in some places on an eight hour day and stabbing our leaders in the back. Our leaders are bound to face the situation and bound to realise that men are going back on Owners' terms. Mr Baldwin said to us at the Downing Street interview, 'If you put forward proposals that are honourable and just, the Government will stand by them'. We have put forward our present proposals and we expected a proper reply to them. Let the Prime Minister tell the House of Commons today whether he thinks the miners' sacrifices are enough or whether he wants them to go lower down to starvation and degradation'.

'I make no apology in the 22nd week of the struggle for the slogan 'not a penny off the pay, not a second on the day'. We have reached the limit of our concessions. I would rather have every pit closed down than that the men should go back on longer hours and lower wages. We have our difficulties. We have to face our own people who are stabbing us in the back. A National Conference is called for next Wednesday so let the rank and file decide. I am prepared to ballot the men who have gone back as to whether they want longer hours or lower wages. We will face the position with a view of keeping the coalfields together and the Federation intact, because that is all important. We will face it with a view to going back together as one body, as we came out together. I want no resumption of work until there has been a ballot vote on the terms on which it is proposed work should be resumed'.

At Radstock on the Saturday, Mr Cook had declared; 'It is a bad job for the nation that the present Prime Minister is a Coal Owner and if Mr Churchill had been left alone without interference from Mr Baldwin there would have been an agreement by now. I am sorry that the miners did not accept the advice of their leaders and endorse the peace proposals of the Bishops and the Churches. The rejection of those proposals was a very grave mistake'.

There was of course an alternative view to that of Mr Cook. His predecessor as Secretary of the **MFGB** Mr Frank Hodges, who was then Secretary of the International Miners' Federation, stated this same week that; '**I think Mr Cook will be the first to go, once the men know how he has fooled them. This, from my point of view is no ordinary personal quarrel. By means of this rejoinder, I hope to reach the ears and minds of our men whose interests are being daily sacrificed upon the altar of Cookism and incompetence. After 21 weeks, the miners' leaders, whom the men pay to lead them, now plead for what they rejected before the stoppage. For what they plead now, the General Council could have got for the asking without one moment's stoppage. This is a gross betrayal of the men's trust – the veriest travesty of leadership'.**

Nationally

There was equal criticism from various members of the public. On the 2nd of October 1926 one such opinion in a national newspaper read; '**The Emergency Act is still in force and several men have been imprisoned for breaking the law, receiving a few weeks' detention. Surely Mr Cook is as bad as any of these offenders. Why not give this agitator the choice of Pentonville or to go for his postponed holiday to his friends in Russia, while the weather gets colder and we are coal-less? District settlements are absolutely necessary; Durham and Northumberland men freely say so and yet they do as Mr Cook orders. He is a prize-winner of sheep-dog trials until balloting is permitted on the question of going back or staying where they are'.**

As Mr Cook implied at the Speech House, the **MFGB** special Conference was held on Wednesday and Thursday the 29th and 30th of September 1926 after Prime Minister Baldwin had dismissed their proposals of the 21st of September 1926. Having reviewed the numbers of men returning to the pits (which was 81,178 nationally), it was decided to call a ballot of the membership as to whether they would accept the Government proposals of the 17th of September 1926. To put pressure on the miners, the Prime Minister had sent a letter on the eve of that Conference saying that their offer would be withdrawn if they decided against their proposals.

The ballot result, announced at a Delegate Conference on the 7th of October 1926 was against the proposals by a vote of 737,000 to 42,000. This prompted the Conference to harden their resolve and to vote on a South Wales Federation resolution to;

1. call out the safety men,
2. to call for an embargo on imported coal,
3. to ask the Trade Unions to introduce a levy for financial help,
4. to ban the practice of 'outcropping'.

The resolution was carried by 589,000 to 199,000

It was agreed that before this resolution could be acted upon, it had to be balloted in each District. The result was announced on Friday the 15th of October 1926;

For the resolution 460,150,
Against the resolution .... 284,336.
Majority in favour .... 175,814.

And so the new policy was approved.

Those Districts voting against were Yorkshire, Nottinghamshire, Leicestershire, Northumberland and the Midlands. Although a later ballot in Nottinghamshire agreed to abide by the **MFGB's** policy and withdrew all men who had returned to work.

The Forest of Dean miners voted for the resolution.
Of course, in order for this new policy to be successful, the **MFGB** needed the cooperation of the T.U.C. General Council. They met with Prime Minister Baldwin on October the 26th 1926 who said that he was still prepared to abide by his 17th of September offer of District Settlements and a National Tribunal if the T.U.C. would mediate. They in turn reported back to the **MFGB** who emphasised they would stick to their revised policy.

At their meeting on the 2nd and 3rd of November 1926, the T.U.C. made a decision that they were unable to co-operate with the **MFGB** on an embargo on imported coal but would agree to a voluntary levy of at least one penny per day from all of its members until the dispute came to an end. They also agreed to give the miners an immediate donation of £10,000 out of Congress funds.

Forest of Dean

During October 1926, the numbers of men returning to the pits increased from 2,715 at the first weekend to over 4,000 by the beginning of November 1926. These figures exclude around 550 safety men who were already working. These figures were reflected nationally where the numbers of returning miners had reached 237,547 by the 10th of November 1926. Mr Arthur Cook's visit to the Speech House did nothing to stop the flow of men returning to work and the **MFGB** even sent an envoy in the person of Mr Vernon Hartshorn M.P. to the Forest to try and stem the tide. He was at some time earlier, the fiery leader of the South Wales Miners' Federation but had now become a Labour M.P. However, his efforts came to nothing and he briskly retreated back to London.

Jack Williams was so determined to keep men from returning to work that at the beginning of October 1926 he persuaded the **FODMA** to set an example to expel its members who had gone back to work. A number of men were involved including Harry Hale and Dan James, both checkweighmen at Lightmoor Colliery and Frank Matthews who was a checkweighman at Cannop.

By the end of October 1926 all collieries in the Forest were working the same number of shifts as before the strike began and at the Crawshay's Cinderford collieries, the 1,300 returning miners were given a bonus of £1 per week – boys getting 10shillings.

The Lydney Tinplate Works which had been idle due to lack of coal and steel bars were able to restart production during the first week of November 1926. Steel had been secured in small quantities from the Continent and a load of 5,000 tons of coal had arrived at Sharpness docks from America. Local coal was only available on a hand to mouth principle but nevertheless they were able to take on 500 men and start up eight rolling mills.

Nationally

When, on the 29th and 30th of September 1926, the **MFGB** had adopted their latest policy, the Government tightened up their control by means of the Emergency Powers Act, intent on creating a further division between miners and their leaders. Union leaders such as Arthur Cook and Herbert Smith were banned by police from holding public meetings and reinforcements were called in to quell any disturbances. However, when a deputation comprising representatives of the T.U.C., Labour M.P.'s and the Miners' Federation met with the Home Secretary on the 3rd of November 1926, they were assured that there was no general ban applied to meetings addressed by officials of the Miners' Federation.

At the beginning of November 278,130 miners had returned to work. The Nottinghamshire, Derbyshire and the Midlands, miners had been returning to work since the middle of August with numbers as high as 21,500 in August 1926 and 60,600 by the end of September 1926. In one of the Nottinghamshire Districts, a return to work at the Digby pit was encouraged by a local Labour M.P. George Spencer who was subsequently hauled before a meeting of the **MFGB** to answer for his actions. Amid a barrage of abuse, he managed to qualify his actions at the Delegate meeting on October the 7th 1926 and ended by saying; **'I don't regret it and I do not plead extenuating circumstances. I believe I did the best day's work in my life for these men and you can pass your sentence'.** He was accused of being a 'blackleg' by persuading men to defy the Federation and return to work. He was then duly voted out of the Conference by an overwhelming majority. On the 15th of October 1926 when the results of a ballot of Nottinghamshire miners as to whether they were in favour of abiding by the **MFGB's** policy against 'blacklegging' and withdraw from the pits, there was a majority of 11,456 in favour. Consequently, the Nottinghamshire Miners' Association suspended 25 of its Delegates including Mr George Spencer M.P. However, not to be discouraged, Spencer and the suspended Delegates were already negotiating with their local Coal Owners on terms for a return to work.

Memorandum of Settlement

It was now more than obvious that the strike was collapsing and with no support from the T.U.C. to force an embargo on imported coal, the **MFGB** was forced to consider a compromise. On Friday the 5th of November 1926 they asked the T.U.C. mediation committee to let the Government know that they were prepared to accept District Settlements subject to certain principles being satisfactory. This was relayed to the Prime Minister and talks continued between the parties. Eventually the Government produce 'the General Principles which the Coal Owners are prepared to follow There were four General Principles but they were not favourable to th **MFGB** who rejected them saying that they contained no safeguards fo national principles or co-ordinating District Agreements. They als contained no reference to working hours. Talks continued between th parties but eventually ended in deadlock.

Eventually, on Thursday the 11th of November 1926, the **MFGB** Specia Conference authorised their Executive Committee to continue negotiation 'unfettered'. On Friday the 12th of November 1926 the Government issue a **'Memorandum of Settlement'** which outlined the terms for a return t work. When details were analysed, the Conference decided to ask th Districts their decision as to whether they were a basis for settlement. The voted to accept.

The miners themselves however, rejected the terms by a vote of 460,80 to 313,200 so the Conference decided to recommend all their Districts t open their own negotiations with the Coal Owners subject to guidelines or the general principles sent out by the Conference. Districts were als advised not to commit themselves to a settlement until Conference ha received reports of negotiations from all Districts. The reports were in or Friday the 26th of November 1926 but not all were satisfactory to the **MFGB** Conference so they declined to approve settlements that included longe working hours.

Eventually consent was given for Districts to make their own agreements with the Coal Owners and by Monday the 29th of November 1926, most coalfields were back at work. South Wales Yorkshire and Durham stayed out but by Tuesday the 30th of November 1926, all had returned to work.

Forest of Dean
In the Forest of Dean 5,002 men had signed on but only 4,515 were working out of an original 6,520 - the 487 had yet to be found jobs. During November 1926 the **FODMA** expelled two more of their loyal members for defying the Union policy by returning to work. Enos Taylor was on the Finance Committee of the **FODMA** and a loyal and prominent member of the Union. He was a checkweighman at Foxes Bridge Colliery. The other was Ernest Brain, a member of the Political Committee who was also a checkweighman at Foxes Bridge.

The Coal Owners would not negotiate a local settlement with those who had not already signed on for work and so around 1,500 men including the **FODMA** representatives were not only excluded from talks, but also from returning to their jobs.

On Wednesday the 8th of December 1926 a meeting was finally arranged at the Speech House between the Coal Owners and representatives of the miners who were at work, led by Jack Williams. In the room the atmosphere was frosty and the Coal Owners asked the men to state their case. Jack Williams requested a seven hour day or seven and a half if possible and would accept a lower minimum wage for a shorter working day. He also requested the reinstatement of the men still unemployed.

The Coal Owners insisted on an eight hour day but conceded seven hours on Saturdays. This was promised with a review after three years. Skilled miners' wages per shift were to be 60% on the 1921 Standard or 9s. 10.5d. for December 1926 and January 1927, 50% for February 1927 or 9s. 3.5d., 40% for March 1927 or 8s. 8d., 33% for April 1927 or 8s. 3d. per shift - being the pre-strike rate for a seven hour day. Thereafter, wages were to be governed by District ascertainments. The minimum wage was set at 25% above the 1921 Standard for an eight hour day. No concessions or promises of safeguards against victimisation were given in respect of the unemployed men.

The Coal Owners wanted an agreement signed that day but Jack Williams argued for time to consult the miners with a recommendation for approval. The miners' representatives were given six days in which to agree to the proposals.

 On a raw and foggy Sunday morning the 12th of December 1926 at the Speech House, the **FODMA** President David Organ and the Agent Jack Williams addressed a crowd of no more than 450 of the 6,500 men involved in the dispute. In his opening address, the President of the **FODMA** said; **'Having failed in our attempt to secure a national agreement, negotiations for a District settlement have been going on in the Forest of Dean this past week and we have called this meeting to ask for an endorsement of the best arrangement we can make. The Executive of the Forest of Dean Miners' Association was ignored so far as the making of that agreement and the negotiations were conducted by our Agent and representatives of the men actually in employment at the several collieries. The terms arrived at have been submitted to the**

Executive and that body had no other alternative than to strongly recommend the acceptance of the terms, distasteful as they are. We have been forced into a position of having to make terms with people who have held a cudgel in their hands and it is just a matter of having to accept what they like to enforce upon us'.

Jack Williams said; **'We have arrived at the last stage in the gallant and tragic struggle which the miners of the Forest of Dean have been engaged in for seven months. We met the Owners last Wednesday not however the members of the Executive of the Miners' Association but representatives of the men at work and myself. The terms are distasteful to the men who, at the beginning of May had embarked on a struggle to avoid worse terms than they were then working under'.**

He explained the terms of the agreement yet to be signed and said that around 1,500 men would be excluded from the agreement which included all but two of the Executive Committee of the **FODMA** although some may be taken on as the Owners see fit. He said; **'In no important respect has it been possible to secure amendments favourable to the men. Yet although this District is one of the poorest, these terms are actually better than in some areas'.**

There was an almost unanimous vote to accept the terms of the settlement.

The agreement was eventually ratified at another rather frosty meeting, again at the Speech House on Wednesday evening the 15th of December 1926 and so, after seven months of struggle and near starvation, the miners returned to work unbowed but under an agreement they had fought hard against.

Accidents/Fatalities

On Friday the 8th of January 1926, Mr James Matthews aged 33, a collier from Cinderford, died of injuries received while working at the Harrow Hill Colliery on the 17th of February 1923. On that day, Mr Matthews received injuries to his spine that caused paralysis below the waist. Since that date he had been confined to his bed and attended to regularly by District Nurses who had done all that was possible for him. He died as a result of his injuries and the Coroner recorded that verdict.

On Wednesday the 3rd of February 1926, Mr George Parsons of Ruardean, a collier aged 63 and married with four children was killed by a fall of rock and earth while working underground at the True Blue Colliery near

Ruardean. Mr Parsons was reported to have been a keen sportsman and rugby player and was allegedly concerned in the affair of the killing of two performing bears belonging to a Frenchman in April 1889.

A sad story – but linked to the search for coal.

On Tuesday the 7th of September 1926, a boy named as Joseph Harry James Blake aged six and a half and from Newtown, Steam Mills died from his injuries, received while helping others in the work of outcropping. An Inquest held at Steam Mills heard that Joseph Blake with his brother Peter and two or three other children were at a plantation near Nofold Green on Monday the 6th of September 1926 where four men were cutting down trees for timber for their outcrop pit nearby. The children were collecting small sticks for firewood and one of the men went off carrying a log by himself. Three of the children also hefted a log weighing about two and a half hundredweight onto their shoulders and marched off to the pit. When they arrived there, they dropped the log to the ground but soon found the child Joseph Blake underneath it. Without the three lads knowing it, the child had followed them and when they dropped the log, it struck him on the head. Dr Sumption of Drybrook attended the child who was then taken home where every help was given. Joseph Blake subsequently died at around 5am on the Tuesday morning from a fracture at the base of the skull. The Jury returned a verdict of accidental death and the parents were sympathised with in the unfortunate accident.

On Monday the 25th of October 1926, Mr Albert Thomas Wellington aged 30 and single of Cinderford Bridge was injured while working underground at the Eastern United Colliery near Ruspidge. He was at his workplace at 5am and at 7.30am, while working with Mr William Bowdler, a fall of half a hundredweight of earth fell onto Mr Wellington. Mr Bowdler was clear of the fall and afterwards Mr Wellington was found in a sitting position with only his hand, a broken finger and arm injured. He was able to walk out of the colliery where his brother took him to the Dilke Memorial Hospital in his motor car. There he complained of abdominal tenderness and was kept in overnight. Early on the Tuesday morning he became much worse and an operation was performed but he died at 6.30pm the same day.

On Friday afternoon the 29th of October 1926, Mr Arthur Thomas Rivers aged 18 from the village of Brithdir in South Wales but living in Drybrook was killed while working in an outcrop pit in the Wet Wood near the New Fancy Colliery. An Inquest held at Parkend heard that Mr Rivers was working the Oaken and Churchway Gale with several other Welshmen and they were given permission to do so by Mr D. Young the Deputy Surveyc provided that the coal produced was for their own use and not for sale. A mentioned earlier, the Gale had been transferred on the 7th of January 192⋅ from the ownership of Mr Sidney Taylor and Mr Gerald Thompson to th⋅ 'O and C' Syndicate Ltd. of Westminster, London. They encouraged th⋅ Welshmen and paid them up to 20 shillings per ton of coal produced bu were soon in trouble with Mr Forster-Brown the Deputy Gaveller fo breaching the rules. The Syndicate were asked to bring the workers int⋅ their employment but the men refused and an order was given for th⋅ operation to cease on the 30th of October 1926, the day after the fatality.

The Inquiry heard from Mr William Gibbs of Brithdir, Glamorgan who saic that Mr Rivers, himself and his two sons were working the outcrop wher the roof caved in without warning and about one hundredweight of debri⋅ trapped Mr Rivers by the feet. He grabbed the arm of Mr Rivers and triec to pull him free but a further fall caused Mr Gibbs to release him and retreat He then went back and removed some of the dirt and found Mr Rivers' hanc and Mr Rivers asked him to remove more dirt from around his face as h⋅ couldn't breathe. Mr Gibbs gave him some encouragement and said the⋅ would have him free soon. Mr Rivers exclaimed that; **'it is impossible'** anc said; **'so long'** before a third fall of several tons fell and Mr Gibbs had t⋅ retreat again. None of that third fall had fallen onto Mr Rivers but it wa⋅ more than an hour before the men could release him. Artificial respiratior was done for two hours without success. Mr Gibbs said that there wa⋅ plenty of timber at the place and that he considered that all precautions hac been taken for the men's safety. The Jury found that death was due to *'suffocation caused by a fall of earth in the outcrop workings'* and found the 'O and C' Syndicate liable owing to their neglect (but not culpable neglect⋅ in not complying with the rules and regulations laid down by the **Coal Mine⋅ Act 1841.**

Chapter 27
The Aftermath

The **Forest of Dean Miners' Association** suffered as a result of the strike and Lockout with no funds and a dwindling membership. Jack Williams was determined to rebuild the Union and continued to fight for the miners' cause despite collieries closing down and fewer and fewer miners being employed. He was a strong opponent of the previously mentioned Butty system and fought for its abolition in the Forest of Dean and within the **MFGB.**

To recap, a Buttyman was in effect a self employed contractor who negotiated a price with the Mine Owner for working a seam or seams of coal. He had several men and boys working under him to help shift the coal from the stall or seam to the surface and to prepare the new underground roadways. The system encouraged bitterness, jealousy and intimidation within the team and by 1930 the first collieries in the Forest to abandon the Butty system were the Princess Royal, Cannop and Waterloo (Arthur and Edward). The workers were eventually paid by a system that paid each member of a team an equal amount of pay. The last of the Forest pits to retain the Butty system was Eastern United where an acrimonious four month exchange and threats of strike action resulted in its abolition in March 1938.

The **FODMA** members expelled during the Lockout were re-instated within the Union although many of the men who stayed out till the end were left to seek alternative employment – unemployment benefit being available to those unfortunate enough not to find work. Most of the **FODMA** Executive was excluded from employment in the pits although some were later taken on again. David Organ for example drew unemployment benefit by walking from Pillowell to Lydney for several weeks, passing his old place of work, the Norchard Colliery, en route. He would often see the colliery manager who would greet him with; **'ow bist getting on then Dave'** and he would reply; **'better than thee bist'.** He did however keep his position as President of the **FODMA** until his retirement in 1939 and co-operated with Jack Williams to restore Union membership and sort out minor disputes and lightning strikes that continued to blight the industry.

Many Forest miners sought work abroad and some found their way across the Atlantic Ocean to the State of Pennsylvania, U.S.A. Some took their families with them and settled there while others later returned home to find work in other occupations – in some cases, away from their native Forest of Dean to other parts of the country.

In 1930, the Government passed the **Coal Mines Act 1930** which, among other things, reduced the amount of hours worked per shift for miners to seven and a half. This meant that the working week would become 45 hours with no further reduction for Saturdays.

After the Lockout, collieries were finding it difficult to mine coal economically. Higher production costs coupled with increased problems with pumping out water saw a gradual closing of many Forest collieries. By the start of WWII, the larger collieries such as Flour Mill at Bream, Crump Meadow near Cinderford, Parkend and Foxes Bridge were gone. As a consequence, the number of miners in the Forest of Dean fell from 6,500 before the General Strike in 1926 to around 4,000 during WWII.

Fig. 110 Northern United Colliery – courtesy of the DHC, Soudley, Cinderford.

One colliery however had bucked the trend with the sinking in 1933/34 of the new **Northern United Colliery.** This was part of the Crawshay enterprise and as a fully modernised pit where the investment was around £100,000, it was intended to reach the Coleford High Delf seam, the highly sought after steam coal. The seam was struck in February 1934 after only six months from the cut of the first sod and was intended to employ up to 1,000 men.

The year 1939 saw the last **Miners' Annual Demonstration** which was held at the Speech House field on the 1st of July 1939. The event was first held at the Speech House in 1872 in the days of Tim Mountjoy and except for the War years, was held annually, usually at the Speech House field.

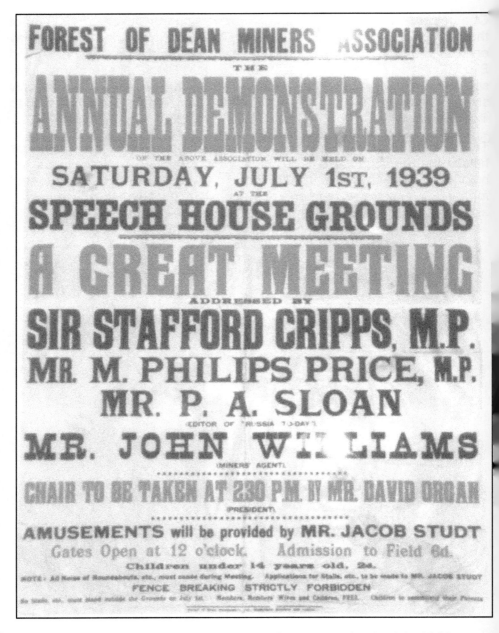

Fig. 111 The last Miners' Annual Demonstration in July 1939

Sadly, 1940 saw the end of the **Forest of Dean Miners' Association** when, in September it became integrated into the South Wales Miners' Federation **SWMF**. This move was instigated by the **MFGB** in May 1939 with a view of strengthening the Trade Union movement in this part of the country where the number of employed miners was falling. The move was fully endorsed by the Executive of the **FODMA.** From then on it was to be known as the **Number 9 Area of the South Wales Miners' Federation** and Jack Williams still retained his position as area Agent.

The Second World War brought again the need for coal and miners became a valued commodity once again. Under Jack Williams' continued leadership, the Union became more persuasive in negotiations with Coal Owners and in 1942 he negotiated an agreement with the Owners where all employed miners were to become members of the Federation – something that had been fought for for over 30 years.

Nevertheless, Forest of Dean pits continued to close – Lightmoor eventually closed in 1940 and New Fancy in 1944, both having produced coal for over 100 years.

It wasn't until the end of WWII when a Labour Government came to power that the miners' hard fought struggle began to bear fruit. The landslide Labour Party victory in the July 1945 General Election saw many objectives of the miners' struggle realised.

Firstly, in 1945 the **Miners' Federation of Great Britain - MFGB** was re-organised into a single Union and became the **National Union of Mineworkers** – the **N.U.M.** Though not generally acknowledged, it was Jack Williams who moved the first ever resolution for its formation. Initially it

Fig.112 Jack Williams on his retirement

failed to get approval but by continually moving the same resolution year after year, Conference eventually adopted it.

And secondly, the Labour Party under the leadership of Clement Attlee were committed to Nationalisation and introduced the **Coal Industry Nationalisation Act 1946** which received the *Royal Assent* on the 12th of July 1946. On the 1st of January 1947, Britain's pits were taken into the hands of the Government, away from the Coal Owners and Companies that had owned them. The **National Coal Board** was born and the day was known as **'Vesting Day'.**

More collieries began to close after WWII, as the cost of raising a ton of coal became too expensive to be economical. As mentioned earlier, the cost of pumping water out of the pits was an ever increasing problem with flooding becoming more regular. Coal seams were also getting thinner and more difficult to extract coal. Ironically, it was estimated that there was still enough coal in the Forest to last for over 100 years. However, men were also drifting away from the pits in ever increasing numbers to find better cleaner and better paid employment in many of the Trading Estate factories springing up in the district. Norchard Colliery near Lydney was the first to close in 1957 although the Pillowell Norchard was still getting coal for the Lydney Power Station.

Jack Williams retired in November 1953 at the age of 65. With him went the position of Miners' Agent with the responsibility for the District being in the capable hands of his assistant Mrs W.G. Jewell. She continued as Finance Officer and Compensation Secretary and liased closely with the Forest of Dean Executive of the **National Union of Mineworkers.**

Fig.113   Official Banner of the Forest of Dean District of
the National Union of Mineworkers.

Eastern United at Ruspidge closed in January 1959 and Waterloo (Arthur and Edward) at Lydbrook followed in December 1959. Cannop, one of the largest collieries in the Forest employing over 1,000 men and boys closed in September 1960 and the Princess Royal at Bream closed in March 1962. The last of the deep collieries, Northern United near Brierley closed in December 1965 while the Pillowell Norchard also closed in December 1965.

Of course, that was not the end of the matter as the fight for better working conditions and wages continued – but that's another story.

Milton Keynes UK
Ingram Content Group UK Ltd.
UKHW042001281024
450365UK00003B/74